End-to-End Data Science with SAS®

A Hands-On Programming Guide

James Gearheart

sas.com/books

Contents

About This Book

What Does This Book Cover?

Hello, my name is James, and I'm an addict. I'm addicted to data science books, web courses, instructional videos, blogs, data science podcasts, predictive modeling competitions, and coding. This addiction takes up the majority of my mental energy. From the time that I wake up until I fall asleep (and all through my dreams), I'm generally thinking about data science concepts and coding. I'm going to bet that many of you are in a similar situation. If so, I'm sure that you have been as frustrated as I have been about the massive hole in the instructional data science market.

> *It is essential that a data scientist who is working in a SAS environment be able to develop and implement machine learning models in ANY SAS environment.*

The market is overrun with data science books for Python, R, and Hadoop. These books provide an overview of data science and in-depth instructions on the various machine learning models, and they provide the associated development code for those particular programming languages. Although these books are great resources for data scientists, they do not offer direct programming instruction to the most popular programming language in the business community. SAS is used by 95% of Fortune 100 companies, and these companies are the leading employers of data scientists. There is an incredible opportunity to fill the need of professional data scientists for hands-on machine learning training with real-world examples.

The unfortunate reality for many SAS programmers is that we often do not have access to the latest and greatest SAS products. SAS Enterprise Miner, SAS Visual Analytics, SAS Forecast Server, and SAS Viya are all incredible products, but they are not universally available to all SAS programmers. It is essential that a data scientist who is working in a SAS environment be able to develop and implement machine learning models in any SAS environment. Even if data scientists have access to SAS Viya, it is incredibly beneficial for them to have a solid understanding of the programming code that drives the models that they develop in SAS Viya.

This book, *End-to-End Data Science in SAS®,* provides all SAS programmers insight into the models, methodology, and SAS coding required to develop machine learning models in any industry. It also serves as a reference for programmers of any language who either want to expand their knowledge base or who have just been hired into a data scientist position where SAS is the preferred language.

The goal of this book is to provide clear and practical explanations of the data science environment, machine learning techniques, and the SAS code necessary for the proper development and evaluation of these highly desired techniques. These explanations are demonstrated with real-world business applications across a variety of industries. All code and data sets are publicly available in a dedicated GitHub repository.

Is This Book for You?

If you are interested in this book, then you (or most likely the organization that you work for) have SAS installed on your computer. However, not all SAS installations are created equal. Some programmers work in Base SAS (also called PC SAS). Others have a variety of SAS software available to them:

- SAS Enterprise Guide
- SAS Enterprise Miner
- Visual Analytics
- SAS Studio
- SAS Viya

> *We are limited only by our ingenuity.*

This list is just a sample of the many SAS products available. In addition to these products, there are several software components that SAS offers:

- SAS/ACCESS software
- SAS/ETS software
- SAS/IML software
- SAS ODS Graphics Editor
- SAS/OR software
- SAS/STAT software

Your company's IT department generally dictates the SAS products that you have and the software components that are available to you. If you desperately want SAS Viya or SAS/ETS, you will often have to "fight the power" to get it. I sincerely hope that you can access one or many of these SAS products because they are awesome, and they will make your life as a data scientist much easier and much more productive. However, if you are like me and you have to develop predictive models without the benefit of all the toys that SAS has to offer, then this book is what you have been waiting for.

SAS Software Requirements

The minimum requirement for the majority of procedures detailed in this book is SAS 9.2 with SAS/STAT installed. This requirement should cover most SAS users. With this minimum requirement, we will be able to develop:

- Linear regressions
- Logistic regressions
- Clustering
- Decision trees

Some of the more advanced procedures will require SAS Enterprise Miner to be installed. These procedures will include:

- PROC HPFOREST
- PROC TREEBOOST
- PROC SVM

Don't panic! Just because you are limited to Base SAS with SAS/STAT installed does not mean that we are limited to the predefined procedures that come with SAS/STAT. We are limited only by our ingenuity. I will include methods of how to perform some of these more advanced procedures by developing them from scratch, using only the procedures available in SAS/STAT. The code to create these procedures from scratch can get pretty complicated, but I'll provide step-by-step explanations and all code will be available in the repository.

Programming Knowledge Assumed

If you only have experience working with Microsoft Excel spreadsheets, then don't worry; we can get you up and running in SAS. However, if you've never worked with data in any capacity, including Excel spreadsheets, then maybe this book isn't for you.

I will assume that you have some experience writing basic formulas. For example, in Excel:

```
=AVERAGE(B12: B32)
=SUM(A1: A14)
```

I will also assume that you can perform basic computer commands such as create a new file, save a file, open a file, and so on.

As long as you have met these minimum requirements and have a desire to learn awesome new skills that are guaranteed to increase your value to any organization, then we are good to go.

Icons used in this book

Warning

This icon indicates a warning or a difficult subject

Decision Time

This icon indicates a decision that the data scientist has to make

Example Code and Data

All data used for examples in this book have been accessed through public-use data repositories. These repositories provide a wide range of data sets that span across a variety of disciplines. The code that is demonstrated in the book is primarily created by the author. Any code that has been shown that was not created by the author has been cited with the appropriate credit to the developer. There is a fantastic community of SAS developers who openly share their code with the world. I strongly encourage you to search the web and connect with these communities on the SAS website, GitHub, Stack Overflow, and several other communities.

You can access the example code and data for this book by visiting the GitHub repository at https://github.com/Gearhj/End-to-End-Data-Science.

SAS University Edition

This book is compatible with SAS University Edition. If you are using SAS University Edition, then begin here: https://support.sas.com/ue-data.

We Want to Hear from You

Do you have questions about a SAS Press book that you are reading? Contact us at saspress@sas.com.

SAS Press books are written *by* SAS Users *for* SAS Users. Please visit sas.com/books to sign up to request information on how to become a SAS Press author.

We welcome your participation in the development of new books and your feedback on SAS Press books that you are using. Please visit sas.com/books to sign up to review a book.

Learn about new books and exclusive discounts. Sign up for our new books mailing list today at https://support.sas.com/en/books/subscribe-books.html.

Learn more about this author by visiting his author page at http://support.sas.com/gearheart. There you can download free book excerpts, access example code and data, read the latest reviews, get updates, and more.

Author Acknowledments

I would like to thank SAS for allowing me the opportunity to publish this book through SAS Press. It is an honor to be part of the SAS author community. I would also like to give special thanks to my editor Suzanne Morgen for her patience and her incredible eye for detail.

Additional thanks are given to all of the reviewers who painstakenly reviewed raw chapters and provided needed critical feedback:

- Christopher Battiston
- David Ghan
- Funda Gunes
- Sunil Gupta
- Mark Jordan
- Robin Langford
- Premkumar Varma

I would still be a poor musician in Warren, Ohio if it were not for Lorin Ranbom, Mitali Ghatak and the Health Services Reseach Section at the Ohio Department of Jobs and Family Services who took a chance on hiring me right out of college. Thanks to Dan Hecht, Donna Bush, Lora Summers, Kendy Markmen, Dave Dorsky, Hope McGonigle, Tracy Cloud and Eric Edwards for introducing me to SAS and providing me all of the support that I needed.

A continuous thank you to the best SAS programmer that I ever met, Matt Bates. I cannot count how many times that I bothered Matt about how to perform tasks from the mundane to the insanely complex. He has always come through for me and I am eternally grateful.

A huge thank you to Mihai Gavril, Vijay Narapsetty, Dan Gedrich, and Jay Das for providing a work environment that is collaborative, innovative and focused on excellence. I couldn't ask for a better team.

Thank you to my parents Richard and Lou Ann Gearheart for all of their love and support and my brothers Scott, Glen, Kenny, George, and Tod. You have always been there for me.

My beautiful son, Jacob Gearheart, is the pride of my life and I am amazed every day with your wit, charm, intelligence, and kindness. I pray that I will be more like you every day.

And of course, the love of my life, Tanya Gearheart. I must have written you a thousand love letters and none of them have come close to how much that I love you and need you in my life.

You are my entire world and the only reason that I wake up everyday is to spend more time with you. Always, madly.

About The Author

 James Gearheart is an experienced Senior Data Scientist and Machine Learning Engineer who has developed transformative machine learning and artificial intelligence models. He has over 20 years of experience in developing and analyzing statistical models and machine learning products that optimize business performance across several industries including digital marketing, financial services, public health care, environmental services, social security and worker's compensation.

James has been both a data science manager and an individual contributor on projects ranging from logistics, anti-money laundering, CRM, cash demand forecasting, customer segmentation, digital marketing, A/B testing, attribution and attrition. His research interests include applied data science, machine learning, and artificial intelligence.

Learn more about this author by visiting his author page at http://support.sas.com/Gearhart. There you can download free book excerpts, access example code and data, read the latest reviews, get updates, and more.

Chapter 1: Data Science Overview

Introduction to This Book

Over the past decade, there has been an explosion of interest in the application of statistics to the vast amounts of data being generated every second by nearly everyone on the planet. This interest has been driven primarily by tech giants that learned how to monetize this information by providing free services to individuals in exchange for the data that these individuals generate. Every click, tweet, picture upload, page view, like, share, follow, purchase, comment, retweet, email, and logon is stored in vast data warehouses maintained by tech giants and made available to their army of data scientists to turn your data into actionable insights.

You may feel flattered that you have a secret admirer that obsesses about your every click, your interests, your hopes and dreams, your wants, your insecurities, and your wildest fantasies. You may envision tech billionaires like Mark Zuckerberg or Jeff Bezos lying awake at night thinking about you and how to give you exactly what you want. Maybe that image is a bit of a stretch, but these CEOs, and all of their competitors, do have the customer at the center of their business models. This phenomenon is not limited to tech companies. Traditional brick and mortar stores (Walmart, Target, Best Buy), telecommunication companies (AT&T, Verizon, Comcast), medical institutions, entertainment conglomerates, utility companies, and government offices all have teams of data scientists whose sole function is to know what you want before you even know it yourself.

Amazon knows that because of your interest in data science books that you might be interested in this one. Netflix knows that because you binged the entire first three seasons of *Black Mirror* over the past weekend, that you will also be interested in the reboot of *The Outer Limits*. These insights are the result of teams of data scientists who access the information that you have freely provided and develop models that categorize individuals into similar groups based on a variety of attributes. They also develop predictive models that try to determine what you will do or want in the future.

Don't believe me? Here is a quick test. Based on the only information that I have about you (your interest in data science books focusing on SAS), I will assume that you are a male aged between 25 and 40 years old with graduate-level education and live in an English-speaking country. You probably work in a large corporation. Maybe your desk is a bit messy, but you have a method to the madness.

How'd I do? If these guesses were a complete miss, then you must be a unique individual to not fall into any of the traditional demographic and interest categories of data scientists. But I would guess that at least half of these descriptions pertain to you. These guesses might appear to be a bit broad or general. But remember, they are based on only a single general piece of information: your interest in data science books focused on SAS.

Now imagine that I have a database of your entire web history, including all your past purchases, your social connections, your financial statements, your search terms, your emails, and your viewing habits. Imagine that I took all of this information and input it into a complex predictive model that was built with the sole purpose of calculating the probability that you would be interested in a specific product. Imagine that I gathered this same database of information for ten million individuals (a small sample size in the world of digital information where the data sets can contain several trillion data points) and built a deep learning model that calculated the probability that you would be interested in a travel rewards credit card offer with a 2% cashback program.

That's a pretty specifically defined target variable! Given the quantity and quality of information that I have about the population and a well-defined target variable, I should be able to build a predictive model that can calculate, with a reasonable degree of confidence, the probability of an individual responding to this credit card offer. This information could be used to allocate my marketing budget efficiently. I'd probably achieve a higher response rate with this approach than if I spent the budget on a radio commercial broadcast to a broad population. If the response rate of the travel website campaign is 1.5% while the response rate of the radio ad is 0.03%, then our predictive model provided a **50X** lift in response rate! That is one way to optimize your marketing budget.

In this example, all of this data has been used to deliver a highly targeted ad for the right product to the right individual at the right time with the right message. This targeting mechanism is just one example of how data science is used every day by a wide variety of businesses. Major corporations have used data science techniques to target, classify, segment, cluster, recommend, adjust offers, personalize, upsell, cross-sell, influence and predict every aspect of customer behavior.

Minimum Effective Dose

This book will follow the Minimum Effective Dose (MED) method of teaching data science. The goal of this method is to get you up and running with sufficient background information on the various data science techniques and provide you with specific examples and access to real data and also provide SAS code that is thoroughly explained. I do not want you to get bogged down with a bunch of mathematical theories on the inner workings of the procedures. We will touch on the formulas, but I will not drone on about it. If you are interested in a thorough explanation of the mathematics of data science, I suggest that you check out *The Elements of Statistical Learning* by Hastie, Tibshirani, and Friedman. It is the bible of statistical mathematics for the data science community.

So, what does MED mean?

- No math! (well...very little math)
- An understandable and practical explanation of data science methods:
  - Which method to use for a given situation
  - What to watch out for
  - How data science works with real business data (you will not find the standard academic data sets such as the iris data set or the MNIST data set in this book)
- Step-by-step instructions on how to do specific procedures
- How to evaluate the performance of your model:
  - How to apply your model to new data
  - How to understand the SAS code provided

The Current Data Science Landscape

Over the past few years, the job titles for business analysts have changed. These changes in job titles reflect the additional demands of the business analyst. If you were in the business analytics field before 2012, maybe you've had one of these job titles:

- Analyst
- Statistician
- Quant
- Researcher
- Analytical Consultant
- Data Architect
- Database Administrator
- "Data Guy"

Since 2012, many of these job titles have changed to:

- Data Scientist
- Machine Learning Engineer
- Artificial Intelligence Engineer

One of the first questions that you may have is, "what is the difference between a data scientist and an analyst"? The initial answer is that 80% of their work is the same:

- Access data
- Clean data
- Combine data sets
- Summarize data
- Answer business questions
- Create reports

However, data scientists have some exciting tools in their toolbox, including:

- Accessing and using unstructured data: Web scraping, Twitter tweets, Facebook comments, and so on
- Making sense of data that they do not know using unsupervised machine learning methods: Clustering and PCA
- Predicting future outcomes: Forecasting and predictive modeling

These additional functions of the data scientist take their role to a new level by being able to move past the traditional descriptive statistics of reporting and move into the exciting world of predictive analytics, prescriptive analytics, and optimization.

Types of Analytics

Let's look at a few different types of analytics that data scientists should be familiar with.

- **Descriptive Analytics** – This is a retrospective look at what has happened in the past and what is currently happening. Firms generate a lot of descriptive analytics to understand business trends, customer demand, production thresholds, and countless other business metrics. Descriptive reporting is not flashy, but it is the life's blood of all business. Since these are events that have already been realized, this reporting focuses on reporting actual figures along with their associated statistics (averages, standard deviations, and so on).

- **Predictive Analytics** – Historical data is used to make predictions about the future. These are statistical estimates of future possibilities based on historical data. This type of reporting is accompanied by confidence intervals, odds ratios, and probabilities.

- **Prescriptive Analytics** – Also called *optimization*, prescriptive analytics identifies impactful factors and recommends the optimal values of these factors to achieve a predefined result.

SAS created Figure 1.1. This figure breaks down the previous list even further into eight levels of analytics. By increasing the level of intelligence in these analytical products, we are expanding the business value of analytics to the organization. The first four stages are based on reporting functions of analytics, while the last four stages are based on probabilistic functions of analytics. The business value of these functions is incredibly beneficial to businesses.

Figure 1.1: Eight Levels of Analytics

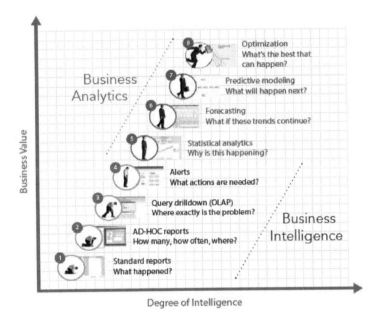

For example, if you are at the horse track and getting ready to place your bet, would you rather have a report on the historical performance of the horses, or would you rather have some probabilistic information on what might happen in the upcoming race? My money would be on the probabilistic report.

Data Science Skills

I'm sure that most of you are as tired as I am of looking at the graphic in Figure 1.2 below. We have seen it on every data science blog, presentation, and instructional medium. Regardless of the ubiquity of the graphic, there is still a clear message that is conveyed. It shows the vital interplay and intersection of three diverse fields that had traditionally been performed separately.

Figure 1.2: Data Science Venn Diagram

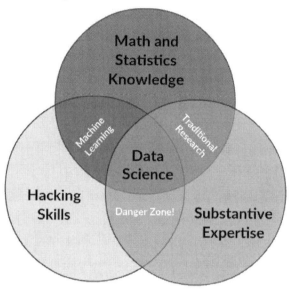

Adapted from: Conway, Drew. (September 2010). *The Data Science Venn Diagram*. Retrieved from http://drewconway.com/zia/2013/3/26/the-data-science-venn-diagram.

The main sections in the diagram in Figure 1.2 are as follows:

- **Computer skills** – represented in the "Hacking Skills" section of the diagram. This skill set is essential for accessing and manipulating structured and unstructured data. Data scientists need to be able to gather data, clean it, merge it with other data sources, prepare it for modeling, and implement machine learning algorithms on this data to answer a specific question.

- **Math and Statistics Knowledge** – A data scientist needs to have the prerequisite statistical background to understand the goal, process, and function of a predictive algorithm.

- **Business knowledge** – represented in the "Substantive Expertise" section of the diagram. In this context, the term "business" can represent any field of study that requires knowledge of that specific environment. Machine learning models are developed to answer business questions. A data scientist needs to have knowledge of that environment to develop the initial business questions that can be modeled. This type of knowledge is critical for knowing what type of data will be required to answer the question, what direction the data should be moving, and what answers are counterintuitive.

The subsections in the diagram in Figure 1.2 are:

- **Machine Learning** – The intersection of "Hacking Skills" and "Math and Statistics Knowledge" excludes the "Substantive Expertise" skill set. This subsection is a reference to computer scientists who can develop sophisticated predictive models based solely on finding correlations in given data sets. Regardless of how sophisticated or accurate these models may be, these models lack the background business knowledge and are therefore prone to spurious correlations, weak inferences and ethical concerns.

- **Traditional Research** – The intersection of "Math and Statistics Knowledge" and "Substantive Expertise" is excluding the "Hacking Skills" section of the graph. Before the application of computers to solve all our daily problems, researchers had to apply mathematical knowledge to their field of expertise to develop theoretical models. If you received your advanced degree before 1995, then I'm talking about you.

- **Danger Zone** – Certainly my favorite section of the graphic. The intersection of "Hacking Skills" and "Substantive Expertise" that excludes the "Math and Statistics Knowledge" highlights the dangerous area of misaligned models, misinterpreted results, and unfounded conclusions.

Introduction to Data Science Concepts

The language of data science is based on a series of concepts that represent the issues that data scientists have to consider when they are developing a project. These terms and definitions are a kind of shorthand for deep theoretical issues that data scientists must consider at each step of their project. For example, if I complain to another colleague that my go-to regression model is not working well on this new project, he might respond, "No free lunch." That doesn't mean that he assumed I was going to steal his lunchbox!

In this section, I will outline some of the most common concepts in data science so that we have a common understanding of these concepts.

Supervised Versus Unsupervised

There are two main categories that machine learning models can fall into. These are supervised and unsupervised models. The presence of a target variable differentiates them. The target variable represents the item that you are interested in. It is also called the response variable. If there is a value that you are trying to predict, you have a supervised method. Supervised models have a target variable, while unsupervised models do not have a target variable.

> Many data science terms are used interchangeably. Predictor variables are also called descriptive variables, independent variables, or input variables. The target variable is also called the response variable or the dependent variable.

Supervised Models

Most of the models that you have been exposed to have been supervised models. These are the main predictive models that filter out your spam, identify your handwriting, recommend your next song, decide which ad to show you, and make a thousand other selections for you every day.

These models include, but are not limited to:

- Regression Models
- Decision Trees
- Random Forests
- Gradient Boosting
- Neural Networks
- Support Vector Machines (SVM)
- K-Nearest Neighbors
- Naïve Bayes Models

Each one of these models is built on a data set that has a target variable along with one to several thousand predictor variables. If a data set contains a target variable, then supervised machine learning algorithms are most commonly used with this type of data. These machine learning algorithms identify the associations between the predictor variables and the target variable. The result is a formula that can be used on new observations where the target value is not known.

For example, if you want to predict the quality ranking of a bottle of wine, then you would generally have a data set that contains several observations that have the ranking of wine for each observation. The quality ranking would be the target variable. The data set would also include several descriptive variables along with the target variable. These descriptive variables describe several different factors that influence the target variable. Table 1.1 shows nine predictive variables that are associated with the target variable "quality."

In mathematical terms, the predictor variable would traditionally be labeled as "X," and multiple predictor variables would be listed as X1, X2, X3, and so on. The target variable would be labeled as "y," so that for each observation of the predictor measurement X_i there is an associated response measurement y_i where i represents the ith observation.

Table 1.1: Wine Quality Data

Fixed Acidity	Volatile Acidity	Citric Acid	Sugar	Chlorides	Density	pH	Sulfates	Alcohol	Quality
8.6	0.23	0.4	4.2	0.035	0.995	3.1	0.53	9.70	5
7.9	0.18	0.37	1.2	0.040	0.992	3.2	0.63	10.80	5
6.6	0.16	0.4	1.5	0.044	0.991	3.5	0.52	12.40	7
8.3	0.42	0.62	19.25	0.040	1.000	3	0.67	9.70	5
6.6	0.17	0.38	1.5	0.032	0.991	3.3	0.55	11.40	7
6.3	0.48	0.04	1.1	0.046	0.993	3.2	0.36	9.60	6
6.2	0.66	0.48	1.2	0.029	0.989	3.3	0.39	12.80	8

In the case of our wine quality prediction example, you could build a regression model that results in a formula like this:

$$Quality = 0.796 + FixedAcidity(0.0349) + VolatileAcidity(-0.8287)$$
$$+ Cholorides(-0.0464) + pH(-0.203) + Sulphates(0.1386)$$
$$+ Alcohol(0.4663)$$

This formula states that the quality score of wine is a function of six main features of the wine. The model determines which features are associated with the wine quality score by assessing the correlation between each feature and the quality score. The model also produces model weights (also called coefficients) that are used to predict the quality score of new bottles of wine that have not been scored yet.

If we were given an information sheet on a brand new bottle of wine that has not been scored for quality, then we would be able to input the information from each of these predictors into our formula and predict the quality of the wine, as shown in Table 1.2.

Table 1.2: Wine Data Set Predictive Weights

		New Wine Info	Predictive Weights
	Model Intercept	Unknown	0.796
	fixed acidity	7.2	0.0349
	volatile acidity	0.22	-0.8287
Predictors	chlorides	0.042	-0.0464
	pH	3.2	-0.203
	sulphates	0.61	0.1386
	alcohol	10.2	0.4663

	Predicted Score
quality (Target)	5.0542

Each value of the new wine information is multiplied by the predictive weight (coefficient) produced by the model. These calculated values are combined with the model intercept to generate a predicted score.

According to our predictive model, this new bottle of wine should have a quality score of 5. Notice that not all the predictive variables were used in the final predictive model. The model retained only the predictors that had a statistically significant relationship with the target variable. Don't worry; these concepts will be explained in detail in the regression modeling chapter of the book.

Unsupervised Models

Unsupervised models are built on data sets that do not have a target variable. This type of analysis is slightly more difficult because of the lack of direction that is usually provided by the target variable. The goal of unsupervised models is inherently different from supervised models. Supervised models are generally constructed to predict the response of future observations or to understand better the relationship between the predictors and the target variable. On the other hand, unsupervised models do not predict anything. They are built to understand the relationship between the given variables. The goal of unsupervised models is to identify naturally occurring groups or classifications of the observations.

The most common types of unsupervised learning models include:

- k-Means Clustering
- Hierarchical Cluster Analysis (HCA)
- Principal Component Analysis (PCA)
- t-distributed Stochastic Neighbor Embedding (t-SNE)

For example, suppose that you have a database of customer attributes and you want to know if you can detect groups of similar customers. These groups could be beneficial in marketing campaigns or for targeting purposes. It is a common practice to run a *k-means clustering algorithm* that will assign each observation to one of *k* groups based on the features that are provided. The "*k*" in k-means clustering represents the number of groups that you want to be assigned. Data points that are relatively close to one another in the feature space are assigned to the same group or cluster.

The takeaway from this section is that the clusters form organically without the direction of a target variable. The relationship between variables is the basis of unsupervised learning.

One of the nice features of clustering algorithms is that they are commonly expressed through visualizations. The clustering algorithm is easily understood in a scatter plot visualization where the observation points can be colored or symbolized according to the cluster that they have been assigned. Figure 1.3 shows a typical clustering model visualization. This visualization demonstrates four distinct groups of observations based on the X and Y features. Each of the groups contains a centroid point that establishes the cluster in the feature space.

Figure 1.3: Clustering Model Visualization

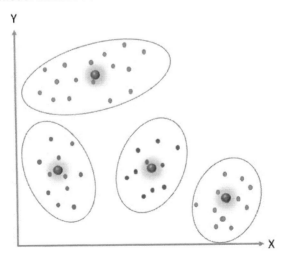

One of the most powerful applications of unsupervised learning models is *dimensionality reduction*. It is not uncommon to have a modeling data set with hundreds of predictors. Although we always want more data, the truth is that more data can lead to more problems. A large number of predictors quickly runs into the curse of dimensionality (explained in detail in the next few sections) and issues of correlation. Dimensionality reduction is the ability to simplify the data without losing too much information.

Algorithms such as *principal component analysis* (PCA) collect correlated variables and merge them into a single feature that represents an important dimension of your data. For example, the square footage of a home and its number of bedrooms are highly correlated. These features can be combined into a single attribute that might represent the family size.

Although the purpose of supervised learning models and unsupervised learning models are inherently different from one another, they often work together. A data scientist can employ unsupervised modeling techniques to develop clusters and perform dimensionality reduction, which will create features that can be used as inputs to a supervised learning model.

Machine Learning Categories

Figure 1.4 demonstrates the high-level categorization of machine learning algorithms. The broad category of machine learning can be broken into supervised learning and unsupervised learning models. Supervised learning can be further broken into classification and regression models. Unsupervised learning can be further broken down into clustering and dimensionality reduction models. Each of these concepts will be explained in detail in the upcoming sections.

Figure 1.4: Machine Learning Categories

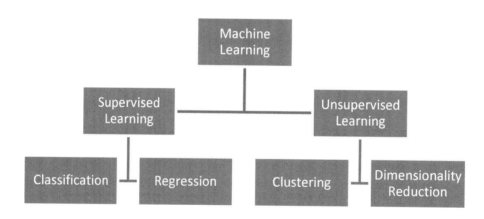

Parametric Versus Non-parametric

Once you examine your data and decide that you are going to build a supervised model, the next step is to try to determine what kind of model will best fit the data. Several methods will be covered later in this book that pertain to variable examination, plotting data, and correlation analysis. When you perform these techniques, you are trying to understand the *functional form* of the relationship between the predictors and the target variable. When you examine the data, you need to ask yourself:

- Is the data linear?
- Is the data clustered?
- Is the data curved?
- Does it look like there is a pattern to the distribution?
- Is the data random?

These methods will provide you with clues as to what type of model you should apply to the data. Figure 1.5 shows two very different types of data distributions. The graph on the left shows a linear relationship between the X and Y variable, while the graph on the right does not display a linear relationship.

When we are trying to decide what type of model to apply to our data, we need to make assumptions about the functional form of the relationship between X and Y. A linear model will attempt to draw a straight line through the data that has the shortest distance between the line and the observation points. If we applied a linear regression model to the first set of data, I think that we would get a decent fit. However, if we applied a linear regression model to the second set of data, we would get a very poorly fit model.

Figure 1.5: Data Distribution Types

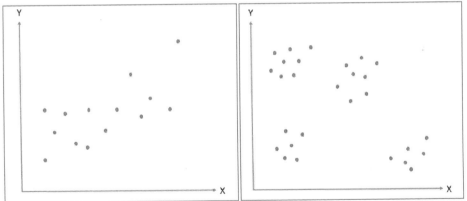

There are two general classifications that models fall into. These are *parametric* and *non-parametric* models.

Parametric Models

Parametric models make an assumption about the functional form of the underlying relationship between the predictors and the target variable. Through your examination of the data, you might determine that there exists a linear relationship between the target and the predictors. In this case, you are assuming a linear functional form:

$$f(X) = \beta_0 + \beta_1 X_1 + \beta_2 X_2 + \cdots + \beta_p X_p$$

Since we assumed that $f(X)$ is linear, then we just need to estimate the coefficients, $\beta_0, \beta_1, \dots \beta_p$. This is most commonly performed through *ordinary least squares* (this concept will be explained in detail in the regression chapter).

Regression models are classified as *parametric* because they reduce the *p*-dimensional function (p is the total number of predictors) down to estimating a given set of parameters.

Parametric models include, but are not limited to:

- Linear regression
- Logistic regression
- Naïve Bayes
- Linear Discriminate Analysis
- Simple neural networks

The benefits of parametric models are:

- **Transparency** – These models are relatively simple and easy to understand. You know exactly what the inputs are and what the coefficients are.

- **They are faster** – Since these models do not have to search through the entire feature space to find an arbitrary *p*-dimensional function, they are much faster to train than non-parametric models.

- **They need less data** – Parametric models can be developed on a limited set of data compared to non-parametric models. Although the coefficients will adjust as more data is added, there is a point of diminishing returns where additional observations will not yield discernable model fit improvements.

Non-Parametric Models

If parametric models assume the functional form of f, then you could probably guess that non-parametric models do not assume the functional form of f. These models are free to learn any functional form of the data because they are not constrained by assumptions. Without the restrictions of a predetermined functional form, these algorithms attempt to estimate a function that gets as close as possible to the training data but will generalize well to unseen data. The significant advantage of non-parametric models is that they can potentially fit a much wider range of functional forms than parametric models.

For example, a nearest neighbor's model does not assume any functional form of the data. It just looks for observations in close proximity to one another in the feature space, regardless of how the data is distributed. The only assumption that is made is that observations close to one another in the feature space have a similar target value.

Non-parametric models include, but are not limited to:

- k-Nearest Neighbors
- Decision Trees
- Complex Neural Networks
- Support Vector Machines (SVM)

The benefits of non-parametric models are:

- **Flexibility** – These models do not assume the functional form; therefore, they can detect a wide range of functional forms.
- **Accuracy** – These models generally result in more accurate models.

Non-parametric models can be applied to linearly distributed data. The disadvantages of applying a non-parametric model to a data set that could be modeled by a parametric model are:

- **Data requirements** – Non-parametric models generally require more data to adequately train a model. If the size of the data set is limited, the parametric model will provide a more accurate model fit.
- **Training Time** – Since non-parametric models do not assume the functional form of the data, these models have to search the p-dimensional feature space to assess the best model fit.
- **Transparency** – Many types of non-parametric models are called *black-box* models because it is difficult to understand how the model prediction is constructed. The parametric model can be easily understood by examining the weights of the coefficients. Most non-parametric models do not output model weights and are therefore difficult to interpret.

Table 1.3 provides a summary of the differences between parametric and non-parametric models

Table 1.3: Parametric versus Non-Parametric Models

Model Type	Data	Speed	Transparency	Functional Forms	Accuracy
Parametric	Less	Fast	Transparent	Limited	Less
Non-Parametric	More	Slow	Black Box	Unlimited	More

Regression Versus Classification

Variables can fall into one of two main categories. *Quantitative* variables take on numerical values. These values are continuous values (1.1, 1.2, 1.3 ...). Examples of these types of variables are height, weight, money, distance, time, and any other quantity that can be expressed as a value.

Variables can also be *qualitative*. These variables represent a value in a category. For example, a home price variable could be categorized as high, medium, or low. A person's gender can be categorized as male, female, or other. Any descriptive label can be made into a qualitative variable.

Machine learning models can be categorized as either *regression* models or *classification* models. This categorization depends on whether the target variable is quantitative or qualitative. If a data set has a target variable that is a continuous value, such as "annual income," then the machine learning model that is built on this data set will be a regression model. On the other hand, if a target variable is qualitative, such as "yes" or "no," then the machine learning model will be a classification model.

The terms "regression" and "classification" can lead to some semantic problems and muddy our understanding of these models. A linear regression model will most likely have a continuous target variable; however, a logistic regression model will often have a binary target variable. Even though they both have the term "regression" in their name, they are performing two very different calculations. A linear regression model is a regression model, while a logistic regression model is actually a classification model.

Also, many machine learning algorithms can perform both regression and classification functions. Decision trees, k-nearest neighbors, neural networks, and random forests can all be applied to either quantitative or qualitative target variables.

My best advice is not to get caught up in the names of the models. Once you understand how each of the models function and their relative strengths and weaknesses, you will have a much better feel for which model to use in a given situation.

Table 1.4 provides some general descriptions of regression and classification models.

Table 1.4: Regression and Classification Models

	Regression	**Classification**
General Description	Regression means to predict the output **value** using training data	Classification means to output the group into a **class**
Example	Regression to predict the **value** ($ amount) of an insurance claim using training data	Classification to predict the **type** of an insurance claim (fraud vs non-fraud) using training data
Target Variable	If it is a real number/continuous, then it is a regression problem	If it is a discrete/categorical variable, then it is a classification problem

Overfitting Versus Underfitting

The concepts of overfitting and underfitting are some of the most important issues that data scientists have to understand. A considerable amount of a data scientist's work is spent evaluating whether their model is overfitting or underfitting the data. To understand these concepts, we first need to understand the difference between the terms "signal" and "noise."

Every machine learning model attempts to capture the underlying relationship between the target variable and the predictor variables. If a relationship exists, then the model should identify this relationship and use it to predict new cases. However, in every data set, there exists a certain amount of random error. This random error can come from variables that have only a weak association or no association at all with the target variable. It can also come from outliers, skewed data, and a myriad of other data issues. This random error is called "noise."

Overfitting

When a machine learning model describes the random error (noise) rather than the underlying relationship of the predictors and the target, the model is said to be overfitting. Overfitting often occurs when a model is too complex for a given set of data. If the machine learning model incorporates too many predictors relative to the number of observations, it will begin to model the random error instead of the desired underlying relationship. The overfitted model will be highly tuned to the data set that it was developed on (called the training data set). However, it will not generalize well to new data. This lack of generalization will lead to poor model performance on new data.

Let's look at a quick example. In the finance world, we often use a customer's FICO score to determine credit worthiness. The FICO score is a three-digit number between 350 and 800 that is calculated and reported by the credit bureau agencies and represents a customer's payment history, credit tenure, credit delinquencies, and many other financial factors. We can construct a very simple data set based on the relationship between a customer's FICO score and their income (Figure 1.6).

Figure 1.6: Simple Linear Relationship

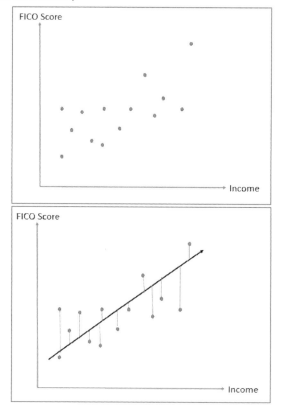

The graph on the top of Figure 1.6 shows a scatter plot graph of the distribution of FICO score and income. We can see that there is a positive relationship between the predictor variable (Income) and the target variable (FICO score). Although there is a positive relationship, it is not a one-to-one perfectly fit relationship. We can see that there is a general upward trend, but it does not look like a perfect match between the two variables.

The graph on the bottom of Figure 1.6 shows a linear trend line and error bars that demonstrate the residual error of the linear model. If you remember your Statistics 101 class, several different lines can be fit to this data set, but the best fit is the one that has the lowest total residual errors. We can easily find this by calculating the distance between the observation and the line; then we square this difference to make sure that we have positive values and then we add them all together to get the total residual error.

So, you might ask yourself, what if I created a polynomial model (a curved line created from polynomial variables) where my line goes through every data point? That would mean that I would have a total residual error of zero. That would be awesome! Unfortunately, that would not be awesome. Even though you would be meeting your goal of reducing the residual error, your model would be so highly tuned to the data set that it was developed on that it would not generalize well to new data.

Figure 1.7 provides a visual example. The graph on the left shows a polynomial line that goes through all data points and has a residual error rate of zero. However, the graph on the bottom shows new data points represented as stars. The polynomial line does not provide a good prediction for these new data points, but the linear prediction does provide a good estimate of the predicted value. Using the linear model, I can predict the value of a customer's FICO score if I am given their income. If I used the polynomial line, my prediction would be much worse.

Figure 1.7: High Degree Polynomial Model

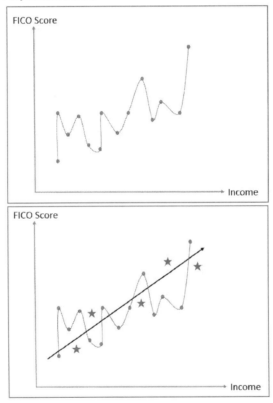

There are several methods to detect overfitting, and there are easy solutions to this important issue. These methods will be described in detail later in the book, but a few highlights are:

- Cross-validation
- Simplifying the model by reducing the number of parameters or reducing your higher-order polynomial
- Regularization

- Cleaning your data set by finding and fixing the outliers and skewed data elements
- Getting more data (more observations, not necessarily more parameters)

Underfitting

The concept of underfitting is the polar opposite of overfitting. In the case of underfitting, the model is not identifying the underlying relationship between the predictors and the target. It is not detecting the signal that is present in the data. In layman's terms, you have a weak model.

If we use the same example as we did in the overfitting demonstration, we can see that the linear model is actually underfitting the data. Figure 1.8 compares the residual error generated from the linear model to the residual error generated from a lower-degree polynomial model. This moderate polynomial model captures some of the dynamic relationships between the predictor and the target that the linear model does not capture. The overall residual error of the moderate polynomial model is lower than the linear model; therefore, it is a better fit.

Figure 1.8: Lower Degree Polynomial Model

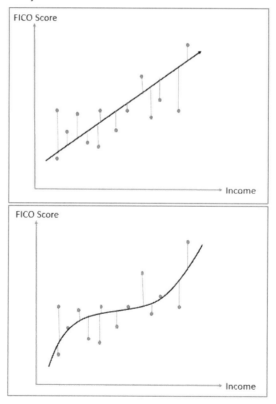

There are methods to address underfitting the data. These include:

- Increasing model complexity. Either through more parameters, feature engineering, or selecting a more powerful modeling algorithm
- Decreasing regularization (reducing the constraints on the model)

Batch Versus Online Learning

Machine learning models can be further classified into either "batch" or "online" learning models. The difference between these types of models is whether the model can learn from an incoming stream of new data.

Batch Models

In batch models, the algorithm (the model equation that we use to predict our target values) has been previously developed, and new observations are scored according to a predefined model. The positive aspect of this model is that since it has been previously developed, the learning algorithm can consider all the available training data and take as long as necessary to output a scoring algorithm. Some deep learning models have been known to run for over a month before the final model weights are constructed.

By developing the model before implementation, the data scientist can try several different approaches and conduct various types of tests to determine the efficacy of the model prior to implementation. If a data scientist wants to use new data for a batch model, then they would have to train a completely new model from scratch on this new data set.

It is common to train a new data set weekly or even every night on the most recent data available. As long as the modeling pipeline is established and new data can be imported, cleaned, prepared for modeling, modeled, and evaluated, then new models can be implemented relatively seamlessly.
Batch models generally require a lot of data, computational resources, and time to process. These requirements can result in a substantial cost to an organization. Due to these resource issues, model designs have been developed that are able to learn incrementally.

Online Learning Models

A solution to the resource requirements of batch models is to instead feed the model either a continuous stream of new data or to feed the model small batches (called "mini-batches") of data. This data can be evaluated by the model algorithm and quickly discarded after it has been used. This model design is great for data environments that receive a constant stream of data such as web clicks or stock prices. An online learning model can adapt quickly to changes in the data stream.

One of the main cautions with this type of system is that these models need to be continuously monitored because they are so sensitive to new data. New data can be erroneous, or it can be purposefully harmful (online attacks, fraud, spamming, bad sensors, system gaming, and so on). This type of new data can have a detrimental impact on an online learning model.

Data scientists generally combat these types of runaway scenarios in two ways:

1. **Continuously monitor model results** – Data scientists build systems to monitor model results in real time. These systems will have threshold levels that trigger a warning if a value meets or exceeds a given level.
2. **Adjust the learning rate** – In this context, the learning rate is a measure of how fast the model incorporates new data and adjusts the model results based on this new data. This adjustment can be a delicate balance because if you set the learning rate too high, the model will adapt to new data very quickly and you can get runaway results. However, if you set the learning rate too low, then the model will not pick up on new trends in the data and this could defeat the purpose of implementing an online learning model.

Bias-Variance Tradeoff

Now it's time to talk about one of the most essential concepts in machine learning. A large part of the work that a data scientist does is directly related to the concept of the bias-variance tradeoff.

A data scientist needs to be able to determine which type of algorithm they will apply to a given business problem and how complex that algorithm needs to be. Even a simple model such as a simple linear regression with one predictor variable can become complex if we transform that single variable into a higher-order polynomial. For example:

Simple: $FICO\ Score = Income(x)$
Complex: $FICO\ Score = Income(x)^{10}$

Even though each of the models contains only one variable, the higher-order polynomial is considered a complex model.

Model complexity can be increased by:

- Increasing the number of predictors
- Feature engineering
- Variable transformations
- Interaction terms
- Model construction
    - Number of branches in a decision tree
    - Regularization value in a regression model
    - Number of hidden nodes in a neural network

- ○ Value of C in an SVM
- ○ Many, many, many others

The goal of a data scientist is to develop a model that captures the signal in the data while being able to generalize well to new unseen data. Although this might sound easy, there is an unfortunate tradeoff that must occur. To understand this tradeoff, we must define the concepts of *bias* and *variance*. Fortunately for us, these concepts are closely related to *underfitting* and *overfitting* that we just covered a few pages ago.

Bias

Bias occurs when we make simplistic assumptions about the data or apply simplistic models to a data set. These simplistic models are not able to adequately identify the underlying signal in the data. The models will underfit the data and result in non-optimal model predictions.

For example, the data represented in Figure 1.8 shows a linear model fit to the data on the top while a polynomial model is fit on the bottom. The model on the top suffers from high bias because the model is not adequately representative of the underlying data. It suffers from a systemic lack of fit due to poor model choice. As we increase model complexity by transforming the predictor variable into a polynomial, the model will begin to better represent the underlying signal in the data. This increase in model complexity reduces the bias of the model.

Variance

Variance is the exact opposite problem compared to bias. High variance occurs when you are overfitting the data by applying too many or too strong of data transformations to the training data, or you are using an overly complex model to a data set that does not require it. For example, the predictive model demonstrated in Figure 1.7 shows a high variance model. It is highly overfit to the data and cannot be generalized to new observations.

A common-sense explanation of why we use the term *variance* is that if we **vary** the underlying training data (that is, changed it over and over), we would get very different models each time that we changed the underlying data. This is called "high variance." This type of model is capturing the noise in the data and not representing the signal.

So, how do we know when we have the right balance of model complexity? Figure 1.9 shows the tradeoff between bias and variance. When model complexity is low, we have a high bias. This is because a more complex model will generally capture the underlying relationship in the data better than a very simple model. A simple model with high bias will have a high total model error.

Figure 1.9: Optimal Model Complexity

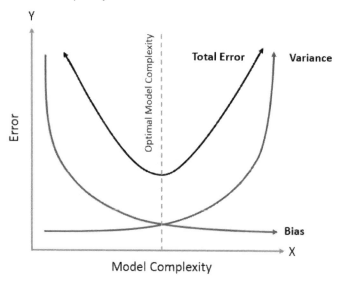

On the other hand, an overly complex model will have a high variance. This model is so highly tuned to the training data that it does not generalize well to new observations. An overly complex model with high variance will also have a high total model error.

There exists a balance point where the total model error is reduced to its lowest possible point. This point is the point of *optimal model complexity*. Although this is not the point with the lowest possible bias or the lowest possible variance, it is the balance point between the two. Of course, your next question has to be, *how do I find the point of optimal model complexity*?

Training and Testing Data Sets

An important technique in data science that is reviewed in detail later in the book is to split your data set into two sections. These sections are called the "training data set" and the "testing data set." As a rule of thumb, about 70% of your data will be in the *training* data set. This is the data set that you will use to build your model. The remaining 30% of your data will be in your hold-out *testing* data set. This is the data set that you will apply your model to and evaluate the results.

There are two important caveats to creating your training and testing data sets:

1. The data needs to be randomly assigned to either the training or testing data set. This randomization will avoid selection bias. If the data is not randomly sampled, then the resulting sample data set is not representative of the population intended to be analyzed.

2. No peeking! You are not allowed to evaluate the test data set prior to building the model on the training data set. Any information that you get from investigating the test data set could influence how you build the model on the training data set. This type of

insider knowledge would not be available once the model is in production. This type of cheating can lead to significant performance differences between a model development environment and a production environment.

Figure 1.10 demonstrates how the training and testing data sets are associated with the concepts of underfitting, overfitting, bias, variance, signal, and noise. If we look at the left side of the graph, this section represents models with low complexity (think of a simple linear regression model). When we evaluate the performance of the model when it is applied to both the training data set and the testing data set, there is a high error rate. This simple model does not capture the underlying signal in the data. There is high bias because the model is not capturing the signal and there is low variance because the model results will not change much if we pulled a different sample to build the model.

As we move to the right and increase model complexity, both the training data set error rate and the testing data set error rate begin to fall. As we increase the model complexity, we are capturing more of the signal in the data. A result of increasing model complexity is that the model bias will begin to fall while the model variance will begin to increase. This effect is because we are capturing more of the signal in the data, but the model is becoming more specified to the underlying training data. If we had pulled a different random sample to create the training data, we would get a slightly different model. However, because we are better able to identify the signal in the data, the training error rate and the testing error rate begin to fall.

Figure 1.10: Bias-Variance Tradeoff

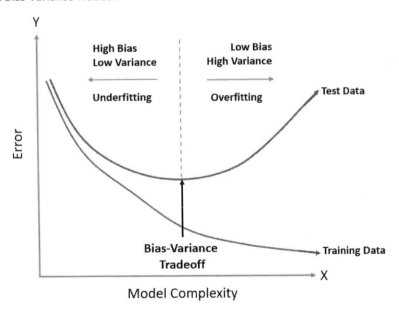

Model Complexity

As we continue to increase model complexity, both the training error rate and the testing error rate will continue to fall until we hit the point of optimal model complexity. At this point, the model captures the signal in the data, and the testing error rate is at its lowest point. Once we increase model complexity beyond the optimal point, the testing error rate will begin to increase. This increase occurs because the model is now overfit to the training data and is starting to not generalize well to unseen data.

Warning

Interestingly, the training data error rate will continue to fall as we increase model complexity. This is where many inexperienced data scientists fall into trouble. Watching the error rate on your training data set continue to fall as you increase model complexity can give you a false sense of accomplishment. It's easy to fool yourself into believing that you are really nailing it! Be aware that you are actually overfitting your model to the training data set and it will result in very high error rates when your model goes into production and is applied to unseen data.

Step-by-Step Example of Finding Optimal Model Complexity

Ok, that's a lot of words, and if you are like me, then you are easily confused by lengthy explanations. I learn much better through pictures. So let's see a visual example of adjusting a model to reach the optimal model complexity (and thus minimizing the error rate).

Let's revisit our example of predicting a person's FICO score. This prediction can be beneficial for marketing or for dynamically adjusting offers based on a person's credit score. Our background business knowledge of how FICO scores are created leads us to believe that we will need predictive variables related to a person's income, payment history, overall balance, and length of credit history. This list of variables should give us a good predictive model to try to determine a new customer's FICO score.

Step 1 – Simple Linear Regression

Figure 1.11 shows a simple data set that has been divided into training data (dots) and testing data (stars). The first model that was constructed is a simple linear regression. We can think of this model in the form of:

$$FICO\ Score = Intercept + Income(x) + \varepsilon$$

Remember that for linear regression models, we will have the target variable (FICO Score), the model intercept, the coefficient (Income), and the error term (ε).

This simple linear regression with a single predictor variable will result in a high error rate for both the training and test data sets. It captures some of the general signal in the data, but it is not dynamic to the true relationship of the underlying data.

Figure 1.11: Simple Linear Regression

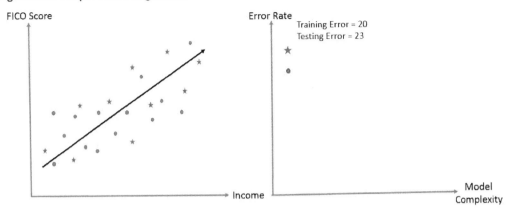

Step 2 – Linear Regression with Two Variables

Figure 1.12 demonstrates the effect of adding another predictor term to the model. In addition to the Income term, we have added a Payments term to the model:

$$FICO\ Score = Intercept + Income(x) + Payments(x) + \varepsilon$$

By considering a person's payment history in addition to their income, we can get a better prediction of their FICO score. The new model shows that the additional predictor term lowered both the training and the testing error rate. Since the testing error rate has decreased, we can be confident that the addition of the new predictor term benefits our model.

Figure 1.12: Linear Regression with Two Variables

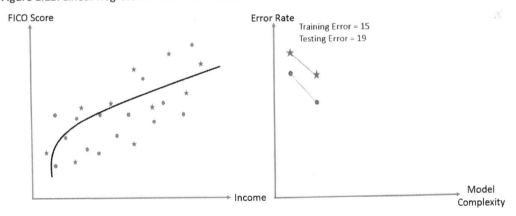

Step 3 – Linear Regression with Three Variables

Figure 1.13 shows the effect of adding a third predictor to the model. The Balance term represents a person's outstanding balance across their accounts. The updated model equation contains all three predictor terms:

$$FICO\ Score = Intercept + Income(x) + Payments(x) + Balance(x) + \varepsilon$$

Figure 1.13: Linear Regression with Three Variables

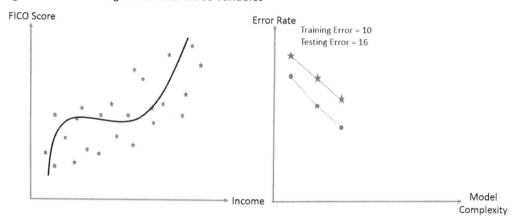

The addition of the Balance term allows the model to adjust and capture more of the signal in the data. This additional variable decreases the error rate in both the training and testing data sets.

Step 4 – Linear Regression with Four Variables

Figure 1.14 shows the effect of adding a fourth predictor term to the model. The addition of the Credit Tenure variable allows the model to adjust to a person's length of credit history. The updated equation is now:

$$FICO\ Score = Intercept + Income(x) + Payments(x) + Balance(x) + Credit\ Tenure(x) \\ + \varepsilon$$

The addition of the Credit Tenure variable lowers the error rate for both the training data and the testing data. We can be confident that the addition of this fourth variable is bringing us closer to optimal model complexity.

Figure 1.14: Linear Regression with Four Variables

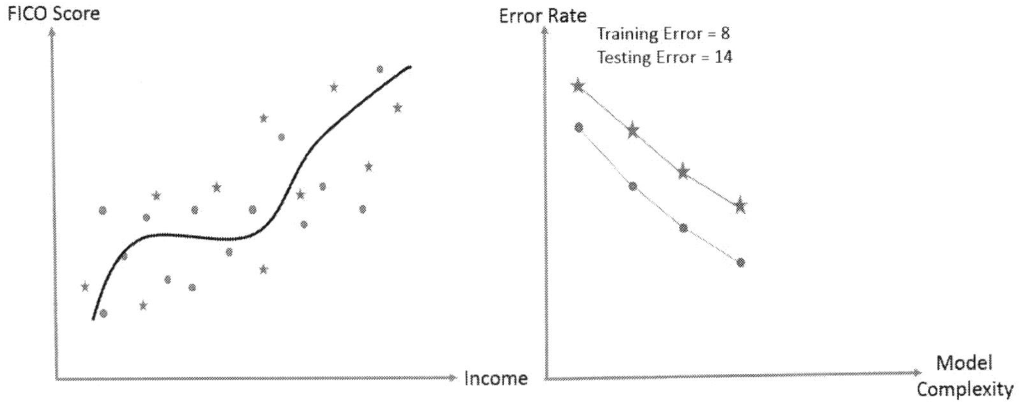

At this point, we have exhausted all the variables that we selected based on our background business knowledge. We now have variables related to income, payment history, overall balance, and credit history. The model is dynamic to the underlying data. It captures the signal in the data and is not overfit to the noise in the data.

What happens if we continue to increase model complexity?

Step 5 – Linear Regression with Five Variables

Figure 1.15 demonstrates the effect of adding a polynomial term of Income to the model. The addition of the squared value of income changes the model equation to:

$$FICO\ Score = Intercept + Income(x) + Payments(x) + Balance(x) + Credit\ Tenure(x) + Income(x)^2 + \varepsilon$$

The model is becoming overly tuned to the underlying training data and is starting to not generalize well to the unseen testing data. This over tuning is demonstrated by examining the error rate of the two data sets. The training rate continues to fall because the model is becoming highly tuned to this data set. It is starting to model the noise along with the signal. However, the testing data error rate has begun to **increase**. This increase is because the model that was developed on the training data is not generalizing well to the testing data. The overly fitted model does a poor job in predicting new cases and results in a higher testing error rate.

Figure 1.15: Linear Regression with Five Variables

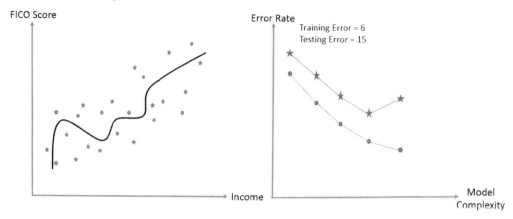

Step 6 – Linear Regression with Six Variables

In order to really drive home the point, we can add a sixth predictor term that is the polynomial of the Balance term. The addition of this term changes our equation to:

$$FICO\ Score = Intercept + Income(x) + Payments(x) + Balance(x)$$
$$+ Credit\ Tenure(x) + Income(x)^2 + Balance(x)^2 + \varepsilon$$

Figure 1.16 demonstrates how overly fit this model has become. The model is now so highly tuned to the training data that it completely misses on the testing data. The training error rate has continued to decrease while the testing error rate has continued to increase.

Figure 1.16: Linear Regression with Six Variables

Step 7 – Optimal Linear Regression Model

This visual demonstration allows us to determine where things went wrong for our model. By evaluating the testing error rate, we can determine that the model with four predictors is the best fit. This model is where the testing error rate is minimized.

$$FICO\ Score = Intercept + Income(x) + Payments(x) + Balance(x) + Credit\ Tenure(x) + \varepsilon$$

Figure 1.17 shows the optimal model complexity for this data set. This model is able to capture the signal in the training data set and use it to accurately predict values in the testing data set.

Figure 1.17: Optimal Linear Regression Model

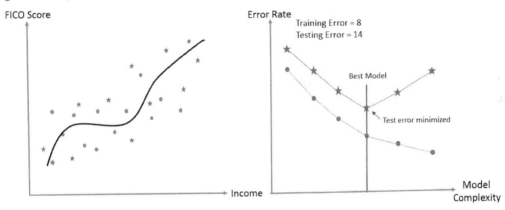

A lot of this book will focus on each concept of finding the optimal model complexity. This simplistic example above looked at a simple linear regression model. In actuality, data scientists need to be able to select a range of model types that would work for their underlying data. This range of model types would need to be narrowed down to one or two model types, and finally, a single model type would be chosen. Then they would need to tune the *hyperparameters* of the selected model in the same manner that we just did above. Hyperparameters are the pre-set parameters of a model that control the performance of the model. These values depend on the model type but may include learning rate, sampling rate, train fraction, alpha, and many other options.

Curse of Dimensionality

The *curse of dimensionality* is problematic because it goes against everything that we've been taught about data, namely, that more data is good. It is a data scientist's job to identify a lot of good data attributes to build a predictive model. Some modeling data sets can have thousands or even millions of predictor variables. This sounds great, right? You may think that you have a nearly endless number of predictors with which to build your model. This idea starts to erode when we think about what the model is actually doing.

If we take a classification model (for example, think about a KNN or decision tree model), we are attempting to identify observations that are close to one another in a certain region of dimensional space. The model will generally count the number of observations in a given region and use those observations to construct a predictor. If a new observation falls within this region, then we can assume that it is similar to the other observations in that region and we can infer a predictive value for the new observation based on the other observations in that space.

Figure 1.18 shows what begins to happen when we increase the number of dimensions. Remember that the number of dimensions is the same as the number of predictors in your model. A model with a single predictor can be visualized by the graph on the left of Figure 1.18. This simple model has only one dimension, so it is common for there to be many variables in a single region. This model has the benefit of many predictor observations to infer values to a new observation, but since it only represents one aspect of the data (the one dimension), it will not tell us much about the new observation.

Figure 1.18: Dimension Increase

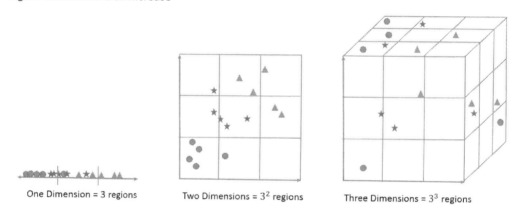

One Dimension = 3 regions   Two Dimensions = 3^2 regions   Three Dimensions = 3^3 regions

The middle graph of Figure 1.18 shows the same observations spread out over two dimensions. The additional dimension adds more information to the data and allows us to infer more information about new variables that appear in a given space; however, there are now fewer observations in a given area because the observations are being distributed across two dimensions rather than a single dimension.

The graph on the right of Figure 1.18 shows the same data spread out over three dimensions. Again, more information is gained by the additional predictor variables (dimensions), but the data is becoming even more dispersed. There are far fewer observations in each region to generate predictions.

Remember that we are distributing our limited number of observations across a feature-dependent dimensional space. The algorithm has to calculate the distance between observation points to identify groups of observations. The Euclidean distance between two Cartesian coordinates is expressed as the following formula, where p is the first coordinate and q is the second coordinate:

$$d(p, q) = \sqrt{\sum_{i=1}^{n} (p_i - q_i)^2}$$

(Sorry for the math, but sometimes it's necessary to explain things sufficiently). This equation shows that for each additional predictor term that we add, the distance between observation points increases. When we continue to add predictors but keep the number of observations constant, the result is a sparse feature space.

Our limited brains have a hard time imagining four-dimensional space, and we cannot really conceive of a 10,000-dimensional space. However, mathematics shows us that the number of observations needed to populate higher-dimensional space at a consistent density increases exponentially. Table 1.5 shows the exponential increase required to maintain an equivalent density in the feature space.

Table 1.5: Consistent Density in High-Dimensional Space

Dimension	Exponential Increase	Observations
1 Dimension	10^1	10
2 Dimensions	10^2	100
3 Dimensions	10^3	1000
n Dimensions	10^n	A whole bunch

Hughes Phenomenon

Hughes Phenomenon describes the tradeoff between the number of predictors in a model and the overall performance of the model. Figure 1.19 provides a graphical display of this concept. Hughes phenomenon simply states that as the number of predictor variables (features) increases, model performance will increase until it reaches the point of the optimal number of features for the given data set. If we add additional features beyond this optimal point while maintaining the same number of observations, the model performance degrades.

Figure 1.19: Hughes Phenomenon

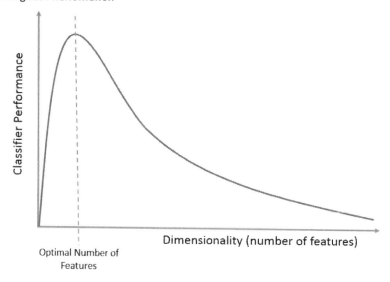

Simply stated, the curse of dimensionality is this: as you add more predictors to your model, you will need to add *exponentially* more observations to maintain model performance.

Transparent Versus Black Box Models

Simple models are easy to explain. For a simple linear regression, you can easily interpret the equation of the line. Nothing is hidden in this type of model. We know exactly what the intercept, coefficient weight, and error terms are. A simple decision tree is also easy to interpret. We can easily see the logic of the decision path and understand how each split point was calculated. The methodology for these models is open for inspection and easily understood. In fact, they are so straightforward that even your manager can understand these models. (Zing! Take that management!)

However, as we increase model complexity, the transparent nature of the model begins to change. Some models, like random forests, take the basic design of a decision tree and add randomization to the construction of many decision trees and summarize their collective predictions. It's not easy to give a solid explanation of what is happening to each variable to generate the result because that explanation changes for each of the hundreds of decision trees in a random forest.

Gradient boosting decision trees compiles the results of many decision trees by systematically taking the residual from the previous tree and using it as the target value for the next tree. In this type of model, the target value is continually changing. This loop is repeated many times over. The result is usually highly accurate, but it is not easy to explain what is happening at the predictor level.

The term "black-box model" describes a type of model that is complex and generates output without clear insight into how the prediction was created. Neural networks have famously become the poster child for black-box models. These types of models work great for image classification; however, there is no clear understanding of what particular factors contributed to the prediction. Was it the curve of the jaw or the angle of the lips or the skin tone of the person or the dress that they are wearing? Although all these factors are considered in a neural network model, you cannot assign a given quantity to a given aspect of the picture. In many cases, a very slight change in an image or a slightly different angle of the image can result in a completely different prediction.

Ethics

Black-box models are a massive concern to machine learning ethicists. As we become increasingly reliant on these types of models due to their incredible predictive accuracy, we are also moving further away from explainability and, consequently, justification of their use. Here is another example of the tradeoffs that are made with machine learning. The tradeoff of explainability and accuracy is not just a theoretical issue. It can have incredible consequences for your daily life.

Imagine that you are charged with a crime. The new AI criminal justice system calculates that you are guilty and automatically assigns you a sentence. You might want to know what reasons it gave to convict you. You might be disappointed if the answer is a cold, "the algorithm said so." That is a dystopian novel scenario with an unquestionable and unfeeling AI overlord determining your fate.

There are many examples of black-box algorithms producing results where we demand an explanation concerning its decision but are not provided one:

- Credit denial
- Identification of a cancerous cyst
- A self-driving car goes off the road
- Criminal sentencing

The ironic reality is that we rely on these black-box models due to their accuracy and automation. They are extremely fast, precise, and accurate. However, the more we integrate these algorithms into our daily lives, the more we will demand a human-level explanation of the model results. It can be a frightening thought that even the model developers who selected the inputs, model design, and the parameters cannot provide a clear explanation of how decisions are made within their own design. But on the bright side, I don't need to manually tag my friends in photos. I guess that's a win.

No Free Lunch

Data scientists have built an array of powerful models that can perform incredible tasks. Some of these model types are continually used to perform the most difficult machine learning tasks. Gradient boosting machines often win predictive modeling competitions and deep neural networks often solve complex image classification problems. You might ask yourself, so which model is the best? If deep neural networks are so great, then why don't we use them on every data problem?

The unfortunate answer is that there is no "skeleton-key model" that would work best for all possible data sets. For many data sets, we make assumptions about the distribution of the data. If a data set appears linear, then we use a linear model. If a data set appears clustered, then we can use a KNN model. However, if we relaxed all assumptions and approached a data set without any preconceived ideas about its distribution, there is no one single model that we can apply to all data sets that would outperform all other models.

This is because models need to be appropriately selected based on the underlying data distribution. Some data sets are linear by design while others are clustered. Some are sparse while some are dense. Some have stable patterns while others are erratic. Each one of these data sets has a specific model type that would work best.

The concept of no free lunch simply means that you cannot take the easy way out and use your trusty neural network model for every problem. For many data sets, a simple linear regression would work much better than a deep neural network. The only way to figure out which model to use is to evaluate the underlying data and make some assumptions about the data distribution. Then you need to select an array of model types that are aligned with that type of data distribution and apply them to the data. Finally, you must compare the results from these different model types and select which one works best for the given data to answer a given problem at a given time frame for a given population.

Chapter Review

This chapter is foundational to your understanding of data science. Nearly all the major concepts and issues of data science have been explained in detail. All these concepts will be used throughout the rest of this book and in every data science project that you will develop. It is very important that you understand these base concepts before you move forward into developing data science projects and constructing modeling algorithms.

Regardless of how well your project is designed or how sophisticated your modeling algorithm is, you will never get away from the underlying concepts explained in this chapter. Every data science project will have to address issues of the bias-variance tradeoff, underlying data distribution, optimal model complexity, the curse of dimensionality, and many other concepts covered in this chapter.

Chapter 2: Example Step-by-Step Data Science Project

Overview

Learning data science is a lot like learning to play a musical instrument. There is a lot of underlying technical theory, but in the end, the only way to learn how to play is to put your hands on the instrument and practice. This chapter will be like a musical recital (or a bar room jam band). It will be a demonstration of approaches and techniques. The goal is to show a real-life example of some of the concepts that we touched on in the introductory chapter and things that we will cover in greater detail in later chapters.

The goal of this chapter is to provide you with a complete data science project. It can be easy to get lost in all the necessary steps, so here is a general outline of the workflow:

- Identify the business opportunity
- Review previous work performed for this problem
- Find data
- Select a performance measure
- Create TRAIN / TEST data sets
- Analyze the target variable
- Analyze the predictor variables
- Develop a modeling data set
- Build predictive models
- Analyze results
- Implement the model

Many of the concepts that are introduced in this chapter will be developed further in the following chapters, which provide deep-dive explanations of specific concepts and techniques. If you are not familiar with a certain term or if a concept is briefly introduced as part of this workflow, please don't worry. These concepts are fully explained in the following chapters.

This chapter will also contain a good amount of SAS code. If you are not familiar with SAS coding, don't worry. The next two chapters will provide a thorough explaination of all the techniques presented in this chapter.

Business Opportunity

Imagine that you are a smart person with some coding skills and you want to make a ton of money with an online business while you work from home and devote very little time to the upkeep of your business. I know, it's a stretch. Who can imagine such a person? *Note: sarcasm does not come across well on the written page.*

Having an entrepreneurial spirit, you have decided to develop a product that could be used to support another much more popular product. This type of product could give you the benefit of an established target audience. This appeals to your lazy nature since you don't have to build an audience from scratch. After a little brainstorming, you've come up with a few ideas:

Amazon

- **Business Need** – Order totals that fall just shy of the $25 threshold for free shipping.
- **Solution** – An online search tool that will return products that will bring your total up to the minimum shipping threshold.

Ticketmaster

- **Business Need** – Concert tickets are expensive and people need to know how much ticket prices will be, so they can save up to see the Van Halen reunion tour.

- **Solution** – An online tool that will predict the cost of a given concert at a given location on a given date.

McDonald's

- **Business Need** – Cold french fries are disgusting.

- **Solution** – An online tool that will predict when fresh, hot fries will be available at any given McDonald's.

These are all brilliant ideas; however, some of them are not feasible.

- Amazon – A quick search reveals that this product already exists. **Strike one.**

- Ticketmaster – You love Van Halen so much that you don't want other people to buy the tickets and leave you at the mercy of scalpers. **Strike two.**

- McDonald's – Data is necessary to build models and you cannot find a database of historical french fry availability times for all possible McDonald's. Maybe there is such a database for Burger King, but you give up out of frustration. **Strike three.**

While you wait for your next brilliant idea to hit you, you decide to list your apartment on the most popular peer-to-peer property rental site, Airbnb, and generate some passive income by renting out your guest bedroom. Airbnb is an online service that lets property owners rent out their properties or rooms to guests.

You log on to Airbnb, set up your account, list the features of your apartment, and upload some photos. Great, you are ready to make some cash. However, the final question that you need to answer for your listing is, how much do you want to charge per night?

You don't know what your apartment is worth per night. You live in New York, so your place has to be expensive, right? But you don't live in an expensive, fashionable neighborhood. It's April, so it is cold and not tourist season. Is there a game or a festival or a concert in your area that might increase demand and, therefore, the price per night that you could charge?

You look at the available listings of the surrounding apartments, but they are not just like yours. Some are bigger or smaller, in different areas, and offer different features. You are about ready to give up out of frustration.

Suddenly, inspiration hits. This is it! This is the business opportunity that you've been looking for. You could develop an interactive web tool where people could input the features of their home, and it would give them the optimal Airbnb per diem price for a given location, date, and specific home features. Brilliant!

Initial Questions

Now that you have your brilliant idea, you need to answer these four initial questions:

- What is the business opportunity?
- Do we have the data to support this project?
- What type of work has been done previously on this type of problem?
- What does a solution look like?

What is the business opportunity?

A quick web search shows that there are approximately 4 million homes listed on Airbnb in 194 countries. Although this is very encouraging news, you want to focus only on the United States. Further research shows that there are nearly 600,000 listings in the United States. That's great news; however, you are a cautious researcher, and you discover that there is an average of three listings per host on Airbnb. So, your total market population is about 200,000 property owners.

You have the choice of different pricing options for your product:

- Charging a one-time fee for an estimate
- Charging a monthly membership fee for unlimited estimates
- Forgoing the fee in favor of ad revenue

I'm sure that you can think of plenty of other ways to monetize your product, but we need to focus on developing the product.

Do we have the data to support this project?

After some web hunting, you hit the jackpot! You have discovered a project titled *Inside Airbnb,* where raw Airbnb data is made publicly available for several cities in the United States and other cities around the world (www.insideairbnb.com). Murray Cox created this project to shed light on the ongoing debate concerning the impact of Airbnb on housing dynamics. Due to Airbnb being so tight-lipped about their data, it looks like this data was scraped from the web. Thanks, Murray!

Decision Time

Here is your first decision point. How much of this problem do you want to take on? You are fairly confident that each city will have its own housing dynamics that are unique to that area. You decide that you want to focus your data analysis on New York City. This is where you live, and you are familiar with the dynamics of the city. It is a reasonable approach to start with an area that you are familiar with and expand once you have proven that you are able to model that environment successfully.

We will look at the data in detail in a little while, but our initial look shows that the data is organized into two categories: *Listings* and *Calendar.* The listings data set contains descriptions of the physical, geographical, and host-related attributes of each property listed in New York City as of December 6, 2018. The calendar data set contains records of the nightly prices for the following 12 months for the majority of the listings. Both of these data sets encode relevant information that could potentially be determining factors in the pricing of these properties.

Great, so we have a business plan and data to support our project. Now let's see what kind of similar work has been done in this area. We don't want to reinvent the wheel.

What type of work has been done previously on this type of problem?

Since the inception of the "shared economy," there have been dozens of articles and scholarly papers written about Airbnb along with other peer-to-peer homestay networking sites. Although you have reviewed several of these papers, two of these studies appear to be the most relevant for your project.

Study #1

The online article titled "Predicting Airbnb Listing Prices with Scikit-Learn and Apache Spark" by Nick Amato was published on April 20, 2016 on the Mapr blog site. This article details the construction of a predictive model using the Python Scikit-Learn package in combination with Apache Spark for performance enhancement. The author uses the GradientBoostingRegressor predictive model in combination with the GridSearchCV cross-validation technique on the Apache Spark system to achieve an error of $21.43 rental price per night.

Takeaway

This article provides an excellent step-by-step look at developing several predictive models and assessing the accuracy of those models. The author also demonstrated how the large modeling data set produced processing issues. He had to rely on Apache Spark to increase processing efficiency and to allow the full range of exhaustive search methods to be employed on model development. So, let's remember that the combination of the listings and calendar data sets produces a very large data set that requires significant processing power to manipulate.

Study #2

In "Neighborhood and Price Prediction for San Francisco Airbnb Listings," Emily Tang and Kunal Sangani explore data from the *Inside Airbnb* project, containing a complete set of 7,029 listings of properties for rent on Airbnb in San Francisco as of November 2, 2015.

Rather than attempting to predict price as a continuous variable, a binary response variable for the price is created that indicates whether the predicted price is above or below the median price in the data set. This method has the advantage of simplifying both the price prediction task and the evaluation of the goodness of the model. However, the disadvantage of this approach is that simple linear regression is no longer a suitable option to model the price response variable and that the results of the prediction are of limited usefulness, especially for the application of suggesting pricing to hosts.

Additionally, in the data cleaning phase, all observations in neighborhoods containing 70 or fewer listings are removed. While this reduces the burden on the neighborhood classifier, it also restricts the model's usefulness to neighborhoods with a relatively high number of listings.

Takeaway

The final models for both price and neighborhood have impressive predictive power. In the test set, prices are categorized to the correct group (either above or below the median) with approximately 81% accuracy, while neighborhoods are categorized with 42% accuracy. While this performance seems good, the authors note that discretization of the predicted price into smaller bins is likely necessary for most applications, and is a promising direction for future work.

What does a solution look like?

We have done our homework and reviewed different approaches. We have gotten some insights into the data from previous researchers, and we have learned some best practices from these researchers. There seem to be benefits to both a continuous target variable and a binary target variable approach. The decision of our modeling approach will be driven by what we want the solution to look like.

Decision Time

The next decision point is establishing what is the problem that we are trying to solve. Do we want to construct this as a regression or a classification problem? We can quickly realize that the problem that we are trying to solve is a continuous target variable problem. Airbnb requires customers to list an exact amount that they will charge per night for their home. This is not a binary type of yes or no problem. We need to be able to generate a continuous dollar value.

Now that we have established what our target variable type will be, we have a couple of options on modeling types:

1. **Transparent model** – Regression model.
   a. Pros – The benefit of this type of model is that it will produce a dollar value for each feature of a home (demonstrated by coefficient weights). Customers will be able to know exactly what each feature contributes to the total cost per night value of their home.
   b. Cons – These types of models are traditionally not as accurate as more complex modeling types. This can result in property owners charging too little or too much for their nightly rate.
2. **Black box model** – This will be a more complex type of model (random forest, neural network, gradient boosting decision tree, and so on.)
   c. Pros – The benefit of this type of model is that it generally produces much more accurate predictions. This could provide the homeowner with the best possible listing price for their property.

d. Cons – Although we will be able to determine the most important features that go into determining the nightly rate, we will not be able to provide a "cost per feature" in the same manner that we can with a regression model.

We have established the business model, identified a data set, learned best practices from other researchers, and envisioned our implementation. Not a bad start. But before we start fantasizing about sipping piña coladas on our Playa Del Carmen vacation paid for by this amazing business, we have more work to do.

Get the Data

We have outlined an opportunity; however, we also have a lot of decisions to make in order to bring this project to life. These decisions are not made in the dark. A general rule of data science is to let the data guide you. So, let's get some data.

There are two ways to get the data.

1. You could go to the source *Inside Airbnb* data set and pull the data directly from their site. It is an excellent site that provides a lot of background information, insights, and many data attributes. You should definitely go to this site and check it out (www.insideairbnb.com).

2. I have downloaded the New York City *Inside Airbnb* data sets: **Listings** and **Calendar,** and I've placed them in our dedicated GitHub repository. These are the two main data sets that we will use for our analysis.

For the sake of consistency, I suggest that you use the data contained in our GitHub repository. The *Inside Airbnb* site updates their data often, so there is a good chance that the data that is currently on their site will be different from the data that we will be analyzing as part of this project. If you want to recreate this analysis to get a feel of the flow of data science (highly recommended), then use the data in our GitHub.

Web data that relies on user input is notoriously messy. People use inconsistent naming conventions (NY vs. New York vs. NYC), and they are generally terrible at spelling. I have taken the liberty of cleaning up the data by standardizing the naming conventions used in specific fields, creating logical and consistent formats for each variable, and I've eliminated all of the descriptive text fields. These descriptive text fields are generally very big fields, and they eat up a lot of memory and processing power.

We can always use the descriptive text fields later if we want to expand our analysis to include Natural Language Processing techniques to create variables developed from the text. But for now, let's move forward with the numeric and categorical fields in the cleaned data sets.

Download the data from GitHub and place it in your local data folder. Once you have the data, you will need to import the data into SAS. The data import code is below in Program 2.1. Please don't make fun of my terrible file naming convention.

Program 2.1: Import Data

```
FILENAME REFFILE 'C:\Users\James Gearheart\Desktop\SAS Book
Stuff\Data\listings_clean.csv';

PROC IMPORT DATAFILE=REFFILE
      DBMS=CSV
      OUT= MYDATA.Listings;
      GETNAMES=YES;
RUN;

PROC CONTENTS DATA=MYDATA.Listings; RUN;
```

For those of you who are new to SAS programming, this code might look a bit confusing. Don't worry; I will give a breakdown of each part of the code in the next chapter that focuses on learning to code in SAS. Remember, the purpose of this chapter is to give you a look at the steps and the decision path of an example data science project.

Output 2.1: Data Contents Overview

The CONTENTS Procedure

Data Set Name	WORK.LISTINGS	Observations	49056
Member Type	DATA	Variables	54

The first two rows of the PROC CONTENTS output show that there are 49,056 observations with 54 variables in the **Listings** data set. The PROC CONTENTS procedure also produces a list of variables and attributes. Since there are 54 variables in this data set, I will not list all of them here.

Remember the old real estate saying, "Location, location, location." Your model will be highly sensitive to the location of the property. When your data science problem is location specific, it is a good idea to generate a map graphic of your data.

Program 2.2: Create Geographic Map

```
ODS GRAPHICS / RESET WIDTH=6.4in HEIGHT=4.8in;

PROC SMAP plotdata=WORK.Listings;
      openstreetmap;
      scatter x=longitude y=latitude /
markerattrs=(size=3 symbol=circle);
RUN;

ODS GRAPHICS / RESET;
```

Figure 2.1: Output of Program 2.2

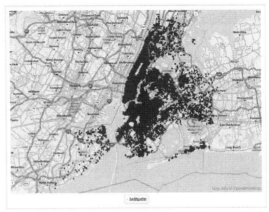

SAS does an excellent job of creating picture-perfect maps with a few lines of code. They are highly customizable with the ability to create choropleth maps and bubble maps along with lots of other customizable features.

For additional information, you can group the data points by a categorical feature. The code below in Program 2.3 shows the Airbnb listings color-coded by the Neighborhood Group feature.

Program 2.3: Create a Color-Coded Map

```
 /*Neighborhood Group Map View*/
ODS GRAPHICS / RESET WIDTH=6.4in HEIGHT=4.8in;

PROC SMAP plotdata=WORK.Listings;
      openstreetmap;
      scatter x=longitude y=latitude /
      group=neighbourhood_group_cleansed
      name="scatterPlot" markerattrs=(size=3 symbol=circle);
      keylegend "scatterPlot" /
      title='neighbourhood_group_cleansed';
RUN;

ODS GRAPHICS / RESET;
```

Figure 2.2: Map View by Neighborhood

The map view that is grouped by neighborhood in Figure 2.2 provides an easy visual snapshot of the data. We can see that Manhattan and Brooklyn appear to have a majority of the listings while The Bronx and Staten Island have relatively few listings.

Select a Performance Measure

To be a successful data scientist, you need to be brutally honest with yourself. It is easy to cheat a little bit here and there by:

- Cherry-picking test cases

- Analyzing the TEST data set to learn information that will be included in the model

- Selecting a more favorable performance measure

Decision Time

A *performance measure* is a metric that is used to determine how well a process is achieving a defined outcome. In the context of predictive modeling, performance measures provide an objective method of assessing model accuracy. Before you start developing your model, you need to first decide on a performance measure that fits your target variable, and that is aligned with the goal of your model. One of the most common performance measures for a continuous variable is the Root Mean Squared Error (RMSE). This metric measures the squared distance between the predicted and the actual observation.

$$RMSE(X, h) = \sqrt{\frac{1}{m_i} \sum_{i=1}^{m} (h(X^{(i)}) - y^{(i)})^2}$$

One important fact to keep in mind with this measure is that it severely penalizes large misses. This requires extra diligence on the upper and lower end predictions where large errors are common.

The RMSE is the performance measure that we will use to assess the performance of our model. The target value is a continuous variable (price), and our goal is to minimize the error distance between our predicted value and the actual value of price.

Train / Test Split

Before we start investigating the data and making any adjustments, we first need to split the data into TRAIN and TEST data sets. Remember, that we are attempting to simulate a real-world environment where we do not know anything about the data that the final model will be applied to. It would not be realistic to make all of our adjustments and learn everything that we can from the full data set and then split it into TRAIN and TEST data sets. It is a common mistake that data scientists make, which they pay for later when their implemented model does not perform as expected.

We create the TRAIN and TEST data sets by using the PROC SURVEYSELECT procedure. This is a great tool to use that allows you to set your sampling rate (SAMPRATE). I want an 80/20 split between my TRAIN and TEST data sets, with 80% of the data going to the TRAIN data set. Although there is no hard-and-fast rule as to what the sampling percentage should be, the 80/20 split is a standard amount.

The PROC SURVEYSELECT procedure also gives you the option of specifying which sampling strategy you would like to apply. For this project, I want to apply a simple random sample without replacement. This sampling method is accomplished with the METHOD = SRS statement.

Finally, I want to establish a seed. This specifies the initial seed for random number generation. In the model development stage of the project, we want to make sure that we create the same data set every time we run our code. The establishment of a seed is a great way to ensure that you can replicate your results.

You can use any number for a seed value. I use 42 because Douglas Adams showed us that 42 is the "Answer to the Ultimate Question of Life, the Universe, and Everything" in his "Hitchhiker's Guide to the Galaxy" series.

Program 2.4: Develop an 80/20 Split Indicator

```
/*Split data into TRAIN and TEST datasets at an 80/20 split*/
PROC SURVEYSELECT DATA=MYDATA.Listings SAMPRATE=0.20 SEED=42
       OUT=Full OUTALL METHOD=SRS;
RUN;
```

The PROC SURVEYSELECT procedure simply adds a field to the existing WORK.Listings data set. The Selected field is a binary variable that is coded as a 1 or 0. The 20% of observations that are randomly selected will have an indicator of 1, while the remaining 80% will have an indicator of 0.

The output of the PROC SURVEYSELECT procedure provides you with a summary statement of the chosen parameters. The Sample Size column shows the number of observations that were randomly selected by the algorithm. A quick confirmation shows that 9812/49056 = 20%.

Output 2.2: PROC SURVEYSELECT Summary Output

The SURVEYSELECT Procedure

Selection Method	Simple Random Sampling

Input Data Set	LISTINGS
Random Number Seed	1234
Sampling Rate	0.2
Sample Size	9812
Selection Probability	0.200016
Sampling Weight	4.999592
Output Data Set	FULL

We can create our TRAIN and TEST data sets by simply outputting records to each data set according to the value of the Selected field. Once the data is appropriately distributed to the data sets, we can drop the Selected variable.

Program 2.5: Create the TRAIN and TEST Data Sets

```
DATA TRAIN TEST;
    SET Full;
        IF Selected=0 THEN OUTPUT TRAIN; ELSE OUTPUT TEST;
        DROP Selected;
RUN;
```

One of the nice features of SAS is that the log provides you with a lot of information. Once Program 2.5 is submitted, you can check the log to confirm that the TRAIN and TEST data sets are the expected sizes and that there are no errors in the processing.

```
NOTE: There were 49056 observations read from the data set WORK.FULL.
NOTE: The data set WORK.TRAIN has 39244 observations and 54 variables.
NOTE: The data set WORK.TEST has 9812 observations and 54 variables.
NOTE: DATA statement used (Total process time):
      real time              0.09 seconds
      cpu time               0.07 seconds
```

Great! Now that our data is appropriately split, we can set aside the TEST data set and **not look at it** until we have developed our model and are ready to test it on our hold-out sample.

Target Variable Analysis

The next step in the development of our project is to identify and analyze the target variable.

Warning

We will take the time to review the target variable analysis in detail. It is **critically important** that you thoroughly explore your target variable and understand the content of this variable. We will make critical decisions that will affect the construction of the modeling data set and our end results.

The target variable requires a different approach than the predictor variables due to two main factors:

1. **Missing and nonsensical values** – It is inadvisable to infer these types of values for the target variable. It is common practice to infer missing values for predictor variables; however, you should not do it for your target variable.

2. **Predictors can be collapsed or dropped** – We will have lots of different choices to make with predictor variables. These include inferring values, regrouping, or dropping these variables. However, we have only one target variable, so we cannot drop it or change the fundamental nature of the variable by inferring values. We can transform the variable in different ways, but these methods cannot change the fundamental nature of the variable.

Let's start by focusing on the cross-sectional data in the TRAIN data set. We are attempting to predict the per diem rate of Airbnb listings in New York City as of 12/06/2018. The data set contains a few different price variables for us to choose from:

- Price
- Weekly price
- Monthly price
- Security deposit
- Cleaning fee
- Extra guest fee

The Price variable looks like the right one to use for our model. The other variables relating to cost are important pieces of information that we might use later, but for now, we will investigate our selected target variable.

The PROC UNIVARIATE procedure is a great way to investigate a continuous variable. A few simple lines of code will result in a lot of information about the distribution and range of a continuous variable.

Program 2.6: Investigate the Target Variable

```
PROC UNIVARIATE DATA=TRAIN;
       VAR Price;
       HISTOGRAM;
RUN;
```

This code calls the PROC UNIVARIATE procedure on the TRAIN data set. We have specified that we want to look at the Price variable. We have also requested that the output produce a histogram of the Price variable.

The output of the PROC UNIVARIATE procedure contains a lot of information, so let's look at it one section at a time.

The first section of Output 2.3 shows that the data contained 39,242 observations and that the average value for price is $152.15. However, you immediately see an issue with this variable. The standard deviation is larger than the mean value. This difference indicates that there are some big outliers that are pulling the average price up. We also see that the skewness is very high. The skewness measures the symmetry of the data. As a general rule of thumb, you want the skewness of the data to be between -1 and 1. This range would indicate a normal distribution of the data. Since the skewness of our target variable is about **20X** greater than we would want, we will probably have to transform the variable to create a normal distribution.

Output 2.3: PROC UNIVARIATE Moments Table

Moments			
N	39242	Sum Weights	39242
Mean	152.158937	Sum Observations	5971021
Std Deviation	224.655808	Variance	50470.2319
Skewness	20.2516236	Kurtosis	692.368482
Uncorrected SS	2889046579	Corrected SS	1980502372
Coeff Variation	147.64549	Std Error Mean	1.1340758

The next section of the PROC UNIVARIATE output shows the basic statistical measures. This section contains the average value of the Price variable (mean, median, and mode) along with measures of variability (std dev, variance, range, and interquartile range).

Output 2.4: PROC UNIVARIATE Basic Statistical Measures Table

Basic Statistical Measures			
Location		Variability	
Mean	152.1589	Std Deviation	224.65581
Median	110.0000	Variance	50470
Mode	150.0000	Range	10000
		Interquartile Range	109.00000

There is a significant difference between the mean and median values. This difference is further evidence that outlier values are affecting the mean value. The range metric shows us the difference between the highest and lowest value. There is a $10,000 per diem range for price. Wow, that high end must be an awesome place to live.

Output 2.5: PROC UNIVARIATE Quantiles, Extreme Observations, and Missing Values Tables

Quantiles (Definition 5)	
Level	Quantile
100% Max	10000
99%	750
95%	355
90%	270
75% Q3	179
50% Median	110
25% Q1	70
10%	50
5%	40
1%	30
0% Min	0

Extreme Observations			
Lowest		Highest	
Value	Obs	Value	Obs
0	37561	9999	9490
0	35638	10000	4323
0	31895	10000	19705
0	25756	10000	36663
0	23968	10000	36951

Missing Values			
Missing Value	Count	Percent Of All Obs	Missing Obs
.	2	0.01	100.00

The final section of the PROC UNIVARIATE output (Output 2.5) contains more information about the details of the variable distribution, along with outliers and missing values.

The first section of Output 2.5 shows the quantiles of the variable. This contains the minimum and maximum values as well as values at certain percentage cutoff points. The maximum value for the Price variable is $10,000 while the minimum is $0.

At this point, we need to ask ourselves a question. Does it make any sense that someone would charge $0 per night to stay at their house? Maybe they are very lonely and just want some company. It is probably just the result of bad data entry.

We also see that in the missing values section of the output, there are two observations with missing price data. This is actually good news. Usually, user-entered data is messier than this. These statistics show that less than 1% of the data would need to be either adjusted or deleted. We will make those decisions in the near future.

On the high end of the distributions, we see that the 99% cutoff value is $750. There is a massive difference between the 99% and 100% values. That top 1% of observations are extreme outlier data points.

The final piece of output that we can examine is the histogram of the Price variable. The distribution chart gives a visual demonstration of the statistics that we just reviewed.

The histogram (Output 2.6) shows a highly skewed distribution with a very long right-sided tail. The story that this chart tells us matches perfectly with the skewness value of 20.25 that we see in the statistics table above. All of this information tells us that the Price variable has significant outliers on the high end that we need to fix before we can do any modeling.

Output 2.6: PROC UNIVARIATE Histogram

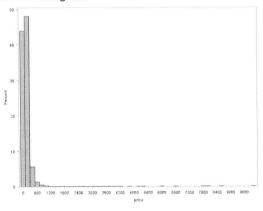

Decision Time

Here is one of the main decision points that we need to address that will affect the rest of our project. We must determine which observations we will keep to establish our modeling data set. Extreme outliers are a big problem in model development because they pull the predicted value in a manner that is not representative of the majority of the data.

The old example of the effect of outliers is if you have 100 people in a room, their average net worth might be $50,000 per person. However, if Bill Gates walks into the room, suddenly the average net worth is now $100,000,000 per person. Bill has skewed the average net worth due to his extreme outlier position of net worth. The only way to establish an accurate average net worth is to kick Bill out of the room.

The moral of the story is that we need to throw out some observations for the model to be uninfluenced by extreme outliers. As a general rule of thumb, we can exclude the top 1% and the bottom 1% of target values if they are determined to be extreme outliers or nonsensical data.

An important note is that we are excluding only these observations because of the outlier nature of the *target* variable. When we see outliers in the predictors, we will have the option to set max and min thresholds and recode those values.

So, we have investigated the target variable and determined that values with missing or $0 entries do not make sense. We have also investigated the high-end values, and we have determined that a cutoff point of $750 would eliminate extreme outliers. Let's code it up...

Program 2.7: Limit the Data and Create the Log Adjusted Target Value

```
/* Eliminate outliers and create log transformed price variable */
DATA Price;
      SET TRAIN;
      WHERE 30 le Price le 750;
      Price_Log = LOG(Price);
RUN;
```

The log shows us that the adjusted data set contains 38,523 observations. The original data set contained 39,241; therefore, we have lost only 715 observations. The majority of these excluded observations were for properties that have a $0 per diem rate.

```
NOTE: There were 38503 observations read from the data set WORK.TRAIN.
      WHERE (Price>=30 and Price<=750);
NOTE: The data set WORK.PRICE has 38503 observations and 55 variables.
NOTE: DATA statement used (Total process time):
      real time            0.07 seconds
      cpu time             0.03 seconds
```

Although our target variable is much cleaner now that we have established our upper and lower boundaries, we expect that the distribution of the data will still be skewed to the right. A PROC UNIVARIATE procedure developed on the Price variable shows a right tail skewness with a value of 2.13. (See Output 2.7.)

Output 2.7: PROC UNIVARIATE Moments Table and Histogram

Moments			
N	38523	Sum Weights	38523
Mean	139.432754	Sum Observations	5371368
Std Deviation	102.003105	Variance	10404.6335
Skewness	2.13093031	Kurtosis	6.25960269
Uncorrected SS	1149751926	Corrected SS	400807291
Coeff Variation	73.15577	Std Error Mean	0.51970075

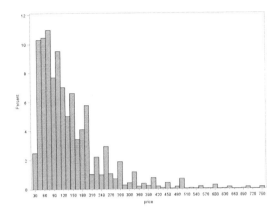

In anticipation of this skewness, I created a log-transformed version of the Price variable in the previous DATA step (Program 2.7). This approach will transform the Price variable into a normally distributed variable. A PROC UNIVARIATE developed on the log-transformed Price variable shows a skewness value of 0.26.

Output 2.8: PROC UNIVARIATE Moments Table and Histogram on the Log-Adjusted Target Variable

Moments			
N	38523	Sum Weights	38523
Mean	4.72611784	Sum Observations	182064.238
Std Deviation	0.63728462	Variance	0.40613169
Skewness	0.26686149	Kurtosis	-0.3983477
Uncorrected SS	876102.048	Corrected SS	15645.0049
Coeff Variation	13.4843151	Std Error Mean	0.00324693

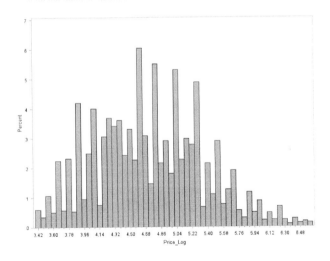

Great! We now have a data set where we have eliminated extreme outliers and nonsensical values. We have also transformed our target variable into a normally distributed variable. Remember that we can always transform the log value of a variable back to its original scale by taking the exponential of the log value. But for now, we are ready to move on to investigating the predictor values.

Predictor Variable Analysis

Before we begin to analyze the predictor variables, it's a good idea to take a moment to think about what the goal of the project is and how we would envision a completed project. We want to develop a tool that property owners could use to give them the optimal per diem price for their property on Airbnb. The predictor variables will be the values that property owners enter to describe the features of their property. You have the option of including additional features based on regional factors (tourist attractions, crime rate, events, and so on), but for now, we will focus on the data that we have already gathered.

Under this scenario, we could make some assumptions:

- We can expect that the traditional home features will be significant in the model:
  - Location
  - Property type
  - Number of people the property will accommodate
  - Number of beds, baths, rooms, and so on
- Some data will not be available at the point of application:
  - User review scores
  - Review volume

This is a good example of the difference between a data scientist and a machine learning engineer. The machine learning engineer will generally use all possible data attributes and create the most predictive model possible by focusing on minimizing the performance metric on the TEST data set.

The data scientist has to use business knowledge to throw out data. This might sound crazy to you. We have all been trained that more data is better. However, to actualize our vision of the final project, we need to limit the data to attributes that will be available at the point of application. Although the data set contains lots of features about current properties on Airbnb, we will not be able to use all of these features.

Modeling Considerations

Another important topic that we need to consider as we investigate our predictor variables is the issue of model design. We haven't determined what type of model we will eventually put into production. However, we will need to take different approaches to our predictor variables based on what type of model that we will implement. Here are our choices:

- **Parametric Model** – This would be some form of a regression model where we know the functional form of the model. This type of model will require us to do a thorough evaluation of the predictor variables and make adjustments based on:
  - **Data quality** – missing data and outlier values will need to be adjusted.

- o **Correlation** – predictor variables that are correlated will need to be identified and adjusted.

- o **Categorization** – character variables with many levels will need to be collapsed into smaller categories.

- o **Scaling** – regression models do not perform well when the numeric values are on different scales. For example, the home price could be a range of $15K to $500K, while the same model will have "number of bathrooms" that range from 0 to 5.

- **Non-parametric Model** – These types of models do not assume a functional form and can, therefore, adapt to a much greater range of functional forms. These models are not (generally) sensitive to the issues that are problematic for regression models. For example, it is often advantageous to feed the raw data into a tree-type model and allow the algorithm to determine categorization and split points.

We will start the analysis of the predictor variables with a regression model in mind. We can always use the raw variables later to build a non-parametric model.

Numeric Variables

The first step to understanding the predictor variables is to separate the numeric and categorical variables. We will need to perform different types of analysis depending on the construct of the variables.

A PROC MEANS statement can give us a quick overview of the numeric variables. This procedure will not work for categorical variables, so we specify that we want to keep only the numeric variables in the KEEP statement.

Program 2.8: Investigate Numeric Data with PROC MEANS

```
PROC MEANS DATA=Price (KEEP = _NUMERIC_) N NMISS MIN MAX MEAN MEDIAN STD;
RUN;
```

Output 2.9: PROC MEANS Output

Variable	N	N Miss	Minimum	Maximum	Mean	Median	Std Dev
id	38523	0	2515	30567057	16,260,626.19	16911171	9,227,822.87
host_id	38523	0	2571	229305072	53,988,568.16	25412718	62,967,997.00
host_since	38518	5	17771	21523	20,077.54	20097	780.03
host_listings_count	38518	5	0	2310	11.93	1	92.37
zipcode	37970	553	10001	112208	10,664.64	11103	948.47
latitude	38523	0	40.499794	40.911695	40.73	40.7241486	0.05
longitude	38523	0	-74.240843	-73.710233	(73.95)	-73.956755	0.04
accommodates	38523	0	1	16	2.86	2	1.82
bathrooms	38462	61	0	17	1.16	1	0.46
bedrooms	38488	35	0	11	1.17	1	0.73
beds	38492	31	0	21	1.54	1	1.04
square_feet	359	38164	0	5000	708.33	650	612.81
price	38523	0	30	750	139.43	110	102.00
weekly_price	5349	33174	85	12000	857.91	700	621.87
monthly_price	4707	33816	500	36000	2,850.75	2400	1,953.74
security_deposit	24326	14197	0	5100	281.36	150	498.69
cleaning_fee	29858	8665	0	600	65.79	50	53.61
guests_included	38523	0	1	16	1.51	1	1.10
extra_people	38523	0	0	300	14.06	0	23.22
minimum_nights	38523	0	1	1000	6.76	3	17.53
maximum_nights	38523	0	1	2147483647	56,911.84	1124	10,941,792.14
availability_30	38523	0	0	30	7.69	4	9.52
availability_60	38523	0	0	60	21.04	15	21.39
availability_90	38523	0	0	90	35.18	28	34.12
availability_365	38523	0	0	365	124.47	64	137.80
number_of_reviews	38523	0	0	571	22.33	5	41.15
first_review	30569	7954	17818	21524	20,771.45	20918	617.22
last_review	30570	7953	18572	21524	21,292.31	21474	353.72
review_scores_rating	29764	8759	20	100	93.90	96	8.14
review_scores_accuracy	29734	8789	2	10	9.61	10	0.80
review_scores_cleanliness	29745	8778	2	10	9.27	10	1.05
review_scores_checkin	29711	8812	2	10	9.75	10	0.68
review_scores_communication	29733	8790	2	10	9.76	10	0.67
review_scores_location	29706	8817	2	10	9.51	10	0.76
review_scores_value	29706	8817	2	10	9.38	10	0.87
calculated_host_listings_count	38523	0	1	174	4.83	1	16.72
reviews_per_month	30569	7954	0.01	20.33	1.43	0.78	1.67
Price_Cat	38523	0	50	750	141.90	100	103.45
Price_Log	38523	0	3.4011974	6.6200732	4.73	4.7004804	0.64

Some of these variables, we can safely ignore. The ID and Host_ID variables are unique identifiers, so as long as the number missing (NMISS) value is 0, we do not need to investigate these any further. We can also ignore the Latitude and Longitude variables because they are useful only for mapping, and we can ignore the Price and Price_Log variables since we analyzed them extensively in the previous section.

Exclude Certain Predictors

Several numeric variables will not be available at the point of application. We will assume that users of our tool will be listing new properties and not ones that already contain user review scores.

Therefore, we will exclude the following variables:

- Number of reviews
- Review scores rating
- Review scores accuracy
- Review scores cleanliness
- Review scores check-in
- Review scores communication
- Review scores location
- Review scores value
- Reviews per month
- First review
- Last review
- Host since

We will also exclude the calculated_host_listing_count because this is a system-generated variable that will not be available at the point of application. It appears that the host_listing_count variable is be a reasonable substitute for this variable, but we will need to work with it because the max value (2310) and the standard deviation (92) appear to be very high.

Numeric Missing Values

Decision Time

A common decision that data scientists have to make is how to handle missing values. Several of the variables have missing values. This issue is especially problematic for regression models. Regression models will exclude any observation with a single missing value. This exclusion can result in a highly biased model. Therefore, we need to make some decisions on what to do with these variables.

A quick look at each of the variables in Table 2.1 that have some missing values shows that the percentage of missing values ranges from nearly all of the values (square_feet = 99.1%) to almost none of the values (host_listings_count = 0.0%).

Table 2.1: PROC MEANS Missing Data Analysis

Variable	N	N Miss	Missing Percent	Suggested Imputation Method
square_feet	359	38164	99.1%	Exclude
security_deposit	24326	14197	36.9%	Set missing to zero
cleaning_fee	29858	8665	22.5%	Set missing to zero
zipcode	37970	553	1.4%	Infer based on neighborhood
bathrooms	38462	61	0.2%	Global median
bedrooms	38488	35	0.1%	Global median
beds	38492	31	0.1%	Global median
host_listings_count	38518	5	0.0%	Global median

We will take a missing value imputation approach based on the nature of the variable and the volume of missing values.

- **Square_feet** – Since nearly all of the observations are missing, this variable adds very little information to the data set. It is an absurd approach to try to impute nearly all of the values. We will exclude this variable from the model.

- **Security_deposit and cleaning_fee** – The logical reason that these values are missing is that these properties do not require a security deposit or cleaning fees as a condition of their rental agreement. We will set these missing values to zero.

- **Zipcode** – It doesn't make sense to impute ZIP codes with a mean value. Instead, we can identify the correct correlation between the neighborhood and ZIP code and apply it to neighborhoods with missing ZIP code values.

- **Bedrooms, bathrooms, beds, host listing count** – There are very few observations where there are missing values. We can impute their value with the global mean.

Numeric Adjustments

Decision Time

Some of the most important decisions that data scientists will make concerning their projects is whether or not they will make adjustments to the predictor variables. These adjustments can include imputing values, setting thresholds, scaling, and excluding variables. This section reviews some of those decision points for our numeric variables.

Host_listings_count – This variable is highly skewed, with some property owners listed as having over 2,300 properties available on Airbnb. This skewness could be a data entry issue, or it could be actual data; we don't really know. Either way, we will need to adjust this variable to deal with the skewness of its distribution.

Further analysis of this variable shows that there are differences between property owners who have a single property compared to those that have between two and ten properties and those who are major property owners who have more than ten properties. I have created a categorical variable for these levels and discarded the original numeric variable.

Table 2.2: Frequency Distribution of Newly Created Variable

host_count_cat	Frequency	Percent	Cumulative Frequency	Cumulative Percent
Level 1	23569	61.18	23569	61.18
Level 2	12294	31.91	35863	93.10
Level 3	2660	6.90	38523	100.00

Additional fees – It does not make intuitive sense that the fees charged for a security deposit, cleaning, and extra people would affect the base per diem rate for the property. You could make the argument that these fees suggest a level of quality of the property, but they are entirely subjective and not an inherent feature of the property. These fees could be modeled separately, and you could generate suggested fee amounts for your customers. For now, we will choose to exclude them from modeling.

Zipcode – This is a tricky feature to deal with. ZIP code is obviously a strong predictive factor because our background business knowledge tells us that location is a primary driver of the per diem rate. However, for our data set, there are 187 different ZIP codes. For our regression model approach, this severely inflates the degrees of freedom in the model, and we are confronted with the curse of dimensionality. (See the previous chapter for an overview of this topic).

Other categorical features provide similar information. These include neighbourhood_cleansed, neighbourhood_group, and city. The inclusion of ZIP code could lead to overfitting. For our regression model approach, we need to make a decision about which location variable to use. I would suggest that the location variables with over 20 levels result in a sparse modeling space and that we would benefit by using the neighbourhood_group_cleansed variable with five levels. The other location variables will be retained for other modeling approaches.

Maximum_nights and minimum_nights – These are highly skewed data attributes with glaring data entry errors. These variables were capped at the 99% value. For maximum nights we set an upper threshold of 1125, and for the minimum nights, we set an upper threshold of 31.

Beds, bedrooms, and bathrooms – Each of these variables have outliers associated with them. For example, the beds variable has a maximum value of 21 while the 99th percentile is just five beds. We will need to cap these variables at their 99th percentile to avoid the severe outliers affecting the model. Therefore, the beds variable is capped at 5, the bedrooms variable is capped at 4, and the bathrooms variable is capped at 3.

Collinearity Analysis

One of the founding assumptions of regression models is that the predictor variables need to be independent (not correlated with one another). This assumption is important because if two or more variables are closely related, it is difficult to separate the individual effects of those variables on the response variable. In the end, collinearity reduces the accuracy of the estimates of the regression coefficients because it inflates the standard error of those coefficients.

The table below provides a good rule of thumb for interpreting correlation coefficients. Any correlation coefficient above 0.7 or below -0.7 is considered highly correlated.

Table 2.3: Correlation Table

Size of Correlation	Interpretation
0.9 to 1.0 (-0.9 to -1.0)	Very high correlation
0.7 to 0.9 (-0.7 to -0.9)	High correlation
0.5 to 0.7 (-0.5 to -0.7)	Moderate correlation
0.3 to 0.5 (-0.3 to -0.5)	Low correlation
0.0 to 0.3 (0.0 to -0.3)	Negligible correlation

SAS provides two great ways to identify multicollinearity through the CORR and REG procedures. PROC CORR creates a correlation matrix that contains the correlation coefficient for each variable combination.

> Here is a good SAS trick. You can create a global variable that contains all of the variables in a data set and places them into a single macro variable. The code below shows how you can call a CONTENTS procedure and retain the names of the variables from that procedure and place them into a separate data set. Then an SQL procedure is created that places those variables into a macro variable that is called with an ampersand (&). Now, you just need to call the macro variable rather than writing each of the variable names over and over!

Program 2.9: Place All Variable Names into a Macro Variable

```
/* Create global numeric variables */
PROC CONTENTS NOPRINT DATA=Clean (KEEP=_NUMERIC_ DROP=id host_id latitude
longitude Price Price_Log) OUT=var1 (KEEP=name);
RUN;

PROC SQL NOPRINT;
     SELECT name INTO:varx separated by " " FROM var1;
QUIT;

%PUT &varx;

/* Create correlation analysis */
PROC CORR DATA=Clean;
     VAR &varx.;
RUN;
```

PROC CORR uses the numeric variables that I kept in the macro variable. The default correlation statistic is the Pearson's r. The results of the procedure are below. I have color-coded the top 10% of high and low correlation values.

Table 2.4: Correlation Table

	accommodates	availability 30	availability 60	availability 90	availability 365	bathrooms	bedrooms	beds	guests included	maximum nights	minimum nights
accommodates		0.05	0.10	0.11	0.15	0.31	0.63	0.77	0.57	0.04	(0.02)
availability 30	0.05		0.88	0.80	0.56	0.04	0.03	0.04	0.03	0.01	0.22
availability 60	0.10	0.88		0.97	0.70	0.05	0.06	0.09	0.09	(0.01)	0.18
availability 90	0.11	0.80	0.97		0.75	0.05	0.06	0.10	0.10	(0.01)	0.18
availability 365	0.15	0.56	0.70	0.75		0.07	0.08	0.14	0.12	0.07	0.27
bathrooms	0.31	0.04	0.05	0.05	0.07		0.37	0.31	0.18	0.03	0.04
bedrooms	0.63	0.03	0.06	0.06	0.08	0.37		0.65	0.42	0.01	0.01
beds	0.77	0.04	0.09	0.10	0.14	0.31	0.65		0.49	0.03	0.01
guests included	0.57	0.03	0.09	0.10	0.12	0.18	0.42	0.49		(0.02)	(0.07)
maximum nights	0.04	0.01	(0.01)	(0.01)	0.07	0.03	0.01	0.03	(0.02)		0.06
minimum nights	(0.02)	0.22	0.18	0.18	0.27	0.04	0.01	0.01	(0.07)	0.06	

Variables are considered highly correlated if the correlation coefficient is above 0.7 or below -0.7. The bottom 10% of correlation values are highlighted in green. We can see that negative correlation is not a problem since the strongest negative correlation is -0.07.

For the positively correlated variables, we see that there are several cases where the correlation coefficient is above 0.7. It makes sense that the availability variables are highly correlated. If a property is available within 30 days, it would also be available within the next 60, 90, and 365 days. Also, the correlation between accommodates and beds makes sense. If a property has a high number of beds, it can accommodate more people.

Variance Inflation Factor

Let's look at the correlation between these features from a different angle. We can create a REG procedure with the VIF option that will give us the variance inflation factor for each variable in the model. The variance inflation factor is calculated by dividing the ratio of variance in a full model by the variance of a model with a single variable. The lowest possible value for a VIF is 1, but a good rule of thumb is that you want your VIF to be less than or equal to 5.

The PROC REG code with the numeric macro variable and the VIF statement is included below in Program 2.10. I also added the COLLIN statement that produces a collinearity diagnostic.

Program 2.10: Variance Inflation Factor in a PROC REG

```
PROC REG DATA=WORK.CLEAN PLOTS=ALL;
      model Price_Log= &varx /
      selection=forward VIF COLLIN;
RUN;
```

Output 2.10: Parameter Estimates Table with the VIF values

Parameter Estimates						
Variable	DF	Parameter Estimate	Standard Error	t Value	Pr > |t|	Variance Inflation
Intercept	1	4.17157	0.00909	458.67	<.0001	0
accommodates	1	0.18535	0.00257	72.00	<.0001	2.96810
availability_30	1	0.00758	0.00069356	10.93	<.0001	5.92921
availability_60	1	-0.00246	0.00077869	-3.15	0.0016	37.69913
availability_90	1	-0.00053214	0.00038769	-1.37	0.1699	23.78118
bathrooms	1	-0.04456	0.00682	-6.53	<.0001	1.17824
bedrooms	1	-0.03798	0.00530	-7.17	<.0001	1.97189
beds	1	0.03115	0.00493	6.32	<.0001	2.79022
guests_included	1	0.01810	0.00304	5.96	<.0001	1.53053
maximum_nights	1	0.00005528	0.00000511	10.81	<.0001	1.00969
minimum_nights	1	0.00398	0.00032250	12.34	<.0001	1.06874

We can see in Output 2.10 that the VIF for the availability_60 and availability_90 variables are off the charts! If we think about what these variables are telling us about the property, we might interpret them as a measure of demand. I believe that we could safely exclude the availability of 60, 90, and 365 variables and still retain the necessary information that we get from the single availability_30 variable.

Warning

However, the problem of correlation is just beginning for this data set. We plan on creating additional variables (called *feature engineering*), and we plan on adding polynomial variables to the model. All of these variables will have some degree of correlation with the other variables that they are built on. So, instead of trying to find all of the variables that are correlated and throwing them out one at a time, we will instead introduce a regularization option to the predictive model. The concept of regularization is examined in detail in the regression chapter of this book. A regularization model is a model that introduces a shrinkage parameter to the algorithm. This parameter constrains the model to ensure that the model does not overfit the data.

The two main options for regularization are RIDGE and LASSO regression. For this project, we will use LASSO regression. The LASSO approach adds an absolute value bias term to the regression function. This approach reduces the negative effects of multicollinearity and consequently the model's variance. This approach has the effect of setting the coefficients to zero if they are not relevant. We will review the LASSO methodology in detail later in the book, but for now, we just need to understand that it is a method that reduces the effects of multicollinearity in our model.

At this point, you might start realizing that data science is not just taking all of your data and throwing it into an XGBOOST model (hey, they win all the time on Kaggle) and minimizing your test error metric. That approach works well for modeling competitions and in academics, but if you are building predictive models to support a real-world business venture, there are a lot of decisions that have to be made that might work against your ability to minimize your test metric.

The question that you have to ask yourself is, "what is my goal"? Minimizing a test metric is not the goal. Building a business that is valuable to your customers by providing them with the most **actionable** information possible is your goal.

Scatter Matrix

An additional method of analyzing our numeric variables is to produce scatter plots of each variable's relationship with the target variable. SAS provides a great visual demonstration of these relationships with the scatter matrix graph.

This graph contains a series of scatter plots and allows the researcher to easily see the relationships that each of the numeric predictor variables has with the target variable. We can also see the relationship that the numeric predictors have with one another.

Output 2.11: Scatter Matrix

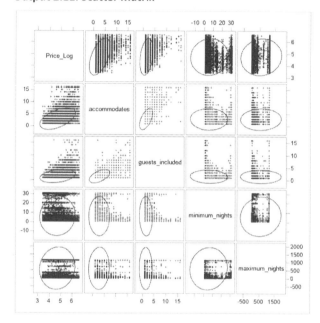

In Output 2.11, we can already see the strong positive relationship between the price and accommodates variables, as well as between price and guests included.

Program 2.11: Scatter Plot Matrix

```
PROC SGSCATTER DATA=Clean;
    TITLE 'Scatter Plot Matrix';
    MATRIX Price_Log accommodates guests_included minimum_nights
maximum_nights/
        START=TOPLEFT ELLIPSE = (ALPHA=0.05 TYPE=PREDICTED) NOLEGEND;
RUN;
```

Feature Engineering

Feature engineering is the process of creating additional variables based on your current variables. It is not just adding new features to your data set; it is the result of taking the time to actually think about your variables and what information they contain and then squeezing even more value from them.

For example, the code below creates two new variables based on the accommodates, beds, and bathrooms variables. When we think about real estate pricing and what features a potential renter is looking for when they are viewing Airbnb listings, we might consider that they are making their decision not only on the total number of beds, bathrooms, and total accommodates values. They are considering the "beds per accommodates" and the "bathrooms per accommodates" rates.

Program 2.12: Feature Engineering

```
/*      Feature Engineering */
IF beds not in (., 0) then
        beds_per_accom = accommodates / beds;
else beds_per_accom = 0;

IF bathrooms not in (., 0) then
        bath_per_accom = accommodates / bathrooms;
else bath_per_accom = 0;
```

If a property states that it can accommodate 12 people, but it only has a single bathroom, that can severely affect demand and therefore, could be a powerful feature to include in our model.

Polynomial Variables

Not all relationships between the target and predictor variables are linear. In fact, most of the time, they are not linear. The addition of polynomial variables to the model provides the model the opportunity to capture the non-linear relationships in the numeric variables.

It does not make sense to create polynomial variables for binary numeric indicators. So we will generate only polynomial variables based on the continuous numeric variables that we have already decided to keep in the regression modeling data set.

Program 2.13: Create Polynomials

```
poly_accom = accommodates**2;
poly_bath = bathrooms**2;
poly_guests = guests_included**2;
poly_min = minimum_nights**2;
poly_max = maximum_nights**2;
poly_avail = availability_30**2;
```

Standardize Numeric Variables

The final adjustment that we need to consider for numeric variables is related to the issue of scale. If you look at the scatter matrix graph, you can see that the scales are different for each variable. Variables with a much higher scale will have a stronger influence on the model than variables with a lower scale. For example, the variable maximum_nights will have an artificially inflated influence on the model results compared to guests_included.

An easy way to adjust the numeric variables to account for differences in scale is to standardize them. There are several different methodologies for standardization, and we will cover several of them in a later chapter. If you run a PROC UNIVARIATE on the predictor variables, you will find that they all have different scales and that several of them are significantly skewed. An easy way to take care of both of these issues is to log transform these variables.

Output 2.12: Scaled Scatter Plot Matrix

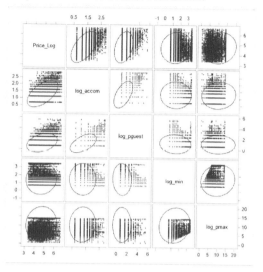

Program 2.14 creates log transformations out of the raw numeric data. Notice that I add one to each of the variables. This adjustment is because if the value for a variable is zero, the log transformation is undefined. This situation creates a missing value. (Remember that observations with missing values are excluded from the regression algorithm). So if we add one to the value, it changes the zero to one, and when we take the log of one, the value is zero. This slight global shift results in all of the variables shifting one unit positive, which does not affect the outcome; however, it does ensure that there are no unforeseen missing values in the data set.

Program 2.14: Create Log Transformations

```
/*Standardize variables with log transformation*/
log_accom    = log(accommodates +1);
log_bath     = log(bathrooms +1);
log_bedrooms = log(bedrooms +1);
```

The scatter matrix of the log variables is shown in Output 2.12. Notice how the scale of the variables has been changed (particularly the maximum_nights variable). Also, the distribution of the variables has been centered as a result of the log transformation.

We have done a lot of work on the numeric variables.

- We have investigated the distribution of these variables and have made decisions concerning upper and lower thresholds.

- We have identified variables that would not be available at the point of application and therefore, we have excluded them from further consideration.

- We have identified missing values and applied the proper inference for each variable.

- We have binned continuous variables and created categorical variables where necessary.

- We have performed a correlation analysis and decided to use a LASSO regression model design to account for multicollinearity.

- We have created new variables through feature engineering.

- We have developed polynomial variables to identify non-linear relationships.

- We have scaled the variables through log transformation.

Not too bad, but we are just getting started! I hope that you didn't actually believe that you just take your raw data and throw it into a deep learning neural network model, and it magically gives you the perfect answer. Regardless of how much I wish that were true, actual predictive modeling takes a lot of preliminary data analysis and decision making before any modeling takes place.

Let's push forward and look at the character variables.

Character Variables

We have applied a variety of different techniques to analyze and adjust the numeric variables. Those techniques included PROC MEANS and PROC UNIVARIATE. Those techniques work great for numeric variables, but they do not work well for character variables. The primary method of analysis for character variables is the FREQ procedure.

We can analyze the character variables by retaining them in the KEEP statement of PROC FREQ.

Program 2.15: Frequency Distribution on Character Variables

```
PROC FREQ DATA=Clean (KEEP= _CHARACTER_) ORDER=FREQ; RUN;
```

The FREQ procedure creates a table of information that contains each level of a categorical variable along with the frequency of observations, the percent of total observations, the cumulative frequency, and the cumulative percent of observations. An example PROC FREQ output for the room_type variable is shown below in Output 2.13.

Output 2.13: PROC FREQ Output

room_type	Frequency	Percent	Cumulative Frequency	Cumulative Percent
Entire home/apt	20539	53.32	20539	53.32
Private room	17272	44.84	37811	98.15
Shared room	712	1.85	38523	100.00

Depending on the type of machine learning algorithm that you apply to your data set, character variables are processed differently.

- **Regression Models** – Categorical variables that have a high number of categories (levels) can be very problematic. For each level, there is an additional degree of freedom for a regression model. You can think of each level as its own variable. So, if a categorical variable has 100 levels, then it is equivalent to adding 100 individual variables to your modeling data set. You can easily see that this leads to the curse of dimensionality (very sparse data sets due to too many dimensions).

- **Tree-Based Models** – The levels of character variables are automatically grouped together to determine the optimal split points. These types of models do not require you to collapse the levels since the algorithm does it for you. The drawback is that you will not get detailed information for each of the categorical levels.

I will assume that we will build both regression models and decision tree models to compare them. For the regression modeling data set, I will indicate which imputation method we should use to prepare the data for modeling.

A summary table of the categorical variables along with the number of levels that each variable has and my suggested imputation method is included below.

Host-dependent fields – These fields are related directly to the host and their relationship with Airbnb. They also include fields that describe requirements that hosts can select. These are binary fields (two levels) with no missing values, so we do not need to impute these values. These include:

- Host_is_superhost
- Host_has_profile_pic
- Host_identity_verified
- Instant_bookable
- Require_guest_profile_picture
- Require_guest_phone_verification

Table 2.5: Table of Character Variables

Character Varible	Levels	Suggested Imputatio Method
host_is_superhost	2	Nor
host_has_profile_pic	2	Nor
host_identity_verified	2	Nor
neighbourhood_cleansed	223	Excluc
neighbourhood_group_cleansed	5	Nor
city	133	Excluc
is_location_exact	2	Excluc
property_type	29	Collaps
room_type	3	Nor
bed_type	5	Nor
instant_bookable	2	Nor
require_guest_profile_picture	2	Nor
require_guest_phone_verification	2	Nor

Location fields – These fields have many levels, and they are strongly correlated with one another. They range from 5 to 223 levels. Even though location variables are highly significant for property valuation, we would not be able to use all of these variables for regression models. All of these variables are telling us the same thing, namely, where the property is located. We can expect that if we leave these variables in the model, that it will overfit to the TRAIN data set and not generalize well to the TEST data set.

If we included the variables zip, city, neighbourhood_cleansed, and neighbourhood_group_cleansed as variables in a regression model, these four variables would result in thousands of additional levels of stratification for our model (the curse of dimensionality)! However, all of these variables could be offered to a tree-based model, and the algorithm will group the levels into categories that have the optimal split point for the leaf of the tree.

Decision Time

Since we are developing a regression model first, let's decide that the categorical variables with over 20 levels are not suitable for our model. Luckily, we still have the neighbourhood_group_cleansed variable that has five levels that we can retain for our regression model.

Property type – This variable has multiple levels; however, 97% of the observations are captured by the top 5 variables. The remaining 24 levels can be collapsed. I used the method of identifying levels with similar rates associated with the target variable. This is an interesting use of PROC MEANS using the categorical variable in the CLASS statement.

Program 2.16: Identify Levels with Similar Target Value Rates

```
PROC MEANS DATA=Clean;
      CLASS Property_Type;
      VAR Price;
RUN;
```

The results of this analysis show that the remaining 24 levels can be collapsed into two groups that have a clear delineation between levels with an average price above $200 per night and those with an average price below $200 per night. We can collapse these levels into two groups within a DATA statement.

Program 2.17: Collapse Categorical Levels

```
DATA TRAIN_ADJ;
      SET Clean;

IF Property_Type in ('Apartment', 'House', 'Townhouse', 'Loft',
'Condominium') THEN Property_CAT = Property_Type;
      ELSE

IF Property_Type in ('Houseboat', 'Resort', 'Tent', 'Serviced ap',
'Aparthotel', 'Hotel', 'Boat', 'Other', 'Boutique ho') THEN Property_CAT =
'Group 1';
      ELSE Property_CAT = 'Group 2';

      IF host_has_profile_pic = ' ' then
            host_has_profile_pic = 'f';
```

```
IF host_identity_verified = ' ' then
        host_identity_verified = 'f';

IF host_is_superhost = ' ' then
        host_is_superhost = 'f';
DROP Property_Type is_location_exact calendar_updated host_response_rate
host_response_time;
RUN;
```

A frequency distribution applied to the newly developed Property_CAT variable shows the collapsed levels in Output 2.14.

Output 2.14: Frequency Distribution of Newly Formed Categories

Property_CAT	Frequency	Percent	Cumulative Frequency	Cumulative Percent
Apartment	30985	80.43	30985	80.43
Condominium	1062	2.76	32047	83.19
Group 1	853	2.21	32900	85.40
Group 2	450	1.17	33350	86.57
House	2705	7.02	36055	93.59
Loft	1185	3.08	37240	96.67
Townhouse	1283	3.33	38523	100.00

Dummy Variables

No, I am not insulting these variables. A dummy variable is a binary variable that is created to represent inclusion in a category. For example, you can have a single smoking category in your model that contains the values smoker and non-smoker. We can create a dummy variable for these categories and have a smoke_ind variable with values of 1 or 0 to indicate if an observation is classified as smoker. It would be repetitive to have a non-smoker_ind variable because any smoker_ind value of 0 would necessarily be a non-smoker.

For the character variables that we have decided to keep in the modeling data set, we will create dummy variables for each level of those variables. For example, the five levels of the bed_type variable can be used to create five individual dummy variables:

Program 2.18: Dummy Variable Creation

```
IF bed_type = 'Airbed' then b_air = 1; else b_air = 0;
IF bed_type = 'Couch' then b_couch = 1; else b_couch = 0;
IF bed_type = 'Futon' then b_futon = 1; else b_futon = 0;
IF bed_type = 'Pull-out Sofa' then b_pullout = 1; else b_pullout = 0;
IF bed_type = 'Real Bed' then b_real = 1; else b_real = 0;
```

We will follow this procedure for the following character variables:

- Bed_type
- Neighbourhood_group_cleansed
- Room_type
- Host_is_superhost

- Host_has_profile_pic
- Host_identity_verified
- Instant_bookable
- Require_guest_profile_picture
- Require_guest_phone_verification
- Host_count_CAT
- Property_CAT

In comparison, the character variables were easier to analyze and adjust than the numeric variables. We do not need to worry about correlation or outliers or transformations or scaling any of the character variables. We just need to make sure that there are not too many levels and that they make intuitive sense for the purposes of our model. The modeling algorithm will determine which character variables are significant.

Adjusting the TEST Data Set

We have spent a good amount of time exploring the TRAIN data set and making several adjustments. We need to apply these same adjustments to the TEST data set so that the model can be properly applied to our hold-out TEST data set and our results analyzed.

Let's try to remember everything that we did to adjust the TRAIN data set to prepare it for regression modeling.

- Log-transformed the target variable (price)
- Set thresholds on the target variable where the price is not missing, and it is not equal to $30 or greater than $750
- Inferred missing values of zipcode with cross-referenced ZIP codes by neighbourhood_cleansed
- Set missing values of security_deposit and cleaning_fees to 0
- Set missing values of bathrooms, bedrooms, and beds to 1
- Set upper limits of bathrooms to 4, bedrooms to 5, and beds to 5
- Set missing values of host_listing_count to 1
- Created a categorical variable for host listing count that groups values into three categories
- Set an upper limit for maximum_nights to 1125 and minimum_nights to 31
- Collapsed the property_type variable
- Created feature engineering variables
- Created polynomial variables

- Created dummy variables from categorical variables
- Log-transformed the numeric variables

Although we dropped several variables from the TRAIN data set, we do not need to worry about dropping those variables from the TEST data set. Any variable that is not retained by the modeling algorithm based on the TRAIN data set will not affect the TEST performance metric. Basically, the model will ignore all of the variables that we had previously dropped.

> **An important note:** It is a best practice to create a macro that automatically applies these adjustments to any data set with a similar structure.
>
> I used the DATA step in the code contained in the GitHub repository because I wanted to make sure that everyone can easily see the IF-THEN statements and understand how each of our decision points has been applied to the TEST data set.

Building a Predictive Model

Finally! This is what we came here for! You have suffered through 30 pages of boring data analysis and tedious data adjustments just to get to the glamorous world of predictive modeling. I appreciate your patience. There is an old saying that 80% of a data scientist's time is spent investigating the data, and 20% is devoted to modeling. I think that the split is closer to 90/10. Either way, let's talk about how to develop our models.

Baseline Models

A baseline model is considered a very simple model with a few data elements and a simple model design. Many people use a simple linear regression for a baseline model. It is a quick and easy way to establish a model without the need for feature engineering and hyperparameter tuning. However, I would suggest that we take a step back and look at an even more basic type of model based on simple averages.

Examining the error rate produced by simple averages can give us the most basic baseline model possible. We will simply calculate the target variable's global average for all of the TRAIN data set's observations and use it as the predicted value.

Let's take this concept a step further and create three basic averages.

- **Global average** – a single value for all observations in the TRAIN data set.
- **Neighbourhood_Group_Cleansed average** – Neighbourhood Group average for the five levels of this variable.
- **Neighbourhood_Cleansed average** – Neighbourhood average for the 223 levels of this variable.

The code used to create these averages and the predicted error rate is contained in the GitHub repository.

The Root Mean Squared Error (RMSE) was calculated by the formula:

$$RMSE = \sqrt{\frac{1}{m_i} \sum_{i=1}^{m} (Price - Avg\_Price)^2}$$

We used the raw Price variable instead of the log-transformed Price variable for two main reasons:

1. We have not created a model yet, so we don't have to worry about skewed data.
2. We want an easy-to-understand error metric.

The table of information and the associated bar chart below shows how badly these predictors perform.

Table 2.6: Baseline RMSE Performance Metrics

	Baseline Global Avg	Baseline Neigh Group Avg	Baseline Neigh Avg
TRAIN	$ 102.11	$ 96.84	$ 90.32
TEST	$ 101.21	$ 96.09	$ 89.26

Figure 2.3: Bar Chart of Baseline RMSE Performance Metrics

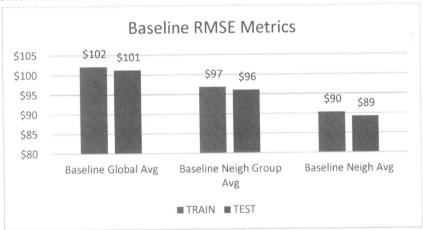

Wow, these are bad models. The RMSE values are extremely high. An interpretation of these errors could be that if you have a property where the correct per diem rate is $300, the global average model would suggest a price of $139.26 because that is what the predicted price is for every property. This results in a residual error of $160.74. I would not pay a cent for this service.

One good takeaway from this example is that as you add more information to your model, your residual error will decrease. The global mean contains very little information and therefore has the highest error rate. The only way to get a worse error rate is to calculate a random price between $30 and $750 (because that is our price range) and use that as the predicted price. Just out of curiosity, I did just that, and the RMSE for a random price prediction is $356.10.

As we add more information by creating average prices for the neighbourhood_group_cleansed and the neighbourhood_cleansed variables, our error rate steadily decreases. However, even though there is an improvement, these models are still terrible.

But this does provide us an opportunity to demonstrate the power of predictive modeling.

Modeling Approach

There are two different approaches to model building. The first is a very cautious approach where the model developer intentionally selects variables for model inclusion and understands how each variable will contribute to the final predicted value. This approach is often used when a model needs to be highly interpretable.

The second type of approach is used when the model developer doesn't have to understand how the variables contribute to the final predicted value. The primary goal for this type of model is predictive accuracy.

Both of these types of models are valuable, depending on the business question that they address and the environment in which they will be implemented. For example, if this is a government model that predicts the amount of public assistance that a region will receive, then that model had better be highly interpretable. There will be a lot of scrutiny concerning the inputs, methodology, and outputs of the model.

However, if the model is an image recognition model, then there is not currently as much scrutiny in understanding how the model came to a specific predicted value. The main concern here is accuracy. No one will really care how you got the correct image classification; they are only concerned that it is accurate.

We will develop both types of models to demonstrate the benefits of these different approaches.

Regression Models

Most of the data analysis and transformations that we performed prior to modeling were specifically designed to prepare the data for regression modeling. To have a successful regression model, you need to understand the content and distribution of each variable as well as how these variables relate to one another.

The parametric functional form of the regression model performs optimally when the following conditions are met:

- Missing values and outliers are identified, and the appropriate imputations and limitations are performed.

- The individual data attributes are not skewed (this is why we created the log transformations).

- The predictors are not correlated with one another (this is why we developed our correlation analysis).

- The categorical variables are collapsed and converted to dummy variables.

General Linear Model

The GLMSELECT procedure performs effect selection within the framework of general linear models. This approach is a very flexible procedure that has a wide variety of selection methods and output options. The procedure allows you to customize your model by specifying the inclusion criteria, stopping criteria, evaluation metrics, and many other options.

The first step of developing this model is to create a macro (see the Advanced SAS Programming chapter) that contains all of the variables that we want to offer to the model. This code creates a macro variable called **lasso_var** that we will use as the predictor for the GLMSELECT procedure.

Program 2.19: Create Macro Variable

```
****************************************************;
/* GLM Linear Regression MODEL                   */
****************************************************;
%let lasso_var = log_accom log_bath log_guest log_min log_max log_avil30
log_bedsper n_bronx n_brooklyn n_manhattan n_queens r_entire r_private
h_super h_profile h_verified b_couch b_futon b_pullout b_real instant
require_pic require_phone
hcount_level1 hcount_level2 hcount_level3 p_apart p_condo p_group2 p_house
p_loft p_townhouse n_staten r_shared b_air p_group1 poly_accom poly_bath
poly_guests poly_min poly_max poly_avail;
```

To generate the evaluation plots, we first make sure that the ODS GRAPHICS ON statement is included. I will not provide a detailed description of each of the selections in the PROC GLMSELECT statement at this point because we will cover them in detail in the linear regression chapter of this book.

Program 2.20: PROC GLMSELECT Model

```
PROC GLMSELECT DATA=WORK.TRAIN_FINAL
OUTDESIGN(ADDINPUTVARS)=Work.reg_design
      PLOTS(stepaxis=normb)=all;
      MODEL Price_Log=&lasso_var. /
selection=lasso(stop=&k choose=SBC);
      OUTPUT OUT = train_score;
      SCORE DATA=TEST_FINAL PREDICTED RESIDUAL OUT=test_score;
run;
```

A few things to note about this code:

- The top line of the PROC GLMSELECT statement includes the OUTDESIGN statement. This statement saves the list of selected effects in a macro variable (&_GLSMOD), and this macro variable can be used later.

- I have specified the plots that I want to use to evaluate the model.

- I specify that I want to use the macro variable **lasso_var** to predict the value of **price_log.**

- I have specified that I want to use a LASSO regularization selection methodology and use the Schwarz's Bayesian Criterion (SBC) for stopping.

- I specify that I want to output the scored TRAIN data set.

- I specify that I want to score the TEST data set and output the predictions and residuals.

Output 2.15: GLMSELECT Model Output

Now we can reap the benefits of all the time and thought that we put into evaluating our predictor variables.

The model output shows the order in which each variable was introduced to the model and its associated SBC value. Since 42 variables are introduced to the model, I have limited the LASSO selection summary to the top ten variables.

			LASSO Selection Summary	
Step	Effect Entered	Effect Removed	Number Effects In	SBC
0	Intercept		1	-34899.918
1	r_entire		2	-42967.758
2	log_accom		3	-52616.589
3	n_manhattan		4	-65761.068
4	p_group1		5	-65787.808
5	log_bath		6	-66113.548
6	poly_accom		7	-66552.058
7	poly_avail		8	-66844.552
8	n_queens		9	-67046.090
9	p_loft		10	-67309.313
10	poly_guests		11	-68037.425
11	r_shared		12	-68229.853

The stepwise selection summary shows us that the r_entire variable is the most influential individual predictor of price_log. The remaining variables are listed in order of predictive power.

The graphical output below shows the effect sequence of each of the variables. This is basically the order in which they have been added to the model as well as their standardized coefficients and their associated SBC values.

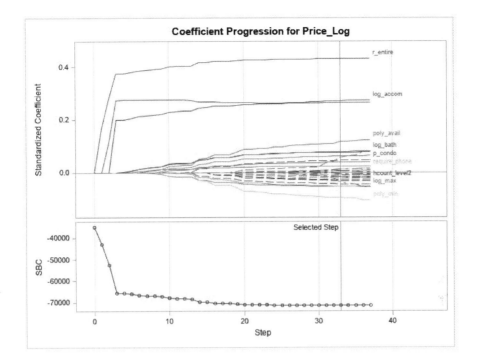

This is looking pretty good. We have built a modeling data set and fed that information into our GLMSELECT LASSO model, and the algorithm gave us the optimal cut point of which variables are statistically significant. That is academically satisfying. However, our regression model was not built to provide us with an A+ in our STATS101 class; it is built with the goal of providing value to our business customers. So, let's examine the details and make some decisions.

Looking at the coefficient progression plot above, we can see that the first four variables add a lot of predictive power to the model. That is to be expected. We are starting at zero information and adding information to our model, so we should expect to see significant gains within the first few variables. However, the information gains quickly level off. The fifth through the tenth variables add slightly more value, and we get diminishing returns for each variable that is added after that.

Let's look at it another way. We can build the same GLMSELECT LASSO model, but we can add the variables one at a time and calculate the RMSE score each time a variable is added. Then we can assess the impact on both the TRAIN and the TEST data sets. By doing this, we will be able to see where the optimal variable cutoff is for the hold-out TEST data set.

The code is a bit lengthy, but I'll show you the top part that starts the loop:

Program 2.21: Add Variables One at a Time to the GLMSELECT Model

```
%macro do_glm;
      %do k=1 %to 42;

PROC GLMSELECT DATA=WORK.TRAIN_FINAL
OUTDESIGN(ADDINPUTVARS)=Work.reg_design
                    PLOTS(stepaxis=normb)=all;
                    MODEL Price_Log=&lasso_var. /
                    selection=lasso(stop=&k choose=SBC);
                    OUTPUT OUT = train_score;
                    SCORE DATA=TEST_FINAL PREDICTED RESIDUAL
                    OUT=test_score;
             run;

      %end;
%mend;

%do_glm
```

Notice that I've created a macro with a DO loop inside of it. This process creates a range of values from 1 to 42. The DO loop starts with the first variable in the **lasso_var** macro variable and cycles through to the last variable in that list. Each cycle of the loop adds the next variable from the sequential list to the model.

An important point to know is that the variables have been sorted based on the order of importance as determined in the previous GLMSELECT LASSO model. This order is important because we are looping through the variables and adding them in order from the most significant to the least significant.

So, in essence, we are running the GLMSELECT LASSO model 42 times. The remaining part of the code that is contained in the GitHub repository calculates the RMSE for the TRAIN and the TEST data sets and appends them to a master RMSE table.

The chart below shows the calculated RMSE values for the TRAIN and the TEST data sets. This looks similar to the SBC chart above in which we see large gains in the first few variables, but diminishing returns for our additional variables.

Figure 2.4: Calculated RMSE Values for TRAIN and TEST Data Sets

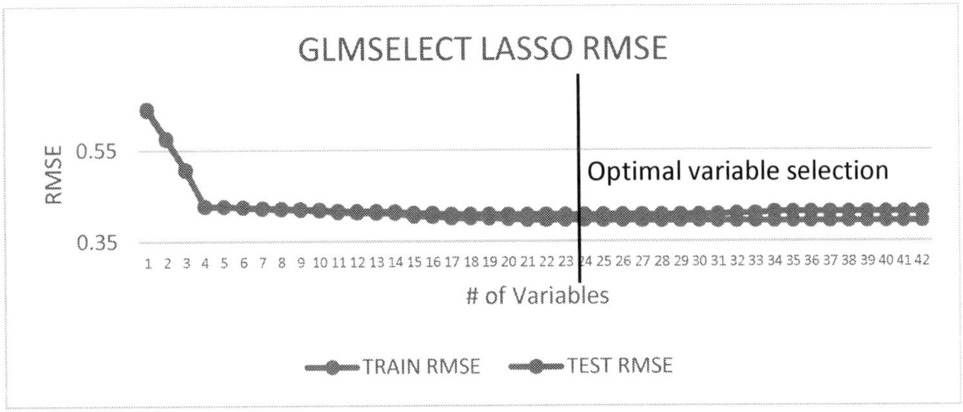

This analysis shows us that the model begins to overfit at the point where the 25th variable is entered into the model. This point is where the RMSE of the TEST data set begins to increase. Notice that the TRAIN RMSE continues to decrease (or at least level off) as we add more variables to the model. This is exactly what we learned in the first chapter about the bias-variance tradeoff.

So, now we have two perspectives of the GLMSELECT LASSO model. The first is generated when we run the model and evaluate the model output for the TRAIN data set. This perspective states that there are 33 statistically significant variables in the data set.

The second perspective looks at the bias-variance tradeoff and shows the difference in the RMSE on the TRAIN versus the TEST data set. This perspective shows that there are 24 statistically significant variables in the model that can be used before overfitting occurs.

Both of these perspectives are technically correct; however, we are building a business model, and one of the important considerations with this type of model is for it to be parsimonious.

Parsimonious Model

A parsimonious model is a model that accomplishes the desired level of explanation with the fewest number of predictor variables. This idea stems from the principle of Occam's razor. This principle is a philosophy that states that one should not make more assumptions than the minimum needed.

A quick look at Table 2.7 shows that the first four variables provide a lot of information to the model. The remaining 38 variables add marginal amounts of information to the model. We can attempt to quantify the impact of each additional variable by calculating the percentage decrease in the TEST RMSE for each variable.

Table 2.7 shows that the first four variables have a significant impact on the TEST RMSE. However, the impact quickly dissipates after the fourth variable is added to the model.

Table 2.7: RMSE Analysis

Variable Number	TRAIN RMSE	TEST RMSE	% Decrease in TEST RMSE
1 r_entire	0.636	0.639	
2 log_accom	0.572	0.575	10.0%
3 n_manhattan	0.505	0.507	11.8%
4 p_group1	0.426	0.426	15.9%
5 log_bath	0.426	0.426	0.1%
6 poly_accom	0.424	0.424	0.4%
7 poly_avail	0.421	0.422	0.5%
8 n_queens	0.420	0.421	0.3%
9 p_loft	0.418	0.420	0.2%
10 poly_guests	0.417	0.419	0.3%

When we look at a comparison between the model suggested by the TRAIN vs. TEST RMSE that recommended 24 predictor variables, and the parsimonious model that suggests only four variables, the TEST RMSE of the 24 variable model is 0.40776 while the TEST RMSE of the four-variable model is 0.42649. This is a difference of (-0.01873). You can argue that that difference is marginal at best.

Bootstrapped Model

We can take one last look at the GLMSELECT LASSO model before we move on to a non-parametric model. The question that we need to address is whether our model results are the result of a particularly lucky data set that just happened to produce a good value for us. The underlying issue is whether the model is stable across multiple draws of the data.

A bootstrapped model repeatedly samples the modeling data set and builds a model on each one of the samples. The models are then averaged together to create final estimates for the coefficients. The code below creates the bootstrapped model.

Program 2.22: Bootstrapped GLMSELECT Model

```
%let parsi_var = r_entire log_accom n_manhattan p_group1;

ods noproctitle;
ods graphics / imagemap=on;
proc glmselect data=WORK.TRAIN_FINAL
outdesign(addinputvars)=Work.reg_design
        plots=(EffectSelectPct ParmDistribution criterionpanel
        ASE) seed=1;
        model Price_Log=&parsi_var. /
        selection=stepwise(select=sbc);
        modelAverage nsamples=1000 tables=(EffectSelectPct(all)
ParmEst(all));
        output out = train_score;
        score data=TEST_FINAL PREDICTED RESIDUAL out=test_score;
run;
```

A few notes on Program 2.22:

- I selected the top four variables from the parsimonious model and placed them into a macro variable called **parsi_var.**

- We are still using the LASSO selection methodology and choosing based on SBC.

- We are creating 1000 samples with replacement and averaging the coefficients across all of the samples.

Output 2.16a: Bootstrap Model Effect Selection

Effect Selection Percentage	
Effect	Selection Percentage
r_entire	100.0
log_accom	100.0
n_manhattan	100.0
p_group1	100.0

The output of the bootstrapped methodology provides us with a lot of information. The effect selection percentage shows us the percentage of the samples where a specific variable was significant. Output 2.16 confirms that each of the four predictor variables was significant in every one of the 1000 sample models.

The next part of the bootstrap model output shows the average parameter estimates across all of the 1000 sample models. This approach produces not only the coefficient estimate but also the standard deviation as well as the estimate quartiles. These values can be instrumental in understanding the estimated range for each of the predictor variables.

Output 2.16b: Bootstrap Model Parameter Estimates

Average Parameter Estimates					Estimate Quantiles		
Parameter	Number Non-zero	Non-zero Percentage	Mean Estimate	Standard Deviation	25%	Median	75%
Intercept	1000	100.00	3.579733	0.008495	3.573782	3.579831	3.585600
r_entire	1000	100.00	0.528617	0.005183	0.524949	0.528538	0.532151
log_accom	1000	100.00	0.548113	0.007360	0.543052	0.548296	0.553436
n_manhattan	1000	100.00	0.352190	0.004481	0.349142	0.352213	0.355395
p_group1	1000	100.00	0.357221	0.019295	0.344579	0.357775	0.370157

Finally, the bootstrap model output contains a graphical distribution for each of the parameter estimates, as well as the intercept.

This graphic shows the distribution of intercept and coefficients' calculated value for the 1000 samples. This is a nice real-world example of the central limit theorem.

Output 2.16c: Bootstrap Model Parameter Distributions

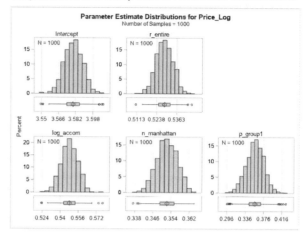

Decision Time

The final decision that we need to make concerning the regression model is to decide which regression model we should use.

Our choices are the full linear regression model with 33 statistically significant variables, the linear regression model based on the TRAIN/TEST evaluations with 24 statistically significant variables, and the parsimonious bootstrapped model with four statistically significant variables.

The benefits of the parsimonious model outweigh the marginal predictive benefits from the other two regression models. I suggest that we move forward with the parsimonious bootstrapped linear regression model with four variables.

Non-Parametric Models

When we first approached the modeling process for our Airbnb model, we made the initial assumption that we were going to build a regression model. Under this assumption, we made several changes to the data:

- Categorized some numeric variables
- Collapsed some character variables
- Standardized our numeric variables
- Created dummy variables for our character variables
- Excluded character variables with too many levels

These are all necessary steps when building a regression model. The result of this process is a modeling data set that contains normally distributed target and predictor variables and a series of binary variables that the regression model can easily read into the algorithm and produce coefficients for every significant variable in the final modeling output. These adjustments provide us with a transparent model where we understand how each variable is incorporated into the model and we have the final coefficient weights for every variable. Nothing is left unexplained about how we derived a prediction for a specific observation.

As we learned in the first chapter, there is another approach to modeling. A **non-parametric** model does not assume a specific functional form. This type of model can adapt to a wide range of functional forms. A linear regression model assumes that the relationship between the target variable and the predictors is linear (thus the name). Non-parametric models such as decision trees, support vector machines, neural networks, and several others do not assume that the relationship between the target and the predictors is linear.

Non-parametric models are very flexible and produce highly accurate predictions, but at the cost of transparency. For example, a gradient boosting decision tree model can often produce significantly lower test metric scores than a linear regression model, but there is no clear visibility into how the algorithm produces these results. We will delve into the details of these algorithms and their outputs later in the book, but for now, let's apply some of these modeling types to our Airbnb data set and compare their predictions to the linear regression model.

For our comparisons, we will limit the non-parametric modeling types to tree-based models. There could be additional benefits in building other non-parametric types of models, but let's focus on the tree-based models for this example.

Modeling Data

One of the big advantages of tree-based models is that we do not have to worry about the distribution of the predictor variables. In the previous section, we spent a lot of time analyzing each variable and making several changes to prepare the data for modeling. Tree-based models do not require that the numeric variables are normally distributed, and there is not an issue with categorical variables having too many levels. This is because the decision tree algorithm segments the predictor space into several simple regions.

The algorithm identifies the variable and split point that minimizes the Residual Sum of Squares (RSS). We will review the decision tree methodology in detail later in the book, but for now, we need to understand that the decision tree approach is fundamentally different from the linear regression approach. The decision tree assesses each variable, both numeric and categorical, and makes optimal selections of variable split points that reduce the RSS for the predictor space. Numeric variables are split at some point across a continuous spectrum, while the levels of the categorical variables are grouped together in optimal groupings that reduce the RSS.

Because the levels of categorical variables are grouped, we do not need to worry about variables such as ZIP code that have a couple of hundred levels. The algorithm will assess this variable and identify the optimal groupings of this variable into two categories that split the predictor space. For example, if a categorical variable has 100 levels, the decision tree might group 95 of these variables into one category and the remaining five variables into another category. These categories do not need to have an equivalent number of levels in each group.

Decision Tree

The first type of tree-based model that we will explore is a simple decision tree. This methodology constructs a single decision tree on the full TRAIN data set, and we can apply the resulting model to the hold-out TEST data set. This type of model is called a *recursive binary splitting* model. This is because the methodology begins with a single variable and splits the predictor space into two (binary) spaces, and then the algorithm evaluates each of the resulting predictor spaces and applies the same splitting methodology recursively (over and over).

This methodology is called "greedy" because it selects the best split at each branch of the tree. It never looks ahead and makes split decisions that would produce a better outcome in the end.

Since we can now utilize the full Airbnb data set, we can start by accessing the data set that we built prior to creating all the dummy variables. This data set contains all the categorical variables before collapsing them and transforming them into binary dummy variables.

The code below gathers the numeric and character variables from the data set that was created before creating the dummy variables, and it places the numeric and character variables into two separate macro variables. This will be helpful later when we need to make different specifications for each variable type.

Program 2.23: Create Numeric and Character Macro Variables

```
/*Create macro variable for numeric variables*/
PROC CONTENTS NOPRINT DATA=TRAIN_ADJ (KEEP=_NUMERIC_ DROP=id
host_id price price_log)
     OUT=VAR3 (KEEP=name);
RUN;

PROC SQL NOPRINT;
     SELECT name INTO: tree_num separated by " " FROM VAR3;
QUIT;
%PUT &tree_num;

/*Create macro variable for character variables*/
PROC CONTENTS NOPRINT DATA=TRAIN_ADJ (KEEP=_CHARACTER_
     DROP=Property_CAT)
     OUT=VAR4 (KEEP=name);
RUN;

PROC SQL NOPRINT;
     SELECT name INTO: tree_char separated by " " FROM VAR4;
QUIT;
%PUT &tree_char;
```

The resulting data set contains 43 variables that are a mix of the raw numeric variables, the log-transformed numeric variables, the feature engineered numeric variables, and the polynomial numeric variables as well as the raw character variables without any level collapsing. These variables are presented in Table 2.8.

Table 2.8: Variable Listing

Numeric Variables		Character Variables
accommodates	log_bathper	bed_type
availability_30	log_bedrooms	city
availability_60	log_beds	host_count_cat
availability_90	log_bedsper	host_has_profile_pic
availability_365	log_guest	host_identity_verified
bath_per_accom	log_max	host_is_superhost
bathrooms	log_min	instant_bookable
bedrooms	maximum_nights	neighbourhood_cleansed
beds	minimum_nights	neighbourhood_group_cleansed
beds_per_accom	poly_accom	property_type
guests_included	poly_avail	require_guest_phone_verification
log_accom	poly_bath	require_guest_profile_picture
log_avil30	poly_guests	room_type
log_bath	poly_max	zip
	poly_min	

We will present all of these variables to the decision tree algorithm and allow it to select the optimal variable and split points that will result in the lowest RSS value.

Although this process allows much more freedom to the modeling algorithm, it also requires significantly more processing power compared to the linear regression methodology. As we increase our complexity by adding randomization and boosting to the decision tree, we will consequently increase the processing power necessary to develop these models. This might not be an issue with a data set of this size, but as you try to apply these techniques to larger data sets, you will run into issues of processing power and memory space. Luckily, SAS has a couple of features that help you split your modeling tasks across different computer cores that can help alleviate this issue.

To create a single decision tree, I have opted to use PROC HPSPLIT. This is a high-performance decision tree algorithm that has lots of options for customization. The code below develops a single decision tree on the TRAIN data set and outputs a scoring code file that can be applied to the hold-out TEST data set for evaluation.

Program 2.24: Simple Decision Tree Model

```
ODS GRAPHICS ON;

PROC HPSPLIT DATA=WORK.TRAIN_ADJ seed=42;
   CLASS &tree_char.;
   MODEL price = &tree_char. &tree_num.;
   OUTPUT OUT=hpsplout;
   CODE FILE='C:\Users\James Gearheart\Desktop\SAS Book
Stuff\Data\hpsplexc.sas';
run;
```

Notes on the decision tree code:

- I am building the model based on the TRAIN_ADJ data set. This is the data set that contains all of the numeric and character variables appropriate for modeling.

- I included a SEED statement to ensure reproducible results.

- The CLASS statement contains all of the character variables.

- The target variable is PRICE_LOG, and the predictor variables are the two macro variables that contain all of the numeric and character variables.

- The code file outputs a SAS program that contains all of the splitting logic. This file can be applied to other data sets for scoring.

One of the main cautions of tree-based models is that they are prone to overfitting. If they are not controlled, they will create a model with 100% accuracy on the training data and not generalize at all to other data sets. Luckily, SAS has default values built into the PROC HPSPLIT that regulate the model. The model developer can customize these values. If you want to select a different pruning method or max tree depth, you certainly have those options available to you.

Output 2.17a: PROC HPSPLIT Model Information

Model Information	
Split Criterion Used	Variance
Pruning Method	Cost-Complexity
Subtree Evaluation Criterion	Cost-Complexity
Number of Branches	2
Maximum Tree Depth Requested	10
Maximum Tree Depth Achieved	10
Tree Depth	10
Number of Leaves Before Pruning	781
Number of Leaves After Pruning	248

The first section of the model output contains information about the construct of the model. Output 2.17a shows the default modeling criteria as well as the default hyperparameters that were used to build the decision tree. We will review each of these criteria in the decision tree chapter of the book, but for now, we need to understand that each of these criteria and the associated hyperparameters are implemented to regularize the decision tree model so that it does not produce a highly overfitted model that represents only the training data set.

Output 2.17b: PROC HPSPLIT Cost Complexity

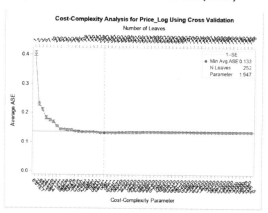

The next section of the model output is a graphical representation of the impact on the average squared error for each leaf of the decision tree. This graphic looks very similar to the graphical analysis of the linear regression model that shows the reduction in the SBC for each variable added to the model.

If we were to decide that we wanted to use a single decision tree for our final solution, we would have the option of reducing the number of variables based on the premise of parsimony, just like we did with the linear regression model. This could provide us with a transparent model with a few features that are competitive with our linear regression model.

The next item produced by the PROC HPSPLIT procedure is the visual representation of the decision tree. This is what we are all accustomed to thinking about when we hear the words "decision tree." The visualization begins at the root value of the full data set and begins the splitting process. The first split of the decision tree starts with the room_type variable. (Hey, that's the same variable that was most important in the linear regression model!)

Output 2.17c: PROC HPSPLIT Tree Visualization

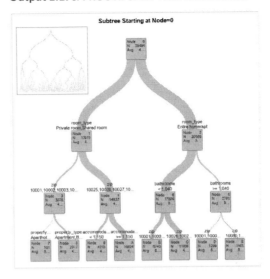

Output 2.17d: PROC HPSPLIT Variable Importance

Variable Importance			
	Training		
Variable	Relative	Importance	Count
room_type	1.0000	81.3833	5
zip	0.5174	42.1064	50
bathrooms	0.3478	28.3035	4
accommodates	0.2538	20.6511	16
neighbourhood_cleansed	0.2214	18.0164	28
bedrooms	0.2111	17.1836	13
property_type	0.1664	13.5387	20
neighbourhood_group_cleansed	0.1257	10.2322	3
guests_included	0.1097	8.9250	14
availability_90	0.1000	8.1407	14

The algorithm continues the splitting process independently at each node of the tree. Notice at the third level of the tree, the left side is split on the zip variable while the right side is split on the bathrooms variable.

Also, a variable can be used several times throughout the splitting process. Just because the zip variable was used at the third level does not mean that it cannot be used again later on down the tree.

The next piece of information produced by PROC HPSPLIT is a table of variable importance. This table is similar to the "Effect Entered" table produced by the linear regression in that it tells us what the most important variables are as they relate to the target variable. Notice that the variables in this table and the order in which they appear are similar to the variables in the "Effect Entered" table in the linear regression output.

The decision tree model easily handles the multiple level categorical variables such as zip and neighbourhood_cleansed. These variables contain a lot of information about housing prices because they are specific to a location. The linear regression could not use them because they contain too many levels; however, the decision tree easily utilizes the information contained in these variables by grouping them by the optimal split point.

We can use the scoring code produced by PROC HPSPLIT to score the hold-out TEST data set. This is easily accomplished in a DATA step where the scoring code is brought in with an INCLUDE statement.

Program 2.25: Apply Decision Tree Model to Hold-out TEST Data Set

```
DATA TEST_SCORED;
  SET TEST_ADJ;
  %INCLUDE 'C:\Users\James Gearheart\Desktop\SAS Book
Stuff\Data\hpsplexc.sas';
RUN;
```

We can now run the same algorithm that I developed for assessing the RMSE for the linear regression model and apply it to our decision tree model. Remember that this code is contained in the GitHub repository.

The table below shows the calculated RMSE value for the TRAIN and TEST data sets for different modeling methodologies.

Table 2.9: Model RMSE Table

	Linear Regression LASSO	Simple Decision Tree	Random Forest	Gradient Boosting
TRAIN	0.426	0.342		
TEST	0.426	0.364		

An observant reader might stop me right here and accuse me of an unfair comparison. The linear regression model is the parsimonious model that has a reduced number of variables. What if we reduced the variables in the simple decision tree? How would they compare then? Luckily, my data-centered OCD forces me to make a simple decision tree with the top ten variables based on relative variable importance for comparison to the parsimonious linear regression model.

As you can probably guess by now, a parsimonious simple decision tree model does not lose a lot of predictive power. The RMSE for the TRAIN data set is still 0.342, while the RMSE for the TEST data set increases very slightly to 0.366. The takeaway from this analysis is that the application of a parsimonious simple decision tree to the Airbnb data set performs better than the parsimonious linear regression model. This increase in performance is because the underlying data structure is non-linear.

Now that we have discovered the non-linear nature of the data, we can develop a few more tree-based models. You are obviously observant enough to see in the table above that we are going to build a random forest and a gradient boosting decision tree model.

Random Forest

An issue that we touched on when we developed the simple decision tree is that it is greedy in nature. That means that it selects the best variable and split point that reduces the RSS of the predictor space and then moves on to the next branch of the tree. Although this methodology makes optimal decisions at each branch of the tree, it never looks forward and makes decisions at an individual branch that might not be optimal for that particular branch but would benefit the overall RSS further down the tree. The random forest approach was developed to alleviate this issue.

A random forest is an "ensemble" modeling approach. This means that several models are brought together to create a single prediction. For a random forest to be developed, the TRAIN data set is sampled with replacement at a specified sampling rate many times. For our example, the TRAIN data set contains 38,527 observations. If I set the sampling rate to be 60%, then 23,116 randomly chosen observations will be in the sampled training data set. The remaining 40% of the observations will be in a hold-out data set that will be used to calculate the "out-of-bag" (OOB) error metric. The OOB is the mean prediction error for each sampled training data set. You can think of this as a mini TRAIN/TEST environment where a decision tree is developed on the sampled training data set and applied to the hold-out OOB test data set.

The randomization of selected observations is not the only randomized part of a random forest. For any data set, there are usually one or two variables that overpower the remaining variables. These are the variables that are most strongly correlated with the target variable. If these variables are included in a simple decision tree, they will be the top nodes of the tree and dominate the initial splitting decisions. A clever way that the random forest mitigates this issue of variable dominance is to randomly select a subset of the total number of possible variables to include in a given decision tree.

In our Airbnb example, there are 43 variables available to present to the algorithm. A rule of thumb for building a decision tree is to set the number of randomly selected predictor variables to the square root of the total number of predictors. The square root of 43 is 6.557, so we will round up and specify that we want seven randomly selected variables to be included with each decision tree.

Since this is a recursive procedure, we also need to specify how many times we want the algorithm to build these randomly selected trees. Keep in mind that the larger the number of trees that you specify, the more processing power will be required of your computer system.

The code below develops a random forest that consists of 500 randomly sampled trees, each with seven randomly sampled predictor variables. Each one of these trees is different due to the randomization of the observations and the predictors.

Program 2.26: Random Forest Model

```
proc hpforest data=WORK.TRAIN_ADJ
        maxtrees= 500 vars_to_try=7
        seed=42 trainfraction=0.6
        maxdepth=20 leafsize=6
        alpha= 0.1;
        target price_log/ level=interval;
        input &tree_num. / level=interval;
```

```
        input &tree_char. / level=nominal;
        ods output train_scored fitstatistics = fit;
        SAVE FILE = "C:\Users\James Gearheart\Desktop\SAS Book
Stuff\Data\rfmodel_fit.bin";
run;
```

Notes on Program 2.26:

- I am building the model based on the TRAIN_ADJ data set. This is the data set that contains all of the numeric and character variables appropriate for modeling.

- I specify that I want to build 500 trees (MAXTREES) and have 7 predictors in each tree (VARS_TO_TRY).

- I specify that I want 60% of the data (TRAINFRACTION) to be used as the sampled training data set.

- I included a SEED statement to ensure reproducible results.

- There are separate INPUT statements for the numeric and character variables.

- The target variable is PRICE_LOG, and the target is specified to be an interval variable.

- The code file outputs a SAS program that contains all of the splitting logic. This file can be applied to other data sets for scoring.

The first section of the random forest output contains a summary of the hyperparameter settings for the model. I have specified a few of these settings in the code while others I left set to their default values. From this list, you can see that there are a multitude of ways to customize your algorithm, and the interaction of these settings can result in widely different predictive values. If you were to choose to move forward with the random forest and select this modeling algorithm as the model to drive your business, you would have to develop a *grid search* that loops through different combinations of these hyperparameters to find the subset that performs best on your hold-out TEST data set.

Output 2.18a: Random Forest Model Information

Model Information	
Parameter	Value
Variables to Try	7
Maximum Trees	500
Actual Trees	500
Inbag Fraction	0.6
Prune Fraction	0 (Default)
Prune Threshold	0.1 (Default)
Leaf Fraction	0.00001 (Default)
Leaf Size Setting	6
Leaf Size Used	6
Category Bins	30 (Default)
Interval Bins	100
Minimum Category Size	5 (Default)
Node Size	100000 (Default)
Maximum Depth	20
Alpha	0.1
Exhaustive	5000 (Default)
Rows of Sequence to Skip	5 (Default)
Split Criterion	Variance
Preselection Method	Loh
Missing Value Handling	Valid value

The next section of the model output provides the fit statistics for each of the 500 decision trees. I have presented only the first ten trees here for a demonstration. We can see that the output contains the cumulative results of including each additional tree to the overall random forest model. As each unique tree is added to the assessment, the number of leaves increases while the average squared error decreases for both the training (train) and testing (OOB) data sets.

Output 2.18b: Random Forest Fit Statistics

	Fit Statistics		
Number of Trees	Number of Leaves	Average Square Error (Train)	Average Square Error (OOB)
1	460	0.13828	0.14921
2	850	0.13147	0.15695
3	1287	0.12339	0.14969
4	1692	0.11944	0.14323
5	2114	0.11818	0.14052
6	2502	0.11638	0.13664
7	2954	0.11590	0.13560
8	3349	0.11608	0.13469
9	3760	0.11489	0.13220
10	4141	0.11499	0.13158

One of the strong selling points of using a random forest is that due to the development of the OOB testing data set, there is no need to have a formal TEST data set. This is because the OOB data set acts as a de facto testing data set. We could, in theory, use our full data set to build the random forests (both TRAIN and TEST). However, there is still a lot of benefit to having a traditional hold-out TEST data set. This will provide you with a better assessment of how the model will perform in a real-world setting.

Decision Time

So, here we have another tradeoff with model development. Should you combine your TRAIN and TEST data sets to produce a random forest on your largest possible number of observations? More data nearly always produces better modeling results. Or do we split our full data set into separate TRAIN and TEST data sets and develop our random forest solely on the TRAIN data set and evaluate the results on the hold-out TEST data set? The assessment of a hold-out data set nearly always provides a better assessment of model performance. Unfortunately, there is no objectively correct answer.

The final section of the model output is the Variable Importance table. This table orders the predictive variables based on each variable's contribution to the reduction in the Mean Squared Error (MSE). The Variable Importance table lists all of the variables that were presented to the algorithm. I have included only the top 10 here for demonstration purposes.

Output 2.18c: Random Forest Variable Importance

	Loss Reduction Variable Importance				
Variable	Number of Rules	MSE	OOB MSE	Absolute Error	OOB Absolute Error
room_type	8736	0.065551	0.06561	0.060477	0.060468
accommodates	5003	0.020250	0.01987	0.016458	0.016055
neighbourhood_cleansed	12486	0.022034	0.01955	0.021983	0.019443
log_accom	3949	0.019323	0.01894	0.015619	0.015240
log_bathper	4219	0.015752	0.01558	0.013816	0.013573
neighbourhood_group_cleansed	7085	0.015150	0.01500	0.013547	0.013336
bath_per_accom	4215	0.013662	0.01325	0.012032	0.011679
poly_accom	4465	0.013207	0.01288	0.010830	0.010469
bedrooms	6234	0.011992	0.01169	0.009503	0.009140
city	4807	0.011852	0.01159	0.010663	0.010379

These variables look very similar to the ones that were highly significant in the linear regression and the decision tree models. Maybe we should start believing that room_type is the most significant aspect of Airbnb per diem pricing in New York City as of December 2018. The other variables are similar to the top ten variables in the other two models that we have developed.

In our previous models, we looked at the incremental value of each additional variable, and we made decisions on selecting a subset of those variables based on parsimony. However, that approach is not really applicable to random forest models. The random forest approach is considered a black box model because we cannot state specifically the value of each variable to the overall prediction. That is because of the random selection of the observations and the random selection of the predictors. The random forest averages together the results of hundreds of decision trees, so we cannot state the value of a single predictor. Any given predictor was not present in a certain percentage of the hundreds of decision trees. We can state the overall average variable importance based on MSE, but we cannot state how a specific variable is used to construct the final predictor because it varies based on the random construction of each composite decision tree.

I subjected the random forest to the RMSE scoring algorithm (found in the GitHub repository). The results show a marginal improvement over the simple decision tree.

Table 2.10: Model RMSE Table

	Linear Regression LASSO	Simple Decision Tree	Random Forest	Gradient Boosting
TRAIN	0.426	0.342	0.332	
TEST	0.426	0.364	0.348	

We can more clearly see the cost-benefit tradeoff of increasing model complexity. As our models increase in complexity, we can see a reduction in the TEST scoring metric, but at the cost of explainability.

Gradient Boosting

The gradient boosting model design was developed from a fundamentally different approach than the traditional decision tree and random forest approaches. Rather than developing a single deep tree (many nodes and branches) or a random collection of deep trees, this approach produces a series of shallow trees (called "weak learners") sequentially.

This approach begins with a single decision tree that is limited to two to eight levels. This is called a weak learner because it does not produce very good predictions by design. This shallow structure produces somewhat large residuals for each observation. But here is the brilliance of this model design, the next tree in the sequence uses the *residuals* from the previous tree as the target value. You are probably saying, "That's crazy talk, why in the world would you do such a thing?"

The problem with a traditional decision tree is that it is a greedy learner, which leads to non-optimal predictions. The shallow sequential design of the gradient boosting approach allows the model to learn slowly. Each shallow sequential decision tree is fitted on the residuals from the previous tree. Once a given decision tree is created, it is not modified. Each tree is added into the fitted function that updates the residuals that are the target values for the next shallow tree in the sequence. This approach slowly improves the function with increased weight on the areas of high residual values.

We will review the gradient boosting approach in more detail later in the book (are you sick of hearing me say that over and over?), but for now, we need to understand that this approach is methodologically different from the traditional decision tree and the random forest approach. The caution of this approach is that we are truly in the black box model territory now. This modeling approach has a different target value for each iteration of the algorithm!

I used PROC TREEBOOST to develop the gradient boosting model. This procedure allows the model developer to adjust nearly every aspect of the gradient boosting algorithm.

One note of caution when implementing a gradient boosting model is that it is resource-intensive. When you develop a random forest model, the trees are developed independently, so the algorithm can develop several trees at a time across multiple cores. However, with a gradient boosting algorithm, the trees are developed sequentially. This means that you cannot gain processing efficiency by spreading the task across many cores. In the end, this algorithm takes some time to run, so once you click the Run button, go make a sandwich and come back to it later.

Program 2.27: Gradient Boosting Model

```
PROC TREEBOOST DATA=TRAIN_ADJ
        CATEGORICALBINS = 10
        INTERVALBINS = 400
        EXHAUSTIVE = 5000
        INTERVALDECIMALS = MAX
        LEAFSIZE = 100
        MAXBRANCHES = 6
        ITERATIONS = 500
        MINCATSIZE = 50
        MISSING = USEINSEARCH
        SEED = 42
        SHRINKAGE = 0.1
        SPLITSIZE = 100
        TRAINPROPORTION = 0.6;
        INPUT &tree_num. / LEVEL=INTERVAL;
        INPUT &tree_char./ LEVEL=NOMINAL;
        TARGET PRICE_LOG / LEVEL=INTERVAL;
        IMPORTANCE NVARS=50 OUTFIT=BASE_VARS;
        SUBSERIES BEST;
        CODE FILE="C:\Users\James Gearheart\Desktop\SAS Book
 Stuff\Data\BOOST_MODEL_FIT.sas"
        NOPREDICTION;
        SAVE MODEL=GBS_TEST FIT=FIT_STATS
 IMPORTANCE=IMPORTANCE RULES=RULES;
 RUN;
```

Notes on Program 2.27:

- The model is developed on the TRAIN_ADJ data set.
- I have specified that there are a maximum of 6 branches (MAXBRANCHES) for each decision tree.
- I am building 500 sequential decision trees (ITERATIONS).
- The learning rate is set to 0.1 (SHRINKAGE).
- I am using 60% of the data to train each of the decision trees.
- I am outputting the code file to score other data sets.
- I am creating data sets for the fit statistics, variable importance, and splitting rules.

The first output data set that we can look at is the fit statistics data set. This data set shows the fit metrics for each of the 500 created decision trees. I've shown the top 10 iterations for demonstration purposes. You can see that the Sum of Squared Error (SSE), the Average Squared Error (ASE), and the Real Average Squared Error (RASE) all decrease for each added iteration of the algorithm.

Output 2.19: Gradient Boosting Fit Statistics

_ITERATIO...	_NOBS_	_SUMW_	_NW_	_MAX_	_SSE_	_ASE_	_RASE_	_DIV_	_DFT_
1	38527	38527	11	1.95032586	14012.073794	0.3636949099	0.6030712312	38527	38527
2	38527	38527	25	2.0059089186	12707.904461	0.3298441213	0.5743205736	38527	38527
3	38527	38527	39	2.0565679196	11617.741241	0.3015480375	0.5491338976	38527	38527
4	38527	38527	53	2.1020742957	10730.841615	0.2785278276	0.5277573568	38527	38527
5	38527	38527	74	2.1323291929	9875.0993561	0.2563163329	0.506276933	38527	38527
6	38527	38527	87	2.1725602261	9238.8951474	0.2398031289	0.4896969766	38527	38527
7	38527	38527	117	2.1949622272	8634.0416426	0.2241036583	0.473395879	38527	38527
8	38527	38527	131	2.229398199	8164.2688285	0.2119103182	0.4603371788	38527	38527
9	38527	38527	157	2.2567640909	7729.3533942	0.2006217301	0.4479081715	38527	38527
10	38527	38527	184	2.2919046506	7351.6142027	0.1908171984	0.4368262794	38527	38527

Table 2.11: Gradient Boosting Variable Importance

The next output data set that we can inspect is the variable importance table. This table is constructed in the same manner as the variable importance table that we saw in the random forest output. This table contains the relative importance for each variable presented to the algorithm. I have presented the top 10 variables in Table 2.11.

NAME	Number of Rules	Relative Importance
room_type	102	1.00
accommodates	110	0.65
zip	583	0.61
neighbourhood_cleansed	292	0.41
neighbourhood_group_cleansed	60	0.25
bedrooms	78	0.24
bathrooms	30	0.23
log_min	233	0.21
availability_90	254	0.20
availability_365	401	0.18

We can see that room_type is the top-ranked variable for the gradient boosting model. The variables accommodates and zip are also highly predictive of the target variable. At this point, I think that we can declare room_type as the winner for the most predictive variable for Airbnb per diem price for New York City as of December 2018!

A final comparison of the calculated RMSE metric on the TRAIN and hold-out TEST data set shows that the gradient boosting algorithm generates the lowest RMSE score for all of our developed models.

Table 2.12: Model RMSE Table

	Linear Regression LASSO	Simple Decision Tree	Random Forest	Gradient Boosting
TRAIN	0.426	0.342	0.332	0.314
TEST	0.426	0.364	0.348	0.334

This isn't too much of a surprise. Once we discovered that the simple decision tree performed substantially better than the linear regression model, we knew that a non-parametric approach was superior to a parametric approach. The underlying data is non-linear.

The gradient boosting model generally produces the most accurate predictions of all the recursive binary splitting (decision tree) algorithms. This is because it reweights each decision tree based on the residuals of the previous tree. It actually focuses the algorithm on fixing the big mistakes generated from the previous decision tree, and it does not focus on the parts where the previous tree got the prediction very close to the actual target value.

Decision Time

Decision Time

Now that we have developed several different predictive models, we need to decide which model we would use to run our Airbnb price generator business. It is tempting to say that since the gradient boosting algorithm generated the lowest error metric that we should obviously use that model. It would give the customer the most accurate, and consequently, the most competitive and profitable price estimate. However, if we use this model, we really cannot provide the customer with any detailed information about the price estimate.

As a customer, you may want to know what factors contribute to the per diem rate. This holds especially true if you are in the business of property arbitrage. This is a business model where investors lease many properties with the goal of listing them on Airbnb (or other short-term property rental sites) in an attempt to collect rents above their monthly lease fees. Airbnb strongly discourages this behavior. But if this is your business model, it would be highly valuable for you to have detailed information about what factors contribute to per diem pricing. This way, you could acquire properties that have the features that maximize your profit.

A gradient boosting model would not provide that level of information because there is very little transparency to this model. We know which features are important, but we cannot assign a specific dollar value for each significant feature.

The random forest model also suffers from a lack of transparency. The estimates are highly accurate, but we cannot assign values at the feature level.

This leaves us with choosing between the linear regression model and the simple decision tree. The simple decision tree will provide the customer with a clear logic path to a given prediction. They could understand quite clearly how the estimate was generated and how each factor contributes to the final predicted value. This type of model is easy to understand and has the added benefit of visibly demonstrating variable importance by showing which variables are at the top of the tree. It also allows the customer to see how important location data is by allowing multiple-level categorical data like the zip code and neighbourhood_cleansed variables to be included in the model. There is a strong case for using the simple decision tree for our modeling algorithm.

However, there are two main reasons that I would select the linear regression model:

1. **Transparency** – The business value that we are providing is information. This information is much more than the final predicted per diem rate. The linear regression model provides detailed information on the per-unit value for each feature in our model. I believe that is what our customers really want.

2. **Accuracy** – Although the linear regression model's RMSE score is higher than the tree-based models, it is actually not too far off from them. When we transform the RMSE of the log adjusted price target variable back into its standard form, we can see in Table 2.13 that the average residual price for the linear regression model is $1.53 while the gradient boosting model's average residual price is $1.40. I am willing to give up $0.13 in accuracy in order to have full transparency.

Table 2.13: True Dollar Error Estimates

	Linear Regression LASSO	Simple Decision Tree	Random Forest	Gradient Boosting
TRAIN	$ 1.53	$ 1.41	$ 1.39	$ 1.37
TEST	$ 1.53	$ 1.44	$ 1.42	$ 1.40

One thing to keep in mind is that these error metrics are based on the average error. We know that properties on the high end and the low end of the price range will have larger residuals due to there being in the top and bottom decile of price categories. The distribution of residuals for these properties has heavier tails for the linear regression model than they do for the gradient boosting model.

Output 2.20 and 2.21 below show the quantile table and the histogram for the linear regression model and the gradient boosting model for comparison. You can easily see that the gradient boosting model produces a tighter distribution of residuals. At nearly every point in the quantile table, the linear regression model has larger residual values.

Another measure to quantitatively confirm that the gradient boosting model has a tighter distribution than the linear regression model is the kurtosis value found in the summary statistics output of the PROC UNIVARIATE procedure. The kurtosis measures the sharpness or the peak of a distribution curve. The kurtosis value for the linear regression model is 1.14, while the kurtosis for the gradient boosting model is 2.21.

Output 2.20: Linear Regression Quantiles

Linear Regression Quantiles	
Level	Quantile
100% Max	2.660
99%	1.147
95%	0.687
90%	0.515
75% Q3	0.256
50% Median	-0.027
25% Q1	-0.271
10%	-0.493
5%	-0.627
1%	-0.904
0% Min	-1.431

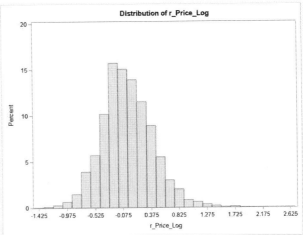

Output 2.21: Gradient Boosting Quantiles

Gradient Boosting Quantiles	
Level	Quantile
100% Max	2.677
99%	0.969
95%	0.566
90%	0.405
75% Q3	0.191
50% Median	-0.018
25% Q1	-0.205
10%	-0.381
5%	-0.503
1%	-0.778
0% Min	-1.402

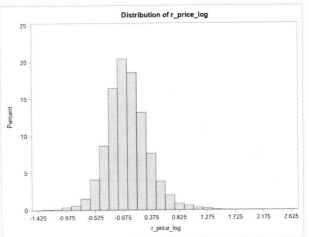

This analysis has shown that the linear regression model performs worse than the gradient boosting model consistently across the entire range of predictions. The gradient boosting model provides better predictions at the high and low end of actual target values.

Decision Time

At this point, we have another decision to make. We could go back to the beginning of the analysis and stratify the data into three price ranges (high, medium, and low), and we could build separate models for each of these price ranges. There is little doubt that these stratified models would result in better price predictions on the high and low ends and probably in the middle range as well. There is no guarantee that this solution would provide better estimates, but for the sake of due diligence (and my data OCD), I would consider developing the stratified models.

The other option is to accept the models that we have developed and put one into production. Often in the real world, a data scientist does not have the luxury of time to iterate through every possible modeling approach.

Implementation

Every implementation process is different because it depends on the purpose of the model and the environment of the deployment. For our example, we developed a linear regression model that will be used to estimate per diem property prices based on user input. This model will be deployed on our own website. The big advantage that we have here is that we have complete control over the deployment and do not have to rely on a corporate IT team to deploy the model for us.

We can take advantage of this deployment environment by incorporating user selection drop-down boxes that force the user to select a predetermined category. This grants us total control over the range of input values.

Due to the simplicity of our parsimonious linear regression model, we can easily hard code the scoring algorithm directly into the HTML code of our website. The bootstrapped version of our model provides us with the 25% threshold, the median value, and the 75% threshold. This could provide the customer with an acceptable range of values that they can use to price their property.

$$25\% \; Threshold = 3.5737 + Room \; Type(0.5249) + Accommodates(0.5430)$$
$$+ \; Neighborhood(0.3491) + Property \; Type(0.3445)$$

$$Median = 3.5798 + Room \; Type(0.5285) + Accommodates(0.5482)$$
$$+ \; Neighborhood(0.3522) + Property \; Type(0.3577)$$

$$75\% \; Threshold = 3.5865 + Room \; Type(0.5321) + Accommodates(0.5534)$$
$$+ \; Neighborhood(0.3553) + Property \; Type(0.3701)$$

The customer has to select only the appropriate drop-down boxes and the algorithm will generate pricing estimates for each of their selections. The result would include a summary price estimate for a low, medium, and high pricing strategy as well as per unit dollar values for each selected feature.

Congratulations! You have just developed a data-driven online business. Ok, now it's time to book the flight to Playa Del Carmen and get ready to sip the piña coladas on the beach. But before you go, remember that you have to a few other things that you need to do:

- Trend the pricing estimates across the calendar year with the information contained in the **Calendar** data set.

- Develop pricing models for each city.

- Develop the website with integrated scoring logic.

- Develop a program that monitors your predictions.

- Market your product to potential Airbnb property listers.

- Develop a program that monitors your predictive accuracy.

- Tune the modeling algorithm based on historical accuracy.

Chapter Review

The goal of this chapter was to give you a thorough review of all the steps involved with a data science project. Even though each of the steps were covered in detail, there will still be many unexpected obstacles and challenges that you will face when developing your own data science project. Although the general workflow may be relatively consistent across projects, the details and implementation will vary greatly.

It is very important to understand the underlying methodology and the general reasoning as to why choose one analytical methodology or one modeling algorithm over another. The following chapters will cover these issues in detail.

Chapter 3: SAS Coding

Overview

I am going to assume that if you bought a book on data science in SAS that you have some familiarity with the SAS programming language. If you do have some experience in SAS coding, then this chapter will be a refresher on common SAS coding techniques. If you do not have much experience in SAS coding, then you may have to spend a little extra time studying this chapter and trying out the programming concepts yourself on the data that I've provided in the GitHub repository.

I will break the SAS coding concepts into four sections:

- Get data
- Explore data

- Manipulate data

- Export data

Regardless of what industry or academic program that you are in, these four areas of SAS coding will cover about 80% of what you will need to know to sufficiently work with data.

Warning

An important programming note to understand before we begin developing SAS code is that SAS does not incorporate "white space formatting." In many other programming languages, the programmer is required to indent four spaces or use a tab to begin or continue a process. SAS does not require the programmer to do this. Although a programmer could either continuously write all their code on a single line or they could put as much white space as they wish between each statement, it is a best practice to use standard formatting to make your code easy to understand.

Get Data

The first step in any analytical project is to get the data. This section will explore the various methods of getting data into the SAS environment.

Structured and Unstructured Data

The first step in any data project is to get the data. Data can come in many forms and from many environments. To simplify the complex subject of data gathering, I will focus on structured data that is contained in existing databases and unstructured data that is contained in text files.

Structured data looks like a spreadsheet. It has defined rows and columns, and it can be stored in many structured environments like SAS tables, Microsoft Excel spreadsheets, and Microsoft Access tables. Structured data can also be stored in database management systems (DMBS) such as Teradata, Microsoft SQL Server, Apache Hadoop, and many others.

Unstructured data does not have defined columns. This data includes text files, JSON files, and weblogs. Some unstructured data may look as if it is structured (for example, a tab-delimited text file), but the computer just sees a long string of text with delimiters. This data would need to be brought into a structured environment for it to be manipulated and analyzed.

The first step to working with either structured or unstructured data is to put the data into a SAS table. A SAS table is a structured data file that has defined columns and rows. This data file has the extension .sas7bdat.

A SAS table has columns and rows with the variable names in the first row and the data in the following rows. Although the structure is similar to a spreadsheet, there are a few SAS specific rules for a SAS table:

- SAS column names can be between 1 and 32 characters in length.

- SAS column names must start with either a letter or an underscore. (They cannot begin with a number.)

- SAS column names cannot contain special values.

- SAS column names can be uppercase, lowercase or mixed case.

- You cannot mix character and numeric data types within the same column.

- Numeric columns are always stored with a length of 8 bytes (which equates to 16 digits).

- Character columns can be any length between 1 and 32,767 bytes (one byte per character).

SAS Libraries

A SAS library is a collection of data files that are of the same data type and in the same location. For example, a SAS library can be constructed to contain all the Teradata files. Another SAS library can be built to contain all the Hadoop files, while another SAS library can be built to hold all your locally stored text files. Many SAS programs will have several library statements at the beginning of the program to construct pathways to all the various data files that you will need for your project.

You can create a SAS library with a LIBNAME statement. The general structure of a LIBNAME statement is:

LIBNAME *libref engine "path";*

Let's look at each part of the LIBNAME statement:

- **LIBNAME** – This is the keyword reference that calls the LIBNAME procedure.

- *libref* – This is the user-defined name of the library. You can name it whatever you want as long as it is eight characters or less, starts with a letter or an underscore, and includes only letters, numbers, and underscores in the name.

- *engine* – An engine is a set of "behind-the-scenes" instructions for reading structured data. Different types of data environments require different engines. Therefore, SAS has different engines for Excel, Teradata, Hadoop, and several others. SAS also has the Base SAS engine to read in SAS tables. The Base SAS engine is the default engine that SAS uses when an engine is not specified in the LIBNAME statement.

- *path* – The path is the location of the data that you want to read. This location is relative to the installation of the SAS environment. If you have SAS installed on your local computer, you can specify a path to a local file. If you have SAS installed on a server, then your paths must be relative to the server.

For example, I have a folder on my desktop that I've labeled "SAS Book Stuff," and within this folder, I have another folder that I've labeled "Data." This folder is where I put all of the data that I will use for my examples. The Windows file path for this folder is: C:\Users\James Gearheart\Desktop\SAS Book Stuff\Data.

I can create a SAS library that I will call "MYDATA."

Program 3.1: Establish a Library Pathway

```
LIBNAME MYDATA BASE "C:/Users/James Gearheart/Desktop/SAS Book
Stuff/Data";
```

Warning

An important thing to notice is that the pathway in the LIBNAME statement in the UNIX/Linux environment requires you to use the forward-slash "/" instead of the backslash "\" that you normally see in a Windows environment.

Notes on Program 3.1:

- I use the LIBNAME statement to create the library.
- I have specified that the libref that I will use is MYDATA.
- I am using the Base SAS engine (although I do not need to specify it because it is the default engine).
- I am specifying the path to my local folder (making sure that I use the forward slash).

SAS libraries are a great way to manage your data environment. They can act as pointers to existing locations that contain similar data files, or you can use SAS libraries to create a place to store files that you create through your programming code permanently. By placing data into a library, the data files become permanent until you choose to delete them.

PROC IMPORT

Now that we have established a library to house our data, let's get some data to populate the library. The code below imports a comma-delimited text file called listings_clean.csv into our newly created MYDATA library.

Program 3.2: Import Data with PROC IMPORT

```
FILENAME REFFILE 'C:\Users\James Gearheart\Desktop\SAS Book
Stuff\Data\listings_clean.csv';

PROC IMPORT DATAFILE=REFFILE
      DBMS=CSV
      OUT= MYDATA.Listings;
      GETNAMES=YES;
RUN;
```

Let's examine each piece of the above code:

- I have used the FILENAME statement to create a path to the data that I want to import. I have called this pathway REFFILE. Notice that that pathway uses the backslash in the file path.

- The IMPORT procedure reads **unstructured data** from an external source and writes it into a SAS data set.

- The DATAFILE statement specifies the file reference that I created in the FILENAME statement. You can choose not to use a separate file reference and instead use the file path.

- The DBMS statement specifies the type of information that you want to import. An important note is that since the data file that we are importing has a .csv extension, we do not need to specify that the delimiter is a comma. PROC IMPORT can identify that this type of delimited external file contains comma-separated data values.

- The OUT statement specifies where the imported data will be placed and what it will be labeled. This example shows that we are putting the data in our newly created MYLIB library, and we are assigning the data to the name "Listings."

- The GETNAMES statement imports variable names from the first row of the imported data set.

The MYDATA library permanently contains the Listings data set. Even if you delete your MYDATA library reference or shut off SAS completely, the Listings data set will still exist in the location that you specified. This is because the libref is merely a pointer to the data. You can delete the pointer, but the data remains until you choose to delete it.

WORK Library

You certainly do not want to permanently keep every data set that you work with throughout your project. Some data files are meant to be temporarily used as part of a process flow and then discarded. Data files consume a lot of computer memory, so you should be judicious in deciding which ones you want to retain after your SAS session is finished.

The WORK library is a temporary library that is automatically created by SAS at the beginning of a SAS session. The files that are written to the WORK library are deleted at the end of the SAS session. If a data file is created and does not contain the reference to a specific library, then this data file is placed into the WORK library.

A programmer can either specify the WORK library directly, or they can infer the WORK library by not providing a specific library. The code below shows two examples of placing the MYDATA.Listings data into a temporary WORK library labeled "Test."

Program 3.3: Place Data into a WORK Library

```
DATA WORK.TEST;
  SET MYDATA.Listings;
RUN;
```

```
DATA TEST;
  SET MYDATA.LISTINGS;
RUN;
```

The first example explicitly states the WORK library while the second example implicitly states the WORK library by not specifying a library.

If you were to restart your SAS session, the MYDATA.Listings data set would still exist; however, the WORK.Test data would not exist.

DATA Step

SAS libraries are a great way to access structured data. The easiest example to understand is copying an existing SAS table from one library to another SAS library. If a SAS table exists in another SAS library, you can copy it into a new library with a DATA step:

Program 3.4: Place Data into a SAS Library

```
DATA MYDATA.DEMOGRAPHICS;
  SET ORG.DEMOGRAPHICS;
RUN;
```

The above code accesses the data set named "DEMOGRAPHICS" that is found in the ORG library previously created by someone else and creates a copy of it in your MYDATA library. We have chosen to keep the same name of the file, but we could have decided to call it whatever we wanted. We will explore the DATA step in more detail in the "Manipulate Data" section of this chapter, but for now, it is important to know that existing SAS tables can easily be copied from one library to another.

Server Connections

Most data scientists work in corporations where data is not stored locally or in Excel files. In the era of big data, data files are generally stored on servers that the data scientist will need to connect to and navigate the correct pathway to access and select the data that they need.

The following code establishes a connection to a specific set of tables on a Teradata server.

Program 3.5: Establish a Connection to a Teradata Server

```
%INCLUDE '~/pw/userinfo.sas';
LIBNAME MY_TERA TERADATA USER="&sysuserid" PASSWORD="&pw"
SERVER="TERADATA_SERVER" SCHEMA=SPECIFIC_AREA
```

Let's look at each piece of the above code:

- In this example, the %INCLUDE statement uses a Linux/UNIX path. This is because this example assumes that you are connecting to a Teradata server in a Linux environment. Linux paths are also compatible with SAS University Edition and most SAS Viya installations.

- It is vitally important to protect your sign-on information. The %INCLUDE statement points to a protected file that contains your username and password information. This file is not to be shared with anyone else. This step is not necessary to connect to servers, but it is highly recommended that you do not directly insert your username and password information into your programs. The tilde (~) indicates the home directory.

- The LIBNAME statement is used to create a library that we will call MY_TERA.

- The TERADATA statement is used to access the Teradata engine that will connect to the Teradata server.

- The USER and PASSWORD statements pull information from the %INCLUDE file to establish your access privileges.

- SERVER specifies the name of your organization's Teradata server. This can also be called with the TDPID statement which is an alias for the SERVER statement.

- The SCHEMA statement points to a specific collection of tables on the Teradata server. Servers will usually have several different schemas that contain different types of data tables.

Pulling data from corporate servers is a bit trickier than using a simple PROC IMPORT. The data found in these servers are generally massive in scale. These data sets can range from a few gigabytes up to the petabyte and exabyte scale. The data contained in these servers are usually not in SAS tables. You will need to access the specific data that you need and bring it into the SAS environment and place it into a SAS table. Let's look at an example piece of code:

Program 3.6: PROC SQL Connection to Teradata Server

```
PROC SQL;
        CONNECT TO TERADATA(USER="&sysuserid" PASSWORD="&pw"
                SERVER="TERADATA_SERVER" SCHEMA=SPECIFIC_AREA
                MODE=TERADATA);
        CREATE TABLE MYLIB.WEBLOGS AS SELECT *
FROM CONNECTION TO TERADATA
                (SELECT a.*
                        FROM SPECIFIC_AREA.TABLE_NAME AS a
                            WHERE date >= '2017-12-01'
                );
QUIT;
```

Notes on Program 3.6:

- The SQL procedure implements the Structured Query Language (SQL) in SAS. SQL is a widely used programming language that accesses existing data structures and creates data tables.

- The CONNECT TO statement uses the same connection specifications that we used to establish a connection to the Teradata server.

- SQL provides the option to create a table or a view. We are creating a table named "WEBLOGS" in the MYLIB library that we have previously created. This table is a permanent data set that is a SAS table.

- The AS SELECT * FROM statement tells SQL where we want to get the data to populate the MYLIB.WEBLOGS data set that we are creating.

- The CONNECTION TO TERADATA statement specifies that we are pulling data from our newly established Teradata connection.

- The remainder of the code within the parentheses is standard SQL coding that we will explore shortly. It is important to note that because the data contained in servers is massive, it is important to limit your data pull. In this example, I am using a WHERE statement to select only the observations that occur after a specific date.

We have just seen a few examples of how to get data into a SAS environment. The LIBNAME statement helps you create a place to put data. PROC IMPORT, the DATA step, and PROC SQL are just a few of the many ways that you can populate your library with SAS tables. Now that we have some data to play with, we will need to explore the data.

Explore Data

After you have successfully gathered some data, you will need to know some information about your data, such as:

- Number of columns
- Number of observations
- Format for each column

PROC CONTENTS

The CONTENTS procedure shows the contents of a specified SAS table. The procedure writes the contents to an output file and provides a summary of the information in the Results window of your SAS environment.

Program 3.7: Explore the Contents of a Data Set

```
PROC CONTENTS DATA=MYDATA.Listings; RUN;
```

The output contained in the Results window has three parts. The first two parts provide summary information about the data set, including when it was created, where it is stored, and the owner of the data set. In this example, we can see that the MYDATA.LISTINGS data set contains 49,056 observations and 54 variables. It was created on March 2nd, 2019, and the file size is 21MB.

Output 3.1: PROC CONTENTS Output

Data Set Name	MYDATA.LISTINGS	Observations	49056
Member Type	DATA	Variables	54
Engine	BASE	Indexes	0
Created	03/02/2019 19:29:38	Observation Length	440
Last Modified	03/02/2019 19:29:38	Deleted Observations	0
Protection		Compressed	NO
Data Set Type		Sorted	NO
Label			
Data Representation	WINDOWS_32		
Encoding	wlatin1 Western (Windows)		

Engine/Host Dependent Information	
Data Set Page Size	65536
Number of Data Set Pages	332
First Data Page	1
Max Obs per Page	148
Obs in First Data Page	132
Number of Data Set Repairs	0
ExtendObsCounter	YES
Filename	C:\Users\James Gearheart\Desktop\SAS Book Stuff\Data\listings.sas7bdat
Release Created	9.0401M6
Host Created	W32_7HOME
Owner Name	Awesomeness\James Gearheart
File Size	21MB
File Size (bytes)	21823488

The third and final section of the output of Program 3.7 shows the individual columns in the SAS table along with their format information. This table provides an alphabetic list that contains the variable name, type, length, format, and informat information.

Output 3.2: PROC CONTENTS Output

Alphabetic List of Variables and Attributes				
# Variable	Type	Len	Format	Informat
19 accommodates	Num	8	BEST12.	BEST32.
35 availability_30	Num	8	BEST12.	BEST32.
36 availability_60	Num	8	BEST12.	BEST32.
37 availability_90	Num	8	BEST12.	BEST32.
38 availability_365	Num	8	BEST12.	BEST32.
20 bathrooms	Num	8	BEST12.	BEST32.
23 bed_type	Char	13	$13.	$13.
21 bedrooms	Num	8	BEST12.	BEST32.
22 beds	Num	8	BEST12.	BEST32.
53 calculated_host_listings_count	Num	8	BEST12.	BEST32.
34 calendar_updated	Char	13	$13.	$13.
50 cancellation_policy	Char	27	$27.	$27.
12 city	Char	8	$8.	$8.
29 cleaning_fee	Num	8	BEST12.	BEST32.
31 extra_people	Num	8	BEST12.	BEST32.
40 first_review	Num	8	MMDDYY10.	MMDDYY10.

Although there are 54 variables in the MYDATA.LISTINGS data set, I have elected to show only the first 16 variables. From this list, you can see that there is a mix of character and numeric variables. The numeric variables are mostly in the BEST12. format with the exception being the first_review variable. This variable is a date field and is formatted in the MMDDYY10. format.

The character variables are individually formatted to their specific length. It is important to inspect the format of character variables. These variables are often stored in formats that are unnecessarily large and consume a lot of computer resources.

PROC FREQ

The FREQ procedure is used extensively by data scientists to understand the contents of both character and numeric variables. This procedure produces one-way to multi-way frequency distributions of data elements. For a single variable, the default settings of the procedure will provide a list of unique observations and the frequency at which they occur. This default setting will also provide the individual percentage of total observations, the cumulative frequency of observations, the cumulative percent of observations, and the total number of missing values.

Warning

Be cautious with using PROC FREQ on numeric data. If your numeric variable has decimal points or has values greater than 100, this procedure can easily produce extremely long tables of information. To explore continuous data with PROC FREQ, first can use a DATA step with the ROUND function to round values up to a whole number. Alternatively, you can apply a format to create numeric bins for frequency analysis.

The example below shows a standard FREQ procedure called on the Listings data set contained in the MYDATA library. The TABLES statement requests a one-way to multi-way crosstabulation table for the specified variables.

Program 3.8: Frequency Distribution Example

```
PROC FREQ DATA=MYDATA.LISTINGS;
        TABLES neighbourhood_group_cleansed;
RUN;
```

Output 3.3: PROC FREQ Output

neighbourhood_group_cleansed	Frequency	Percent	Cumulative Frequency	Cumulative Percent
Bronx	928	1.89	928	1.89
Brooklyn	19968	40.71	20896	42.60
Manhattan	22564	46.00	43460	88.60
Queens	5273	10.75	48733	99.35
Staten Is	320	0.65	49053	100.00
Frequency Missing = 3				

By default, the data is sorted in alphabetical order. It is often useful to have the data sorted in order of frequency from high to low. The ORDER statement controls the order in which the data is sorted.

Program 3.9: Ordered Frequency Distribution Example

```
PROC FREQ DATA=MYDATA.LISTINGS ORDER=FREQ;
      TABLES neighbourhood_group_cleansed;
RUN;
```

Output 3.4: Ordered Frequency Distribution Example Output

neighbourhood_group_cleansed	Frequency	Percent	Cumulative Frequency	Cumulative Percent
Manhattan	22564	46.00	22564	46.00
Brooklyn	19968	40.71	42532	86.71
Queens	5273	10.75	47805	97.46
Bronx	928	1.89	48733	99.35
Staten Is	320	0.65	49053	100.00
Frequency Missing = 3				

PROC FREQ can also create crosstabulation tables for two or more variables. The following code shows the crosstabulation between the variable neighbourhood_group_cleansed and the variable room_type. The code also specifies that I want to suppress the column, row, and overall percentage information from the output. Finally, I also want to create a temporary output data set of this crosstabulation that I will name "room_freq."

Program 3.10: Crosstabulation Example

```
PROC FREQ DATA=MYDATA.LISTINGS ORDER=FREQ;
      TABLES neighbourhood_group_cleansed * room_type /
      NOCOL NOROW NOPERCENT OUT=room_freq;
RUN;
```

Output 3.5: Crosstabulation Output

Table of neighbourhood_group_cleansed by room_type					
		room_type			
		Entire home/apt	Private room	Shared room	Total
neighbourhood_group_cleansed					
Manhattan	Frequency	14102	8028	434	22564
Brooklyn	Frequency	9540	10046	382	19968
Queens	Frequency	1958	3110	205	5273
Bronx	Frequency	314	577	37	928
Staten Is	Frequency	143	172	5	320
Total	Frequency	26057	21933	1063	49053
Frequency Missing = 3					

The FREQ procedure has several options to evaluate the statistics of a given set of variables. These options include:

- Chi-square tests and measures

- Measures of association

- Binomial proportions and risk differences for 2 x 2 tables

- Odds ratios and relative risks for 2 x 2 tables

- Tests for trend

- Tests and measures of agreement
- Cochran-Mantel-Haenszel statistics

Each of these topics is certainly worthy of its own chapter. However, this chapter has a "Getting Started with SAS" level of detail. I recommend that the reader go to the SAS Support Documentation for further information: https://support.sas.com/en/documentation.html

PROC UNIVARIATE

The UNIVARIATE procedure produces descriptive statistics for numeric data. This procedure provides a lot of information about the distribution of the data and the measures of centrality. These include the mean, median, and mode along with the standard deviation, range, and interquartile range. PROC UNIVARIATE is used extensively by data scientists to investigate the distribution of numeric data and assess the need to transform variables into a normal distribution.

The code below shows a simple UNIVARIATE procedure to be run against the Listings data set contained in the MYDATA library. We are specifying that we want to see the descriptive statistics for the "price" variable contained in that data set. We also have specified that we want to see a histogram of the "price" variable by including the HISTOGRAM statement.

Program 3.11: PROC UNIVARIATE Example

```
PROC UNIVARIATE DATA=MYDATA.LISTINGS;
  VAR Price;
  HISTOGRAM;
RUN;
```

The first section of the output from the procedure is contained in Output 3.6a. This table shows the total number of observations (N), the central point of the data (Mean), the distribution of the data (Std Deviation) along with several additional statistics that describe the distribution of the data. This table provides an excellent overview of the selected variable that will be detailed in the following sections of the PROC UNIVARIATE output.

Output 3.6a: PROC UNIVARIATE Output – Moments Table

Moments			
N	49053	Sum Weights	
Mean	152.301653	Sum Observations	
Std Deviation	227.800206	Variance	
Skewness	20.4539323	Kurtosis	
Uncorrected SS	3683275463	Corrected SS	
Coeff Variation	149.571723	Std Error Mean	

The second section contains the Basic Statistical Measures. This valuable table provides additional information on the measures of centrality including the median and the mode. This table also provides additional information on the distribution of the data including the range and the interquartile range.

Output 3.6b: PROC UNIVARIATE Output – Statistical Measures

Basic Statistical Measures			
Location		Variability	
Mean	152.3017	Std Deviation	227.800:
Median	110.0000	Variance	5189
Mode	150.0000	Range	100(
		Interquartile Range	109.000(

The third section of the output contains the Tests for Location. PROC UNIVARIATE produces a test statistic for the null hypothesis. The null hypothesis is the point at which the mean or median is equal to a given value of μ. This statistic is a two-sided test with the default value of $\mu = 0$.

The fourth section of PROC UNIVARIATE provides a table of the quantiles of the data. This table provides a deeper look of the distribution by providing the values of the data at predetermined percentage markers. The example shows that the range of the price variable is from 0 (0% Min) to 10,000 (100% Max) with a median value of 110 (50% Median). This table also provides data values that mark the first and third quartile of the data distribution as well as various high and low percentage markers.

The quantile table is extremely valuable because it gives the researcher a concise table of information describing the distribution of the data. This table can serve as a decision point as to whether a variable has outliers, needs to be capped on the high or low ends, or needs to be transformed into a normally distributed variable.

The fifth section of the PROC UNIVARIATE output provides the Extreme Observations table. This table shows the top five and bottom five observation values and their associated observation number. This table allows the researcher to quickly see if there is a single high or low outlier or if there are several values on the high or low end of the spectrum.

Output 3.6c: PROC UNIVARIATE Output – Tests for Location

Tests for Location: Mu0=0				
Test		Statistic	p Value	
Student's t	t	148.0755	Pr > |t|	<.0001
Sign	M	24514	Pr >= |M|	<.0001
Signed Rank	S	6.0095E8	Pr >= |S|	<.0001

Output 3.6d: PROC UNIVARIATE Output – Quantiles

Quantiles (Definition 5)	
Level	Quantile
100% Max	10000
99%	750
95%	355
90%	272
75% Q3	179
50% Median	110
25% Q1	70
10%	50
5%	40
1%	30
0% Min	0

Output 3.6e: PROC UNIVARIATE Output – Extreme Observations

Extreme Observations			
Lowest		Highest	
Value	Obs	Value	Obs
0	42926	9999	13960
0	38781	10000	10346
0	31405	10000	12395
0	31397	10000	17985
0	31339	10000	20017

The final default table produced by the UNIVARIATE procedure is the Missing Values table. This table provides an overview of the volume of observations that have missing values for the selected variable. This table also provides the percentage of observations that have missing values. This information is very important because it tells the researcher how big of an issue that missing values are for the selected variable. As a rule of thumb, if missing values are less than 20% of the total observations, then you can infer the missing values through a variety of methods. If the missing values are greater than 20% of the total observations, then you may need to take an alternative approach that we will discuss in the "Create a Modeling Data Set" chapter.

We have also decided to include a histogram graphic that is not part of the default PROC UNIVARIATE output. The histogram shows a graphical demonstration of the data distribution. The example shown in Figure 3.1 shows a highly skewed price variable with extreme high-end outliers. This data would need to be adjusted before it could be used for modeling.

Output 3.6f: PROC UNIVARIATE Output – Missing Values

Missing Values			
Missing Value	Count	Percent Of All Obs	Missing Obs
.	3	0.01	100.00

Figure 3.1: PROC UNIVARIATE Histogram Output

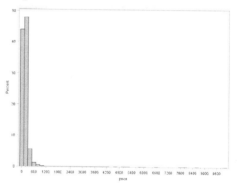

PROC MEANS

The MEANS procedure is another way to calculate descriptive statistics for your data set. This procedure allows you to select the types of statistical features that you would like to include in the output. The procedure provides you with the flexibility to stratify the data and create output data sets of the calculated statistics.

The following code calls the MEANS procedure on the Listings data set contained in the MYDATA library. The programmer has the option of specifying the variables that they want to investigate through the use of the VAR statement. If no VAR statement is included, the PROC MEANS will calculate the default statistics for all the numeric variables in the selected data set.

Program 3.12: PROC MEANS Example

```
PROC MEANS DATA=MYDATA.LISTINGS;
  VAR price accommodates bathrooms;
RUN;
```

The output data shown in Output 3.7 shows the default statistics generated from PROC MEANS.

Output 3.7: PROC MEANS Output

Variable	N	Mean	Std Dev	Minimum	Maximum
price	49053	152.3016533	227.8002064	0	10000.00
accommodates	49053	2.8903635	1.8965131	1.0000000	16.0000000
bathrooms	48977	1.1740613	0.4884138	0	17.0000000

We can expand the MEANS procedure to include additional statistics that we specify. The following code specifies that I want the output to show the number of observations (N), the number of missing values (NMISS), the minimum value (MIN), the maximum value (MAX), the mean and median values (MEAN, MEDIAN) as well as the standard deviation (STDDEV).

Program 3.13: PROC MEANS with a CLASS Statement

```
PROC MEANS DATA=MYDATA.LISTINGS
  N NMISS MIN MAX MEAN MEDIAN STDDEV;
  CLASS room_type;
  VAR price accommodates bathrooms;
  OUTPUT OUT=list_stats;
RUN;
```

The CLASS statement stratifies the data by the selected variable. The output will contain the selected statistics for each level of the variable in the CLASS statement.

Output 3.8: PROC MEANS with a CLASS Statement Output

room_type	N Obs	Variable	N	N Miss	Minimum	Maximum	Mean	Median	Std Dev
Entire home/apt	26057	price	26057	0	0	10000.00	208.8284146	160.0000000	251.8221308
		accommodates	26057	0	1.0000000	16.0000000	3.7491269	3.0000000	2.0988856
		bathrooms	26037	20	0	16.0000000	1.1796290	1.0000000	0.4976853
Private room	21933	price	21933	0	0	10000.00	89.0778279	70.0000000	178.8739211
		accommodates	21933	0	1.0000000	16.0000000	1.9267770	2.0000000	0.9309658
		bathrooms	21880	53	0	17.0000000	1.1629799	1.0000000	0.4465495
Shared room	1063	price	1063	0	0	1800.00	71.1825024	49.0000000	112.6109271
		accommodates	1063	0	1.0000000	16.0000000	1.7215428	1.0000000	1.2280374
		bathrooms	1060	3	0	8.0000000	1.2660377	1.0000000	0.9006227

Output 3.8 shows the output for the expanded MEANS procedure. The selected statistics are calculated for each level of the CLASS variable.

The final element created from the MEANS procedure is the output data set. The OUTPUT statement specifies the statistics to be stored in the data set specified in the OUT option. The default output includes the N, MIN, MAX, MEAN and STD statistics. These are the same defaults as the unspecified PROC MEANS output.

The OUTPUT statement creates the output data set shown below (Output 3.9). It is important to note that the output data set has two distinct levels as specified by the _TYPE_ field. The output where _TYPE_ = 0 provides summary statistics for the entire data set. The output where _TYPE_ = 1 provides the calculated statistics for each of the levels specified in the CLASS statement.

Output 3.9: PROC MEANS with a CLASS Statement Output Data Set

	room_type	_TYPE_	_FREQ_	_STAT_	price	accommodat...	bathrooms
1		0	49053	N	49053	49053	48977
2		0	49053	MIN	0	1	0
3		0	49053	MAX	10000	16	17
4		0	49053	MEAN	152.30165331	2.8903634844	1.1740612941
5		0	49053	STD	227.80020636	1.8965131441	0.488413772
6	Entire home/apt	1	26057	N	26057	26057	26037
7	Entire home/apt	1	26057	MIN	0	1	0
8	Entire home/apt	1	26057	MAX	10000	16	16
9	Entire home/apt	1	26057	MEAN	208.82841463	3.7491269141	1.1796289895
10	Entire home/apt	1	26057	STD	251.82213078	2.0988856445	0.4976853482
11	Private room	1	21933	N	21933	21933	21880
12	Private room	1	21933	MIN	0	1	0
13	Private room	1	21933	MAX	10000	16	17
14	Private room	1	21933	MEAN	89.077827931	1.9267770027	1.1629798903
15	Private room	1	21933	STD	178.87392106	0.9309657566	0.4465494929
16	Shared room	1	1063	N	1063	1063	1060
17	Shared room	1	1063	MIN	0	1	0
18	Shared room	1	1063	MAX	1800	16	8
19	Shared room	1	1063	MEAN	71.182502352	1.7215428034	1.2660377358
20	Shared room	1	1063	STD	112.61092708	1.2280374425	0.9006226775

PROC SUMMARY

The last procedure that we will look at in the "Explore Data" section of this chapter will be PROC SUMMARY. The SUMMARY procedure can calculate summary statistics for a data set much in the same manner as PROC MEANS and PROC UNIVARIATE. The default PROC SUMMARY creates an output data set that is very similar to what we have just seen in the default MEANS procedure.

Program 3.14: PROC SUMMARY Example

```
PROC SUMMARY DATA=MYDATA.LISTINGS;
  VAR price accommodates bathrooms;
  OUTPUT OUT=list_sum;
RUN;
```

Output 3.10: PROC SUMMARY Output Data Set

	TYPE	_FREQ_	_STAT_	price	accommodat...	bathrooms
1	0	49056	N	49053	49053	48977
2	0	49056	MIN	0	1	0
3	0	49056	MAX	10000	16	17
4	0	49056	MEAN	152.30165331	2.8903634844	1.1740612941
5	0	49056	STD	227.80020636	1.8965131441	0.488413772

The code displayed in Program 3.14 produces the output data set in Output 3.10. This data set is identical to the information that we receive in the default MEANS procedure.

So, you have to ask yourself the question, why would I need to use PROC SUMMARY if I already have ways of getting that information? Good question.

As you can probably tell by the title of the procedure, the SUMMARY procedure can summarize information in many different ways. For example, if you have an ID variable, you can summarize specific information at the ID level and create a summary output data set. Program 3.15 below shows a SUMMARY procedure at the ID level to create a summary data set.

If a SUMMARY procedure includes a BY statement, the data will need to be sorted by that variable prior to the SUMMARY procedure.

Program 3.15: PROC SUMMARY with a BY Statement

```
PROC SORT DATA=MYDATA.LISTINGS OUT=list_sort;
  BY host_id;
RUN;

PROC SUMMARY DATA=list_sort;
  BY host_id;
  VAR price accomodates bathrooms;
  OUTPUT OUT=list_sum SUM=;
RUN;
```

After the data has been sorted, the PROC SUMMARY code is developed to specify that the procedure will use the sorted data and summarize the price, accommodates, and bathrooms variables. These variables will be summarized at the host_id level, and an output data set will be created named list_sum. The SUM=; option in the OUTPUT statement suppresses the statistics from the output data set. The first ten rows of the final data set are shown in Output 3.11.

Output 3.11: PROC SUMMARY with a BY Statement Output Data Set

	host_id	_TYPE_	_FREQ_	price	accommodat...	bathrooms
1	.	0	3	.	.	.
2	2571	0	1	182	4	1
3	2758	0	3	234	9	3
4	2782	0	2	200	2	2
5	2787	0	8	667	42	8
6	2845	0	2	324	3	2
7	2881	0	2	118	4	4
8	3211	0	1	90	2	1
9	3227	0	1	150	4	1
10	3563	0	1	35	1	1

This data set shows the summarized information at the host_id level. The _FREQ_ column shows how many observations are included in the host_id summary. For example, on line 5, we can see that host_id 2787 has eight observations. This can be interpreted as "Host ID # 2787 has eight properties listed on Airbnb in NYC as of Dec 5th, 2018. These properties can accommodate a total of 42 people at a total nightly price of $667."

It is useful to create a summary data set and perform statistical analysis on the summarized data or to take it a step further and create a clustering algorithm on this information. We will explore this idea further in the unsupervised modeling chapter.

Manipulate Data

At this point, you have gathered some data, created a library to store your data, imported the data into your library, and explored the contents of the data. This is a great start! However, data is rarely useful in its raw form. We often have to do things to the data to prepare it for reporting or modeling. This process can include filtering the data, appending it with additional data sets, creating new variables, and many, many other adjustments that are necessary prior to extracting actionable information from our data.

DATA Step

The DATA step is considered "home base" in SAS programming. This is where much of your data adjustments will take place. Many of the techniques that we will be discussing will take place within a DATA step. The DATA step is the primary method of creating a SAS data set, merging two or more data sets, creating variables, filtering data, and many more data manipulation techniques.

Behind the scenes, the DATA step executes in two phases:

1. **The Compilation Phase** – This initial phase has three important functions:
   a. Checks the SAS syntax for errors and then translates your SAS code into machine code.
   b. Initializes the program data vector (PDV). This is a logical area in memory where SAS builds a data set one observation at a time. This data set contains each column that you referenced in the DATA step and its attributes. These attributes include the column name, type, and length. The compilation phase establishes the rules for the PDV based on your code. This includes which records will be read into the PDV. This phase also creates a one-row temporary data set of empty columns that will be populated during the execution phase.
   c. Creates descriptor information. This is the table metadata that is created by the compilation phase. This table metadata will be used as a rules engine in the execution phase of the DATA step.

2. **The Execution Phase** – This phase occurs as a loop through the input data set.
   a. Initializes the PDV. The general structure and the rules of the PDV were created in the compilation phase of the DATA step. The newly created program variables are set to missing in the PDV.
   b. Reads a single row from the input table into the PDV. You can use a SET, INPUT, MERGE, UPDATE, or MODIFY statement to read data into the PDV.
   c. Executes processing statements and updates values in the PDV. This step performs all the logical functions that you have specified in the DATA step.
   d. At the end of the statements specified in the DATA step, SAS writes an observation to the output SAS data set.
   e. Returns to the top of the DATA step and performs the same process on the next row of data in the input table.

f. The DATA step is finished when the process has iterated through each row of the input data set.

So, now that we understand how data is processed through the DATA step, let's look at some of the cool stuff that we can do with this statement.

Filtering Data

One of the most common techniques performed on data sets is to filter out records that are not needed for your analysis. The two most widely used functions for filtering data are the WHERE and IF statements.

Both the WHERE and IF statements select observations that meet a particular condition. The main difference between the WHERE and IF statement is that the WHERE statement restricts the volume of observations that are initially read from the input table. A WHERE statement is preferred when the condition is not dependent upon rows other than the current, due to its efficiency.

For example, Program 3.16 shows the creation of a temporary data set named TEST that is built from the input table MYDATA.Listings. The WHERE statement restricts the observations that are initially read from the MYDATA.Listings data set to include only those that met the logical condition that was stated in the WHERE statement.

Program 3.16: Filtering Data with a WHERE Statement

```
DATA WORK.TEST;
  SET MYDATA.LISTINGS;
  WHERE accommodates le 4;
RUN;

NOTE: There were 42565 observations read from the data set
MYDATA.LISTINGS.
      WHERE accommodates<=4;
NOTE: The data set WORK.TEST has 42565 observations and 54 variables.
NOTE: DATA statement used (Total process time):
      real time           0.31 seconds
      cpu time            0.07 seconds
```

The log output shows that 42,565 observations were read from the input table. In contrast, let's look at the IF statement to perform the same type of filtering.

The same restrictions can be implemented with an IF statement, as demonstrated in Program 3.17.

Program 3.17: Filtering Data with an IF Statement

```
DATA WORK.TEST;
  SET MYDATA.LISTINGS;
  IF accommodates le 4;
RUN;
NOTE: There were 49056 observations read from the data set
MYDATA.LISTINGS.
NOTE: The data set WORK.TEST has 42565 observations and 54 variables.
```

```
NOTE: DATA statement used (Total process time):
      real time            0.03 seconds
      cpu time             0.03 seconds
```

The log output shows that all 49,056 observations were read from the input table. The IF statement then selected 42,565 observations that met the logical condition specified in the IF statement.

This might not seem like too big of a difference to you. However, consider that most corporate data sets contain millions of records with thousands of columns. Rather than reading all of them into temporary memory and then performing your logical conditions, it is much more efficient to only read in the observations that meet the logical condition. This method can be the difference between a program taking five minutes to run or five hours to run.

SAS Operators

SAS operators can be used to filter data, create new variables, and perform calculations on existing data. We can classify SAS operators into three broad groups:

- Arithmetic operators

- Conditional operators

- Logical operators

The arithmetic operators are mathematical expressions that can be applied to numeric data. Table 3.1 provides a list of arithmetic operators along with examples of their application.

Table 3.1: Arithmetic Operators

Symbol	Definition	Example	Result
**	exponentiation	a**3	raise A to the third power
*	multiplication	2*y	multiply 2 by the value of Y
/	division	var / 5	divide the value of VAR by 5
+	addition	num + 3	add 3 to the value of NUM
-	subtraction	sale - discount	subtract the value of DISCOUNT from the value of SALE

Conditional operands establish a comparison, operation, or calculation between two variables. These operands can be applied to both numeric and character variables. The application of these operands to numeric data is straightforward. It establishes a conditional mathematical relationship between the two variables, just as one would expect. However, when you apply these conditional operands to character data, the comparison will always yield a numeric result (0 or 1). Character operands are compared character by character from left to right. Character order depends on the collating sequence, usually ASCII or EBCDIC, used by your computer.

For example, in the EBCDIC and ASCII collating sequences, G is greater than A; therefore, this expression is true:

Gray ▶ Adams

Table 3.2: Conditional Operands

Symbol	Mnemonic Equivalent	Definition	Example
=	EQ	equal to	a=3
^=	NE	not equal to	a ne 3
-=	NE	not equal to	a-=3
~=	NE	not equal to	a~=3
>	GT	greater than	a>3
<	LT	less than	a<3
>=	GE	greater than or equal to	a>=3
<=	LE	less than or equal to	a<=3
	IN	equal to one of a list	a in (3, 4, 5)

SAS can also implement logical (Boolean) expressions to link sequences of comparisons. These expressions can be applied to both numeric and character variables.

- If both quantities linked by the AND operator are true, then the result of the AND operation is 1 (true).

- If one of the qualities linked by the OR operator is true, then the result of the OR operation is 1 (true).

- The result of putting NOT in front of a quantity whose value is 0 (false) is 1 (true).

Table 3.3: Logical Expressions

Symbol	Mnemonic Equivalent	Definition
&	AND	(a>b & c>d)
|	OR	(a>b | c>d)
!	OR	(a>b ! c>d)
^	NOT	(a>b ^ c>d)
~	NOT	(a>b ~ c>d)

Program 3.18 provides an example of using each of the SAS operators within a DATA step.

Program 3.18: SAS Operators Examples

```
DATA WORK.TEST;
  SET MYDATA.LISTINGS;

  /*Specify length of new character variable*/
  LENGTH bath_count $8.;

  /*Limit the data imported into memory with a
  symbol operand*/
  WHERE accommodates ^= 0;
```

```
/*IF-THEN statement with mnemonic operand*/
IF bathrooms EQ 1 THEN bath_count = 'Single';
ELSE bath_count = 'Multiple';

/*Calculation with arithmetic operand*/
poly_bath = bathrooms**2;

/*IF-THEN with logical condition*/
IF (accommodates >= 5 AND bathrooms GE 2)
THEN big_house = 1; ELSE big_house = 0;
RUN;
```

Program 3.18 demonstrates the ability to utilize SAS operands to limit data, filter observations and create new variables all within a single DATA step.

IF-THEN/ELSE Logical Statements

SAS evaluates IF-THEN statements and determines if the result of a logical expression is true or false. If the result is true, SAS executes the statement defined in the THEN statement. If the statement is false, SAS continues to the statement defined in the ELSE statement.

In the code shown above (Program 3.18), the IF-THEN / ELSE logical statement follows a pattern:

1. Evaluates the arithmetic expression "IF bathrooms EQ 1".
2. If this value is true, SAS executes the THEN statement and creates a character variable named bath_count and sets the value to "Single".
3. If the value is false, SAS executes the ELSE statement and sets the bath_count to "Multiple".

SAS also allows the programmer to link together multiple IF-THEN / ELSE statements.

SAS Dates

SAS provides the programmer with the flexibility to perform calculations on date values. Dates are stored as numeric values in SAS. This value represents the number of days between January 1, 1960, and a specified date. Any date value before January 1, 1960, is stored as a negative value, while dates after January 1, 1960, are stored as positive values. These date values account for all leap year days.

Figure 3.2: SAS Date Values Example

Calendar Date	Jan 1 1959	Jan 1 1960	Jan 1 1961
SAS Date Value	-365	0	366

The SAS code below demonstrates several different processes that can be applied to SAS date values. These processes include visualizing the date value in various ways through the FORMAT statement, performing arithmetic operations with the BETWEEN and DATDIF functions, and extracting information from date values with specific date functions.

Program 3.19: SAS Date Formats Examples

```
DATA dates;
      set MYDATA.Listings;

      WHERE first_review BETWEEN '01JAN2018'd AND '30APR2018'd;

      date_fmt1 = first_review;
      date_fmt2 = first_review;
      date_fmt3 = first_review;
      day   = day  (first_review);
      week  = week (first_review);
      month = month(first_review);
      year  = year (first_review);

      btw_dates = DATDIF(first_review, last_review, 'ACT/ACT');

      KEEP date_fmt1 date_fmt2 date_fmt3 first_review
          last_review
                day week month year btw_dates;
      FORMAT date_fmt1 DATE. date_fmt2 DATE9.
          date_fmt3 WEEKDATE.;
RUN;
```

- The WHERE statement performs an arithmetic calculation to identify dates between the two date values specified with a BETWEEN – AND statement.

- Three new variables were created that are each equivalent to the first_review variable. Each of these new variables were treated with a different FORMAT statement to demonstrate different visualizations of the same date value.

- The day, week, month, and year date functions were implemented to create variables specific to these aspects of the first_review field.

- The DATDIF function performs an arithmetic calculation that outputs the number of days between dates. The ACT/ACT specification tells SAS to use the actual number of days between the specified dates.

Output 3.12: SAS Date Values Examples

first_review	last_review	date_fmt1	date_fmt2	date_fmt3	day	week	month	year	btw_dates
02/12/2018	08/04/2018	12FEB18	12FEB2018	Monday, February 12, 2018	12	6	2	2018	173
01/01/2018	11/21/2018	01JAN18	01JAN2018	Monday, January 1, 2018	1	0	1	2018	324
01/08/2018	05/05/2018	08JAN18	08JAN2018	Monday, January 8, 2018	8	1	1	2018	117
01/01/2018	09/30/2018	01JAN18	01JAN2018	Monday, January 1, 2018	1	0	1	2018	272
01/21/2018	01/21/2018	21JAN18	21JAN2018	Sunday, January 21, 2018	21	3	1	2018	0
01/03/2018	01/03/2018	03JAN18	03JAN2018	Wednesday, January 3, 2018	3	0	1	2018	0
04/14/2018	10/08/2018	14APR18	14APR2018	Saturday, April 14, 2018	14	14	4	2018	177
04/12/2018	10/07/2018	12APR18	12APR2018	Thursday, April 12, 2018	12	14	4	2018	178
01/02/2018	01/02/2018	02JAN18	02JAN2018	Tuesday, January 2, 2018	2	0	1	2018	0
01/04/2018	11/30/2018	04JAN18	04JAN2018	Thursday, January 4, 2018	4	0	1	2018	330

The output shown in Output 3.12 demonstrates the different manipulations that we have performed on the date variables.

- The DATE. format presents the first_review variable as 12FEB18.

- The DATE9. format presents the first_review variable as 12FEB2018.

- The WEEKDATE. format presents the first_review variable as Monday, February 12, 2018.

- The DAY function returns the numeric day of the month.

- The WEEK function returns the numeric week of the year.

- The MONTH function returns the numeric month of the year.

- The YEAR function returns the year.

- The DATDIF function returns the number of days between the two specified dates.

This example is just a small sampling of the formats that can be applied to any date value, and this example just scratches the surface on the functions that can be applied to date values. I encourage everyone to look through the SAS documentation for a complete review of SAS date, time, and datetime values: https://support.sas.com/en/documentation.html.

Merging Data Sets

A single data set rarely contains all the information that you will need for your data science project. A data scientist will often have to bring together information from various data sources to create one or more data sets that will be used for their analysis. There are multiple ways in which you can combine data sets in SAS, but we will focus on the two most common methods:

- PROC SQL
- SAS MATCH MERGE

PROC SQL

Structured Query Language (SQL – pronounced "sequel") is a commonly used programming language that is supported by many other programming languages (SAS, Python, R, Scala, and so on). Due to the ubiquity of this language, it is a great investment of your time to learn the basics of SQL. The PROC SQL statement in SAS enables you to do the following:

- Retrieve data stored in tables and views
- Manipulate data and create new variables
- Create new data sets and views

The difference between a table and a view is that the table contains data while the view contains no data. The view is a stored query expression that reads data values from its underlying tables dynamically.

There are four main sections to a SQL procedure:

1. Specify the data set that you want to create.
2. Select and create variables to populate your data set.
3. Identify the table or tables that you want to pull the data from.
4. Specify any conditional logic to limit the data pull.

The following code provides an example of creating a new data set in the MYDATA library that I will name "Combine." This data set will contain a mixture of raw, renamed, and created variables from two data sets that I've joined together through a common variable available in both tables. Certain logical conditions have also limited the data.

Program 3.20: PROC SQL with Logical Conditions Example

```
PROC SQL;
      CREATE TABLE MYDATA.Combine AS
      SELECT  a.host_id,
                  a.room_type,
                  a.price AS base_price,
                  b.price AS calendar_price,
                  CASE
                        WHEN a.price GE 150 THEN 'Expensive'
                        ELSE 'Cheap'
                        END
                        AS price_cat,

                  b.date AS calendar_date

            FROM MYDATA.Listings AS a
            LEFT JOIN MYDATA.Calendar AS b
                  ON a.listing_id = b.listing_id
                        WHERE a.host_id IS NOT NULL
                        AND a.bedrooms GT 1
                        AND b.date BETWEEN '01JAN2019'd AND
'30JAN2019'd;
QUIT;
```

One of the main benefits of SQL language is that it is very easy to understand because it reads like common language. Even if you are not a programmer, you can probably understand through the naming conventions that I am creating a table called MYDATA.Combine, and I am selecting some variables from the MYDATA.Listings and the MYDATA.Calendar tables and limiting it to specific instances.

Let's look at each step of the SQL code:

*   PROC SQL – this tells SAS that you are about to write some SQL code.
*   CREATE TABLE AS – this step specifies that you will create a table rather than a view. You have the option of creating a temporary table or a permanent table with the use of a library statement.

- SELECT – this step specifies which variables that you want to include in your output data set and allows you to create new variables.

  ○ You can select all the variables from a specified data set through the use of the "*" symbol (for example A.* will select all of the variables from the table assigned to the alias A).

  ○ You can rename a variable by including an AS statement. This method is a quick and easy way to rename variables, especially variables that have identical names in different tables but have different values (for example, the variable name could be found in both tables A and B; however, in table A it represents company name, and in table B it represents customer name. It would be beneficial to rename the variable to specify the meaning of name).

  ○ You can create new variables with the use of the CASE-WHEN-THEN-ELSE statements. The CASE statement selects values if certain conditions are met. You can use an arithmetic, logical, or conditional statement to specify your selection method. The CASE statement allows you to define your conditions, specify the output data, and create a variable name, all within the same CASE statement.

- A comma separates each of the selected variables. The final variable **does not** have a comma following the variable name.

- FROM – specifies a table from a specific database that you will use to either populate your SAS table or limit data that will be included in your SAS table

- JOIN – when you have more than one data source, the JOIN statement tells SAS how to merge the two data sets. There are three main options to join tables:

  ○ INNER JOIN – retains records that match a common variable in **both** tables

  ○ OUTER JOIN – retains records that match a common variable in the **specified** table (right or left)

  ○ FULL JOIN – retains records contained in **either** table

- WHERE – you can specify conditions that limit the data to include in your SAS table.

SAS Match-Merge

If your data sets are already in SAS tables, the SAS match-merge process provides you with the flexibility of all of the functions available in a DATA step with the ability to combine multiple data sets on a common variable as defined in the BY statement.

Program 3.21: SAS Match-Merge Example

```
PROC SORT DATA=MYDATA.LISTINGS;
  BY listing_id;
RUN;

PROC SORT DATA=MYDATA.CALENDAR;
  BY listing_id;
RUN;
```

```
DATA Left Right Left_Outer Inner;
  MERGE MYDATA.LISTINGS (IN=a) MYDATA.CALENDAR (IN=b);
  BY listing_id;

  IF a THEN OUTPUT left;
  IF b THEN OUTPUT Right;
  IF a AND NOT b THEN OUTPUT Left_Outer;
  IF a AND b THEN OUTPUT Inner;

RUN;
```

Program 3.21 demonstrates some important aspects of the match-merge process.

1. Each data set that will be merged must be sorted by the common variable that the data sets will be joined on (the BY variable).
2. The use of the IN statement assigns each of the data sets to a group that will control the matching conditional logic. These groupings will be control points for how the data will be joined.
3. You can create multiple data sets in a single DATA step through the use of the OUTPUT statement.
4. The matching logic is controlled by the IF-THEN logic applied to the groupings assigned in the IN statement.
   a. LEFT JOIN – IF a
   b. RIGHT JOIN – IF b
   c. LEFT OUTER JOIN – IF a AND NOT b
   d. INNER JOIN – IF a AND b

Table 3.4: Comparing Merge Techniques

Comparing Merge Techniques			
Description	**Visual**	**SQL**	**DATA Step**
FULL OUTER JOIN Select all rows from both tables		SELECT * FROM Table AS a FULL OUTER JOIN Table AS b ON a.ID = b.ID	DATA Full; MERGE table_a (in=a) table_b (in=b); BY ID; RUN;
LEFT JOIN Select all rows from the left table and matching rows from the right table		SELECT * FROM Table AS a LEFT JOIN Table AS b ON a.ID = b.ID	DATA Full; MERGE table_a (in=a) table_b (in=b); BY ID; IF a; RUN;
INNER JOIN Select rows that appear in both tables		SELECT * FROM Table AS a INNER JOIN Table AS b ON a.ID = b.ID	DATA Full; MERGE table_a (in=a) table_b (in=b); BY ID; IF a AND b; RUN;

PROC SORT

Sorting data is an essential part of data management. Many SAS procedures require you to sort the data before committing to a BY statement within a certain procedure such as MERGE or

PROC MEANS. The SORT procedure provides you with an easy and flexible method of sorting your data with options to customize your output.

The standard PROC SORT simply calls the SORT procedure on a specified data set and sorts it by a specified variable:

Program 3.22: PROC SORT Example

```
PROC SORT DATA=MYDATA.LISTINGS;
  BY listing_id;
RUN;
```

Program 3.22 will sort the data contained in the MYDATA.Listings data set by the listing_id variable. This code will replace the existing MYDATA.Listings data set with a data set with the exact same values only sorted in ascending sequence by the variable specified in the BY statement.

In contrast, the Program 3.23 utilizes the OUT statement to create a new data set that contains the same data elements found in the data sets specified in the DATA statement; however, the new data set is sorted by the variable specified in the BY statement while the original data set is left unchanged. This PROC SORT also utilizes the DESCENDING option to change the order of the sort.

Program 3.23: PROC SORT with DESCENDING Option

```
PROC SORT DATA=MYDATA.LISTINGS OUT=list_sort;
  BY DESCENDING listing_id;
RUN;
```

The final example of PROC SORT is demonstrated below. This version includes the NODUPKEY statement. This statement is used to de-duplicate a data set by one or multiple variables. It is a good practice to use an OUT statement when you are performing a de-duplicated sort to maintain the original full data set.

Program 3.24: De-duplicated Sort with DESCENDING Option

```
PROC SORT NODUPKEY DATA=MYDATA.LISTINGS OUT=list_sort;
  BY DESCENDING listing_id;
RUN
```

Export Data

Data in a vacuum is useless. What I mean by that is there should be a purpose to all the data manipulations that you have performed. You might have successfully accessed data, read it into a SAS table, filtered, summarized, and manipulated the data. However, all those data manipulation techniques are all means to an end. If you are performing all those actions to answer a question, then we will need a way to share that answer with an audience. The three main methods of moving data from the SAS environment to an environment outside of SAS are exporting, reporting, and graphing.

PROC EXPORT

The first method of sharing data will focus on exporting a SAS data set to an external environment. This method is generally used to move data from a SAS table to an Excel file, CSV file, or Access database. However, there are multiple output formats that you can write your data to including JMP, SPSS, Stata, Lotus 1-2-3, tab-delimited, and many more.

PROC EXPORT reads in a SAS data set and writes the data to an external data file. In the example below, PROC EXPORT is used to access an existing SAS data set named MYDATA.list_sort and write the contents of that file to an external file.

Program 3.25: PROC EXPORT Example

```
PROC EXPORT DATA=MYDATA.list_sort
      OUTFILE="C:\Users\James Gearheart\Data\list.xls"
      DBMS=EXCEL REPLACE;
      SHEET="list";
RUN;
```

A few notes on Program 3.25:

- PROC EXPORT is called to write data from a SAS table into an external file.

- The DATA statement specifies the data set to be exported.

- The OUTFILE statement specifies where you would like to place the newly created data. This statement also allows you to specify the name and format of the output file.

- The DBMS statement specifies the type of external data file that the PROC EXPORT will create. This step is where you can select from a wide range of data formats including Access, JMP, dBASE, and many others.

- The REPLACE statement specifies that if the data set already exists, then it should be replaced with the newly exported data.

- The SHEET statement is specific to the EXCEL format and allows you to name the sheet in the newly created Excel workbook.

Warning

If you need to write a large amount of data from a SAS environment to a CSV file, SAS has created a high-performance macro that can efficiently move larger quantities of data to a CSV file. The SAS utility macro that is already included in SAS is called %DS2CSV. Although we will cover macros in the next chapter, it is important to demonstrate this export methodology in the "Export Data" section of the book.

Program 3.26: SAS Utility Macro Example

```
%DS2CSV(DATA=MYDATA.Listings, RUNMODE=B,
CSVFILE="C:\Users\James Gearheart\Data\listings.csv");
```

A few notes on Program 3.26:

- The above code calls the %DS2CSV SAS utility macro.

- The DATA statement specifies the file that you would like to export.

- The RUNMODE statement allows the option of running the macro in batch or server mode.

  ○ Batch mode (RUNMODE = B) means that you are submitting the %DS2CSV macro in the SAS Program Editor.

  ○ Server mode (RUNMODE = S) is used with Application Dispatcher programs and streaming output stored processes.

- The CSVFILE statement specifies the location and name of the export file.

PROC REPORT

PROC REPORT is a highly flexible procedure that enables a programmer to control the content and format of data to be displayed in a text-based or ODS (Output Delivery System) report. This procedure writes output to the Results window of the SAS programming environment.

The REPORT procedure provides you the ability to control the order of variables that you would like to include in your report as well as if and how they are summarized, and the format in which the results are displayed. Program 3.27 provides an example of the REPORT procedure that builds a summarized report for the MYDATA.Listings data set.

Program 3.27: PROC REPORT Example

```
PROC REPORT DATA=MYDATA.LISTINGS ;
  TITLE 'Summarized AirBnB Report';
  COLUMN bed_type room_type price;
  DEFINE bed_type / GROUP 'Bed Type';
  DEFINE room_type / GROUP ORDER=FREQ DESCENDING 'Room Type';
  DEFINE price / MEAN FORMAT=DOLLAR10.2 'Average Price';
RUN;
```

Notes on Program 3.27:

- The REPORT procedure is called to create a summarized report of the MYDATA.Listings data set.

- The TITLE statement is used to create a title to be displayed in the output.

- The COLUMN statement is used to specify the variables to be displayed in the report and the order in which they will appear.

- The DEFINE statement defines how to use and display a report item. The associated GROUP statement specifies that the report should summarize the data for each level of the DEFINE specified variable.

- The single-quoted statement after the GROUP statement specifies how the variable will be labeled in the report.

- The ORDER = FREQ statement specifies that the variable identified in the DEFINE statement will be ordered according to the frequency of occurrence. The DESCENDING statement specifies that the order frequency will be descending in the report.

- The MEAN statement for the numeric variable price specifies that the report will contain the mean value of price as defined by the proceeding GROUP statements.

Output 3.13: PROC REPORT Output

Summarized AirBnB Report

Bed Type	Room Type	Average Price
Airbed	Entire home/apt	$213.89
	Private room	$95.63
	Shared room	$90.50
Couch	Entire home/apt	$416.28
	Private room	$69.33
	Shared room	$56.89
Futon	Entire home/apt	$145.05
	Private room	$70.82
	Shared room	$95.14
Pull-out Sofa	Entire home/apt	$146.89
	Private room	$89.16
	Shared room	$71.42
Real Bed	Entire home/apt	$209.17
	Private room	$89.23
	Shared room	$70.30

Graphs

One of the most common methods of sharing data with a broad audience is through the use of graphs. When done correctly, graphs provide a quick visual representation of the underlying data that is clear, concise, and easy to understand. PROC SGPLOT enables you to create an incredible variety of graphs, including bar charts, line charts, scatter plots, pie charts, and many others. I will briefly demonstrate the programming code and the associated output for a few of the most commonly utilized graphs.

Histograms

A histogram is a visual display of a continuous variable's distribution that is grouped into defined ranges. This graph can demonstrate the range of values as well as the volume of observations at each point in the distribution. A histogram is commonly used to visually demonstrate a continuous variable's minimum value, maximum value, and mean value, as demonstrated by the volume of observations at those points.

Program 3.28 demonstrates the SAS code used to create a histogram of the log adjusted price variable that we used in the case study example. This code will create the histogram and define the bin ranges that comprise the histogram. It will also create a density curve that shows a smooth continuous curve for the distribution of the numeric values.

Program 3.28: Distribution Plot Example

```
PROC SGPLOT DATA=WORK.TRAIN_ADJ;
  HISTOGRAM Price_Log / BINWIDTH= 0.25;
  DENSITY Price_Log;
  TITLE 'Distribution of Log Adjusted Price';
RUN;
```

Notes on Program 3.28:

- The SGPLOT procedure is called to create a visual display of the TRAIN_ADJ data set located in the WORK library.

- The HISTOGRAM statement specifies the type of graph to be created. The HISTOGRAM statement can only be applied to numeric variables. The Price_Log variable is specified to be represented in the histogram.

- The BINWIDTH statement allows the programmer to specify the width of the categorical bins that are created by the HISTOGRAM statement. This statement is optional because SAS will determine a bin width value by default.

- The DENSITY statement creates a density curve for the distribution of numeric values.

- The TITLE statement is used to create a title to be displayed in the output.

Output 3.14: Distribution of Log-Adjusted Price

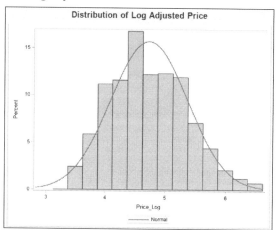

Output 3.14 shows the distribution of the Price_Log variable. This chart demonstrates how the log transformation of the continuous Price variable results in a normally distributed variable.

Bar Charts

Bar charts show the distribution of a categorical variable. The volume of observations for each level of a categorical variable is represented as vertical rectangular bars. SAS provides many options to customize bar charts, including grouping, stacking, and selecting an output statistic.

Program code 3.29 creates a bar chart on the case study data. The data will represent the average log price grouped by neighborhood and room type.

Program 3.29: Bar Chart Example

```
PROC SGPLOT DATA=WORK.TRAIN_ADJ;
  VBAR neighbourhood_group_cleansed /
  RESPONSE=Price_Log GROUP= room_type STAT=MEAN;
  YAXIS LABEL='Mean Log Price';
  XAXIS LABEL='Neighbourhood Group';
  TITLE 'Mean Log Price of Room Type by Neighbourhood Group';
RUN;
```

Notes on Program 3.29:

- PROC SGPLOT is called to create a visual display of the TRAIN_ADJ data set located in the WORK library.

- The VBAR statement specifies the type of graph to be created. The VBAR statement can only be applied to character variables. The neighbourhood_group_cleansed variable is specified to be represented in the histogram.

- The RESPONSE statement allows the programmer to specify the output statistic that is created by the VBAR statement. This statement is optional because SAS will report the volume of observations by default.

- The GROUP statement is optional and allows the programmer to create a stacked bar chart using another categorical variable.

- The STAT statement is optional because SAS will report the volume of observations by default.

- The TITLE statement is used to create a title to be displayed in the output.

Output 3.15: Bar Chart Example Output

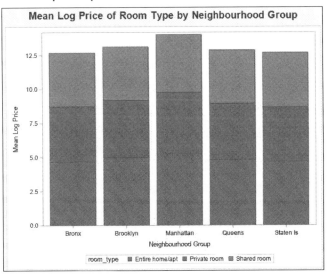

Output 3.15 shows the mean log price grouped by neighborhood and stacked by room type. This chart demonstrates how the average price varies by the categorical variables.

Line Charts

Line charts are called *series plots* in SAS. These charts are most often used to show the trend of a numeric variable over time. The value of a numeric variable is plotted for each date over a range of time. Each of the plotted values is connected by a line. This methodology allows the researcher to demonstrate the change in the variable over time.

Program 3.30 first prepares a data set to be graphed with a line chart. The DATA step selects three unique identifiers from the MYDATA.Calendar data set and creates separate price variables for each Listing ID. This data is then sorted by the Listing ID and Date fields. The SGPLOT procedure is incorporated to develop the series plot on the adjusted data set.

Program 3.30: Line Chart Example

```
DATA CAL;
  SET MYDATA.Calendar;
  WHERE Listing_id in (21456, 2539, 5178);
  IF listing_id = 21456 THEN price_1 = price;
  IF listing_id = 2539 THEN price_2 = price;
  IF listing_id = 5178 THEN price_3 = price;
run;

PROC SORT DATA=CAL; BY listing_id date; run;

PROC SGPLOT DATA=CAL ;
  SERIES X=date Y=price_1 / LEGENDLABEL='Listing 21456';
  SERIES X=date Y=price_2 / LEGENDLABEL='Listing 2539';
  SERIES X=date Y=price_3 / LEGENDLABEL='Listing 5178';
  YAXIS LABEL= 'Daily Price';
  XAXIS LABEL= 'Date';
  TITLE 'Price Per Night';
RUN;
```

Notes on Program 3.30:

- The SGPLOT procedure is called to create a visual display of the adjusted MYDATA.Calendar data set.

- The SERIES statement specifies the type of graph to be created. The SERIES statement can be applied only to numeric variables. The date variable is selected for the x-axis while the newly created price variable is selected for the y-axis. This process is repeated for each of the price variables that we want to be represented in the chart.

- The LEGENDLABEL allows you to specify how the data will be referred to in the associated legend.

- The TITLE statement is used to create a title to be displayed in the output.

Output 3.16: Line Chart Example Output

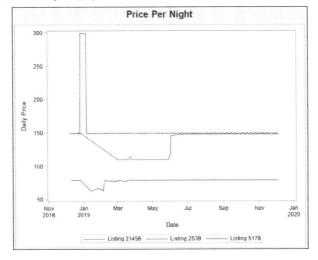

Output 3.16 shows the daily price for each of the selected listings over a defined time period. This chart highlights different pricing strategies for each of the listings, with one of the listings doubling its daily rate on the days surrounding New Year's Eve while the other listings choose to drop their rate at that same time period.

Scatter Plots

A scatter plot graphs the observations of numeric variables in relation to one another. These graphs primarily focus on the relationship between two variables represented in a two-dimensional graph. Each observation is represented as a single point in the two-dimensional space.

Program 3.31 uses PROC MEANS to calculate the average price for each value of the ordinal review score variable. PROC SGPLOT is used to create a scatter plot where the review score is on the x-axis, and average price is on the y-axis. Conditional logic is also applied to the data set to retain only those cases where there are greater than or equal to twenty observations for each level of the review score.

Program 3.31: Scatter Plot Example

```
PROC MEANS DATA=MYDATA.LISTINGS;
   VAR price;
   CLASS review_scores_rating;
   OUTPUT OUT= AVG;
RUN;

PROC SGPLOT DATA=AVG (WHERE=(_STAT_='MEAN' and _FREQ_ GE 20));
   SCATTER X = review_scores_rating Y = price;
   YAXIS LABEL= 'Average Price';
   XAXIS LABEL= 'Review Score';
   TITLE 'Average Price by Review Score';
RUN;
```

Notes on Program 3.31:

- The SGPLOT procedure is called to create a visual display of the newly calculated AVG data set created by PROC MEANS.

- The SCATTER statement specifies the type of graph to be created. The SCATTER statement can be applied only to numeric variables. The review_scores_rating variable is selected for the x-axis while the newly created average price variable is selected for the y-axis.

- The TITLE statement is used to create a title to be displayed in the output.

Output 3.17: Scatter Plot Example Output

Output 3.17 shows the relationship between customers' review scores and the average price of a property. This is a great way to quickly demonstrate the relationship between price and quality. This chart provides a visual demonstration that the customer review score has a positive association with price.

Chapter Review

This chapter focused on introducing the SAS programming language and providing you with concepts and sample code to get you up and running in SAS. Each of the concepts that this chapter covered could be the basis for an entire chapter devoted to that concept. There are numerous ways to expand upon each of the demonstrated techniques with a variety of options that SAS has available for you. These options can be utilized to perform nearly any data manipulation and analysis that you would like to develop.

Although a skilled data scientist can use the techniques demonstrated in this chapter to develop some incredible analytical products, the next chapter is designed to increase your programming efficiency, introduce automation, and take your programming skills to the next level.

Chapter 4: Advanced SAS Coding

Overview

We have covered several basic data exploration and data manipulation techniques. These techniques will certainly get you up and running with SAS programming, and you can spend years learning all the various options of each of these techniques and become proficient in these methods. However, there are several additional techniques that can significantly expand and improve a data scientist's codebase. These methods can improve your ability to efficiently manipulate data and take your coding to the next level.

DO Loop

Looping is a convenient way to execute one or more statements, usually over changing parameters. This technique can be a highly efficient method of iterating through different levels of a variable and applying a computation to each level. You can replace a long series of IF-THEN statements with a single DO loop.

A simple example of a DO loop is to iterate over a small set of numbers and perform a calculation on each value in the number set.

Program 4.1: DO Loop Example

```
DATA X;
      DO i = 1 TO 10;
            y = i*2;
            OUTPUT;
      END;
RUN;
```

Notes on Program 4.1:

- The DO loop is performed inside of a DATA step.

- The DO loop starts with a DO statement and contains a TO specification.

- You assign an index variable (in this case, "i") that is assigned a value in each cycle of the loop based on the TO specification.

- The calculation is performed using the current value of the index variable.

- You use the OUTPUT statement to output the current contents of the PDV in each cycle of the loop.

- The END statement marks the end of the iteration. The index value is incremented here.

- The loop iterates until the index variable value is outside of the range.

- The END statement marks the end of the statements within the loop.

The default for the DO loop is to iterate by single whole numbers; however, you have the option of specifying the unit increase in the DO loop with a BY statement.

Program 4.2: DO Loop with BY Statement

```
DATA X;
      DO i = 1 to 10 BY 2;
            y = i*2;
            OUTPUT;
      END;
RUN;
```

This code will loop through values 1 to 10 in increments of 2. So, your "i" values will be 1, 3, 5, 7, 9 and your output values will be 1, 6, 10, 14, 18.

One last option that we will review with the DO loop is the specification that uses WHILE. This statement will stop the DO loop if a certain condition occurs.

Program 4.3: DO Loop with WHILE Statement

```
DATA X;
      DO i = 1 to 10 BY 2 WHILE (y < 15);
            y = i*2;
            OUTPUT;
      END;
RUN;
```

In this example, the DO loop will check before each iteration to see if the condition y < 15 is true. It will continue to process the DO loop while that condition is true. When the condition becomes false, the restriction implemented by the WHILE statement will stop the looping.

ARRAY Statements

Many people find arrays challenging to learn. You are not alone in your struggles. However, the benefits of the ARRAY statement greatly outweigh the learning difficulties. I will attempt to break it down into very simple concepts.

If you have many lines of code in a DATA step where the only change is a variable name, then you will greatly benefit from learning the ARRAY statement. The ARRAY statement is often used in conjunction with a DO loop to perform the same calculation on several different variables, all with just a few lines of code.

Let's learn this concept by example. Let's say you have a data set that has the weight of 100 boxers with each boxer's weight as its own variable. So, you have a data set with 100 columns of weight reported in pounds. However, you have been tasked to report these values in kilograms.

The formula to convert pounds to kilograms is to multiply the number of pounds (x) by 0.45: x * 0.45

Although this is a very easy calculation, you do not want to have to apply it once for each of the 100 variables. That would be 100 lines of code.

An ARRAY statement identifies a group of variables of a similar type that you want to perform an operation on. In our example, that would be all 100 of the boxer's weight variables, and the operation that we would like to perform is to convert the weight as represented in pounds to kilograms. Each item in an array is referred to as an element. Array elements can be referenced using a numeric expression instead of a hard-coded variable name.

There are three essential components to an ARRAY statement

array array-name {n} array-elements ;

1. **Array_name** – This is what you decide to name your array. You can use any valid SAS name.
2. **n** – This is the number of elements in your array. In our example, there are 100 elements.

3. **Elements** – A list of common SAS variables that are part of the array. In our example, the elements are all of the boxer weight columns.

The following code combines an ARRAY statement and a DO loop (they often occur together) to perform the necessary conversion:

Program 4.4: ARRAY Example

```
DATA convert;
      SET boxers;
      ARRAY weight_array [100] weight1-weight100;

      DO i = 1 TO 100;
            weight_array{i} = weight_array{i} * 0.45;
      END;
RUN;
```

Notes on Program 4.4:

- The ARRAY statement is compiled within a DATA statement.

- The ARRAY statement performs the following steps:

    ○ Assigns an array name (weight_array) that will be referenced in the calculation.

    ○ Specifies the number of elements in the array (100 columns).

    ○ Specifies the list of variables that will comprise the elements of the array (weight1 through weight100 from the boxer data set).

- A DO loop will loop through each of the 100 elements contained in the weight_array because the index variable, i, increments from 1 to 100 by 1 and in each cycle of the reference (weight_array{i} will resolve to each element of the array.

- The conversion calculation is executed on each of the elements in the array.

The resulting data set will contain the newly calculated kilogram weight variables. This code works great if you want to overwrite existing variables with a newly calculated variable. However, we often need to keep the original variable as it is and create brand new variables that contain the newly calculated values. This is an easy modification to the code by adding a second ARRAY statement that contains the new variables.

Program 4.5: ARRAY Statement Creates New Variables

```
DATA convert;
      SET boxers;
      ARRAY weight_array {100} weight1-weight100;
      ARRAY kilo_array {100} kilo_weight1-kilo_weight100;

      DO i = 1 TO 100;
            kilo_array{i} = weight_array{i} * 0.45;
      END;
RUN;
```

Notes on Program 4.5:

- The ARRAY statements are compiled within a DATA statement.
- The first ARRAY statement performs the following steps:
    - Assigns an array name (weight_array) that will be referenced in the calculation.
    - Specifies the number of elements in the array (100 columns).
    - Specifies the list of variable that will comprise the elements of the array (weight1 through weight100 from the boxer data set).
- The second array performs the same steps for the newly created variables weight_array1 thorough weight_array100.
- A DO loop will loop through each of the 100 elements contained in the weight_array, perform the conversion calculation and assign the result to the corresponding element of the kilo_array.

The resulting data set will contain all of the original weight variables along with the newly calculated kilogram weight variables.

Note that arrays created with the ARRAY statement exist as the DATA step processes as a way to refer to a series of variables. The arrays are not stored in data sets, only the variables processed or created with arrays.

SCAN Function

The SCAN function is a very easy way to parse text data from character strings. Data sets will often contain fields such as name, address, city, and state, or any character variable where there is more than one piece of information contained in a single variable. The classic example is customer_name. This field can contain first name, last name, and title. Usually, these fields are represented in a consistent order such as "Gearheart, James, Mr.". We will often want to parse out the first name and last name into separate variables. The SCAN function is an easy way to accomplish this.

Program 4.6: SCAN Example

```
DATA names;
  SET dataset;
  first_name = SCAN(customer_name, 2);
  last_name = SCAN(customer_name, 1);
RUN;
```

Notes on Program 4.6:

- The SCAN function is performed inside of a DATA statement.

- The SCAN function has two required arguments:

  - The first argument inside of the parentheses specifies the text field that you would like to parse.

  - The second argument inside of the parentheses indicates the number of the word to be extracted from the text string specified in the first argument.

- SCAN determines where one word ends and the next begins using a pre-defined set of delimiters. If the pre-set delimiters don't delimit words the way you need for your application, you can specify your own list of delimiters as the third argument within the parentheses. If you do choose to specify your own delimiters, only the delimiters specified will be used by the SCAN functions; the original delimiter list is ignored.

FIND Function

The FIND function is another very useful function to apply to text data. This function can scan through a text field and find a specified value. If the function finds the specified value, the function then returns the position of the given value.

The syntax of the FIND function is:

FIND(*string, substring, <modifiers>, <startpos>*)

The FIND function has two required arguments, two optional arguments, and returns a numeric value.

- **String** – this required argument identifies the source text in which you want to search. You can either directly type constant text into the field (the example below), or you can reference a variable containing text.

- **Substring** – this required argument specifies the text that you would like to search for. If this search text is found, the output will specify the position of the text. If not found, the output will be 0.

- **Modifiers** – this optional argument provides flexibility in how FIND is applied to text. For example, you can specify a case-insensitive match or trim away trailing blanks from the search text.

  - **i** – ignores the character case during search

  - **t** – trims trailing blanks

- **Startpos** – this optional argument specifies the starting position of the text search.

Program 4.7: FIND Example

```
DATA chk;
        pos_1 = FIND ("Data Science","nce");
        pos_2 = FIND ("Data Science","sci");
        pos_3 = FIND ("Data Science","sci","i");
        pos_4 = FIND ("Data Science","ata",42);
RUN;

PROC PRINT DATA = chk;
RUN;
```

The output in Table 4.1 shows the results of the above code.

Table 4.1: FIND Output

Obs	pos_1	pos_2	pos_3	pos_4
1	10	0	6	0

Notes on Program 4.7:

- The FIND function is performed within a DATA step.

- The first statement finds the substring "nce" at position 10 in the referenced text string.

- The second statement does not find the substring "sci" in the referenced text string because it is a case-sensitive search.

- The third statement uses the modifier "i" to make the search indifferent to case and therefore finds the substring "sci" starting at the sixth position.

- The fourth statement specifies a starting position past the end of the source string and thus returns 0.

PUT Function

The PUT function is most widely used to convert a numeric value to a character value. This simple function is incredibly valuable and is often used when manipulating data. There are often times when a variable is represented as a numeric value in one database and as a character value in another database. To join these databases, you will need to make the data types of the two variables consistent. The PUT function is an easy way to change a variable value from numeric to character.

The syntax of the PUT function is:

PUT(*source, format.*)

The PUT function has two required arguments.

- **Source** – the variable containing the value (or expression) that you would like to convert
- **Format** –the format that you want to use to convert the variable value to text

Program 4.8: Convert Numeric to Character

```
DATA temp;
  SET dataset;
  id_char = PUT(id_num, $8.);
RUN;
```

The above code creates a new variable id_char by converting the existing numeric variable id_num into a character variable. The first argument identifies the variable that you want to convert, and the second argument specifies that you want to convert the variable to a character format $8.

FIRST. and LAST. Statements

Certain processes happen "behind the scenes" in SAS. These processes are how SAS processes information. I touched on this topic in the explanation of the DATA steps and how the program data vector (PDV) iterates through a data set, line by line, in Chapter 3.

When a DATA step contains a BY statement, the DATA statement creates two temporary indicator variables for each variable in the BY statement. The names of these variables are FIRST.variable and LAST.variable (where "variable" is the name of the associated variable in the BY statement). If you sort the data set by the variables contained in the BY statement, you are able to perform a running calculation iteratively applied to each observation and to perform summary calculations within each BY group.

For example, if we wanted to count the number of observations for each level of a categorical variable, we can use the FIRST.variable LAST.variable statements to calculate a total within each level of the BY variable. Program 4.9 demonstrates this technique applied to the MYDATA.Listings data set to count the number of observations for each level of the variable room_type.

Program 4.9: First. Last. Summary BY Variable

```
PROC SORT DATA=MYDATA.LISTINGS;
  BY room_type;
RUN;

DATA count;
  SET MYDATA.LISTINGS;
  BY room_type;

  IF FIRST.room_type THEN
      count = 0;
  count + 1;

  IF LAST.room_type;
RUN;

PROC PRINT DATA=count NOOBS;
  FORMAT count comma10.;
  VAR room_type count;
RUN;
```

Notes on Program 4.9:

- The data must be sorted by the variable that you will include in the BY statement.

- Within a DATA step, the BY statement controls the operation of the SET statement and sets up the grouping variable.

- SAS creates a FIRST.room_type temporary indicator variable and initializes a count = 0 at the beginning of each level of the BY variable.

  - Because of the presence of the BY statement, when the SET statement reads a row, it checks to see if this is the first row of a group. If so, it sets the value of first.room_type to 1, otherwise it sets the value to 0. It also checks to see if the next row to be read contains another row from the current group. If so, it sets the value of last.room_type to 0, otherwise it sets the value to 1.

  - The value of first.room_type is tested and, if it is 1, the value of count is set to 0.

  - Next, 1 is added to the count variable for every row of data read.

  - In the subsetting IF statement, the value of last.room_type is tested and, if it is 1, the program continues on to excute the RUN statement, outputting a record as the count data. Otherwise, processing returns to the top of the DATA step without outputting a row.

  - The process continues through each level of the room_type variable until no more rows are available in the room_type data set.

- Because we know that there are three distinct values for the room_type variable, we will see three rows output to the count data set.

- The PROC PRINT statement is optional and allows you to create a report displaying the output data set containing the summarized results

The output of the above code is shown in Table 4.2.

Table 4.2: First. Last. Summary Output

room_type	count
Entire home/apt	26,057
Private room	21,933
Shared room	1,063

Macros Overview

We have discussed many ways in which you can manipulate data. SAS offers an incredible number of methods that allow you to ingest, transform, and report data. However, one of the most powerful and often misunderstood methods is the use of macros. Sometimes the terminology can get a bit confusing, so let's make a quick distinction between a macro variable and a macro.

There are two main categories of macros:

- **Macro variable** – This is a variable that is typically defined and assigned a value once and then referenced throughout your program. Usually, a %LET statement is used to define and assign a value to a macro variable.

- **Macro** – This is a named repeatable set of stored SAS code that can be called for execution within SAS programs. The method used to name and define this set of stored statements is to use a %MACRO statement to mark the beginning of the set of statements and a %MEND to mark the end of the set of statements.

Macro Variables

There are two main types of macro variables. When you invoke a SAS program, the SAS system's macro processor generates automatic macro variables that supply information related to the SAS session. These are called *automatic macro variables*.

A user can also create, define, and call their own macro variables. These are called *user-defined macro variables*. These variables can have a maximum of 65,534 characters and must be printable characters. This requirement is because macro variables are essentially a method of dynamically modifying text within the SAS program through the use of symbolic substitution. If the text is not printable, then SAS would not be able to read it and interpret it in its execution.

Automatic Macro Variables

When you invoke a SAS program, the SAS system automatically generates several macro variables that supply information related to the SAS session. This information includes how the data will be processed as well as system information such as the date and time that the session was invoked. You have the ability to access and use these system-generated macro variables as part of your program. Most of these system-generated macro variables begin with the "SYS" prefix. A full list of these automatic macro variables can be found in the SAS documentation.

A common use of the system-generated macro variables is to use them in reporting to specify when the report was created. Program 4.10 incorporates the code that we developed for the PROC REPORT section in the previous chapter; however, we have now added a FOOTNOTE statement that includes automatic macro variables. The system-generated macro variables SYSDAY and SYSDATE9 are used to specify the day and date that the SAS program was invoked. Macro variables are referenced by placing an ampersand (&) before the name of the requested variable. The dot (.) following the macro variable delineates the end of the macro variable reference. This is required if the macro variable reference is not followed by a white space or other character that will otherwise mark the end of the macro variable reference.

Program 4.10: System-Generated Macro Footnote

```
PROC REPORT DATA=MYDATA.LISTINGS ;
  title 'Summarized AirBnB Report';
  COLUMN bed_type room_type price;
  DEFINE bed_type / GROUP 'Bed Type';
  DEFINE room_type / GROUP ORDER=FREQ DESCENDING'Room Type';
```

```
   DEFINE price / MEAN FORMAT=DOLLAR10.2 'Average Price';
   FOOTNOTE "Report for &sysday., &sysdate9.";
RUN;
```

This report will include a footnote that specifies the day and date in which the report was created. If this report is run according to a scheduled process, then the FOOTNOTE statement will detail which day and date that the specific report was created.

Output 4.1: System-Generated Macro Footnote Output

Summarized AirBnB Report

Bed Type	Room Type	Average Price
Airbed	Entire home/apt	$213.89
	Private room	$95.63
	Shared room	$90.50
Couch	Entire home/apt	$416.28
	Private room	$69.33
	Shared room	$56.89
Futon	Entire home/apt	$145.05
	Private room	$70.82
	Shared room	$95.14
Pull-out Sofa	Entire home/apt	$146.89
	Private room	$89.16
	Shared room	$71.42
Real Bed	Entire home/apt	$209.17
	Private room	$89.23
	Shared room	$70.30

Report for Saturday, 25MAY2019

User-Defined Macro Variables

User-defined macro variables allow you to increase your program's efficiency and to increase quality control. User-defined macro variables must begin with either a letter or an underscore and can be followed by letters or digits. These types of macro variables can be used for a variety of purposes, including representing constant text, equations, and null values. They can also be used to refer to another macro variable. The possibilities of these combinations are nearly endless.

Table 4.3: User-Defined Macro Examples

Assignment Type	User-Defined Macro Variable	Purpose	Output
Constant text	%LET animal = DOG;	Create a text reference for a specific value	DOG
Digits	%LET num = 100+200	Create a text reference for specific digits	100+200
Equation	%LET eq = %EVAL(20-15);	Create an equation that resolves to a calculated value	5
Null value	%LET actor = ;	Create a null value for a specific variable	

Assignment Type	User-Defined Macro Variable	Purpose	Output
Macro variable reference	%LET first_name = George; %LET last_name = Washington %LET name = &first_name &last_name;	Create a text reference developed from previously defined macro variables	George Washington

Table 4.3 provides a few examples of user-defined macros based on assignment type. A few items to note about the information contained in Table 4.3:

- The "Digits" assignment demonstrates that the macro does not evaluate the expression 100+200. It treats the expression as character values and therefore the output is "100+200" rather than 300.

- The "Equation" assignment incorporates the %EVAL function to evaluate the expression 20-15. This expression results in the calculated value of 5 as the output value.

- The "Macro variable reference" assignment allows you to create macro variables and then refer to those variables within another user-defined macro variable.

Let's look more closely at a common application of user-defined macro variables. If you have a SAS program that references a particular value repeatedly, it is extremely useful to incorporate macro variables. We often write programs that constantly refer to a certain date or categorical value throughout the program. If we need to update that date value to a new time period, then we will have to search throughout the program and change it at every instance that it is specified. Hopefully, you will not miss one of the instances where it is called and throw off your entire data output!

An easy fix to this problem is to create a macro variable. This technique allows you to specify the value of a variable once, usually at the beginning of your program, and then refer to the macro variable throughout your program. This way, if you need to change the value of the variable, you will need to do it only once, and all of the referred instances of the macro variable will be in line with the new value.

Program 4.11 demonstrates the development of the macro variable and provides an example of how it is called within a DATA step.

Program 4.11: Macro Variable Example

```
%LET date = '01MAY2019'd;

DATA POP;
  SET DATASET;
  IF start_date = &date.;
RUN;
```

Notes on Program 4.11:

- The %LET statement is used to create and define the macro variable. We are creating a macro variable that we have decided to call "date," and we are setting this value to '01MAY2019'd. This statement is telling SAS that every time that the macro variable "date" is referenced, that it should interpret it as "'01MAY2019'd".

- The DATA step is one way of incorporating the newly formed macro variable. You can use and define macro variables anywhere within the SAS program except in data lines used as input to a DATA step through the use of the DATALINES statement. In this example, the macro variable is used to filter the data set to observations where the "start_date" is equal to '01MAY2019'd.

- The macro variable is referenced by placing an ampersand (&) in front of the defined macro variable name. The dot (.) following the macro variable name delineates the end of the macro variable reference. This is required if the macro variable reference is not followed by a white space or other character that will otherwise mark the end of the macro variable reference.

Macros

Macros are reusable pieces of code that perform a function and can easily be updated with new information. You may be familiar with the concept of macros if you have used functions in other programming languages. Table 4.4 demonstrates a simple reusable algorithm developed in the three most popular data science programming languages, R, Python, and SAS. The example algorithm raises the first value by the power of the second value.

Table 4.4: Macro Comparison Table

Language	Programming Code	Output

R Programming	power <- function(x, y) {
	
	  result <- x^y
	
	  print(paste(x,"raised to the power", y, "is", result))
	
	}
	
	power(8,2)
		"8 raised to the power 2 is 64"

Python Programming	def power(x,y):
	
	  result = x**y
	
	  print(x, "raised to the power", y, "is", result)
	
	power(8,2)
		8 raised to the power 2 is 64

Language	Programming Code	Output

SAS Programming	%MACRO POWER(x,y);
	    %LET result = %EVAL(&x.**&y.);
	
	    %PUT &x. raised to the power &y. is &result.;
	%MEND;
	%POWER(8,2);
		8 raised to the power 2 is 64

Now that these functions have been developed, the programmer would merely have to call the name of the function with updated values to get new results.

Table 4.5: Macro Call Examples

Call Function	Output
%power(3,5)	3 raised to the power 5 is 243
%power(10,3)	10 raised to the power 3 is 1000
%power(-7,3)	-7 raised to the power 3 is -343

This simple example demonstrates a powerful programming concept. Complex programs can be developed with symbolic placeholders for values to be input later. This methodology is the path to program efficiency. Reusable code can save a lot of time and be shared with team members to ensure methodological consistency and quality control.

Defining and Calling Macros

The basic structure of a macro contains three necessary parts. The %MACRO statement begins the process by telling the SAS system that you are generating a user-defined macro. The macro name assigns a name to the macro that can be called later. The %MEND statement tells the SAS system that the definition is complete. Program 4.12 demonstrates the basic structure.

Program 4.12: Macro Structure

```
%MACRO <macro_name>;
    programming code;
%MEND;
```

When you submit a macro definition, the macro processer compiles the definition and adds it to the available SAS macros for that session. Once a macro is compiled, user-defined macros are available during the current SAS session. Once the session ends, the user-defined macros will be removed from the available macro list. If you begin a new session, you will need to compile the macro prior to calling it.

Once the algorithm has been compiled, you can call the macro any time by simply calling the macro name. Program 4.13 demonstrates how to call the macro.

Program 4.13: Macro Call Example

```
%<macro_name>;
```

Let's take an in-depth look at the previous example of the polynomial macro and explain each part.

Program 4.14: Polynomial Macro Example

```
%MACRO POWER(x,y);
      %LET result = %EVAL(&x.**&y.);
      %PUT &x. raised to the power &y. is &result.;
%MEND;
```

Notes on Program 4.14:

- The %MACRO statement begins the creation of a user-defined macro.

- The macro is given the name POWER. You can assign any valid SAS name for a macro name.

- The parentheses contain the symbolic placeholders for values to be used in the macro program. These are generally called the "parameters" of the macro. You can use any valid SAS name for the parameters. These parameters will be used in the following macro program. The parameters within the macro will be called by placing an ampersand (&) symbol before the parameter name. In the provided example, the first parameter is called by the value &x. The second value is called by the value &y.

- Once the macro is initiated and the name and parameters are defined, the next step is to develop the content of the macro. You can use any valid SAS programming code within a macro. If you have defined parameters in the parentheses following your macro name, you can use them within the content of the macro.

- The %MEND statement completes the macro process.

Let's take a look at another example of a macro statement developed on the Airbnb data set from our case study. If we had decided that we wanted to implement a discount on Airbnb properties based on room type and price, we can create a macro that performs this calculation without knowing the specific values of room type and price. Program 4.15 provides an example of this code.

Program 4.15: Macro Price Change Example

```
%MACRO SALE(type, price, discount);
  DATA chk;
     SET TEST;
        WHERE bed_type = &type.
        AND price gt &price.;
        discount = price* &discount.;
  KEEP host_id price discount;

  PROC SORT DATA=chk; BY price; RUN;
%MEND;
```

Program 4.15 creates a macro called SALE that contains three parameters. The type parameter will assign a user-defined value that will be used to specify bed type. The price parameter will be used to determine the per diem price of the property. The discount parameter will specify the percentage discount to be applied to the calculation.

The first two values are used to filter the data set to observations that meet these criteria. This data set is then subject to the discount calculation. We can now call the macro by calling the macro name along with values for the parameters. Program 4.16 demonstrates the execution of the macro with the parameters specified.

Program 4.16: Macro Price Change Call

```
%SALE('Real Bed', 100, 0.8);
```

This example limits the data set to values where the room type is specified as "Real Bed" and that the per diem price of the property is greater than $100. This data set is then subjected to a discount rate of 80%.

Now that the macro has been defined, we can easily create new sales strategies by specifying different values for the parameters. Program 4.17 demonstrates different implementations of the user-defined macro.

Program 4.17: Macro Price Change Call Examples

```
%SALE('Real Bed', 100, 0.8);
%SALE('Couch', 50, 0.6);
%SALE('Futon', 75, 0.75);
```

These examples demonstrate how easy it is to change the parameters contained in the macro and develop new output.

Chapter Review

Congratulations on finishing the Advanced SAS Coding chapter! If you are new to programming, these concepts and techniques can be challenging to learn. If you have programmed in other languages, you can probably see similar approaches and coding techniques in SAS that you have used elsewhere. The methods that we have discussed in chapters 3 and 4 comprise most of the hands-on programming that is necessary for data ingestion, manipulation, and analysis. However, there is always more coding to learn. The methods that I have demonstrated are only a small fraction of the possibilities that SAS has to offer to programmers.

Chapter 5: Create a Modeling Data Set

Overview

It is commonly estimated that at least 80% of a data scientist's effort is exerted in the extract, transform, load (ETL) stage of model development. This is a critical stage of model development that is often overlooked because it is not as exciting as applying a range of awesome algorithms to your data and evaluating your model's performance. The ETL process is critical for quality model development because of the GIGO rule: Garbage In, Garbage Out.

Nearly all data sets need to be adjusted in some way before they are ready for modeling. Real data "in the wild" is often very messy. This means that raw data often contains inconsistent formats, spelling errors, data input errors, duplicated fields, null or uniform fields, and many other general data issues. Even if you are employed in a large corporation that has dedicated data engineers that preprocess the data and subject it to standardized data cleaning, formatting, and quality control methods, the data is still not ready for modeling.

The algorithms that are used to develop predictive models perform optimally only if the underlying data is structured in a particular way. The input data needs to be structured so that the algorithm can easily ingest all observations and perform assessments on each predictor variable and the target variable according to the nuances of the model. For example, a decision tree can accept observations that have missing values, while a regression model will exclude any observation that has any missing data. A "nearest neighbors" model performs much better if the predictor variables are adjusted to be on the same scale while the random forest model will see marginal benefit from scaling.

Although every model design has its own particularities as to how to optimally structure the input data, there are common themes and best practices on how to structure a data set for modeling that could benefit nearly all model designs. We touched on several of these techniques in the case study chapter. This chapter will focus on investigating these techniques more thoroughly and provide a deeper dive into why these data adjustments are beneficial and how to perform them.

ETL

ETL stands for Extract, Transform, and Load, which is a process of data preparation:

- **Extract** – Collect data from various sources. These sources can be raw or processed data collected from a variety of different sources, such as:
    - Credit card swipes
    - Input from Tesla sensors
    - YouTube video streams
    - Twitter feeds
    - Corporate databases
    - Government data
    - Survey data
- **Transform** – Change the data depending on business rules and needs. The data transformation may include various operations including but not limited to:
    - Filtering
    - Sorting
    - Aggregating
    - Joining
    - Cleaning
    - Creating calculated fields
- **Load** – The data must be loaded into a destination database. This location is the source data to develop the machine learning model and deploy the model results.

Extract

If you have access to a corporate database that contains all your company's data assets, then the "extract" part of ETL will be much easier for you. You will simply have to connect to the appropriate table within a given database by using one of the many SAS/ACCESS functions and pull the necessary data into a SAS data set for evaluation.

We covered some of the methods of accessing data in Chapter 3: SAS Coding. The most common method of extracting data from corporate servers is by using the SAS SQL passthrough and specifying the type of database (Teradata, Aster, MySQL, and so on) using the MODE specification along with the SCHEMA and the TDPID specifications.

For non-corporate data sets, there are several ways to get data. Many companies will allow you to access certain sections of their data through APIs, and many data sets are available for public use. I'll review a few of my favorite public use data sources:

APIs

There are several ways to extract data from source systems. Many companies allow independent researchers to access their data through an API (application programming interface). An API is (usually) a web-based tool that enables the researcher to connect to a data set that the company makes publically available and extract the information in a JSON or XML format. Companies often have researchers sign a data use agreement and create an account to log in to access the data. These requirements are standard for API data access and provide a minimum level of identification on the part of the user.

Web Scraping

Web scraping is the process of extracting data from a web page. This methodology includes connecting to the web page through an analytical tool (such as SAS), parsing through the page tags to find the necessary information, and extracting the correct information into a data set that can be used by the analytical tool.

Chris Hemedinger wrote an excellent blog post for SAS titled "How to scrape data from a web page using SAS": https://blogs.sas.com/content/sasdummy/2017/12/04/scrape-web-page-data/. This blog post provides example code to pull data directly from web pages.

Web scraping is generally performed in three steps:

- Connect to the web page and access its contents.
  - This step is performed with the PROC HTTP or FILENAME URL procedures.
- Parse the web page contents
  - Performed within a DATA step by utilizing the FIND, SCAN, or regular expression functions using PRXMATCH.
- Repeat across multiple web pages.
  - Usually implemented through macro statements.

Open Source Data Sets

There has been an explosion of web sites that provide a wide array of publically available data. These data sets can range from raw data to highly processed data that is ready to be modeled.

The following sections contain a short list of a few of my favorite sites that contain a wide array of publically available data sets.

Federal and State Data

Nobody has been in the business of supplying data longer than the government. Federal and State data sets are highly standardized, well documented, and have a long history, with some databases having over 100 years of information. The Federal government also provides SAS code for many of their data sets that allows you to access, download, and format the data easily.

U.S. Census Bureau (https://www.census.gov/)

Bureau of Labor Statistics (https://www.bls.gov/data/)

Data.Gov (https://www.data.gov/)

GitHub
(https://github.com/awesomedata/awesome-public-datasets)

This GitHub repository contains an incredible number of publically available data sets from a wide variety of disciplines, including economics, environmental, genomics, astronomy, social media, business and image data sets.

Kaggle
(https://www.kaggle.com/datasets)

Kaggle was the first popular data science competition web site that allows data scientists to compete in predictive modeling competitions for cash prizes. In 2017, Google acquired Kaggle and quickly integrated some of Google's big data products such as Google's cloud storage and its Python notebook interface titled Colab.

Kaggle provides a wide variety of public data sets. Since the purpose of Kaggle is to host machine learning competitions, many of the data sets available have been preprocessed and prepared for machine learning. This preprocessing includes identifying the target variable and splitting the data into train and test data sets.

Kaggle has become an essential tool for learning data science because it allows you to learn in a supportive community that provides a lot of example code. It is also a lot of fun to develop machine learning algorithms and see how well your results rank among other data scientists. Be warned; this can be a very addictive site for the obsessive-compulsive data scientist!

UCI Machine Learning Repository
(https://archive.ics.uci.edu/ml/datasets.php)

The University of California, Irvine, was one of the first major repositories of publically available data. As of this writing, they house nearly 500 data sets from a wide variety of disciplines.

Google Public Data Explorer

(https://www.google.com/publicdata/directory)

When all else fails, Google it. Google's core business is centered on accessing, organizing, and sharing information. In September 2018, Google launched the Dataset Search service. This service is a companion to Google Scholar, which is the company's search engine for academic research and reports. The Dataset Search service allows researchers to search for publically available data through metadata tags that publishers included on their web page.

Data Set

I will use the publically available Lending Club data set to demonstrate the analytical and data transformation techniques that I'll review in this chapter. Lending Club is a peer-to-peer money lending platform in which investors provide funds to borrowers in return for interest income based on a borrower's credit risk profile.

Get the Data

I downloaded the data from Kaggle, but you can find a copy of it in the GitHub repository for this book along with all of the code used throughout the book:

https://github.com/Gearhj/End-to-End-Data-Science

One of the nice things about this data set is that it comes with a data dictionary. A data dictionary is a document that contains definitions for each field in the data set. The level of detail can vary greatly for these types of documents. This particular one lists only the variables in the data set and their common language definition. Other data dictionaries can provide detailed information on the number of observations, the format of each variable, precise definitions for each level of each variable, split points for continuous variables, and the relationship with a predefined target variable. However, this level of detail is rare, so don't get your hopes up.

I downloaded the data from Kaggle and placed it in the data folder that I created on my laptop. I then imported the data into the MYDATA library with Program 5.1.

Program 5.1: Data Load

```
LIBNAME MYDATA BASE "C:/Users/James Gearheart/Desktop/SAS Book
Stuff/Data";

FILENAME REFFILE 'C:\Users\James Gearheart\Desktop\SAS Book
Stuff\Data\loan.csv';

PROC IMPORT DATAFILE=REFFILE
     DBMS=CSV
     OUT= MYDATA.Loan;
```

```
      GETNAMES=YES;
RUN;

PROC CONTENTS DATA=MYDATA.Loan; RUN;
```

Program 5.1 performs four separate tasks.

1. I created the MYDATA library by establishing a connection to the data source.
2. I created a FILENAME that I will use as a shortcut in my import statement.
3. I used a PROC IMPORT to access the data referenced in the FILENAME statement and output it as a SAS data set in the MYDATA library.
4. I ran a PROC CONTENTS on the newly created data to understand the contents.

The CONTENTS procedure shows that the Lending Club data set contains 2.2 million records and 145 variables. I always suggest that the first thing that you should do after you run a PROC CONTENTS is to open the data set and actually look at it. A visual inspection of the data set is worth a thousand lines of data inquiry code.

Let's look at a few sections of the data set and see if we can spot any potential issues with the data.

Output 5.1: Look at Raw Data

	id	member_id	loan_amnt	funded_amnt	pymnt_plan	url	desc	purpose	title
1			2500	2500	n			debt_consolidation	Debt consolidation
2			30000	30000	n			debt_consolidation	Debt consolidation
3			5000	5000	n			debt_consolidation	Debt consolidation
4			4000	4000	n			debt_consolidation	Debt consolidation
5			30000	30000	n			debt_consolidation	Debt consolidation
6			5550	5550	n			credit_card	Credit card refinancing
7			2000	2000	n			debt_consolidation	Debt consolidation

loan_amnt	funded_amnt	funded_amnt_inv	term	int_rate	installment	delinq_2yrs	earliest_cr_line	inq_last_6mths	mths_since_last_delinq	mths_since_last_record	open_acc
2500	2500	2500	36 months	13.56	84.92	0	APR2001	1		45	9
30000	30000	30000	60 months	18.94	777.23	0	JUN1987	0	71	75	13
5000	5000	5000	36 months	17.97	180.69	0	APR2011	0			8
4000	4000	4000	36 months	18.94	146.51	0	FEB2006	0			10
30000	30000	30000	60 months	16.14	731.78	0	DEC2000	0			12
5550	5550	5550	36 months	15.02	192.45	0	SEP2002	3			18
2000	2000	2000	36 months	17.97	72.28	0	NOV2004	1			7

debt_settlement_flag	debt_settlement_flag_date	settlement_status	settlement_date	settlement_amount	emp_title	emp_length	home_ownership	annual_inc	verification_status	issue_d
N					Chef	10+ years	RENT	55000	Not Verified	DEC2018
N					Postmaster	10+ years	MORTGAGE	90000	Source Verified	DEC2018
N					Administrative	6 years	MORTGAGE	59280	Source Verified	DEC2018
N					IT Supervisor	10+ years	MORTGAGE	92000	Source Verified	DEC2018
N					Mechanic	10+ years	MORTGAGE	57250	Not Verified	DEC2018
N					Director COE	10+ years	MORTGAGE	152500	Not Verified	DEC2018
N					Account Manager	4 years	RENT	51000	Source Verified	DEC2018

A quick look at a few sections of the data provides some insights:

- Each row contains a single loan with accompanying data about the loan mechanics (loan amount, interest rate, term, and so on), information about the borrower (income, length of employment, job title), and loan status information (delinquency, collections, on-time payments).

- The Loan ID and Member ID fields are blank (probably to protect private information that could be linked back to the individual).

- Several fields appear to be completely blank. We would verify by running a PROC FREQ or a PROC MEANS on those fields.

- Some fields appear to have missing values. We would determine the number of missing values by running a PROC FREQ or a PROC MEANS on those fields.

- Some fields appear to have repetitive information. The Purpose and Title fields appear to be the same. We would verify this with PROC FREQ.

- There appears to be a lot of information that is not useful for our purposes. Regardless of what your outcome variable is, not all of the available data will be necessary for your model. You will need to select data attributes based on your business expertise, data investigation, and common sense.

Reduce the Size of the Data

The Lending Club data set is not really considered to be "big data." It has a respectable 2.2 million records and 145 variables. That is plenty of data on which to build our models. However, many aspiring data scientists who are reading this book might not have a powerful computer that can process that much data within a reasonable time frame. So, the solution is to sample the data down to a manageable number of observations and variables that can be easily processed by most mid-range laptops.

As long as the data is randomly sampled, the resulting data set should be an unbiased representative sample of the data. This method will ensure that each row has an equal likelihood of being included in the sample. Program 5.2 creates a simple random sample of the data set and specifies that we want to retain 500,000 records.

Program 5.2: Data Sampling

```
PROC SURVEYSELECT DATA=MYDATA.LOAN OUT=LOAN_SAMP
     METHOD=SRS SAMPSIZE=500000 SEED=42;
RUN;
```

Notes on Program 5.2:

- PROC SURVEYSELECT is used to create a random sample of the data.

- The DATA statement specifies which data set that we want to sample and the OUT statement specifies the name of the newly created sampled data set.

- The METHOD statement specifies which sampling method we want to employ. The SRS method is the Simple Random Sampling method.

- The SAMPSIZE statement allows us to specify how many records that we would like to obtain in the output data set.

- The SEED statement allows us to create reproducible results if we need to rerun the program.

Create a Target Variable

Most data sets do not come with a predefined target variable. You will often have to create a target variable based on the purpose of your business need. For example, let's suppose that we work for a financial firm, and we want to develop a model that would predict the probability of a borrower having a bad status on a loan within a given time period. This information could be very beneficial in identifying customers who are about to default on their loans. By identifying these customers, the lender could offer support in the form of deferred payments, loan restructuring, or reduced interest rates. These actions could have the effect of reducing losses due to loan defaults and providing proactive customer service to borrowers struggling with their payments. This would be a win-win!

After looking through all of the 145 available variables, we find a variable titled Loan Status. This variable is defined in the data dictionary as "Current status of the loan." That is not very helpful. However, a quick PROC FREQ on the loan status field shows us that this field contains information on whether a loan is paid, current, late, charged-off, or in default.

Output 5.2: Loan Status Categories

loan_status	Frequency	Percent	Cumulative Frequency	Cumulative Percent
Fully Paid	230812	46.16	230812	46.16
Current	202851	40.57	433663	86.73
Charged Off	58105	11.62	491768	98.35
Late (31-120 days)	4853	0.97	496621	99.32
In Grace Period	1952	0.39	498573	99.71
Late (16-30 days)	828	0.17	499401	99.88
Does not meet the credit policy. Status:Fully Paid	418	0.08	499819	99.96
Does not meet the credit policy. Status:Charged Off	172	0.03	499991	100.00
Default	9	0.00	500000	100.00

One of the first things to notice is that every record has a Loan Status value. There are no missing values for this variable. This is an important aspect to consider because it is inadvisable to impute missing values for the target variable.

When we examine the various levels of the Loan Status variable, we can see that there are three levels that indicate that the loan is in a bad status:

1. Charged Off
2. Does not meet the credit policy. Status: Charged Off
3. Default

Decision Time

We can make a business decision that if a loan has a status of "Late" or "In Grace Period," that it is not the same as being charged-off or in default. This is an important distinction to make because the target variable must represent a unique aspect of the population. Not all loans that are late will be charged off. (We've all missed a payment either by accident or extenuating circumstances.)

Program 5.3 creates a temporary data set in the WORK library called loan_data. This program creates the target variable according to the definition that we outlined above. Since the data set contains one loan per row, I've also created a unique identifier called "row_num." I will be able to use this variable later if I need to reference specific observations.

Program 5.3: Target Variable Creation

```
DATA LOAN_DATA;
  SET LOAN_SAMP;

  IF loan_status in ("Charged Off", "Default",
  "Does not meet the credit policy. Status:Charged Off")
  then bad = 1; else bad = 0;

  ROW_NUM = _N_;

RUN;
```

To verify that we have created the target variable correctly, we can create a PROC FREQ statement on the Loan Status and the newly created BAD variable.

Program 5.4: Frequency Distribution on Loan Status and Target Variable

```
PROC FREQ DATA=LOAN_DATA; TABLES loan_status*bad / NOCOL NOROW NOPERCENT;
RUN;
```

The output displayed in Output 5.3 shows that the new target variable correctly captures each level of the Loan Status variable that we indicated, and the target event rate is 11.65% (58,286 / 500,000). For binary response models, the target event rate is defined as the percent of total observations that have a positive target value.

Output 5.3: Output of Frequency Distribution

Table of loan_status by bad				
		bad		
		0	1	Total
loan_status				
Fully Paid	Frequency	230812	0	230812
Current	Frequency	202851	0	202851
Charged Off	Frequency	0	58105	58105
Late (31-120 days)	Frequency	4853	0	4853
In Grace Period	Frequency	1952	0	1952
Late (16-30 days)	Frequency	828	0	828
Does not meet the credit policy. Status:Fully Paid	Frequency	418	0	418
Does not meet the credit policy. Status:Charged Off	Frequency	0	172	172
Default	Frequency	0	9	9
Total	Frequency	441714	58286	500000

Creating TRAIN and TEST Data Sets

We reviewed the importance of creating separate TRAIN and TEST data sets in the "Data Science Overview" and the "Example Data Science Project" chapters of this book. Therefore, I will not review the importance of splitting your data into TRAIN and TEST sections again, but as a matter of process, we will develop these data sets for the Lending Club example.

Program 5.5 utilizes the SURVEYSELECT procedure to randomly assign a newly created variable called "Selected" to the data set. This variable will determine which observations will be assigned to the TEST group, while the remaining observations will be assigned to the TRAIN group.

Program 5.5: TRAIN/TEST Data Set Split 70/30

```
PROC SURVEYSELECT DATA=LOAN_DATA RATE=0.3
OUTALL OUT=CLASS SEED=42;
RUN;

PROC FREQ DATA=CLASS; TABLES selected; RUN;
```

Program 5.5 specifies that we want to randomly assign 30% of the observations to the TEST group while the remaining 70% of observations will be assigned to the TRAIN group. This split is specified in the RATE statement.

A frequency distribution is a good quality check to ensure that the volume of observations is as expected.

Output 5.4: Frequency Distribution Output

Selection Indicator				
Selected	Frequency	Percent	Cumulative Frequency	Cumulative Percent
0	350000	70.00	350000	70.00
1	150000	30.00	500000	100.00

The newly created Selected variable can now be used to separate the full data set into TRAIN and TEST data sets. Program 5.6 creates these two data sets according to the Selected variable.

Program 5.6: TRAIN/TEST Data Set Creation

```
DATA MYDATA.LOAN_TRAIN MYDATA.LOAN_TEST;
  SET CLASS;
  IF selected = 0 THEN OUTPUT MYDATA.LOAN_TRAIN;
  ELSE OUTPUT MYDATA.LOAN_TEST;
RUN;

PROC FREQ DATA=MYDATA.LOAN_TRAIN; TABLES BAD; RUN;
PROC FREQ DATA=MYDATA.LOAN_TEST; TABLES BAD; RUN;
```

One final quality check is to create frequency distributions for both the TRAIN and TEST data sets to ensure that the event rate is equivalent in both data sets. There will always be a slight variation due to the nature of random sampling. However, the event rate should be within a half percentage point difference between the two data sets. Output 5.5 shows that the TRAIN data set has an event rate of 11.72%, while the TEST data set has an event rate of 11.51%.

Output 5.5: TRAIN/TEST Target Variable Frequency Distribution

bad	Frequency	Percent	Cumulative Frequency	Cumulative Percent
0	308972	88.28	308972	88.28
1	41028	11.72	350000	100.00

bad	Frequency	Percent	Cumulative Frequency	Cumulative Percent
0	132742	88.49	132742	88.49
1	17258	11.51	150000	100.00

So far, we have made a good amount of progress. We have accomplished a few important tasks:

1. We have found an interesting data set to explore.
2. We have imported it into the SAS environment.
3. We have visually explored the data set.
4. We have sampled it down to a manageable number of observations.
5. We have identified an important variable and transformed it into a binary target variable.
6. We have split the data set into separate TRAIN and TEST data sets.

Not a bad start! However, this is just the beginning of the ETL process. Please note that all of the remaining data explorations and transformations will be performed on the TRAIN data set, and then we will later apply the final transformations to the hold-out TEST data set. It is critically important that these steps are separated. Remember that the purpose of splitting the data into TRAIN and TEST data sets is to simulate the process of transforming and scoring new data that will appear in the future.

Variable Selection

The goal of data science is to make informed decisions that are aligned with a business goal. Not all variables are going to be applicable to our stated business goal. Therefore, we need to examine the data set to determine which variables we should include in our modeling data set.

A common approach to data science projects is to include all of the data and let a dimensionality reduction algorithm, such as principal components or a regularization parameter, select which variables to include. These are great methods, and we will explore these techniques later. However, at this stage of data analysis, we first need to determine whether the variables meet a minimum level of quality to be included in the modeling data set. This will include variable analysis to determine:

- Percent of missing values
- Blank fields
- Repetitive fields
- Categorical fields with too many levels
- Variables not aligned with our business goal

Transform

Now that we have gathered some data, we will need to prepare it for modeling. This process will require us to make several critical decisions that will affect how the predictive algorithm will perform. The accuracy of a predictive model is highly influenced by several factors including how we decide to treat missing values, how we adjust for outliers, whether we scale the data, whether we perform feature engineering, and many other decisions that we will make in the "transform" section of ETL.

Missing Values

Missing values is one of the most critical issues of data quality. Nearly every data set has some variables where there are missing values. Not only is the percent of missing values an issue, but also the **reason why** the values are missing. If a variable has 10% of the values missing, that could mean that those missing values represent observations where that variable does not apply to that observation. For example, if the variable is defined as "Number of missed credit card payments," but the data set contains some people who do not have a credit card, that variable will often have a missing value for those observations. It would be a mistake to infer these missing values with a zero because that would imply that these observations have a credit card and have not missed a payment. That is much different from not having a credit card at all.

There are several different definitions of a missing value:

- **Missing** – Data that is not available and there is no way to get it. *Example – Participant doesn't answer a question on a survey.*

- **Not Applicable** – Data that does not apply to the subject in question. *Example – If the person indicates they don't have a driver's license, asking what kind of car they drive wouldn't make sense.*

- **Not Available** – Data that should be obtainable but is, for some reason, not accessible. *Example – Lab data that should be in the patient's chart but is flagged as "Processing".*

- **Not Legible** – May be the same as Not Available, but allows for more granularity. Not Available could be used for data that is delayed or not in the chart. Not Legible is used for situations where handwriting or other documentation issues impede the readability of the data. *Example – Chart review done where a lot of the labs and notes from other doctors were on thermal fax paper (who remembers what that is?) and the text had started to fade. A lot of information was lost as a result.*

- **Prefer not to answer** – Participant does not want to share the information. **The answer cannot be assumed.** *Example – Do you use illicit drugs? (The study team might assume that the answer is actually Yes, but in fact, the person might have used in the past and is concerned about additional questions.)*

- **Don't know** – Particularly useful when an event occurred but the date (or other piece of information) can't be remembered. *Example – Surgery or medication start date. The participant knows they had surgery but can't remember the exact date, or a medication was changed and there is no indication of when the change was made.*

Missing values can also represent **systemic bias**. There could be a specific population or type of product that has a disproportionately large number of missing values. These missing values could be the result of data collection errors, non-inclusion of population subsets, or any number of reasons that would cause a non-random pattern of missing data.

The issue of missing data and the underlying reasons for the missing data is highly specific to a given data set. There is no general solution on how to handle missing data. This is where your business expertise has to come in. Every project will require a unique way to address the issue of missing data. However, we will examine some techniques on how to identify missing data and how to calculate the percent of data that has missing values.

Identifying Missing Numeric Data

A good starting point for identifying missing data is PROC MEANS for numeric data and PROC FREQ for character data. PROC MEANS allows options to specify which statistical values you would like displayed. The ones that I will use are:

- N – Number of observations that are not missing

- NMISS – Number of observations that are missing

- MIN – Minimum value

- MAX – Maximum value

- MEAN – Average value (arithmetic mean)

We can apply PROC MEANS to the TRAIN data set.

Program 5.7: PROC MEANS on Numeric Data

```
PROC MEANS DATA=MYDATA.LOAN_TRAIN N NMISS MIN MAX MEAN;
     VAR _NUMERIC_;
     OUTPUT OUT=LOAN_MEANS;
RUN;
```

The output for this program can be found in Output 5.6. I have manipulated this output by copying the results and putting them into a Microsoft Excel spreadsheet so that I can easily create a "% Missing" column. Currently, SAS does not have that option in PROC MEANS, and although you can certainly develop some code to create that field within SAS, sometimes it's just faster and easier to do a little spreadsheet calculation.

Output 5.6: PROC MEANS Output

Variable	N	N Miss	% Missing	Minimum	Maximum	Mean
loan_amnt	350000	0	0.0%	500	40000	15,034.28
funded_amnt	350000	0	0.0%	500	40000	15,029.20
funded_amnt_inv	350000	0	0.0%	0	40000	15,011.69
int_rate	350000	0	0.0%	5.31	30.99	13.10
installment	350000	0	0.0%	4.93	1714.54	445.73
annual_inc	350000	0	0.0%	0	61000000	77,867.93
dti	349735	265	0.1%	0	999	18.84
delinq_2yrs	349998	2	0.0%	0	30	0.31
inq_last_6mths	349998	2	0.0%	0	33	0.58
mths_since_last_delinq	170692	179308	51.2%	0	188	34.52
mths_since_last_record	55498	294502	84.1%	0	125	72.44

Output 5.6 shows the first 11 rows of the PROC MEANS output. The specified statistics are shown for each numeric variable in the data set. PROC MEANS provides an excellent overview of the data and allows you to detect possible issues with the data easily. For example, the annual_inc variable has a maximum value of 61 million dollars. That seems like an extreme outlier, possibly due to an input error. Also, the dti variable (which stands for "debt to income ratio") has a max value of 999. That does not seem to be a legitimate value for that field, so it could be a special value that indicates a particular aspect of the data, such as "no determinable income" or something like that.

The last two rows of Output 5.6 show a large percentage of the observations for these variables have missing values. For now, we just want to calculate the percentage of missing values for each observation. In a following step, we will make determinations on whether to retain these variables or infer the missing values.

Identifying Missing Character Data

PROC FREQ is widely used to determine the number of missing values for character data. One of the things to keep in mind with character data is that some fields will have several hundred categorical levels for a single variable. This often happens with variables such as "zip code" or open answer fields such as "job title." A PROC FREQ on these variables can easily fill up your memory. If you try to run a PROC FREQ against all character variables for this data set, you will probably get this error message in the log:

```
ERROR: The SAS System stopped processing this step because of insufficient
memory.
```

A quick way to eliminate some of the character variables from the data set is to create a separate data set consisting only of the character variables and then open it up and look at it. You will probably be able to visually determine which variables will have a large number of categorical levels just by looking at the first 100 observations.

Program 5.8: First 100 Observations of Character Data

```
DATA char;
  SET MYDATA.LOAN_TRAIN (OBS=100);
  KEEP _CHARACTER_;
RUN;
```

A quick visual inspection of the character variables shows us:

- **Empty variables** – The id, host_id, and url variables all appear to be empty variables. We can confirm this by running a PROC FREQ directly on these variables.

- **Multiple level variables** – The variables desc, emp_title, and zip_code all have unique values that will result in several hundred categorical levels.

- **Date values** – There are several date values that are formatted as character variables. These variables can easily be reformatted into numeric variables, and we could perform calculations on them to do feature engineering. However, for the sake of brevity, we will remove the date variables from the modeling data set.

Now that we have made the initial cut of the character variables, we can run a PROC FREQ on the remaining character variables to determine the percent of missing observations.

Program 5.9: Frequency Distribution of Remaining Character Variables

```
PROC FREQ DATA=MYDATA.LOAN_TRAIN (DROP=id member_id url emp_title zip_code
earliest_cr_line sec_app_earliest_cr_line desc issue_d title last_pymnt_d
next_pymnt_d last_credit_pull_d debt_settlement_flag_date settlement_date
hardship_start_date hardship_end_date payment_plan_start_date);
    TABLES _CHARACTER_;
RUN;
```

The results of this analysis show us that most of the character variables have complete information (Output 5.7).

Output 5.7: Frequency Distribution Output

term	Frequency	Percent	Cumulative Frequency	Cumulative Percent
36 months	249479	71.28	249479	71.28
60 months	100521	28.72	350000	100.00

grade	Frequency	Percent	Cumulative Frequency	Cumulative Percent
A	67031	19.15	67031	19.15
B	102432	29.27	169463	48.42
C	100523	28.72	269986	77.14
D	50472	14.42	320458	91.56
E	21149	6.04	341607	97.60
F	6489	1.85	348096	99.46
G	1904	0.54	350000	100.00

However, this analysis also shows us that there are specific variables where there is an extremely high percentage of missing values (Output 5.7). For example, the verification_status_joint variable has 95% of the values missing. This is most likely because this variable applies only to borrowers who applied for a joint loan along with a co-borrower.

Other character variables that pertain to "hardship status" have 99.5% of the observations missing. This is most likely because people who are not part of a hardship repayment program do not have a value for this field.

verification_status_joint	Frequency	Percent	Cumulative Frequency	Cumulative Percent
Not Verified	8670	48.66	8670	48.66
Source Verified	5497	30.85	14167	79.52
Verified	3649	20.48	17816	100.00
Frequency Missing = 332184				

hardship_status	Frequency	Percent	Cumulative Frequency	Cumulative Percent
ACTIVE	133	8.33	133	8.33
BROKEN	336	21.04	469	29.37
COMPLETED	1128	70.63	1597	100.00
Frequency Missing = 348403				

Now that we have identified the volume of missing data for each variable, we need to ask ourselves some critical questions:

- Can we find a new data source that has the missing observations?
- Should we remove the rows or columns that have a large proportion of missing values?
- Which method will we use to impute the value of the missing observations?

New Data Sources

If you are working in a corporate environment, then chances are that several databases contain similar information, and some of these databases are more populated than others. You may find a better data source that has nearly complete information. However, the example data set that we received from Lending Club does not have any additional methods of retrieving the missing data, so we will have to work with what we have.

Delete Variables from the Data Set

If a variable has a large proportion of its values that are truly missing (that is, where the missing value is not representing a value such as "not applicable"), then it is inadvisable to try to infer the values of those missing observations. It is a subject of considerable debate among researchers of what the threshold of acceptable missing value percentage should be. Although there is a consensus that the answer will vary depending on the data set and the importance of the variable, there are no clear guidelines on what the cutoff point should be. The current research places that threshold anywhere between 20–40%. Although that seems like a wide range, it does provide us some guidance. For this project, let's split the difference and set our allowable missing observation percentage at 30%.

Since we have previously analyzed the numeric and character variables separately, we can quickly see which variables make the first cut of having less than 30% of their observations missing. There is a total of 79 variables that meet our initial criteria. This list includes 65 numeric variables and 14 character variables.

Let's create a new data set that contains only the variables that have passed this first-level quality check. Program 5.10 creates a new data set called LOAN_LIMIT in the MYDATA library. The KEEP statement retains the unique identifier, the target variable, and a list of variables that we want to retain for further exploration. I have not listed all 79 variables here due to space limitations. Again, this code is in the GitHub repository.

Program 5.10: Limit Data Set to Variables of Interest

```
DATA MYDATA.LOAN_LIMIT;
  SET MYDATA.LOAN_TRAIN;

  KEEP ROW_NUM bad <list of keep variables>;

RUN;
```

Numeric Imputation Methods

Once we have decided which variables to keep, we must try to impute the actual value for the missing value. This imputation is important for several reasons:

- Many machine learning algorithms will drop any observation that has a single missing value in any of the predictor fields.
- If observations with missing values are dropped, this can severely limit the sample size.
- Dropping observations with a missing value can lead to systemic bias.
- There can be a significant loss of information by dropping an entire observation because only one variable has missing values.

If you think of a missing value as a blank space in your data set, then when we impute missing values, we are merely filling in the blank with our best guess as to what that value should be. There are several different methods to impute missing values. These include:

- **Mean** – Replaces missing numeric values with the global average value. This methodology can be further refined by stratifying the data set into categories depending on the nature of the data set and imputing the missing values with the categorical average.

- **Median** – Replaces missing numeric values with the median value. This method can be beneficial for numeric variables with a large standard deviation. For example, the variable income usually has a highly skewed right tail distribution. Unless outliers are adjusted before the imputation occurs, this will pull the mean statistic higher than it should be. The median statistic is not influenced by outliers and can serve as a more stable imputation method for these types of variables.

- **Mode** – The mode is the value that appears most often in a given data set. This method is primarily used to impute missing categorical values. The data can also be stratified into groups, and the mode for the group is used to replace missing values.

- **Regression** – The regression method separates the data set into a group that has missing values and a group that does not have missing values. The group that does not have missing values is used to build a predictive model that predicts the value for the missing value. This method works well for data sets that have only one or two variables that have missing values, but it can be burdensome to try and repeat this method several times for a single data set.

Although there are no general rules of thumb for assessing missing data due to the specific nature of the data set being analyzed, I can offer one piece of advice. If the percentage of missing data is less than 5%, then all imputation methods will produce nearly identical results.

In order to impute missing numeric values with one of the standard statistical values (mean, median, min, max, midrange) the easiest method in SAS is to use PROC STDIZE.

Program 5.11: Standardize Numeric Variables

```
PROC STDIZE DATA=MYDATA.LOAN_LIMIT REPONLY METHOD=mean OUT=Complete_data;
VAR _NUMERIC_;
RUN;
```

Notes on Program 5.11:

- PROC STDIZE is used to impute missing values.

- The REPONLY statement specifies that you do not want to standardize the data, but that you only want to impute the missing values.

- The METHOD statement specifies the statistical measure that you want to use to impute the missing values.

- The OUT statement preserves the original data set and creates a new data set with the imputed values.

- The VAR statement specifies which variables you want to impute. In this case, we have imputed the missing values for all numeric variables.

Although the above method works well for most numeric variables, you should be cautious of applying it to all numeric variables. Most data sets contain some variables that have high outliers. These outliers will result in a large standard deviation for the variable. If you use the mean value to impute missing values for these variables, you can be imputing much higher values than should be expected.

One quick fix for this problem is to impute the **median** value for these variables. I ran a PROC MEANS on the LOAN_LIMIT data set's numeric variables. Output 5.8 shows the top dozen variables sorted by the MAXIMUM value. Notice that the standard deviation is generally much higher than the mean value for these variables.

Output 5.8: PROC MEANS Output

Variable	N	N Miss	Maximum	Mean	Median	Std Dev
annual_inc	350000	0	61000000	77867.93	65000	125,741.07
tot_hi_cred_lim	339071	10929	9999999	177822.11	114352	180,801.19
tot_cur_bal	339071	10929	4772549	142166.52	79272	159,896.52
total_bal_ex_mort	342208	7792	2652799	51005.44	37808.5	49,914.95
total_rev_hi_lim	339071	10929	2013133	34512.45	25400	34,729.46
revol_bal	350000	0	1743266	16618.55	11334	22,733.93
total_il_high_credit_limit	339071	10929	1269783	43704.65	32579	45,094.31
total_bc_limit	342208	7792	1090700	23183.66	16300	23,074.52
avg_cur_bal	339063	10937	477255	13506.63	7367	16,228.13
bc_open_to_buy	338391	11609	371701	11378.23	5431	16,543.67
delinq_amnt	349998	2	249925	13.0350831	0	817.21
tot_coll_amt	339071	10929	215902	218.878462	0	1,664.49

We can impute the missing values for these variables by using the median value instead of the mean value. Program 5.12 contains three separate sections. First, a macro variable is created to identify the outlier variables. Second, PROC STDIZE is called on those variables using the median imputation method. Third, a DATA step is used to merge the data set that imputed missing variables with the mean methodology to the data set that imputed the missing values with the median methodology.

Program 5.12: PROC STDIZE to Impute Median Values for Numeric Variables

```
%let outliers = annual_inc total_rev_hi_lim tot_hi_cred_lim
tot_cur_bal tot_coll_amt total_bal_ex_mort total_il_high_credit_limit
total_bc_limit avg_cur_bal bc_open_to_buy delinq_amnt tot_coll_amt;
```

```
PROC STDIZE DATA=MYDATA.LOAN_LIMIT (keep=ROW_NUM &outliers.)
      REPONLY METHOD=median OUT=Outlier_adjust;
      VAR _NUMERIC_;
RUN;


DATA MYDATA.LOAN_ADJUST;
MERGE Complete_data (drop= &outliers. in=a) Outlier_adjust (in=b);
      by ROW_NUM;
RUN;
```

The final result of all of this tedious data manipulation is a data set where all of the numeric variables have been analyzed for missing values and those values have been imputed with a methodology that is best suited for the distribution of those variables.

Character Imputation Methods

For the Lending Tree data sets, we have retained 14 character variables in our modeling data set. Luckily, there are no missing values for these character variables. However, if there were, it would be very easy to impute those missing values. For character variables, you simply run a PROC FREQ on all of the character variables, such as the example in Program 5.13.

Program 5.13: Frequency Distribution of Character Variables
```
PROC FREQ DATA=MYDATA.LOAN_ADJUST ORDER=FREQ;
      TABLES _CHARACTER_;
RUN;
```

The most common method of imputing character variables is to replace any missing values with the most frequent category for that variable. It is often helpful to stratify the data into specific categories such as age group, income level, region, or some other grouping variable, and replace the missing values for a given level with the most frequent value for that level.

For example, if we wanted to use the variable verification status as our stratifier, we can simply create a crosstabulation table for all the character variables by using the following code:

Program 5.14: Crosstabulation Example
```
PROC FREQ DATA=MYDATA.LOAN_ADJUST ORDER=FREQ;
      TABLES verification_status*(_CHARACTER_);
RUN;
```

This method will provide the categorical volume for each level of all the character variables stratified by verification status. You can then simply replace the missing values with the most frequent categorical level within that group.

Outlier Identification and Adjustments

We touched on the issue of outliers in the section about imputing missing values for numeric variables. It is important to adjust for outliers, not only for imputing missing values, but also because outliers can severely skew your model's estimates.

Figure 5.1 visually demonstrates the impact of a single outlier on model estimates. The graph on the top shows a scatter plot of individual observations for the age and income variables. We can create a simple linear regression line through the data to get an estimate of income given a person's age. Roughly half of the observations are above the regression line, while the other half are below it.

The graph on the bottom shows what happens when Bill Gates enters the room. The extreme outlier of Bill's income skews the model estimate higher than one would expect. Notice that most of the observations are now below the regression line. The single extreme outlier has affected the model estimation for all observation points.

Figure 5.1: Outlier Visualization

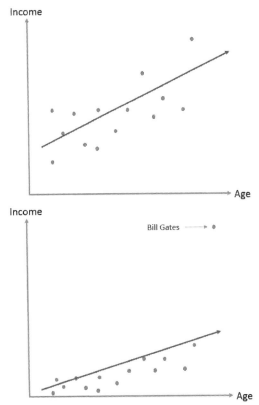

1.5 IQR Rule

One of the most popular ways to adjust for outliers is to use the 1.5 IQR rule. This rule is very straightforward and easy to understand. For any continuous variable, you can simply multiply the interquartile range by the number 1.5. You then add that number to the third quartile. Any values above that threshold are suspected as being an outlier. You can also perform the same calculation on the low end. You can subtract the value of IQR x 1.5 from the first quartile to find low-end outliers.

The process of adjusting for outliers can be tedious if you have several continuous variables that are suspected as having outliers. You will need to run PROC UNIVARIATE on each variable to identify its median, 25th percentile, 75th percentile, and interquartile range. You would then need to develop a program that identifies values above and below the 1.5 IQR rule thresholds and overwrite those values with new values at the threshold.

The following program is a bit complicated, but it automates the process of adjusting a list of continuous variables according to the 1.5 IQR rule. This program consists of three distinct parts:

1. Create a BASE data set that excludes the variables contained in the &outliers global macro that we developed previously. Then create an OUTLIER data set that contains only the unique identifier ROW_NUM and the outlier variables.
2. Create an algorithm that loops through each of the outlier variables contained in the global variable &outliers and apply the 1.5 IQR rule to cap each variable's range according to its unique 1.5 IQR value.
3. Merge the newly restricted outlier variable with the BASE data set.

Program 5.15: Outlier Adjustment Based on 1.5 IQR Rule

```
/*Step 1: Create BASE and OUTLIER data sets*/
DATA MYDATA.BASE;
      SET MYDATA.LOAN_ADJUST (DROP=&outliers.);
RUN;

DATA outliers;
      SET MYDATA.LOAN_ADJUST (KEEP=&outliers. ROW_NUM);
RUN;

/*Step 2: Create loop and apply the 1.5 IQR rule*/
%MACRO loopit(mylist);
      %LET n = %SYSFUNC(countw(&mylist));

      %DO I=1 %TO &n;
            %LET val = %SCAN(&mylist,&I);

            PROC UNIVARIATE DATA = outliers ;
                  VAR &val.;
                  OUTPUT OUT=boxStats MEDIAN=median QRANGE=iqr;
            run;

            data _NULL_;
                  SET boxStats;
                  CALL symput ('median',median);
                  CALL symput ('iqr', iqr);
            run;

            %PUT &median;
            %PUT &iqr;

            DATA out_&val.(KEEP=ROW_NUM &val.);
                  SET outliers;

                  IF &val. ge &median + 1.5 * &iqr THEN
                        &val. = &median + 1.5 * &iqr;
            RUN;
```

```
/*Step 3: Merge restricted value to BASE dataset*/
            PROC SQL;
                CREATE TABLE MYDATA.BASE AS
                    SELECT *
                    FROM MYDATA.BASE AS a
                    LEFT JOIN out_&val. as b
                        on a.ROW_NUM = b.ROW_NUM;
            QUIT;

        %END;
%MEND;

%LET list = &outliers;
%loopit(&list);
```

Notes on Program 5.15:

- A macro variable was previously created in Program 5.15 that contains all of the continuous variables that are suspected of having outliers.

- Separate data sets were created: one that contains all of the outlier variables and one that excludes the outlier variables.

- A macro program is developed to contain the process of looping through the list of variables.

- A macro variable (n) is created that counts the number of variables contained in the macro variable.

- A DO loop is created that starts at the first variable and runs the following program on each variable contained in the macro variable.

- PROC UNIVARIATE identifies the variable's median and interquartile range.

- A macro variable is created to contain the values of the median and interquartile range.

- A DATA step is created to adjust any values that exceed the 1.5 IQR rule on the high end and the low end.

- PROC SQL adds the adjusted variables to the BASE data set.

This program might seem like overkill to you. It could be easier to simply adjust outlier variables one at a time. This is often the case; however, when you have a large number of outlier variables, it is often beneficial to create an algorithm to transform them efficiently and consistently.

Character Data Adjustments

We have spent a lot of time investigating the numeric data and meticulously applying the appropriate transformations to infer missing values and adjust for outliers. Character data has its own standard methodology for adjusting these fields so that they are optimized for modeling. There are two primary concerns for character data: missing values, and too many categories.

Missing Character Data Adjustments

The most often used method to infer missing character data is to simply replace the missing values with the most frequent category. In our example data set, the character data does not have any missing values. However, I can force some values to be missing for demonstration purposes. Program 5.16 creates an example data set where the last 501 rows have missing values for the variable purpose.

Program 5.16: Create Missing Values

```
DATA EXAMPLE;
  SET MYDATA.BASE (KEEP=purpose);
  if _N_ ge 349500 then purpose = '';
RUN;
```

A simple PROC FREQ will provide the volumes for each category of the purpose variable.

Program 5.17: Frequency Distribution

```
PROC FREQ DATA=EXAMPLE ORDER=FREQ; TABLES purpose; RUN;
```

Output 5.9 shows the associated output for this PROC FREQ.

Output 5.9: Frequency Distribution Output

purpose	Frequency	Percent	Cumulative Frequency	Cumulative Percent
debt_consolidation	197882	56.62	197882	56.62
credit_card	79523	22.75	277405	79.37
home_improvement	23288	6.66	300693	86.04
other	21517	6.16	322210	92.19
major_purchase	7809	2.23	330019	94.43
medical	4325	1.24	334344	95.66
small_business	3928	1.12	338272	96.79
car	3792	1.08	342064	97.87
vacation	2339	0.67	344403	98.54
moving	2304	0.66	346707	99.20
house	2134	0.61	348841	99.81
wedding	388	0.11	349229	99.92
renewable_energy	204	0.06	349433	99.98
educational	66	0.02	349499	100.00
Frequency Missing = 501				

Output 5.9 shows that the most frequent category for the variable purpose is debt_consolidation. It represents over half of all entries for this variable. It is a reasonable choice to infer all of the missing values with this category.

Program 5.18: Infer Missing Values with Mode Value

```
DATA EXAMPLE_INFERRED;
  SET EXAMPLE;
  IF purpose = '' THEN purpose = 'debt_consolidation';
RUN;
```

Program 5.18 shows how to replace all missing values for the variable purpose with the most frequent category. This method can be expanded upon by stratifying the data by an important grouping variable. This variable is often something like age, region, or economic group. Then you can take the most frequent category in that group to replace the missing values.

Collapsing Categories

Many programs offer automated functions that will take a categorical variable and transform it into dummy variables. Dummy variables are binary numeric categories that represent whether a variable meets a criterion or not. Although these functions are very helpful and time-saving, they should be used with caution. If you have a categorical variable with 20 categories, this function will create 20 new variables from just this one variable. Imagine that your data set has 10 character variables with 100 levels for each variable. The automated function will create 1000 new dummy variables! As you can see, this method of variable creation can get out of hand very quickly.

I strongly suggest that instead of blindly creating dummy variables for every categorical level, you should inspect the categorical variable and decide whether it is appropriate to collapse the number of categories down to a more manageable level without losing any significant information.

The above data output found in Output 5.9 shows each categorical level for the variable purpose. This variable has 14 levels. However, a quick inspection shows that over 90% of the values are contained in the top three values. It could be appropriate to retain those top three values and create a fourth category that contains all of the remaining categories. Program 5.19 collapses the variable purpose into four categories by creating dummy variables for each of the retained categorical levels.

Program 5.19: Create Dummy Variables

```
DATA char_data;
        SET MYDATA.BASE (keep=row_num _CHARACTER_);

        IF purpose = 'debt_consolidation' then
                purpose_dc = 1;
        else purpose_dc = 0;

        IF purpose = 'credit_card' then
                purpose_cc = 1;
        else purpose_cc = 0;

        IF purpose = 'home_improvement' then
                purpose_hi = 1;
        else purpose_hi = 0;

        IF purpose NOT IN ('debt_consolidation', 'credit_card',
        'home_improvement') then
                purpose_other = 1;
        else purpose_other = 0;
RUN;
```

Transforming the TEST Data Set

At this point, we have developed and applied many different types of data transformations to our training data set. This process includes inferring missing values, capping variables to protect against outliers, and collapsing categorical variables by creating dummy variables. As part of our modeling workflow, all of these processes need to be applied to the hold-out TEST data set. This is to ensure that a model that is derived from the TRAIN data set will be appropriately applied to the TEST data set. Remember that the reason that we split the main data set into TRAIN and TEST data sets is to simulate new data that has not been used to create the predictive model. We will build our predictive models on the TRAIN data set and apply it to the TEST data set. The model fit metrics from the TEST data set will determine the accuracy of the model.

One of the first steps that we did with the TRAIN data set was to determine the percentage of observations with missing observations for each variable. We do not need to recreate this analysis for the TEST data set. We only need to apply the same selections that we made in the TRAIN data set to the TEST data set. Program 5.20 keeps all of the variables that were previously determined to be valid and creates a new TEST data set based on this filter.

Program 5.20: Limit the TEST Data Set to Variables of Interest

```
DATA MYDATA.LOAN_LIMIT_TEST;
  SET MYDATA.LOAN_TEST;

  keep <List of variables from the TRAIN dataset> ;
RUN;
```

Now that we have limited the TEST data set to the same variables that we used in the TRAIN data set, we will simply calculate the summary statistics for the TRAIN data set and use this information to transform the TEST data set. We will use the TRAIN mean and max values to infer the TEST missing values and to cap the TEST max values. These transformations will be identical to what was used to infer missing values and to cap outliers in the TRAIN data set. Program 5.21 creates a PROC MEANS to calculate the TRAIN summary statistics.

Program 5.21: PROC MEANS on TRAIN Data Set

```
PROC MEANS DATA=MYDATA.BASE (DROP=ROW_NUM BAD)
      MIN MAX MEAN MEDIAN;
      VAR _NUMERIC_;
      OUTPUT OUT=VALUES(DROP=_type_ _freq_)
      MIN= MAX= MEAN= MEDIAN= / AUTONAME;
RUN;
```

There are a couple of different ways to apply these summary statistics to a new data set. Some of these methodologies consist of complex programming that is easy to get lost in. To demonstrate the basic concept of value replacement, I will use a brute force method that is fairly easy to understand.

The first step is to create a global variable that contains all of the numeric variable names from the original TRAIN data set. Program 5.22 creates this global variable.

Program 5.22: Create Macro Variable

```
PROC CONTENTS NOPRINT DATA=MYDATA.BASE
KEEP=_NUMERIC_ DROP=ROW_NUM BAD) OUT=VAR4 (KEEP=name);
```

```
RUN;

PROC SQL NOPRINT;
        SELECT name INTO: orig_num separated by " " FROM VAR4;
QUIT;
```

The second step is the brute force part of this process. The output from the previous PROC MEANS statement gives us a data set that contains a single row of information. It contains the MIN, MAX, MEAN, and MEDIAN variables for each of the original variables. Therefore, for the original 62 numeric variables in the TRAIN data set, PROC MEANS created an output data set of 248 variables. Output 5.10 shows a small sample of the output generated from this program. The summary statistic for each of the original numeric variables has been placed into its own variable. Since each of the 62 numeric variables has four statistics (MIN, MAX, MEAN, MEDIAN), there are 248 total summary statistics variables.

Output 5.10: PROC MEANS Output

recoveries_Mi n	collection_rec overy_fee_M...	acc_now_deli nq_Min	tot_coll_amt_ Min	delinq_amnt_ Min	num_accts_e ver_120_pd_...
0	0	0	0	0	0

The brute force approach will replicate this single line to be the same size as the TEST data set. We will then merge the TEST data set with this replicated data set to create a data set where we can easily apply the data transformations to the TEST data set. Program 5.23 replicates the single observations summary statistics data set 150K times to be the same size as the TEST data set.

Program 5.23: Create Data Set of TRAIN PROC MEANS Output

```
DATA class(DROP=i);
        DO i = 1 TO 150000;
                DO j = 1 TO n;
                        SET values NOBS=n POINT=j;
                        OUTPUT;
                END;
        END;
        STOP;
RUN;
```

Program 5.24 merges the TEST data set with the replicated data set.

Program 5.24: Merge Data Sets

```
DATA MYDATA.CHK;
        MERGE MYDATA.LOAN_LIMIT_TEST CLASS;
RUN;
```

The final step of this process is broken into three sections.

1. Create a BASE data set that will contain all the adjusted values.
2. Create a macro that loops through each of the variables and replaces missing values with the associated MEAN value from the adjusted TRAIN data set. Do the same thing to cap the MIN and MAX values of the TEST data set with the MIN and MAX values from the adjusted TRAIN data set. This process protects against high and low outliers in the TEST data set.

3. Create a final data set that retains only the original variables. Drop all the replicated summary statistics variables.

These steps are contained in Program 5.25.

Program 5.25: Replace TEST Missing Values with TRAIN Summary Stats Values

```
/*Create base dataset that will contain all adjusted values*/
DATA mydata.update;
SET mydata.loan_limit_test (KEEP=row_num);
RUN;

/*Loop through variables in the TEST dataset and replace the missing
values with the summary stats MEAN value and cap any values greater than
the MAX value with the MAX value*/
%MACRO loopit(mylist);
        %LET n = %SYSFUNC(countw(&mylist));
        %DO I=1 %TO &n;
                %LET val = %SCAN(&mylist,&I);
                data chk;
set mydata.chk(keep=row_num &val. &val._MIN &val._MAX &val._MEAN);

if &val. = . then &val. = &val._MEAN; ELSE &val. = &val.;
if &val. lt &val._MIN then &val = &val._MIN; ELSE &val. = &val.;
if &val. gt &val._MAX then &val = &val._MAX; ELSE &val. = &val.;

                RUN;

                PROC SQL;
                  CREATE TABLE MYDATA.UPDATE AS
                  SELECT *
                  FROM MYDATA.UPDATE AS a
                  LEFT JOIN chk AS b
                    ON a.ROW_NUM = b.ROW_NUM
                  ;
                  QUIT;

        %END;
%MEND;

%LET list = &orig_num;
%loopit(&list);

/*Retain only the original variables for the numeric TEST dataset and run
a PROC MEANS to validate that everything looks correct*/
DATA MYDATA.UPDATE; SET MYDATA.UPDATE (KEEP=ROW_NUM &orig_num.); RUN;

PROC MEANS DATA=MYDATA.UPDATE N NMISS MIN MAX MEAN MEDIAN;
VAR _NUMERIC_; RUN;
```

The next step of transforming the TEST data set is to apply the same categorical transformations that were developed in the TRAIN data set to the TEST data set. This step is a simple process where you can copy and paste the code that you developed in the TRAIN character data transformation and apply it to the TEST data set. Program 5.26 provides an example.

Program 5.26: Categorical Transformation

```
DATA char_data;
  SET MYDATA.LOAN_LIMIT_TEST (keep=row_num BAD _CHARACTER_);
  IF purpose = 'debt_consolidation' then purpose_dc = 1; else purpose_dc =
0;
  IF purpose = 'credit_card' then purpose_cc = 1; else purpose_cc = 0;
  IF purpose = 'home_improvement' then purpose_hi = 1; else purpose_hi =
0;
  IF purpose NOT IN ('debt_consolidation', 'credit_card',
'home_improvement') then purpose_other = 1; else purpose_other = 0;
RUN;
```

Remember that there are actually several dummy variables that were created to transform all of the character variables. Program 5.26 only provides an example. The full code can be found in the GitHub repository for this book at https://github.com/Gearhj/End-to-End-Data-Science.

The final step in transforming the TEST data set is to combine the adjusted numeric data with the adjusted character data. This will create your final TEST modeling data set.

Program 5.27: Create Final TEST Modeling Data Set

```
PROC SQL;
  CREATE TABLE MYDATA.MODEL_TEST AS
  SELECT *
  FROM MYDATA.UPDATE AS a
  LEFT JOIN char_data AS b
    ON a.ROW_NUM = b.ROW_NUM
      ;
QUIT;
```

Wow, that seemed like a lot of work! The ETL process is the most important and most time-consuming aspect of predictive modeling. Although we demonstrated several data transformations in this example data set, there are many, many more types of data transformations that we could have applied. The next section provides a quick look at some of these data transformations.

Additional Transformations

Data transformations are a common necessity when working with real-world data. This is the process of converting data from one format or structure to a different format or structure. For example, oftentimes, a data set will have a continuous variable formatted as a character variable. It would be difficult to use this variable in a regression model because the model would interpret it as a class variable rather than a continuous numeric input variable (more on those details in the regression chapter). Even if the model could finish processing, the results would look strange. The same issues would occur with a tree-based model. The tree algorithm would assess all the individual values of the character variable individually and group common values onto one side of a split point. Again, this would look very strange and be very difficult to interpret.

Luckily, our example data set for this chapter does not have any variables that are improperly formatted as a character value when they rightfully should be numeric. However, let's look at a couple of common examples of when this issue occurs.

Transforming Character to Numeric Formats

The process of transforming the format of a variable is possibly the most common data transformation technique that all SAS programmers must perform. The main thing to remember is to use a PUT statement when transforming from numeric to character and use an INPUT statement when transforming from character to numeric. Let's look at a couple of examples:

Program 5.28 takes a numeric variable and transforms it into a character variable. In this example, I am only retaining the numeric variable that I want to transform. This is just for increased processing speed. I would normally not limit the data set to a single variable. The program creates a new variable named char_loan that is the exact same value as the loan_amnt variable except that it is formatted as a character variable. I use the PUT statement, and in parentheses, I specify the variable that I want to transform and the format that I want to transform it into.

Program 5.28: Transform Numeric to Character

```
DATA num_to_char;
   SET MYDATA.LOAN_LIMIT (KEEP=loan_amnt);
   char_loan = put(loan_amnt, $8.);
   DROP loan_amnt;
RUN;
```

Program 5.29 demonstrates the opposite transformation. I transform the newly created character variable back into the numeric format. Notice that the only difference is that I am using the INPUT statement with the proper numeric format specified.

Program 5.29: Transform Character to Numeric

```
DATA char_to_num;
   SET num_to_char;
   num_loan = input(char_loan, 8.);
   DROP char_loan;
RUN;
```

Transforming Date Values

Date values are often problematic because of the wide variety of ways that they can be represented. If they are formatted as character variables, then you can simply use the transformation technique that was demonstrated above. The only addition is that you may want to include a FORMAT statement as your final line of code (FORMAT start_date date8.;.).

Another common formatting issue with date values occurs when the data is expressed in a DATETIME format. The variable will look something like this: 01APR2001:12:01:37

This variable shows that the date is 01APR2001 and the timestamp is 12:01:37. It is often useful to separate these variables into distinct date and time variables. Program 5.30 shows an example of separating a datetime variable into distinct date and time variables. This code would be included in a DATA statement.

Program 5.30: Identifying Date and Time Parts

```
date = datepart(datetime);
time = timepart(datetime);
```

One final item that is useful when transforming date values is the ability to create distinct values for year, month, day, and week. When working with time series models, these variables can be incredibly valuable. Program 5.31 demonstrates how to create separate variables for each one of these date values. The resulting data set will contain numeric values for each of the created variables.

Program 5.31: Creating Date Variables

```
DATA date_values;
  SET dataset;
  year  = year(date);
  month = month(date);
  day   = day(date);
  week  = week(date);
RUN;
```

These variables can now be used as either separate inputs to a time series model or you can use them to perform calculations.

Feature Engineering

Feature engineering is the process of creating new variables from the combination or transformation of existing variables. The transformation process that we reviewed above is a type of feature engineering. There are several different types of feature engineering that can be applied to our Lending Club data set. These include combining variables, creating polynomials, creating dummy variables, and several other methodologies. Program 5.32 demonstrates a few of these techniques on the Lending Club data set.

Program 5.32: Feature Engineering

```
DATA new_features;
  SET MYDATA.LOAN_LIMIT (KEEP=installment annual_inc int_rate term);

  /*Create new variable: debt to income ratio*/
  dti = installment / (annual_inc / 12);

  /*Polynomial*/
  int_rate_sq = int_rate**2;

  /*Dummy variables*/
  IF term = '36 months' THEN t36 = 1; ELSE t36 = 0;
  IF term = '60 months' THEN t60 = 1; ELSE t60 = 0;

RUN;
```

Notes on Program 5.32:

- The debt to income variable was created by applying a formula to two of the variables contained in the Lending Club data set. The installment variable is used as the numerator, and the annual_inc variable is divided by twelve to create the denominator. This new variable can be used as a separate feature in the modeling data set.

- The polynomial of the int_rate variable can be beneficial in modeling because it can emphasize the difference between low, medium, and high values. For example, for the base values of 3.4, 9.2, and 17.8, the squared values of these figures are 11.56, 84.64, and 316.84. The separation caused by the polynomial is often valuable. The polynomial also has the benefit of expressing non-linear relationships.

- The character variable term has two values. These values can be separated into two distinct numeric values that are merely binary indicators of those values. Dummy variables are very common and can be extremely valuable in predictive modeling.

Feature Scaling

Feature scaling is the process of transforming the input variables in order to adjust the range and distribution of the data. This process is an essential step for some types of models. For example, a "nearest neighbor" model assigns a value to an observation based on the calculated distance between two or more predictor variables. If the scales of these variables are vastly different, certain variables will overpower other variables. However, if all variables are scaled similarly, then all variables are equally represented in the predictor space. There are two main methods of feature scaling.

Normalization – Applying a transformation to your data so that your transformed data is roughly normally distributed. This method is most commonly performed through log transformation, although there are several other normalization methods.

Program 5.33 shows the simple code to create a log transformation of a continuous variable. This code demonstrates how to create a new variable log_income by applying the log transformation to the existing continuous variable annual_inc. This code is generally included in a DATA step.

Program 5.33: Creating Logarithmic Variables
```
log_income = log(annual_inc);
```

Standardization – This is the process of adjusting the input variables to be on the same scale. The simple formula is to subtract the mean and divide by the standard deviation. This process produces standard scores that tell us the number of standard deviations above or below the mean for that specific variable. This method allows us to compare scores between different types of variables.

Program 5.34 demonstrates the STDIZE procedure. This procedure is highly flexible and allows the data scientist to choose between 18 different standardization methodologies. PROC STDIZE utilizes the STD method of standardization, which is also called the z-score method. This method subtracts the mean from the observation value and divides by the standard deviation to produce a standardized result.

Program 5.34: Create Standardized Variables

```
PROC STDIZE DATA=MYDATA.Loan_limit(KEEP=annual_inc int_rate)
      METHOD=STD OUT=std_vars;
      VAR annual_inc int_rate;
RUN;
```

Let's look at the difference between the original values and the newly standardized values. Table 5.1 shows the first ten observations of the Lending Club data set for the variables int_rate and annual_inc. The set of variables on the left shows the original scale of the variables. Obviously, there is a big difference between the value of an interest rate and the value of the applicant's annual income. These variables have completely different scales.

The set of variables on the right shows the standardized version of these variables. The STD methodology has standardized these variables. Since these variables have now been converted to z-scores, we can compare the variables by plotting them on similar scales (Figure 5.2).

Table 5.1: Comparison of Original and Standardized Values

OBS	Original Variables		Standardized Variables	
	INT_RATE	ANNUAL_INC	INT_RATE	ANNUAL_INC
1	13.56	55000	-1.34	-0.548
2	18.94	90000	1.149	-0.097
3	17.97	59280	0.701	-0.493
4	18.84	92000	1.149	-0.071
5	16.14	57250	-0.15	-0.519
6	15.02	152500	-0.66	0.708
7	17.97	51000	0.701	-0.6
8	13.56	65000	-1.34	-0.419
9	17.97	53580	0.701	-0.566
10	14.47	300000	-0.92	2.609

Figure 5.2: Visualization of Original and Standardized Values

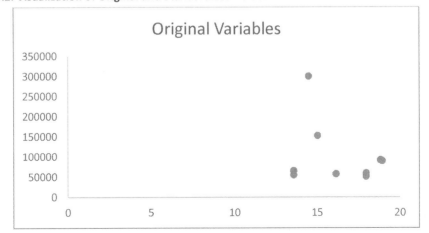

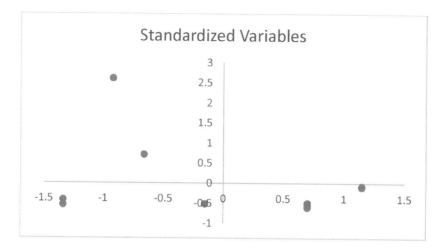

The first scatter plot in Figure 5.2 shows the original scale of the variables. We can see that the annual_inc variable dominates how the data is distributed. However, the second scatterplot shows the standardized variables. This view of the data would be much more beneficial for a nearest-neighbors model because both variables contribute equally to the distribution of the data.

Weight of Evidence

"Win if you can, lose if you must, but always cheat!" – Jesse Ventura

The ETL process is time-consuming. It takes a lot of time to investigate every variable, identify and impute missing values, identify and cap outliers, and apply the appropriate feature scaling technique. Sometimes you are pressed for time, and you need a quick transformation of the data to build a basic model to determine if the project is worth pursuing. Wouldn't it be great if there was a shortcut to all this data processing? Given the opportunity, wouldn't you want to cheat a little?

Welcome to the Weight of Evidence (WOE) transformation.

The WOE expresses the predictive power of an independent variable in relation to the dependent variable. As a general formula, the WOE is calculated by taking the natural logarithm of the division of the percent of non-events and the percentage of events.

$$WOE = \ln \left(\frac{\% \ of \ NonEvents}{\% \ of \ Events} \right)$$

For our example, the Lending Club data set, the dependent (target) variable is labeled as BAD. This is an indicator if a customer had a bad status on a loan defined as a charge-off or a delinquency. The WOE is simply a measure of the separation of "good" and "bad" customers.

$$WOE = \ln \left(\frac{Distribution\ of\ Goods}{Distribution\ of\ Bads} \right)$$

The *Distribution of Goods* is defined as the percentage of good customers in a particular group. The *Distribution of Bads* is defined as the percentage of bad customers in a particular group.

The WOE is a binned procedure. This means that the algorithm creates several bins or numeric ranges of the data and calculates the WOE value for each of these bins. The process is relatively simple:

1. Sort the variable and split it into an equal number of parts. The standard number of bins is either 10 or 20. Therefore, each bin will contain either 10% or 5% of the data.
2. Calculate the number of events and non-events in each bin.
3. Calculate the percent of events and the percent of non-events in each bin.
4. Calculate the WOE by taking the natural log of the % of non-events divided by the % of events.

The WOE score is calculated for each bin. The Information Value is the sum of the percentage of non-events minus the percentage of events multiplied by the WOE value:

$$IV = \sum(\%\ of\ nonevents - \%\ of\ events) * WOE$$

The Information Value is a single metric that describes the strength of the relationship between the dependent and the independent variable.

Let's look at an example. PROC HPBIN is a fast and efficient way to apply the Weight of Evidence and Information Value transformations to your data set. In this example, I have specified that I want to limit the data set to only the total_pymnt variable and that I want 10 bins.

Program 5.35 is split into two parts. The first part creates the mapping algorithm while the second part applies the mapping to the data and creates the WOE bins and Information Value metric.

Program 5.35: Create WOE Transformation

```
PROC HPBIN DATA=MYDATA.BASE (KEEP=total_pymnt) NUMBIN=10;
      INPUT total_pymnt ;
      ODS OUTPUT MAPPING=MAPPING;
RUN;

PROC HPBIN DATA=MYDATA.BASE (KEEP=bad total_pymnt)
      WOE BINS_META=MAPPING;
      TARGET BAD / LEVEL=BINARY ORDER=DESC;
RUN;
```

Output 5.11 shows the results of Program 5.35. You can see that there are 10 bins of information with each bin having a range of values. Each of these bins has metrics for the number of events and non-events. In our example, this can be interpreted as the number of "bad accounts" and the number of "non-bad accounts."

Output 5.11: WOE Output

Range	Non-Event Count	Non-Event Rate	Event Count	Event Rate	WOE	IV
total_pymnt < 6273	108093	84.4%	19987	15.6%	(0.3311)	0.0455
6273 <= total_pymnt < 12547	82081	86.4%	12935	13.6%	(0.1712)	0.0085
12547 <= total_pymnt < 18821	50880	91.1%	4994	8.9%	0.3022	0.0130
18821 <= total_pymnt < 25095	30611	94.1%	1933	5.9%	0.7433	0.0386
25095 <= total_pymnt < 31369	18120	96.1%	742	3.9%	1.1764	0.0477
31369 <= total_pymnt < 37642	9832	97.0%	300	3.0%	1.4706	0.0360
37642 <= total_pymnt < 43916	6847	98.5%	103	1.5%	2.1778	0.0428
43916 <= total_pymnt < 50190	1954	98.8%	23	1.2%	2.4231	0.0140
50190 <= total_pymnt < 56464	455	98.1%	9	1.9%	1.9041	0.0024
56464 <= total_pymnt	99	98.0%	2	2.0%	1.8830	0.0005

Information Value (IV)	0.2490

The Information Values for each of the bins can be totaled for a metric that represents the Information Value of the variable as a whole. This metric represents the strength of the relationship between the predictor and the target variable. The Information Value will range from zero (no predictive relationship) to 1 (complete predictive power).

Table 5.2: WOE Predictive Power Ranges

Information Value (IV)	Predictive Power
<0.02	No predictive value
0.02 to 0.1	Weak predictor
0.1 to 0.3	Medium predictor
0.3 to 0.5	Strong predictor
>0.5	Too good to be true

The WOE and IV algorithm can be applied to all numeric variables in your data set. A general rule is to keep all variables with an IV score greater than 0.1. This is a fast and efficient method of variable selection because you are retaining only the variables that have a strong relationship with the target variable.

Table 5.3 summarizes the pros and cons of the WOE procedure.

Table 5.3: WOE Pros and Cons

Pros	Cons
Handles missing values	Only appropriate for logistic regression modeling
Handles outliers	Hard to interpret values
No need for dummy variables	Creates a step-wise model

The positive aspects of the WOE procedure are pretty straightforward. The negative aspects might need a little explanation.

1. **Only appropriate for logistic regression modeling** – The WOE procedure creates a transformation of the data that is based on the logarithmic value of distributions. This is aligned with the logistic regression output function. Other classification models such as decision trees are not appropriate to use in conjunction with the WOE procedure.

2. **Hard to interpret values** – The output of the WOE procedure is logarithmic transformations of binned data. This output does not have an easy-to-explain common language definition that your manager will understand.

3. **Creates a step-wise model** – The binned procedure of the WOE creates non-continuous categories of information. These binned groups result in a step-wise model rather than a continuous variable model.

Although the limitations of the WOE procedure constrain the applicability of this method, the benefits of the method should not be denied. It is a fast, efficient method that can be used to build a quick logistic regression model and determine the strength of the relationship between the target variable and the predictor variables.

Load

This chapter has focused on the ETL process. We have investigated the Extract and Transform parts, and we are left with the final Load part of the process. Although the Extract and Transform parts required a good amount of explanation and associated code, the Load part is highly dependent on the environment in which you are working. Load refers to loading your final transformed data set into a data warehouse or modeling environment. There are three general types of environments in which the Load step is performed.

Single Machine

If you are a single researcher or a student, then your environment is most likely a single machine in which you have downloaded the data and performed your transformations. You will most likely build and deploy your model in that same environment. In this environment, the Load step is not necessary because the data is already loaded into the environment that you will perform all of the remaining steps of model development and deployment.

Cloud-based Environment

Many data scientists have extracted a data set into a certain environment and performed their transformations on the data. However, the modeling and deployment of the model will be performed in one of the cloud-based environments such as AWS, Azure, IBM, Google, and many other options that offer cloud-based data storage and predictive modeling tools.

For these researchers, once the data has been appropriately transformed in their SAS environment, they would need to export the data (usually as a CSV, txt, or JSON file) and load the data into their selected cloud-based environment.

Corporate Environment

Although the cloud-based environment is rapidly gaining in popularity, the corporate environment is where most data resides. These are data warehouses that only house data for a specific company. These data warehouses are generally owned and operated by that company. In this environment, once you have extracted the data (generally from various databases in the data warehouse) and transformed the data for modeling purposes, you will need to load the data into a database that can be accessed by the appropriate modeling tool.

Even if you have SAS available as the primary analytical tool for your company, you may still have to export your transformed data from your SAS library and load it into an environment that is accessible by other SAS modeling tools such as SAS Enterprise Miner or SAS Viya. The good news is that since these are all SAS systems, there should be no need to export the files in a different format such as CSV or txt. All SAS tools can ingest SAS data sets.

One final note is that even if you have finished the Extract and Transform steps and have continued to build and evaluate your model in your SAS environment, you will still need to export, or Load, the final model output to an environment that can utilize your model output. This is highly dependent on the business purpose of the model. Some models are used to score potential customers on their propensity to apply for a product while other models are used to score customers at the point of application. These are two completely different environments and would require the model to be loaded in the appropriate environment.

Chapter Review

This chapter reviewed the important and time-consuming issues of developing a modeling data set. It is essential that a data scientist thoroughly evaluate their data set and make the transformations that are appropriate for that particular data set. Unfortunately, there is not a standard methodology that will work on all data sets. This is why it is important that a data scientist not only know the coding of how to perform the data transformations, but also the reason why these transformations are necessary. Once your data set is properly prepared, the modeling part will be much easier and much more successful.

Chapter 6: Linear Regression Models

Overview

In the previous chapter, we reviewed the ETL process and all the various data transformations required to prepare a raw data set a modeling data set. This time-consuming process was necessary to ensure that the data is optimized for modeling purposes. Raw data can be rife with missing values, outliers, highly correlated variables, and run-on categories, among many other issues that will cause any modeling algorithm to underperform.

Many of the data transformations that we performed in Chapter 5 were specifically aligned with regression modeling. Now that we understand the theory and practice of ETL, the next step is to do some actual modeling.

Full disclosure: Linear regression models might be my favorite type of predictive model. This may sound strange when there are so many different types of complex models that are extremely interesting and produce extraordinarily precise model results. In comparison, linear regression seems simplistic and outdated. However, linear regression models are the bedrock of machine learning models. These models are fast to train, work well with high-dimensional data, and are highly interpretable. When appropriately developed, these models are often comparable to the more sophisticated machine learning models described later in this book. These models also have the added benefit of transparency, and they provide the business with information on individual variables that can be used to make business decisions.

This chapter will review the structure and implementation of linear regression and expand upon it to include different variations of the regression approach as well as how to use these methods.

Regression Structure

If you remember your Stats 101 course, you probably remember the basic structure of the linear regression model.

Equation 6.1: Linear Regression

$$Y \approx \beta_0 + \beta_1 X_1$$

This equation can be interpreted as the target variable (Y) can be approximately determined ($\approx$) by the combination of an intercept value (β_0) and the value of a single variable (X_1) multiplied by its coefficient (β_1). If you were to look at this graphically, the equation would be represented by a straight line where the intercept value (β_0) crosses the y-axis, and the single variable (X) is represented on the x-axis with the coefficient (β_1) determining the slope of the straight line that connects the two points.

Figure 6.1 should look familiar. We used it before to demonstrate the relationship between two variables back in Chapter 1: Data Science Overview.

Figure 6.1: Simple Linear Regression Visualization

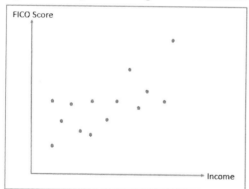
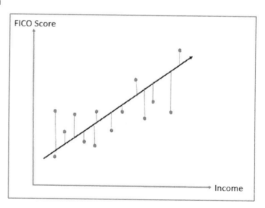

The graph on the left of Figure 6.1 shows a scatter plot graph of the distribution of FICO score and income. This graph demonstrates a positive relationship between the predictor variable (Income) and the target variable (FICO score). Although there is a positive relationship, it is not a one-to-one perfectly fit relationship. We can see that there is a general upward trend, but it does not look like a perfect match between the two variables.

The graph on the right shows a linear trend line and error bars that demonstrate the residual error of the linear model. You can draw many different straight lines through these points; however, the line with the best fit to the data will be the one where the residual error is minimized. The residual error is a summary of the squared value of the distance between each of the observations and the regression line. Equation 6.2 represents the residual sum of squares.

Equation 6.2: Residual Sum of Squares

$$RSS = \sum_{i=1}^{n}(y_i - \hat{y}_i)^2$$

We can construct a simple linear regression that models the relationship between these two variables. Equation 6.3 represents the relationship between FICO Score and Income.

Equation 6.3: FICO Score Regression Equation

$$FICO\ Score \approx \beta_0 + \beta_1(Income)$$

This equation simply states that FICO Score can be approximately determined by an intercept value, and a person's income multiplied by a constant value. Remember that a FICO score is a score created by credit bureaus that represents customer risk based on several personal financial indicators such as credit history, credit tenure, number of open accounts and several other financial metrics.

Let's look at some actual values. Table 6.1 shows a table of values that represents a person's annual income and their associated FICO Score. The top chart of Figure 6.2 graphically represents this table. We can easily see that there is a positive relationship between FICO Score and Income. However, we may want to create an equation to model this relationship. This could help us with estimating a person's FICO Score if the only information that we have is that person's income.

Table 6.1

Income (in thousands)	FICO Score
20	525
25	546
32	545
29	595
45	610
38	635
48	643
70	679
65	585
66	695
90	716
72	728
95	745
88	753
71	770
100	794
95	805
125	826
87	838
113	845

Figure 6.2: Visualization of Income and FICO Table

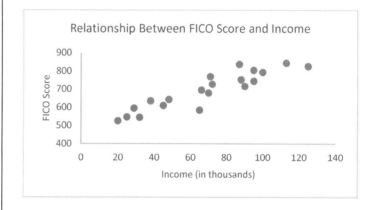

The bottom chart of Figure 6.2 shows a line that represents the linear relationship between FICO Score and Income. The equation y = 480 + 3.1(x) can be interpreted this way. A person's FICO Score can be estimated by the equation 480 plus the value of 3.1 times the person's income, represented in thousands of dollars.

Let's test it out. We can look at the data in Table 6.1 and apply the equation created from the simple linear regression model to produce estimated values. Table 6.2 shows the model results for each observation and the squared residual value.

Table 6.2: Table of Model Results

Income (in thousands)	FICO Score	Model Results	Squared Difference
20	525	542	289
25	546	558	132
32	545	579	1,170
29	595	570	630
90	716	759	1,849
72	728	703	615
95	745	775	870
88	753	753	0
71	770	700	4,886
100	794	790	16
95	805	775	930
125	826	868	1,722
87	838	750	7,797
113	845	830	216

The model results represented in the third column of Table 6.2 have been created by applying the linear regression formula to the Income variable. For example, the first row of data shows that the income for that observation is 20. We can place that value into the equation 480 + 3.1(x) to get 480 + 3.1(20). The result of this equation is 542. The actual value is represented in the second column of the table. In order to calculate the squared difference, we would use the formula $(y_i - \hat{y}_i)^2$. We can input our actual values to get the equation $(525 - 542)^2$. This will get us the squared difference of 289. When we apply the Residual Sum of Square (RSS) formula to the data set, we simply sum all the squared residual values. This gives us a total RSS value of 32,543.

It is important to note that the RSS value does not have any inherent meaning. It can only be interpreted in relation to other RSS values that are calculated from creating other linear predictions for this data set. For example, Figure 6.3 shows a competing linear equation for the same data set.

Figure 6.3: Comparison of Linear Regression Lines

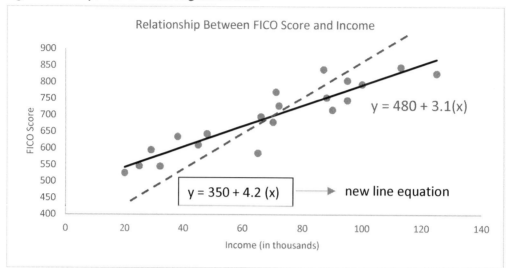

If we again look at the first observation in Table 6.1 and use the new line equation to estimate the target value (FICO Score), we would get 350 + 4.2(20). The result of this equation is 434. We can then take the squared residual for this new predicted value by squaring the difference between the actual value and the predicted value $(525 - 434)^2$. The squared residual for this observation is 8,281. That value is considerably higher than the squared residual value for this observation generated by the original linear regression equation.

If we sum all the squared residuals for this new line equation, the RSS is 115,185. Again, this value does not mean anything by itself. It is only when we compare it to the original line equation's RSS value of 32.543 that we can determine that the original line fits the data better than the new line because the original line has a lower RSS value. This is a tedious way to explain the simple concept that when interpreting RSS values, lower is better.

Gradient Descent

At this point, you may ask how an algorithm chooses a certain set of coefficients for a linear regression model. In the previous example, when the algorithm produced the equation y=480+3.1(x), how did it arrive at these values? The answer is gradient descent.

Gradient descent formalizes the concept of "lower is better" in relation to error metrics. It is a generic optimization algorithm capable of finding optimal solutions to a variety of problems. The concept is very simplistic yet powerful. First, let's define an important term.

Cost function – Measures the performance of a predictive model. This function quantifies the error between the actual value and the predicted value and represents it as a single metric. For example, the Residual Sum of Squares (RSS) is a single error metric produced by a cost function (Equation 6.2).

Gradient descent is a method of applying the cost function to a variety of parameters (for linear regression that would be β) and adjusting these parameters in a way that methodically decreases the cost function (RSS) until it cannot reduce the cost function any further.

The gradient descent algorithm loops through a series of steps to reach a final value. These steps are outlined below.

1. The gradient descent algorithm begins by assigning β a random value. This is called *random initialization*. The cost function is then applied, and the resulting error metric (RSS) is calculated.

2. The gradient descent algorithm will assign a new value for β and calculate the error metric for this value. If the resulting new cost function value is higher than the previous cost function value, then that is considered an inferior result. Remember that lower is better.

3. If the previous result was inferior and the new value was **higher** than the initial value, the gradient descent algorithm will assign a **lower** value for β and calculate the error metric. However, if the previous result was inferior and the new value was **lower** than the initial value, the gradient descent algorithm will assign a **higher** value for β and calculate the error metric. This method is how the gradient descent method decides which direction (higher or lower) to adjust the value for β.

4. If the new error metric is lower than the previous error metric, then the gradient descent will continue to apply a new value to β that is either higher or lower than the previous value depending on whether higher or lower values are resulting in better (lower) error metrics. The amount of adjustment to the value of β is called the *learning rate.*

5. The gradient descent algorithm will stop this process when it cannot find a lower error metric. The minimum error metric is called *convergence.*

We can better understand this concept when we look at it graphically. The left side of Figure 6.4 shows the relationship between the β values and the cost function. The initial random value for β is depicted on the left side of the graph. It should be no surprise that a random value has a high RSS value. When a new value is applied to β, the corresponding cost function decreases. This process is repeated several times until a β value is determined that produces the minimum cost function value.

The right side of Figure 6.4 shows this same concept expressed through tangents. The initial random value has a tangent with a high-degree slope. The phrase *gradient descent* means that the estimate will move in the direction where the slope of the tangent line is less than the previous estimate. This process will continue until a slope of zero is achieved.

Figure 6.4: Gradient Descent Visualizations

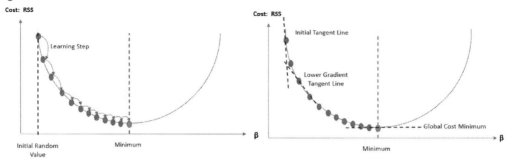

A critical point to note is that the learning rate determines the size of the steps for each of the adjustments to the value of β. The value of the learning rate can have a significant impact on model performance and outcome. For example, if the learning rate is set too low, the algorithm will have to go through many iterations to converge at the final minimum cost function value. This can significantly affect the processing time to run your model. Figure 6.5 graphically shows the impact of a small learning rate.

Figure 6.5: Small Learning Rate Visualization

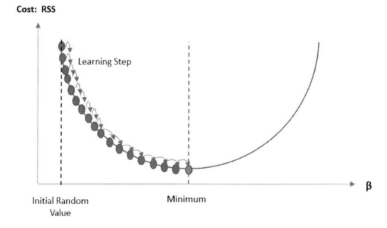

Of course, the opposite can be true where the learning rate can be set too high. Rather than incremental steps, the algorithm takes large steps across the cost curve. This can result in the algorithm being unable to converge at the global minimum. Figure 6.6 graphically depicts this process.

Figure 6.6: Large Learning Rate Visualization

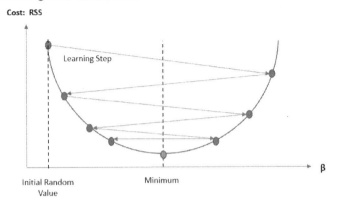

Let's shift from the theoretical to the practical. A few pages ago, in Table 6.2, we showed a table of FICO and Income values and the associated model results for each pair of values. This table was generated by a simple linear regression algorithm that produced the equation y=480+3.1(x). Let's look behind the scenes to determine how the algorithm produced this equation.

Remember that the gradient descent algorithm will provide some initial random values for the intercept and the slope of the line (β). The algorithm will then adjust those values, and the size of those adjustments is called the learning rate.

To simplify the study of this process, let's just focus on the adjustments made to the slope. Table 6.3 contains the results of a gradient descent algorithm, where the learning rate was set to adjust the slope by one point for each iteration. The resulting RSS value is contained in the table.

This table can be represented graphically. Figure 6.7 plots the resulting RSS values for each of the slope values.

Table 6.3: RSS Table

Coefficient	RSS Value
β=7.1	1,817,164
β=6.1	1,034,330
β=5.1	475,949
β=4.1	142,020
β=3.1	32,543
β=2.1	147,518
β=1.1	486,944
β=0.1	1,050,823
β=-0.1	1,190,533
β=-1.1	2,023,754

Figure 6.7: RSS Table Visualization

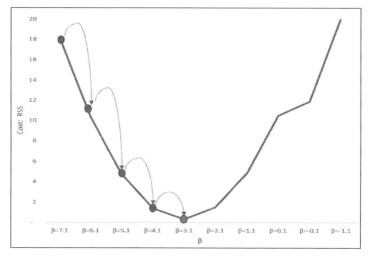

If the initial random value of the slope was set at 7.1 and the learning rate was set where the value of the slope would be adjusted by one point for each iteration, then the resulting gradient descent curve would look like the left-hand side of Figure 6.7. The algorithm would start with a high RSS value and make adjustments that would decrease the RSS methodically. This process would continue until a global minimum was reached. This is the point where any additional adjustments to the slope would not reduce the RSS value.

However, if the learning rate were set too high, the algorithm would produce results that would jump from the left-hand side of the graph to the right-hand side of the graph. This would be inefficient and could result in non-convergence.

Linear Regression Assumptions

Linear regression models are not appropriate for all data sets. For a linear regression model to function properly, the underlying data needs to meet certain criteria. It is often the case that the underlying data does not meet one or more of the requirements and needs to be adjusted.

1. Linear relationship
2. Multivariate normality
3. Little to no multicollinearity
4. No autocorrelation
5. Homoscedasticity

Linear Relationship

Each of the independent variables (predictors) needs to have a linear relationship with the dependent variable (target). A quick way to assess the relationship between two numeric variables is to create a scatter plot between them. Figure 6.8 demonstrates how scatter plots can be used to assess the relationship between the dependent variable (Y) and an independent variable (X).

Figure 6.8: Data Distributions

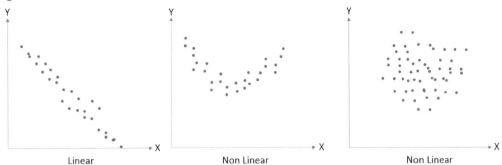

The first chart in Figure 6.8 shows a standard linear relationship between the dependent and independent variables. The general trend of the data shows that as the independent variable (X) increases, the dependent variable (Y) decreases.

Although the middle chart in Figure 6.8 shows a non-linear relationship between the dependent and independent variables, it can still be used in linear regression by creating a polynomial variable that captures the dynamic relationship between these two variables. Instead of using the X variable in its current form, we could square the variable to capture the curve of the general trend between the two variables.

The third chart shows no relationship between the two variables. This variable would not be selected for the linear regression model.

Multivariate Normality

The assumption of multivariate normality states that all variables are assumed to be normally distributed. The normal distribution is a bell-shaped curve where most of the observations are gathered at the mean value. The volume of observations decreases, the further away that they move from the mean value. Figure 6.9 shows the normal distribution and the number of observations contained within the range of one, two, and three standard deviations.

Figure 6.9: Normal Distribution Curve

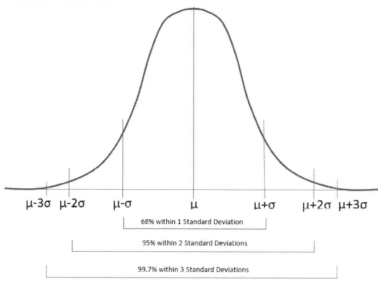

The assumption of multivariate normality can be checked visually with a histogram or a Q-Q plot. Normality can also be checked statistically with a Kolmogorov-Smirnov test. Often, a non-normally distributed variable can be transformed into a normally distributed variable by a non-linear transformation, such as a log transformation.

Multicollinearity

Multicollinearity only occurs in algorithms that have more than one variable. Therefore, it cannot be present in a simple linear regression model. However, for regression models with more than one variable, multicollinearity occurs when two or more explanatory variables are highly linearly correlated.

The problem of multicollinearity: The primary goal of a regression model is to isolate the relationship between each independent (predictor) variable and the dependent (target) variable. Each of the regression model's coefficients represents the mean change in the independent variable given a one-unit change in the dependent variable **holding all other variables constant**.

The problem of multicollinearity is that if two or more variables are highly correlated, changes in one variable necessarily mean changes in a separate variable that is highly correlated with it. This similarity violates the assumption of independence between the variables. When multicollinearity is present, the model cannot estimate the relationship between each of the independent variables and the dependent variable separately because the highly correlated independent variables tend to move in unison.

The consequences of multicollinearity: Multicollinearity can have a severe impact on your model estimates and accuracy:

- The coefficient estimates can change drastically depending on which other variables are in the model. This is because multicollinearity can increase the variance in the coefficient estimates and make the estimates very sensitive to minor changes in the model. The model will become unstable and difficult to interpret. This instability is a sure sign that the variables are not independent.

- The presence of multicollinearity reduces the precision of the coefficient estimates. This weakens the statistical power of the model. The P-values may not be a strong indicator of statistical significance, and the result is that you will not be able to trust the output of the model.

When multicollinearity is present, you will not be able to evaluate each of the variables in your model independently. Small changes in one variable can result in large changes in a separate variable. This can even result in the coefficient estimate sign changing from positive to negative. You will not even trust that a given variable should be retained in the model due to the weakened P-values that are a result of the inflated variance.

How to detect multicollinearity: You can detect multicollinearity using certain tests that are available in the REG procedure. This procedure has the option to produce the following tests: correlation matrix (COLLIN), tolerance (TOL), and variance inflation factor (VIF).

Correlation Matrix – The COLLIN option in a PROC REG can produce a Pearson's correlation matrix that contains the correlation coefficients for each of the variable pairs in the data set. The correlation coefficient needs to be less than 1 in order to be retained in the modeling data set. A good global check to see if there is multicollinearity anywhere in the model is to evaluate the *condition index* produced by the COLLIN option. If any variable has a condition index greater than 30, then there is definitely multicollinearity in the data.

Variance Inflation Factor – This test measures the increase in an independent variable's variance due to other independent variables in the model. This test is produced with the VIF option in PROC REG. Although the issue of where to set the threshold for the VIF varies by project, a good rule of thumb is that the VIF for each of the variables in the model should be less than 5.

Tolerance – The tolerance is the proportion of variance in each independent variable that is not explained by all the other independent variables. This test is produced by the TOL option in PROC REG. The tolerance is defined as 1/VIF.

How to fix multicollinearity: The simplest approach is to remove variables with high VIF values. I suggest removing the variable with the highest VIF value first and then rerunning the model. The new model will have recalculated the VIF values for the remaining variables. One at a time, keep removing each variable that exceeds the VIF threshold until you have a data set where all variables have a VIF value that is lower than your threshold.

A second approach to deal with multicollinearity is to transform the data by centering the data. This approach simply calculates the mean for each independent variable and then subtracts the mean from each observation within that variable. These newly "centered" variables are used in the model. This approach is easily performed in SAS with PROC STDIZE.

Autocorrelation

Autocorrelation is usually an issue that occurs in time series data. Autocorrelation occurs when the *residuals* are not independent of one another. It is common in time series data that the errors in one time period are correlated with the errors in the previous time period. This is a form of lagged correlation. The presence of autocorrelation can drastically reduce the model's accuracy.

The problem of autocorrelation: A positive autocorrelation among the residuals results in the estimate of the error variance being too small. When the error variance is incorrectly small, this results in the confidence intervals being too narrow, and there is a higher probability that the true null hypotheses will be rejected.

A negative autocorrelation among the residuals results in the error variance being too large and consequently, the confidence intervals being too wide. When this occurs, the power of the significance test is reduced.

How to check for autocorrelation: A scatter plot of the residuals can show a pattern of autocorrelation. This scatter plot of residuals should have a random design with no discernible pattern. If autocorrelation is present, you will often see a U-shaped pattern in the residuals or some other curved shaped pattern.

The best way to check for autocorrelation is the Durbin-Watson D test. This test can be produced with the DW option in PROC REG. This test will produce a value between 0 and 4. Values around 2 (between 1.5 and 2.5) indicate that there is no autocorrelation present.

The Durbin-Watson D test is used to detect *first-order* autocorrelation. First-order means that observations that are one unit apart are correlated. Although the Durbin-Watson D test is not designed to test for second-order autocorrelation, this test adequately detects most instances of autocorrelation because most forms of autocorrelation exhibit some form of first-order autocorrelation.

How to fix autocorrelation: Autocorrelation is generally a result of a relevant missing independent variable in the model. So, the first thing that you should do is to think about the variables that you have in your model and try to figure out what other pieces of information could be missing that would explain the variation in your dependent variable.

If you do not have access to more data, then the second approach is to apply a different modeling technique to the data. This would most often be a time series specific model such as an autoregression model. SAS has a long list of time series models that can be used to address autocorrelation. One of my favorites is the AUTOREG procedure.

Homoscedasticity

Homoscedasticity is a fancy way of saying that the variance around the regression line should be relatively constant. Figure 6.10 shows an example plot of a single predictor (X) and the target value (Y). Notice that the observations at the beginning and endpoints of the regression line have a relatively equal distance from the regression line. However, the observations in the middle demonstrate a wide variance from the regression line.

Figure 6.10: Homoscedasticity Visualization

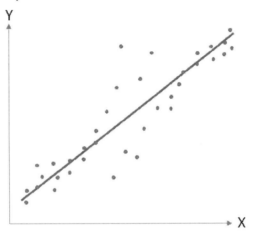

The "noise" around the regression line should be consistent. When the predictor does not have consistent variance, this is called *heteroscedasticity*.

The problem of heteroscedasticity: The goal of an ordinary least squares regression model is to minimize residuals in order to produce the smallest possible standard error. The regression model gives equal weight to all observations; however, when heteroscedasticity is present, the observations with larger variance from the regression line have a greater influence on the model than the observations closer to the regression line. This can result in the standard errors being biased, which will, in turn, lead to incorrect conclusions about the significance of the regression coefficients.

How to check for heteroscedasticity: There are three main tests that check for heteroscedasticity:

> **White test** – The logic of the White test is a bit complicated, but basically, it takes the squared residuals from the original regression model and uses them as additional predictors along with the original independent variables as inputs into a second regression model. The theory is that if heteroscedasticity is present, then the coefficients in the new regression model should not be equal to zero and the R^2 value will be large.
>
> The White test can be called in several different modeling procedures in SAS using the (WHITE) option. The null hypothesis is that the model errors are homoscedastic. The model output will contain a table titled "Heteroscedasticity Test" and this table will

have a P-value. This P-value can be used to accept/reject the null hypothesis of homoscedasticity.

Breusch-Pagan test – This test is very similar to the White test where an initial regression model is created, and the residual output from that model is used as a predictor along with the original independent variable as inputs into a second regression model. The *overall model P-value* (usually found in the ANOVA model output) is used to determine whether the null hypothesis (that the model errors are homoscedastic) should be rejected.

The Breusch-Pagan test can be called in several different modeling procedures in SAS using the (BREUSCH) option.

Lagrange Multiplier test – This test is similar to the White and Breusch-Pagan tests. This test tests for cross-sectional or time effects based on the residuals from a restricted model. It is most often used in conjunction with the Breusch-Pagan test. Due to its ability to detect effects from time series data, it is most often used with time series models such as PROC AUTOREG.

The options (GARCH) and (ARCHTEST) are most commonly used to test for serial correlation in time series data.

How to fix heteroscedasticity: There are three common remedies for heteroscedasticity:

Box-Cox transformation – You can often solve the problem of heteroscedasticity by transforming the dependent (Y) variable with the Box-Cox transformation. This is a method of transforming a variable into a normal distribution. SAS provides an easy method to implement the Box-Cox with the TRANSREG procedure.

Weighted Least Squares – Remember that the underlying issue with heteroscedasticity is that due to the increased variance of some variables, they have more influence (or weight) in the model. You can calculate the weights manually with the following steps:

1. Create an initial simple linear regression model with the target variable and the predictor that displays heteroscedasticity.
2. Calculate the absolute value of the residuals from that model.
3. Create a second simple linear regression model that regresses the predictor variable on the newly created absolute value of the residuals variable.
4. Calculate the weights using estimated standard deviations.

Program 6.1 shows an example of each step of this process.

Program 6.1: Create Weighted Least Squares

```
/*Create initial simple linear regression model*/
PROC REG DATA=example;
  MODEL Y=X;
  OUTPUT OUT=pred RESIDUAL=RESID;
RUN;
```

```
/*Create the absolute value of the residuals*/
DATA abs_resid;
  SET pred;
  absresid = ABS(RESID);
RUN;

/*Create another simple linear regression model*/
/*Regress X on the absolute value of the residuals*/
PROC REG DATA=abs_resid;
  MODEL absresid = X;
  OUTPUT OUT=abs_weights PREDICTED=abs_hat;
RUN;

/*Compute weights using estimated standard deviations*/
DATA weights;
  SET abs_weights;
  weight = 1/(abs_hat**2);
RUN;
```

Rebuild the model with new predictors – Starting over is always the last option; however, sometimes if all else fails, you will need to reimagine your project with new data attributes.

Linear Regression

Simple linear regression is the most basic parametric model that we can develop. This model only has two components; a target variable and a single predictor. This simple structure can be expanded upon to create very complex model designs. However, let's start with the basic simple linear regression and increase its complexity throughout the next several sections.

To provide a hands-on demonstration, we will use the Lending Club data set that we developed in Chapter 5: Create a Modeling Data Set. Remember that this is a real-world data set and not one that was developed for academic purposes. We can expect that the results won't be pretty with perfectly shaped bell curves and sky-high R^2 values.

The target variable that we developed in Chapter 5 was a binary indicator. Regression models require a continuous target variable. So, we need to select a different variable to serve as our target variable.

All data science projects should be focused on solving a single problem. The target variable is a singular representation of that problem. This is the value that you want to predict or understand the driving factors for. So, let's make up a business problem and choose a variable that would help us solve this problem.

Since the Lending Club data set is a loan database and we know that a financial firm generates revenue on the interest income generated on revolving balances, it could be beneficial for a financial firm if they could predict the total outstanding revolving balance for an account and understand the factors that drive the revolving balance.

Analyze the Target Variable

To this end, let's select the revol_bal variable as the target variable. The definition of this variable from the Lending Club data dictionary is "Total credit revolving balance." That appears to be exactly what we are looking for.

The first step is to always investigate the target variable. Program 6.2 creates a PROC UNIVARIATE on the revol_bal variable.

Program 6.2: PROC UNIVARIATE on the Target Variable

```
PROC UNIVARIATE DATA=MYDATA.BASE; VAR revol_bal; HISTOGRAM; RUN;
```

Remember that we transformed the raw Lending Club data set into a fully adjusted modeling data set back in Chapter 5: Create a Modeling Data Set. This data set has been transformed by replacing missing values with the appropriate mean value and capping outliers according to the 1.5 IQR rule. Due to these transformations, we should expect that there will be an unnatural limitation when we examine the summary stats and graphs of the data.

Output 6.1 shows the output from the PROC UNIVARIATE of the revol_bal variable.

Output 6.1: Results of Program 6.2

Moments			
N	350000	Sum Weights	350000
Mean	13873.6356	Sum Observations	4855772455
Std Deviation	9841.44651	Variance	96854069.5
Skewness	0.65896941	Kurtosis	-0.7231103
Uncorrected SS	1.01266E14	Corrected SS	3.38988E13
Coeff Variation	70.9363198	Std Error Mean	16.6350808

Basic Statistical Measures			
Location		Variability	
Mean	13873.64	Std Deviation	9841
Median	11334.00	Variance	96854069
Mode	32713.50	Range	32714
		Interquartile Range	14253

Quantiles (Definition 5)	
Level	Quantile
100% Max	32713.5
99%	32713.5
95%	32713.5
90%	32713.5
75% Q3	20208.0
50% Median	11334.0
25% Q1	5955.0
10%	2934.0
5%	1566.0
1%	123.0
0% Min	0.0

The transformation of the data results in an unnatural pattern where the top 10% of observations all have the same value (32713.5). This is because the top 10% were considered outliers according to the 1.5 IQR rule, and they were capped at that value.

Since the revol_bal variable will be the target variable in this model, we will need to decide on how to treat this variable. The current distribution of this variable is shown in Output 6.2.

Output 6.2: Target Variable Histogram

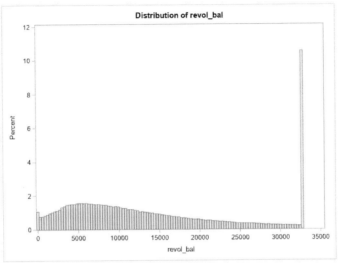

We can obviously see that the top 10% of values have all been capped at a constant value and that this creates a skewed representation of the data. It might be hard to tell from this graph, but the low-end outliers were also capped at zero (no negative values).

These artificial limitations can help the model when the variable is a predictor; however, we must treat the target variable with extra caution since all the predictor variables will be trying to correlate with the target variable.

Decision Time

In this case, I suggest that we limit the data set to observations where the revol_bal variable has values between 10 and 30000. This limitation will avoid any of the consequences of transforming the variable, and we will be able to test the model performance on those values above 30000 once the model has been completed.

Program 6.3 limits the data to observations where revol_bal is between 10 and 30000 and creates a PROC UNIVARIATE on this newly restricted data set.

Program 6.3: Filter Data Based on Target Variable Values

```
DATA base_reg;
  SET MYDATA.MODEL_TRAIN;
  WHERE 10 le revol_bal le 30000;
RUN;

PROC UNIVARIATE DATA=base_reg;
    VAR revol_bal;
    HISTOGRAM;
RUN;
```

Output 6.3 shows the histogram for the revol_bal variable created from the newly restricted data set.

Output 6.3: Revised Histogram of Target Variable

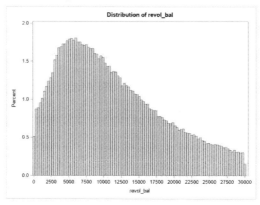

A few things to note about the newly restricted data set and the distribution of the target variable revol_bal:

- The target variable has a fairly widespread that ranges from 10 to 30,000.

- The distribution has a slight right-hand skew.

- The mean value of the target variable is 11,293, but the largest percentage of observations occur around a revol_bal of 6,000.

Because the distribution is skewed to the right, this is called *positively skewed data*. The methods of transformations for positively skewed data are log, square root, and cube root transformations.

If the data was skewed to the left, it would be considered *negatively skewed data*, and it could be transformed with the square (not square root), cube root, and log transformations.

After a bit of experimenting, the square-root method appears to be the transformation that best adjusts the target variable into a normal distribution. Program 6.4 shows the transformation and Output 6.4 shows the resulting histogram.

Program 6.4: Transform the Target Variable

```
DATA base_reg;
  SET MYDATA.MODEL_TRAIN;
  WHERE 10 le revol_bal le 30000;
  sqrt_revol_bal = sqrt(revol_bal);
  DROP revol_bal;
RUN;
```

```
PROC UNIVARIATE DATA=base_reg;
      VAR sqrt_revol_bal;
      HISTOGRAM;
RUN;
```

Output 6.4: Transformed Target Variable Histogram

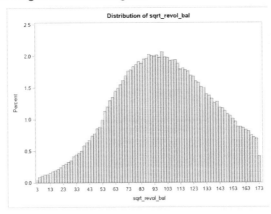

Although the newly transformed target variable has a slightly negative skew, we can see that it is a much better approximation of the normal distribution than the raw variable.

Analyze the Predictor Variables

Now that we have selected the target variable, restricted the data set, and transformed the target variable into a normal distribution, we can now move forward with analyzing the predictor variables. In Chapter 5, we converted all the character variables into numeric representations of those variables. These transformations will make developing a regression model much easier because we will not have to analyze character variables separately, and we do not have to worry about degrees of freedom for those character variables in our regression model.

Continuous Variables

Although there are several continuous variables in our data set, we will want to retain only those that are in line with our business objective. If, for example, we retained the predictor variable revol_util, which is defined as "revolving line utilization rate," this would defeat the purpose of the model. We are trying to find predictors that are independent of the target variable yet are correlated with the target variable. Some variables, such as revol_util, are just a different expression of the target variable, which is defined as the revolving balance. If we were to retain that variable, it would be a nearly perfect predictor, but no new information would be gained.

Decision Time

A data scientist will often have to make decisions on which variables to include in the modeling data set. Not all variables will be appropriate for the business purpose of the model.

Variables that should not be included in a modeling data set include:

- Variables that are a different way of expressing the target variable
- Variables that will cause a spurious correlation
- Variables that would not be available at the point of implementation of the model
- Variables that would not be useful in business decisions

I know that many instructional texts say that you can include all variables and let the modeling algorithm select the significant ones. Although that is one way of building a model, the risk associated with this approach is that you could end up with a model that makes no sense, does not help with solving your business problem, and would not be implementable. With this in mind, we are going to select a few appropriate variables that we will retain in the modeling data set and define the business justification for keeping them. Table 6.4 shows the continuous variables that we will keep.

Table 6.4: Retained Model Variables

Variable	Description	Business Justification
annual_Inc	The self-reported annual income provided by the borrower during registration	Indictor of financial status
bc_Util	Ratio of the total current balance to the high credit/credit limit for all bankcard accounts	Indicator of credit utilization
dti	A ratio calculated using the borrower's total monthly debt payments, divided by the borrower's self-reported monthly income	Indicator of financial status
loan_Amnt	The listed amount of the loan applied for by the borrower	Total loan obligation
mths_since_oldest_il_open	Months since the oldest bank installment account opened	Indicator of credit tenure
mths_since_recent_bc	Months since the most recent bankcard account opened	Indicator of credit-seeking behavior

Variable	Description	Business Justification
pct_tl_nvr_dlq	Percent of trades that were never delinquent	Indicator of credit stability
tot_hi_cred_lim	Total high credit/credit limit	Indicator of overall credit strength

Let's examine these variables and their relationship with the target variable. Program 6.5 develops a global variable called "cont" and a macro that will loop through this list of variables and create a scatter plot of each variable and the target variable. I have retained only 5000 observations so that the scatter plot is not too overwhelming to look at.

Program 6.5: Scatter Plot of Continuous Variables Macro

```
%let cont = annual_inc bc_util dti loan_amnt mo_sin_old_il_acct
mths_since_recent_bc pct_tl_nvr_dlq tot_hi_cred_lim     total_bc_limit
total_rec_int;


%MACRO loopit(mylist);
        %LET n = %SYSFUNC(countw(&mylist));

        %DO I=1 %TO &n;
                %LET val = %SCAN(&mylist,&I);
                        proc sgplot data=base_reg (obs=5000);
                          SCATTER X=&val.
                                        Y=sqrt_revol_bal;
                        RUN;
        %END;
%MEND;
%LET list = &cont.;
%loopit(&list);
```

Let's look at a few examples of the macro output. Output 6.5 shows the output of three continuous variables plotted against the target variable.

Output 6.5: Scatter Plots of Continuous Variables

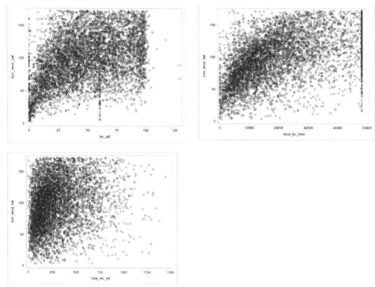

We can see that the first two scatter plots have a positive relationship with the target variable, and this relationship appears to be concave. This could be the result of the target variable being transformed by the square root function. The last graph on the right does not appear to demonstrate a relationship between the predictor variable and the target.

Based on the distribution of observations displayed in the scatter plot graphs, we can infer that a simple linear model will produce skewed residuals. A linear regression line that cuts straight through either of the first two predictors will result in a U-shaped residual plot. Therefore, we can experiment with transforming the predictor variables with a method that would result in a linear relationship between the target and the predictors.

Program 6.6 develops the square root transformation for two of the predictor variables. The full code for all the variables is contained in the GitHub repository.

Program 6.6: Transformation of Predictor Variables

```
data change;
  set base_reg;
  sqrt_annual_inc = sqrt(annual_inc);
  sqrt_bc_util = sqrt(bc_util);
run;
```

We can now create a global macro of the newly transformed square root versions of the continuous variables and run the macro on these variables in the new data set.

Program 6.7: Scatter Plot Macro of Transformed Predictor Variables

```
%let trans = sqrt_annual_inc sqrt_bc_util sqrt_dti sqrt_loan_amnt
sqrt_mo_sin_old_il_acct sqrt_mths_since_recent_bc sqrt_pct_tl_nvr_dlq
sqrt_tot_hi_cred_lim sqrt_total_bc_limit   sqrt_total_rec_int;

%MACRO loopit(mylist);
     %LET n = %SYSFUNC(countw(&mylist));

     %DO I=1 %TO &n;
          %LET val = %SCAN(&mylist,&I);
               proc sgplot data=change (obs=5000);
                 SCATTER X=&val.
                              Y=sqrt_revol_bal;
               RUN;
     %END;
%MEND;
%LET list = &trans.;
%loopit(&list);
```

Let's check out the scatter plots of the same variables that we previously investigated. Output 6.6 shows the square root versions of the same variables shown in Output 6.5.

Output 6.6: Scatter Plots of Transformed Predictor Variables

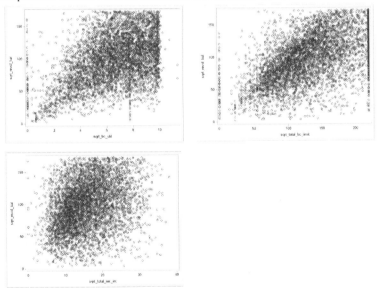

Notice how the first two scatter plots display a linear relationship with the target variable while the third scatter plot displays no relationship between the target and the predictor.

Interval Variables

Interval variables are whole number numeric variables (0,1,2,3, and so on). This type of data is not appropriate for a scatter plot analysis. Instead, we can develop box plots to inspect the data visually. Program 6.8 identifies the variables that would be appropriate for modeling and creates a macro that produces box plots for each of these variables.

Program 6.8: Box Plot Macro for Interval Variables

```
%let box = acc_open_past_24mths app_individual app_joint emp_10 emp_0to4
emp_5to9 emp_NA grade_A grade_B grade_C grade_D grade_E grade_F grade_G
home_mort home_own home_rent     inq_last_6mths int_rate mo_sin_rcnt_tl
months_since_issue mort_acc mths_since_recent_inq num_actv_bc_tl num_bc_tl
open_acc purpose_cc purpose_dc purpose_hi purpose_other recoveries term_36
term_60 ver_not ver_source ver_verified;

%MACRO loopit(mylist);
        %LET n = %SYSFUNC(countw(&mylist));

        %DO I=1 %TO &n;
              %LET val = %SCAN(&mylist,&I);

proc sort data=change (keep=sqrt_revol_bal &val.) out=out; by &val.;

              proc boxplot data-out ;
                    plot sqrt_revol_bal*&val.;
                    inset min mean max stddev /
                          header = 'Overall Statistics'
                          pos     = tm;
                    insetgroup min max /
                          header = "Revol_Bal by &val.";
              run;
        %END;
%MEND;
%LET list = &box;
%loopit(&list);
```

Notes on Program 6.8:

- A global macro labeled "box" is created that contains all the interval variables appropriate for modeling.

- A macro is created that loops through each of the variables.

- The data is sorted by the interval variable.

- A box plot is created for each interval variable compared to the target variable.

Let's check out a few of the box plots created from this macro in Output 6.7.

Output 6.7: Box Plots of Interval Variables

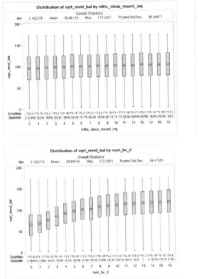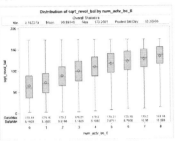

The first chart on the left shows a fairly even level of interaction between the target variable and the predictor. This variable does not tell us much about the target variable, and it will most likely not be picked up in the model.

The second and third charts do show a dynamic relationship between the target and the predictors. As the predictor interval increases, the target variable increases in a nearly linear fashion. We should expect these two variables to be significant in the regression model.

The interval variables do not appear to require any form of transformation. Although it is a common practice to transform continuous variables to make their distribution closer to the normal distribution, it is not normally required for interval variables.

Simple Linear Regression

Simple linear regression is a basic approach that can be used on each of the potential predictor variables to gain more insight into their relationship with the target variable. This type of model contains only the target variable and a single predictor. Program 6.9 creates a simple linear regression model using the target sqrt_revol_bal and the predictor sqrt_total_bc_limit.

Program 6.9: Simple Linear Regression

```
ODS GRAPHICS ON;
PROC REG DATA=change (obs=5000)
        PLOTS(ONLY)=ALL;
        MODEL sqrt_revol_bal = sqrt_total_bc_limit /
                SLE=0.1
                SLS=0.1
```

```
            INCLUDE=0;
      OUTPUT OUT=WORK.REG_PRED PREDICTED=P RESIDUAL=R;
RUN;
```

Notes on Program 6.9:

- The ODS Graphics option is turned on to create charts and graphical output that will help us analyze the model. Notice in the DATA statement that I've specified to select only 5000 observations. This limitation is because the graphical output will not be produced with a high number of observations. The data is random, so using the first 5000 observations should be adequate for our purposes; however, after I made my assessments on the sampled data, I would then run the model on the full data set.

- The REG procedure is used to create a simple linear regression model.

- The PLOTS option is set to ALL. This setting will provide us with all the available graphs associated with the REG procedure.

- The first term in the MODEL statement is the target variable (sqrt_revol_bal). The predictor appears after the equals sign.

- The SLE option specifies the significance level for a variable to enter into the model.

- The SLS option specifies the significance level to be retained in the model. This option is not necessary for a simple linear regression model, but it is very important once we begin to add variables to the model to create a multiple linear regression model.

- The INCLUDE statement specifies that the model should include the intercept value.

- The OUTPUT statement creates an output data set. I have also specified that I want to retain the PREDICTED value and RESIDUAL value.

Output 6.8 contains the output created from the simple linear regression. This output shows that the predictor variable sqrt_total_bc_limit is significantly correlated with the target variable.

Output 6.8: Simple Linear Regression Output

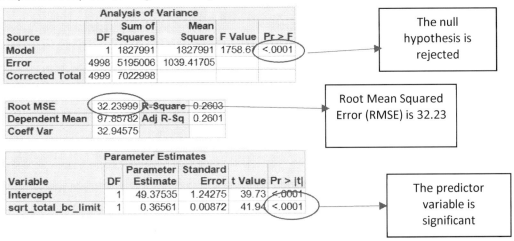

Analysis of Variance					
Source	DF	Sum of Squares	Mean Square	F Value	Pr > F
Model	1	1827991	1827991	1758.67	<.0001
Error	4998	5195006	1039.41705		
Corrected Total	4999	7022998			

The null hypothesis is rejected

Root MSE	32.23999	R-Square	0.2603
Dependent Mean	97.85782	Adj R-Sq	0.2601
Coeff Var	32.94575		

Root Mean Squared Error (RMSE) is 32.23

Parameter Estimates					
Variable	DF	Parameter Estimate	Standard Error	t Value	Pr > |t|
Intercept	1	49.37535	1.24275	39.73	<.0001
sqrt_total_bc_limit	1	0.36561	0.00872	41.94	<.0001

The predictor variable is significant

Analysis of Variance

Output 6.8 shows the summary statistics for the PROC REG model. In the Analysis of Variance section, the null hypothesis that the predictor variable is not significantly related to the target variable is tested. The P-value of less than 0.05 rejects this null hypothesis.

Error Metrics

The next section of the summary statistics output shows the RMSE value of 32.23. This value by itself does not mean a lot, but we will be able to use this value as a baseline when we compare this model to other more complicated models.

This section also contains the R^2 value. The R^2 metric represents the percentage of variation of the observations explained by the model. It is tempting to use this metric to evaluate your model. It is straightforward and easy to understand. However, the R^2 metric has some inherent problems:

- The R^2 metric will always increase when you add more predictors to the model. This is the case even when these predictors are random variables with no relation to the target variable.

- The R^2 metric can misrepresent the strength of the model. It does not measure goodness-of-fit and can be artificially low when the model is completely correct. If the standard deviation of the data is large, the large standard deviation will drive R^2 towards zero even when the model is correctly specified.

- The R^2 metric can be artificially high, even when the model is wrong. This often occurs when the data is clearly non-linear, as demonstrated by a scatter plot of the data. A straight line through the data might capture many observations and produce a high R^2 value, but the most appropriate model would be a non-linear approach.

- If you change the range of your predictor variables, it can have a dramatic effect on the R^2 value.

Parameter Estimates

The final section of the PROC REG summary statistics is the Parameter Estimates section. This section is what we think of when we talk about "the model." This section contains all the values for the linear regression equation. Remember that the basic structure of the simple linear regression model is:

$$Y \approx \beta_0 + \beta_1 X$$

Now, we can add some real variables and values into this general equation:

$$sqrt\_revol\_bal \approx 49.37 + sqrt\_total\_bc\_limit(0.3656)$$

This equation can be interpreted as: the target variable sqrt_revol_bal is predicted to go up by 0.3656 when the predictor goes up by one. Also, if the predictor is zero, the target variable is 49.37. Since these variables are expressed in their square root form, they can be easily transformed back into their raw values by taking the exponential of the square root value.

Output 6.9 shows the graphical output generated from the REG procedure with the ODS Graphics set to ON.

Output 6.9: Fit Diagnostics for sqrt_revol_bal

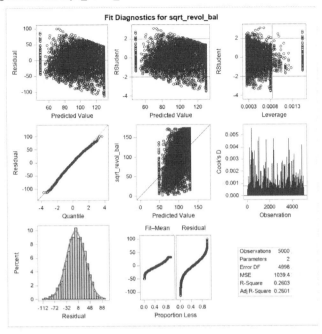

The output provides lots of visualizations of the model output with an emphasis on the distribution of the residuals.

- The top-left chart shows the distribution of the residual by the predicted value. There is a random distribution of the residuals, which indicates to us that the square root transformation was appropriate.

- The middle-left chart shows the Q-Q plot. This plot checks to see whether the predictor variable is normally distributed. The actual distribution is plotted against the theoretical (normal) distribution. If the resulting graph is a straight line, this means that the actual and the theoretical are aligned, but if the resulting graph is curved, this indicates that the predictor is skewed.

- The bottom left chart shows the distribution of the residuals. You want this to look like the normal distribution.

- The middle chart shows the distribution of the predicted values against the target value. Although we can see that the data has been artificially restricted at the high and low ends, the distribution of the data is random.

- The Cook's D graphic is displayed on the middle right. This shows the observations that have a significant influence on the model in relation to the predictor variable.

- A summary of the model output is shown in the bottom-right section of the output. Although this output provides a quick look at some of the model metrics, it is better to look at the information contained in the Analysis of Variance and the Error Metric sections of the model summary statistics to assess your model. Remember that you should not assess your model fit with the R^2 metric. In the case of a continuous linear regression model, the Real Mean Squared Error (RMSE) is a much better metric to use.

Model Evaluation

At this point, we have developed a simple linear regression on a sample data set (remember that we only selected 5000 observations), and we have evaluated the summary metrics for the TRAIN data set. But remember that final model evaluation is performed on the hold-out TEST data set. So, we have a few more steps that we need to perform:

- We will need to recreate the model on the full TRAIN data set.

- We will need to adjust the hold-out TEST data set in the same manner that we adjusted the TRAIN data set.

- We will then apply the full simple linear regression model to the hold-out TEST data set and evaluate the results.

Program 6.10 creates a simple linear regression on the full data set. Since we have already determined that the single variable `sqrt_total_bc_limit` is significant, we can strip down the coding a bit.

Program 6.10: Simple Linear Regression on Full Adjusted Data Set
```
PROC REG DATA=change OUTEST=RegOut;
      MODEL sqrt_revol_bal = sqrt_total_bc_limit
/ SELECTION=STEPWISE;
      OUTPUT OUT=WORK.REG_PRED PREDICTED=P RESIDUAL=R;
RUN;
```

There are two important changes from the original development code in Program 6.10:

- The model is being developed on the full adjusted TRAIN population. The previous simple linear regression model was developed on a 5000-observation sample to provide us insight into the relationship between the target and the predictor. The full model is being developed on the full 300,000-observation data set.

- There is a new option in PROC REG called OUTEST. This option creates an output data set that contains the parameter estimate for the predictor along with the model intercept and a few summary statistics. e will use this output data set to apply to the hold-out TEST data set.

Adjust the Hold-out TEST Data Set

Now that we have created the model, we need to evaluate the performance of the model on the hold-out TEST data set. In order to apply the model, the TEST data set will need to be structured in the same manner as the TRAIN data set. Program 6.11 adjusts the TEST data set using the same restrictions and transformations that we applied to the TRAIN data set.

Program 6.11: Transform the Hold-out TEST Data Set

```
DATA test_reg;
  SET MYDATA.MODEL_TEST;
  WHERE 10 le revol_bal le 30000;
  sqrt_revol_bal = sqrt(revol_bal);
  sqrt_annual_inc = sqrt(annual_inc);
  sqrt_bc_util = sqrt(bc_util);
  sqrt_dti = sqrt(dti);
  sqrt_loan_amnt = sqrt(loan_amnt);
  sqrt_mo_sin_old_il_acct = sqrt(mo_sin_old_il_acct);
  sqrt_mths_since_recent_bc = sqrt(mths_since_recent_bc);
  sqrt_pct_tl_nvr_dlq = sqrt(pct_tl_nvr_dlq);
  sqrt_tot_hi_cred_lim = sqrt(tot_hi_cred_lim);
  sqrt_total_bc_limit = sqrt(total_bc_limit);
  sqrt_total_rec_int = sqrt(total_rec_int);
RUN;
```

This program has created a TEST data set where the observations are limited to cases where the revolving balance is between 10 and 30000. For the remaining observations, the continuous variables were transformed by the square root function.

Now that we have a model and a data set to apply the model to, all we need to do is score this new data set with the simple linear regression model and evaluate the results. Program 6.12 performs these three tasks.

Program 6.12: Apply Simple Linear Regression Model to the TEST Data Set

```
PROC SCORE DATA=test_reg SCORE=RegOut OUT=RScoreP TYPE=parms;
   var sqrt_total_bc_limit;
RUN;

/*Calculate RMSE for the TEST dataset*/
DATA eval;
  SET RScoreP;
  RESIDUAL = (MODEL1-sqrt_revol_bal)**2;
  sqrt_residual = sqrt(residual);
  KEEP row_num model1 sqrt_revol_bal residual sqrt_residual;
RUN;

PROC MEANS DATA=eval N MEAN;
  VAR RESIDUAL sqrt_residual;
RUN;
```

Notes on Program 6.12:

- PROC SCORE is used to apply the model results contained in the RegOut data set to the newly adjusted TEST data set called test_reg. The PROC SCORE code outputs a scored data set called RScoreP that contains all the observations in the TEST data set along with a new variable called MODEL1. This is the model estimated value for each of the observations.

- The DATA step creates the root squared value by applying the simple formula of taking the squared value of the difference between the predicted value (MODEL1) and the actual value (sqrt_revol_bal). The next step is to take the square root of that value.

- The final step is PROC MEANS, which simply calculates the mean value of the sqrt_residual value. This gives us the Root Square Mean Error (RSME).

This evaluation process has resulted in the metrics contained in Output 6.10.

Output 6.10: Results of the Evaluation Process

Analysis of Variance					
Source	DF	Sum of Squares	Mean Square	F Value	Pr > F
Model	1	111701393	111701393	117547	<.0001
Error	304021	288901591	950.26854		
Corrected Total	304022	400602984			

Variable	Parameter Estimate	Standard Error	Type II SS	F Value	Pr > F
Intercept	52.28751	0.14965	116003345	122074	<.0001
sqrt_total_bc_limit	0.38521	0.00112	111701393	117547	<.0001

Summary of Stepwise Selection								
Step	Variable Entered	Variable Removed	Number Vars In	Partial R-Square	Model R-Square	C(p)	F Value	Pr > F
1	sqrt_total_bc_limit		1	0.2788	0.2788	2.0000	117547	<.0001

Variable	N	Mean
RESIDUAL	129960	955.0601235
sqrt_residual	129960	24.2425668

The first three sections of Output 6.10 show the Analysis of Variance and Model Metrics output for the simple linear regression that was developed on the full data set. The final section of output contains the RSME value that was created from the MEANS procedure. The simple linear regression model has an RSME of 24.24 on the hold-out TEST data set. We will use this value as our base metric to compare more complex models to.

Multiple Linear Regression

The review of the structure and output of the simple linear regression gave us a great basis for how to apply the regression algorithm to actual data and what the output looks like. However, you will rarely use a single predictor in a regression model for business decisions. The simple linear regression approach provides a great method to assess a single variable and understand its relation to the target variable; however, we need to explore the method of bringing together a variety of variables where each is correlated with the target variable and get them to work together to tell a holistic story about the data. Welcome to multiple linear regression.

Multiple Linear Regression Equation

The basic equation of the multiple linear regression is merely an expansion of the simple linear regression. The equation still states that the target variable (Y) is approximately modeled as $(\approx)$ the intercept value (β_0) plus the value of a single variable (X_1) multiplied by its coefficient (β_1).

The expansion of the simple linear regression equation merely adds predictors and their associated coefficients to the model. So now, we not only have $(\beta_1 X_1)$, but there are also several additional predictors as part of the equation along with an error term (ε):

Equation 6.4: Multiple Linear Regression Equation

$$Y \approx \beta_0 + \beta_1 X_1 + \beta_2 X_2 + \beta_3 X_3 \ldots + \beta_p X_p + \varepsilon$$

Now that we understand the basic structure of the multiple linear regression model, let's put it into practice. Program 6.13 develops a multiple linear regression model with PROC REG on the "change" data set. Remember that this data set consists of a subset of variables from our modeling data set from Chapter 5, and we have transformed some of the variables by the square root function.

Program 6.13: Multiple Linear Regression

```
ODS GRAPHICS ON;
PROC REG DATA=change (obs=5000) PLOTS(ONLY)=ALL;
      MODEL sqrt_revol_bal = &trans. &box. / SELECTION=STEPWISE
      SLE=0.1 SLS=0.1 INCLUDE=0 COLLIN VIF;
      OUTPUT OUT=WORK.REG_PRED PREDICTED=P RESIDUAL=R;
RUN;
```

Notes on Program 6.13:

- The same basic structure of the PROC REG that was used for the simple linear regression was used for the multiple linear regression.

- The global variables &trans and &box were used to specify the predictor variables. Remember that the &trans global variable contains the list of continuous variables that were transformed by the square root function, and the &box global variable contains the list of interval numeric variables. Keep in mind that it is not necessary to create global variables and use them in the model. You can easily type in each variable directly into the REG procedure.

- The SELECTION statement specifies that I want to use the STEPWISE modeling procedure. The options for this statement are FORWARD, BACKWARD, and STEPWISE. This statement refers to how each of the variables is added to the model.

  o The FORWARD option starts with a single variable, evaluates it, and decides whether to retain the variable in the model. Once the decision is made, the algorithm will assess the next variable and continue the process through the list of variables.

  o The BACKWARD option begins with all variables in the model and makes decisions on which ones to kick out of the model one at a time.

- ○ The STEPWISE option is like the FORWARD option in that it adds one variable at a time to the model. However, at each iteration of variable evaluation, the algorithm evaluates each of the variables that have been retained and makes decisions on whether to keep them in the model.

- ○ So, the difference between the FORWARD and the STEPWISE selection methods is that once a variable is added with the FORWARD method, it remains in the model. When a variable is added with a STEPWISE method, it can be kicked out later in the process due to information contained in new variables.

- The model contains the COLLIN statement to evaluate the collinearity of the model.

- The model contains the VIF statement to create the Variance Inflation Factor metric. This metric will help us evaluate whether there is multicollinearity in the model.

Output 6.11 contains the output created from the multiple linear regression. This output shows that several predictor variables are significantly correlated with the target variable.

Output 6.11: Output Created from Multiple Linear Regression

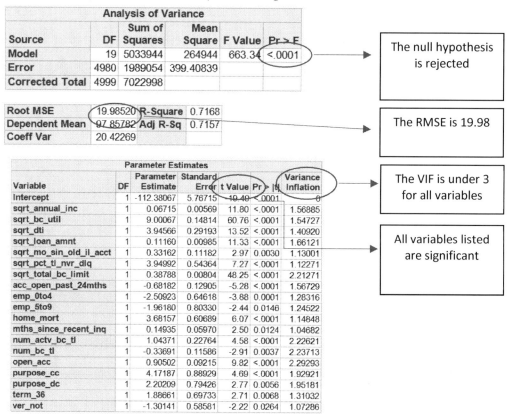

Analysis of Variance					
Source	DF	Sum of Squares	Mean Square	F Value	Pr > F
Model	19	5033944	264944	663.34	<.0001
Error	4980	1989054	399.40839		
Corrected Total	4999	7022998			

The null hypothesis is rejected

Root MSE	19.98520	R-Square	0.7168
Dependent Mean	97.85782	Adj R-Sq	0.7157
Coeff Var	20.42269		

The RMSE is 19.98

Parameter Estimates						
Variable	DF	Parameter Estimate	Standard Error	t Value	Pr > |t|	Variance Inflation
Intercept	1	-112.38067	5.76715	-19.49	<.0001	0
sqrt_annual_inc	1	0.06715	0.00569	11.80	<.0001	1.56885
sqrt_bc_util	1	9.00067	0.14814	60.76	<.0001	1.54727
sqrt_dti	1	3.94566	0.29193	13.52	<.0001	1.40920
sqrt_loan_amnt	1	0.11160	0.00985	11.33	<.0001	1.66121
sqrt_mo_sin_old_il_acct	1	0.33162	0.11182	2.97	0.0030	1.13001
sqrt_pct_tl_nvr_dlq	1	3.94992	0.54364	7.27	<.0001	1.12271
sqrt_total_bc_limit	1	0.38788	0.00804	48.25	<.0001	2.21271
acc_open_past_24mths	1	-0.68182	0.12905	-5.28	<.0001	1.56729
emp_0to4	1	-2.50923	0.64618	-3.88	0.0001	1.28316
emp_5to9	1	-1.96180	0.80330	-2.44	0.0146	1.24522
home_mort	1	3.68157	0.60689	6.07	<.0001	1.14848
mths_since_recent_inq	1	0.14935	0.05970	2.50	0.0124	1.04682
num_actv_bc_tl	1	1.04371	0.22764	4.58	<.0001	2.22621
num_bc_tl	1	-0.33691	0.11586	-2.91	0.0037	2.23713
open_acc	1	0.90502	0.09215	9.82	<.0001	2.29293
purpose_cc	1	4.17187	0.88929	4.69	<.0001	1.92921
purpose_dc	1	2.20209	0.79426	2.77	0.0056	1.95181
term_36	1	1.88661	0.69733	2.71	0.0068	1.31032
ver_not	1	-1.30141	0.58581	-2.22	0.0264	1.07286

The VIF is under 3 for all variables

All variables listed are significant

Analysis of Variance

Output 6.11 shows the summary statistics for the PROC REG model. In the Analysis of Variance section, the null hypothesis that the predictor variable is not significantly related to the target variable is tested. The P-value of less than 0.05 rejects this null hypothesis.

Error Metrics

The next section of the summary statistics output shows the RMSE value of 19.98. When we compare this value to the RMSE generated from the simple linear regression model in the previous section (RMSE: 32.23), we can see that there is a nearly 40% reduction in the RMSE generated by the new model. This is a substantial gain in predictive accuracy due to all the new information that we have gained from the additional variables.

Parameter Estimates

The Parameter Estimates section shows that 19 variables met the critical level of significance to be retained in the model. Although there are no solid rules that dictate how many variables should be retained in the model, we can evaluate the model output and determine the amount of contribution that each variable has made to the final model. Output 6.12 shows two pieces of information generated from the model.

Output 6.12: New Information Generated from the Model

	Summary of Stepwise Selection						
Step	Variable Entered	Variable Removed	Number Vars In	Partial R-Square	Model R-Square	C(p)	F Value	Pr > F
1	sqrt_total_bc_limit		1	0.2603	0.2603	8006.93	1758.67	<.0001
2	sqrt_bc_util		2	0.3924	0.6526	1111.87	5644.51	<.0001
3	open_acc		3	0.0217	0.6743	733.010	332.36	<.0001
4	sqrt_loan_amnt		4	0.0168	0.6911	440.102	271.28	<.0001
5	sqrt_dti		5	0.0068	0.6979	323.051	111.94	<.0001
6	sqrt_annual_inc		6	0.0077	0.7055	189.973	130.30	<.0001
7	sqrt_pct_tl_nvr_dlq		7	0.0025	0.7081	147.197	43.56	<.0001
8	home_mort		8	0.0022	0.7103	110.776	37.65	<.0001
9	acc_open_past_24mths		9	0.0018	0.7120	81.8250	30.51	<.0001
10	num_actv_bc_tl		10	0.0008	0.7129	69.6154	14.04	0.0002
11	purpose_cc		11	0.0008	0.7136	58.2501	13.24	0.0003
12	emp_0to4		12	0.0005	0.7141	50.9400	9.24	0.0024
13	num_bc_tl		13	0.0005	0.7146	44.9134	7.98	0.0048
14	sqrt_mo_sin_old_il_acct		14	0.0005	0.7150	38.9792	7.90	0.0050
15	purpose_dc		15	0.0004	0.7154	34.0290	6.93	0.0085
16	term_36		16	0.0004	0.7158	29.0795	6.93	0.0085
17	mths_since_recent_inq		17	0.0003	0.7162	25.0418	6.03	0.0141
18	emp_5to9		18	0.0003	0.7165	21.4695	5.57	0.0183
19	ver_not		19	0.0003	0.7168	18.5357	4.94	0.0264

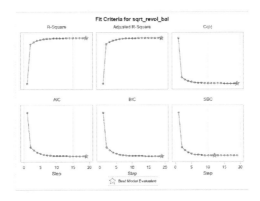

Fit Criteria for sqrt_revol_bal

The table on the top of Output 6.12 shows the order in which each variable entered the model. The order is determined by the overall impact of the model R^2 value with the addition of a specific variable. The chart on the bottom shows a graphical representation of the addition of each variable for several model metrics.

The Fit Criteria graphic shows that the first five variables that entered the model produce substantial gains in model accuracy. The next five variables show additional marginal gains. The remaining variables are statistically significant, but they do not provide much additional predictive weight to the model.

We can use this information to select a subset of variables that provide us the maximum level of predictive accuracy with the minimum number of variables. This approach is called *parsimonious modeling*.

Parsimonious Multiple Regression Model

With the information that we gained in Output 6.12, we can confidently select the top ten variables and use these as the predictors to feed into a new model. Program 6.14 shows the parsimonious model code.

Program 6.14: Parsimonious Linear Regression

```
ODS GRAPHICS ON;
PROC REG DATA=change (obs=5000) PLOTS(ONLY)=ALL;
      MODEL sqrt_revol_bal = sqrt_total_bc_limit sqrt_bc_util
               open_acc sqrt_loan_amnt sqrt_dti
               sqrt_annual_inc sqrt_pct_tl_nvr_dlq home_mort
 acc_open_past_24mths num_actv_bc_tl
         / SELECTION=STEPWISE
             SLE=0.1
             SLS=0.1
             INCLUDE=0
             COLLIN VIF;
      OUTPUT OUT=WORK.REG_PRED PREDICTED=P RESIDUAL=R;
RUN;
```

Instead of using the global variables to define the predictors, I have hard-coded the names of the variables directly into the model equation.

Output 6.13 shows the output generated from the parsimonious model. Notice that the RMSE has increased by only 0.12. This is a barely noticeable difference from the full multiple regression model, but we have only ten variables in the parsimonious model compared to nineteen that we had in the full model.

Output 6.13: Parsimonious Linear Regression Output

Analysis of Variance					
Source	DF	Sum of Squares	Mean Square	F Value	Pr > F
Model	10	5006345	500634	1238.52	<.0001
Error	4989	2016653	404.21987		
Corrected Total	4999	7022998			

Root MSE	20.10522	R-Square	0.7129
Dependent Mean	97.85782	Adj R-Sq	0.7123
Coeff Var	20.54534		

Parameter Estimates						
Variable	DF	Parameter Estimate	Standard Error	t Value	Pr > |t|	Variance Inflation
Intercept	1	-107.95868	5.41508	-19.94	<.0001	0
sqrt_total_bc_limit	1	0.38436	0.00775	49.58	<.0001	2.03316
sqrt_bc_util	1	9.21013	0.14506	63.49	<.0001	1.46597
open_acc	1	0.88760	0.08937	9.93	<.0001	2.13085
sqrt_loan_amnt	1	0.10544	0.00852	12.37	<.0001	1.22884
sqrt_dti	1	4.05306	0.29191	13.88	<.0001	1.39230
sqrt_annual_inc	1	0.06536	0.00562	11.64	<.0001	1.51099
sqrt_pct_tl_nvr_dlq	1	3.99515	0.53979	7.40	<.0001	1.09368
home_mort	1	3.99003	0.59658	6.69	<.0001	1.09659
acc_open_past_24mths	1	-0.75181	0.12671	-5.93	<.0001	1.49313
num_actv_bc_tl	1	0.79364	0.21177	3.75	0.0002	1.90368

The parsimonious approach allows us to retain nearly all the predictive power of the full model with a minimal number of predictor variables. This model can be reduced even further by selecting only the top five variables in the full model. Although I will not show the code and the diagnostic output from this further reduced model, I did create the model and it produced an RMSE of 20.35. In comparison to the full model, there is a difference of only 0.37 units, and when compared to the ten-variable parsimonious model, there is a difference of only 0.25 units.

Apply Parsimonious Model to the Hold-out TEST Data Set

The method of applying the parsimonious model to the hold-out TEST data set is very similar to the steps that we reviewed in the simple linear regression section of this chapter. Therefore, there is no need to go into detail on each part of the process. Program 6.15 demonstrates how the parsimonious model is applied to the adjusted hold-out TEST data set.

Program 6.15: Score and Evaluate the Hold-out TEST Data Set

```
/*Apply the parsimonious model to the full TRAIN dataset*/
%LET parsi_vars = sqrt_total_bc_limit sqrt_bc_util open_acc
    sqrt_loan_amnt sqrt_dti sqrt_annual_inc;

PROC REG DATA=change OUTEST=RegOut ;
    MODEL sqrt_revol_bal = &parsi_vars. / SELECTION=STEPWISE;
    OUTPUT OUT=WORK.REG_PRED PREDICTED=P RESIDUAL=R;
RUN;

/*Apply parsimonious model to the TEST dataset*/
PROC SCORE DATA=test_reg SCORE=RegOut OUT=RScoreP TYPE=parms;
   VAR &parsi_vars.;
```

```
run;

/*Calculate RMSE for the TEST dataset*/
DATA eval;
  SET RScoreP;
  RESIDUAL = (MODEL1-sqrt_revol_bal)**2;
  sqrt_residual = sqrt(residual);
  KEEP row_num model1 sqrt_revol_bal residual sqrt_residual;
RUN;

PROC MEANS DATA=eval N MEAN;
  VAR RESIDUAL sqrt_residual;
RUN;
```

Output 6.14 shows the final output produced by the MEANS procedure.

Output 6.14: TEST Data Set Evaluation Metrics

Variable	N	Mean
RESIDUAL	129960	408.5718289
sqrt_residual	129960	14.6690613

This output shows that the RMSE for the parsimonious model is 14.66. This is a substantial reduction from the RSME of 24.24 generated from the simple linear regression model. At this point, we can make the decision that the parsimonious model provides more precise predictive estimates than the simple linear regression model.

The parsimonious approach is a great way to get the best model with a minimal number of variables. However, it does require a significant amount of model creation, evaluation, update, and reevaluation. Don't you wish that there was an automated process to do all these reductions and evaluations for you? Welcome to regularization models.

Regularization Models

Back in Chapter 1: Data Science Overview, we talked about model complexity and the fact that as model complexity increases, overfitting begins to occur, which leads to poor model performance. The goal of our model development process is to create a model that captures the signal contained in the data but does not model the noise of non-important data attributes. We want to optimize the model complexity. Too little complexity will result in an underfit model, and too much complexity will result in an overfit model.

Regularization models introduce a new term to the model equation that penalizes model complexity by constraining the model coefficients. This new regularization term is called the *shrinkage penalty*. This term is effectively a tuning parameter that allows the model developer to adjust the model complexity as part of the objective function. The tuning parameter shrinks the model coefficients towards zero. This process discourages the objective function from producing an overly complex model.

Remember that the model coefficients were determined by a process that minimizes the loss function. In the case of linear regression models, the loss function is generally the Residual Sum of Squares (RSS) as defined in Equation 6.5.

Equation 6.5: Residual Sum of Squares

$$RSS = \sum_{i=1}^{n} (y_i - \hat{y}_i)^2$$

The regularization approach simply adds a penalty term to the RSS equation. This penalty term is usually denoted as lambda (λ) and is applied to each of the model coefficients. There are two main types of regularization approaches, ridge and lasso regression. They each express the lambda term differently in the loss function, so let's examine them separately.

Ridge Regression

The ridge regression approach applies the penalty term to each of the *squared values* of the model coefficients. Equation 6.6 shows the additional penalty term in the RSS equation:

Equation 6.6: Ridge Regression RSS

$$RSS + \lambda \sum_{j=1}^{p} \beta_j^2$$

This equation states that for all instances where $\lambda \geq 0$, the squared value of the model coefficients will be multiplied by the factor of λ. If $\lambda = 0$, then the equation is the same as the general least squares equation. However, as λ increases, the impact of the shrinkage penalty increases. The result of this shrinkage is that the model coefficients will approach zero.

An important fact to keep in mind is that the ridge regression method will never shrink the model coefficients all the way to zero. The coefficients can become very small, and as a result, they will not be significant in the model. However, the ridge regression model will still contain all the predictive variables that were initially fed into the algorithm and create coefficients for all of them.

This is a very different approach from the "best subset" approach that we used in the multiple regression model example where we selected the model attributes using the STEPWISE model option. This approach selected only a subset of predictors that met our selection criteria.

Program 6.16 shows PROC REG updated with the RIDGE option. Rather than applying a single value for the ridge tuning parameter, we can select a range of values and evaluate the results to determine the best value for the tuning parameter.

Program 6.16: Ridge Regression Model

```
ODS GRAPHICS ON;
PROC REG DATA=change OUTEST=b RIDGE=0 to 1 by .05
      PLOTS(ONLY)=ALL      ;
      MODEL sqrt_revol_bal = &trans. &box.;
      OUTPUT OUT=WORK.RIDGE_PRED PREDICTED=P RESIDUAL=R;
RUN;
```

Notes on Program 6.16:

- The OUTEST option creates a data set that contains the parameter values for each value of the ridge tuning parameter. This data set demonstrates that the value for each parameter decreases as lambda increases.

- The RIDGE option contains a range of values starting at 0 and continues through 1 in intervals of 0.05.

Output 6.15 shows the resulting ODS output from the ridge regression model. The top part of the graph shows the Variance Inflation Factor (VIF), while the lower part of the graph shows the standardized coefficients.

Output 6.15: Ridge Regression VIF Output

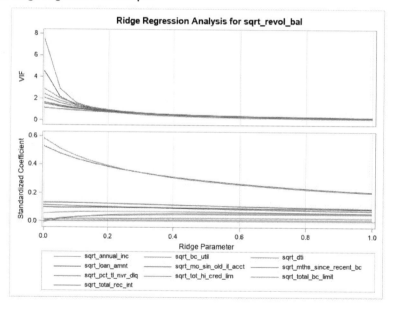

It appears that when the tuning parameter is set to 0.01, the VIF decreases to under 3 for all predictors shown in the chart, and these predictors have leveled out to a constant standardized value. If you have several input variables in your regression model, the output will contain several charts with groups of about 10 variables in each chart.

Apply Ridge Regression Model to the Hold-out Test Data set

Now that we have developed the ridge regression model, we can apply the model to the hold-out TEST data set. The process is the exact same process detailed in the parsimonious model section, so I will not recreate the code here. The ridge regression RSME is shown in Output 6.16.

Output 6.16: Ridge Regression Evaluation Metrics

Variable	N	Mean
RESIDUAL	129960	392.3806346
sqrt_residual	129960	14.4115384

We can see that the RSME for the ridge regression model is 14.41. This score is slightly better than the parsimonious model that has an RMSE of 14.66. This metric gives us evidence that the ridge regression model has provided us a marginally better prediction than the parsimonious model.

Pros and Cons of the Ridge Regression Model

Pros – One of the major benefits of the regularization method is that you do not need to determine whether the data set contains multicollinearity and make the necessary adjustments prior to modeling. The tuning parameter will shrink the model coefficients and will, in turn, reduce the model variance. This reduction is why we see the VIF metric decreasing for each of the predictors as the tuning parameter increases.

Cons – The ridge regression method retains all the input variables that were fed into the regression algorithm. Although many of the model variables have very small coefficients that have little to no impact on the model output, those variables are still in the model. The reason for this retention is because regularization models do not require a significance level for entry into the model, such as the SLE option in the STEPWISE selection method PROC REG that we developed in Program 6.16.

One of the main benefits of the parsimonious model is that it selects the fewest number of variables that have the equivalent predictive power as a full unconstrained multiple linear regression model. The ridge regression model has the benefit of ingesting all predictors and can deal with multicollinearity using the regularization parameter; however, all predictors are retained in the final model.

What if there was a way to ingest all predictors and let the model deal with multicollinearity and retain only a significant subset of those predictors? Welcome to Lasso Regression.

Lasso Regression

The lasso regression approach applies the penalty term to each of the *absolute values* of the model coefficients. Equation 6.7 shows the additional penalty term in the RSS equation.

Equation 6.7: Lasso Regression RSS

$$RSS + \lambda \sum_{j=1}^{p} |\beta_j|$$

This equation states that for all instances where $\lambda \geq 0$, the *absolute value* of the model coefficients will be multiplied by the factor of λ.

The important difference between ridge regression and lasso regression is that while the ridge regression punishes weak predictors by shrinking their coefficients to very small values, the lasso approach can shrink coefficients to zero. This is effectively a *variable reduction* method.

In SAS, the lasso regression method is not available in PROC REG. Instead, we will use PROC GLMSELECT. This is a flexible procedure that is a general linear model (GLM) and allows the data scientist to choose from a variety of selection methods (SELECT). Thus, the name GLMSELECT.

Program 6.17 develops the lasso regression model using PROC GLMSELECT.

Program 6.17: Lasso Regression Model

```
PROC GLMSELECT DATA=change PLOTS(UNPACK)=ALL;
       MODEL sqrt_revol_bal = &trans. &box.
       / SELECTION=lasso(CHOOSE=CP) STATS=ALL;
       SCORE DATA=test_reg OUT=test_pred PREDICTED RESIDUAL;
RUN;
```

Notes on Program 6.17:

- PROC GLMSELECT is used to create a multiple linear regression model on the adjusted TRAIN data set called "change".

- The SELECTION option is set to "lasso." The additional option of CHOOSE=CP tells the regression algorithm that the selected model will be the one that optimizes the Mallows's Cp metric.

- PROC GLMSELECT can score a separate data set within the procedure. There is no need for a separate PROC SCORE. The SCORE DATA option allows us to score the adjusted hold-out TEST data set and output the results by specifying the OUT statement.

The output of the GLMSELECT procedure is slightly different from PROC REG output. Although it will still provide you with detailed information contained in the Analysis of Variance table, it will also provide a list of fit metrics, including the RMSE, AIC, BIC, and Mallows's Cp metrics. Output 6.17 demonstrates several of the model outputs.

Output 6.17: Lasso Regression Output

Analysis of Variance				
Source	DF	Sum of Squares	Mean Square	F Value
Model	23	279659491	12159108	30562.7
Error	303999	120943493	397.84175	
Corrected Total	304022	400602984		

Parameter Estimates		
Parameter	DF	Estimate
Intercept	1	-100.549448
sqrt_annual_inc	1	0.061663
sqrt_bc_util	1	8.685230
sqrt_dti	1	4.195944
sqrt_loan_amnt	1	0.090220
sqrt_mo_sin_old_il_a	1	0.068476
sqrt_pct_tl_nvr_dlq	1	3.189254
sqrt_total_bc_limit	1	0.416312
sqrt_total_rec_int	1	0.040369
acc_open_past_24mths	1	-0.459470
emp_10	1	1.318478
emp_0to4	1	-1.121406
emp_NA	1	0.815892
grade_A	1	-1.378976
home_mort	1	1.359464
home_own	1	0.162840
mo_sin_rcnt_tl	1	0.042014
mort_acc	1	0.676488
mths_since_recent_in	1	0.040696
num_actv_bc_tl	1	0.426201
open_acc	1	0.853865
purpose_cc	1	2.341450
purpose_hi	1	-2.379450
purpose_other	1	-2.001271

Root MSE	19.94597
Dependent Mean	99.88145
R-Square	0.6981
Adj R-Sq	0.6981
AIC	2123947
AICC	2123947
BIC	1819924
C(p)	2409.36275
SBC	1820177
ASE	397.81034

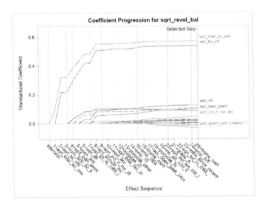

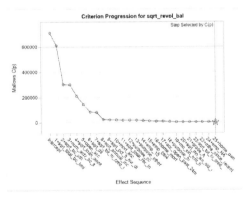

Notice that the Parameter Estimates table in Output 6.17 contains 23 predictors that are retained in the model. Compare this to the full list of 46 variables retained in the ridge regression model. This difference shows that the lasso regression method is a variable reduction method.

This list can be reduced even further by specifying the number of variables that you would want to keep in the model output. If, for instance, you want to retain only 10 variables in your model, you can specify it in the SELECTION option of PROC GLMSELECT. Program 6.18 shows the updated SELECTION statement.

Program 6.18: Lasso Selection Method

```
SELECTION=lasso(CHOOSE=CP STEPS=10) STATS=ALL;
```

This selection option will result in a model that contains only 10 predictors.

Apply Lasso Regression to the Hold-out TEST Data Set

The final step to evaluating the performance of the lasso regression model is to evaluate the RMSE of the hold-out TEST data set. The one minor update to the evaluation code is that the model prediction results are contained in a field p_sqrt_revol_bal. The p_ indicates that this is the predicted value. The updated program is demonstrated in Program 6.19.

Program 6.19: Evaluate the RMSE of the Hold-out TEST Data Set

```
DATA eval;
  SET test_pred;
  RESIDUAL = (p_sqrt_revol_bal-sqrt_revol_bal)**2;
  sqrt_residual = sqrt(residual);
  KEEP row_num model1 sqrt_revol_bal residual sqrt_residual;
RUN;

PROC MEANS DATA=eval N MEAN;
  VAR RESIDUAL sqrt_residual;
RUN;
```

The resulting RMSE is displayed in Output 6.18. This shows that the lasso regression approach results in an RMSE of 14.51 for the adjusted hold-out TEST data set.

Output 6.18: Evaluation Metrics for Hold-out TEST Data Set

Variable	N	Mean
RESIDUAL	129960	395.7292650
sqrt_residual	129960	14.5149556

At this point, you may want to compare the RMSE values that we gathered from the simple, parsimonious, ridge, and lasso regression models. Of all these models, the ridge regression model results in the lowest RMSE for the hold-out TEST data set.

However, that does not imply that the ridge regression method is necessarily superior to all the other modeling types that we explored. The only conclusion that we can draw from this exercise is that for this given data set and with the assumptions and transformations that we applied to the data, the ridge regression resulted in the lowest RMSE for the specific hold-out TEST data set.

Although predictive accuracy is one of the main goals of model development, it does not necessarily mean that it is the only factor to consider when choosing which model to select as your production model. In this example, the ridge regression has 46 variables and is only marginally more predictive than the parsimonious and lasso regression models. A data scientist would certainly have a strong argument for selecting a more concise model to move into a production environment.

You are not bound by one metric as to which model you have to select. The decision of which model to choose is a balance of model accuracy, interpretability, efficiency, control, business impact, and business acceptance.

Chapter Review

The goal of this chapter was to introduce you to the concept of linear regression and demonstrate several methods of producing linear regression models in SAS. We started with the simplest approach (simple linear regression) and continued to increase the model complexity by adding more predictors and demonstrating different modeling techniques. Each of the model approaches that were demonstrated had their own strengths and weaknesses, and it is the job of the data scientist to determine the correct modeling approach for a given project.

Linear regression models are a go-to modeling approach when it is important to understand which variables are significant in the modeling algorithm and how each of the predictors affects the predicted outcome. This is why linear regression models are very popular in any business that has a significant amount of model oversight (finance, insurance, health care, government, and so on).

These types of models are also suitable for very large data sets, especially data sets that contain very high dimensional data. The parametric modeling approach is highly efficient and can produce modeling results in a fraction of the time that more complex modeling methods would take.

There are entire textbooks devoted to regression methods. We discussed only a few of the many possible methods, and we discussed only a few of the options that are available for those models. Linear regression models are highly flexible, efficient, and provide specific information for every predictor in the model. The transparency of this modeling algorithm makes it one of the most important modeling techniques in the data scientist's toolbox.

Chapter 7: Parametric Classification Models

Overview

In the last chapter, we focused on linear regression models. Two important characteristics define those models. 1.) They are designed to support a quantitative target variable. 2.) They assume a functional form ($Y \approx \beta_0 + \beta_1 X_1$); therefore, they are categorized as parametric models.

Linear regression models are constrained to fit the data by utilizing the linear regression equation. The constraint of an assumed functional form is what makes the linear regression model so powerful. The equation is transparent and models the data quickly because it only has to fit the data to a predetermined functional form. In later chapters, we will review the non-parametric models that are incredibly versatile and powerful but come at the cost of computational resources and processing time.

Although linear regression models are powerful, they are not appropriate to use in many situations. The primary decision point concerning what type of model to use is often driven by the nature of the target variable. Remember that the linear regression model is appropriate for *quantitative* dependent variables. What if the dependent variable is *qualitative*?

Qualitative variables are often binary (yes or no, 1 or 0, on or off), but they can also be multi-level categories (1st, 2nd, 3rd) or (red, yellow, green). Notice that these categories do not need to be numeric. They are often descriptive categories that we will need to transform into numeric representations of the data.

There are specialized models that are designed to predict a categorical dependent variable while retaining a predetermined functional form. This chapter will focus on two of these models: **Logistic Regression** and **Linear Discriminant Analysis**.

Classification Overview

Classification problems are prevalent in the modeling world. In fact, it is often more important to determine whether an event will occur rather than the exact time or value of the event. Some examples include:

- Will a viewer click on an ad?

- Will a borrower default on a loan?

- Will this new drug lower a patient's blood pressure?

- Is this transaction fraudulent?

- Which one of three locations should the company drill for oil?

The answer to each of these examples can be represented as a binary or multi-level categorical response. We can still structure our modeling data set in the same manner that we reviewed in Chapter 5: Creating a Modeling Data Set, the only difference will be the selection or creation of the dependent target variable. The modeling data set will still contain several independent predictor variables that we will use to try to determine the outcome variable. So, if nearly everything is the same as the linear regression model, why not just use the linear regression model to predict categorical outcomes?

Difference Between Linear and Logistic Regression

As stated previously, the main difference between linear and logistic regression is the structure of the dependent variable. Linear regression assumes a quantitative numeric variable while logistic regression assumes a qualitative categorical target variable. Figure 7.1 demonstrates an example distribution of values for these modeling types.

Figure 7.1: Linear vs. Logistic Regression Data Distributions

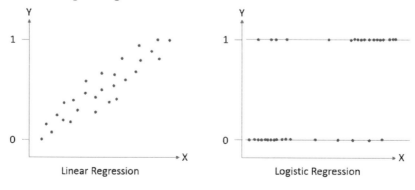

In this example, the linear regression model can take on any value between zero and one. Let's assume that the target value represents "the percentage of tickets sold (Y) given a certain discount rate (X)." This value can be 0% or 31% or 73% or 100% or any value in between.

The figure on the right shows an example binary distribution for a logistic regression model. Let's assume that the target value represents "sale or no sale." There are no values in between "sale" (represented as a 1) and "no sale" (represented as a 0) given a certain discount rate (X).

If we were to try and model a binary outcome with a linear regression model, we would get some confusing results. Figure 7.2 compares the modeling approaches of linear and logistic regression on the binary target variable.

Figure 7.2: Linear vs. Logistic Models on a Binary Outcome

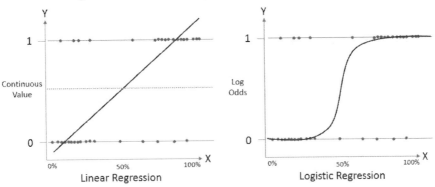

The linear regression model aims to minimize the Residual Sum of Squares (RSS) for the data. The underlying functional form of the model assumes that the dependent variable (Y) is a continuous value. Under this assumption, the straight line is the best fit for the data. We could actually use the linear regression model to make predictions of the data by stating any predicted value above the green dotted line will make a purchase and any value below the green dotted line will not make a purchase.

One of the problems with this approach is that as you approach the highest or lowest values for the predictor, the logic of the linear regression breaks down. Notice that as the value of X nears 0%, the predicted value of a purchase is negative, and as we approach the high end of X, the predicted value is greater than one. Neither of these outcomes is possible because they lie outside of the [0,1] range.

Maybe we are just being picky and overly academic about the use of the linear regression model. We could simply state that all predicted values greater than one will be capped at one, and all predicted values less than zero will be capped at zero. Problem solved, right? Unfortunately, not.

There are **three main reasons** why we should not use linear regression on classification problems:

1. The issue of probabilities being greater than one or less than zero as described above.
2. Homoscedasticity – One of the assumptions of linear regression is that the variance of Y is constant across values of X. However, for binary models, the variance is calculated as the proportion of positive values (P) times the proportion of negative values (Q). The variance is therefore (PQ). This value varies across the logistic regression line. For example, at the midpoint of the logistic regression line when P = 0.5 then Q = 0.5, the variance is PQ = 0.25. However, on the far end of the logistic regression line when P = 0.1 and Q = 0.9, then variance is PQ = 0.09.
3. Linear regression assumes that the residuals are normally distributed. Because a classification problem has a binary target, this assumption is hard to justify.

Logistic Regression

A better approach is to model the binary outcome variable as a **probability** that the event will occur. This probability is represented as the S-curved regression line in Figure 7.2. The formula for this line is much different from the linear regression formula, but it does share some similarities.

Equation 7.1: Linear Regression

$$Y \approx \beta_0 + \beta_1 X_1$$

Equation 7.2: Logistic Regression

$$p(X) = \frac{e^{\beta_0 + \beta_1 X}}{1 + e^{\beta_0 + \beta_1 X}}$$

The logistic regression equation (Equation 7.2) contains four main parts:

1. p(X) represents the probability of a positive value (1), which is also the proportion of 1s. This is the mean value of Y (just like linear regression).
2. Since this is a logistic model, we should expect to see the base value of the natural logarithm (e) represented in the model.
3. The value β_0 represents P when X is zero (similar to the linear regression intercept value).
4. The value β_1 adjusts how quickly the probability changes with changing X a for single unit (similar to the β_1 value in linear regression)

The logistic regression equation is called the *logistic function,* and we use this function because it produces outputs between 0 and 1 for all values of X, and it allows the variance of Y to vary across values of X.

Loss Function

In the linear regression chapter, we described the process of how the β values were determined by the process of minimizing the cost function of RSS through the process of gradient descent. For logistic regression, since we are dealing with an *S-curved* logistic regression line, there is no mathematical solution that will minimize the sum of squares as we did with the linear regression model. For the logistic regression model, the β values are determined through the process of **maximum likelihood**.

Remember that we are dealing with probabilities. The term *likelihood* represents a conditional probability of P(Y|X), the probability of Y given X. The parameters of the logistic regression function (β_0 and β_1) are determined by selecting values that the predicted probability $\hat{p}(x_i)$ of a value for each observation corresponds as closely as possible to the observation's actual value.

Therefore, *maximum likelihood* means that we are selecting values for β_0 and β_1 that result in a probability close to one for all ones and a probability close to zero for all zero values. This is called maximum likelihood because we are attempting to maximize the likelihood (conditional probability) of the model estimate matching the sample data.

Data

In Chapter 5: Create a Modeling Data Set, we developed a modeling data set with a binary target variable. We should be familiar with this data set by now. We have extensively examined the variables in Chapter 5, and we used the data set to develop our linear regression models in Chapter 6: Linear Regression Models. Let's finish off our tour of parametric models by using this same data set to demonstrate the development and interpretation of parametric binary classifiers.

For those of you who skipped Chapters 5 and 6 (shame on you), the data set is the Lending Club loan database. This data set represents loan accounts sourced from the Lending Club website and provides anonymized account-level information with data attributes representing the borrower, loan type, loan duration, loan performance, and loan status.

The target variable is a bivariate indicator labeled "bad," and it is an indicator for loan accounts that resulted in a loan status of "Charged Off," "Default" or "Does not meet the credit policy: Charged Off." All of these loan status categories represent losses to the loan issuer.

The data set was split into separate TRAIN and TEST data sets using a 70/30 split ratio. The predictor variables have been modified to cap outliers according to the 1.5 IQR rule. We have also identified variables with less than 30% of their observations having missing data, and we inferred the missing values according to a process appropriate for that data type. We then created dummy variables for the categorical variables and developed several new variables through feature engineering techniques. If you have any questions on how to perform these data transformations, check out Chapter 5.

Data Restriction

Now that we have our base modeling data set constructed, we need to make a final decision prior to modeling. Since our data set is the full list of loan accounts since the inception of the Lending Club database, we need to understand that there is an initial ramp-up period that will have a low volume of loans, and we also need to realize that loans do not go bad right away. There will be a lag between application and eventual delinquency. Figure 7.3 shows the trend in the number of accounts with a bad status over the eleven-year history of the Lending Club data set.

Figure 7.3: Lending Club Account Trend

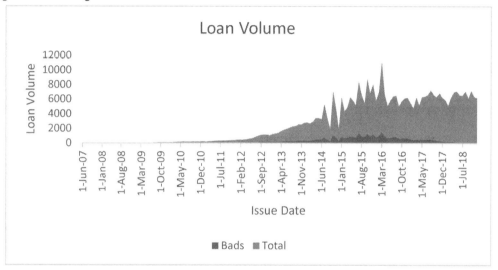

We can easily see that the ramp-up period for the data set extends from inception to around the beginning of 2012. Throughout this time period, loan volume is very low. If we were to include this time period in our modeling data set, it would not be adequately representative of the loan type and volume that we would expect at the point of model implementation. Figure 7.4 isolates the volume of accounts with a bad status for the Lending Club data set.

Figure 7.4: Lending Club Bad Status Trend

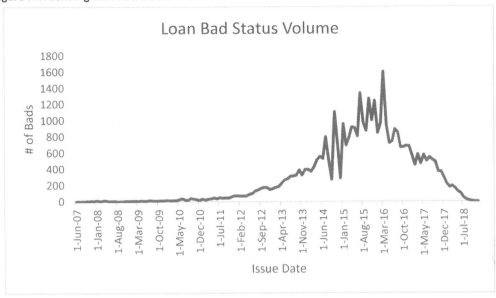

This graph shows that the number of bads (accounts with a bad status) starts to increase around the beginning of 2012 and reaches its peak in March 2016 after which the number of bads decreases through the end of the time period.

What is a data scientist supposed to do with this information? These charts give us insight into the nature of the target variable. We now understand that there is a clear ramp-up period where a small number of loans are being issued, and during that time, the number of bad loans is very low. This situation is most likely because loans do not go bad right away. There is generally a lag between the time period of loan issuance and delinquency. We can also see this occurring in the later time periods where the number of bads is decreasing in the later months. This is most likely because these loans have not had enough time to go bad.

If we are to build a model that adequately represents the true bad rate, I would choose a tight time frame where the loans have enough volume, and they have enough time to have gone bad. For our modeling purposes, I will restrict the data to loan issue dates between Jan 1, 2015, and Dec 31, 2015. That will give us a solid one-year period of representative loan volume.

Program 7.1 limits the training data set to the specified time period and develops a frequency distribution for the "bad" variable.

Program 7.1: Limit Data Set by Time Frame

```
DATA TRAIN;
  SET MYDATA.MODEL_TRAIN;
  WHERE '01JAN2015'd le issue_date le '01DEC2015'd;
RUN;

PROC FREQ DATA=TRAIN; TABLES BAD; RUN;
```

Output 7.1: Target Value Frequency Distribution

bad	Frequency	Percent	Cumulative Frequency	Cumulative Percent
0	53498	81.99	53498	81.99
1	11754	18.01	65252	100.00

Output 7.1 shows that 18.01% of loans issued in the specified time period result in a bad status.

Visualization

The first step to any modeling process is to visualize the data. This step will help you to understand the relationships between the predictors and the relationship between each predictor and the target variable, but there is another, often-unspoken, reason to visualize the data. With the visualization, you can gain an *a priori* idea of how well a model can separate the positive target values from the non-positive target values.

With just one look, you can often know before you do any modeling whether there is a clear separation between the binary target values, in which case you could expect strong modeling results. If there is not a clear separation between the binary target values, you can expect that your model will not be as strong.

Output 7.2 shows a scatter plot graph that shows the relationship between the predictor variables loan_amnt and int_rate. This graph also represents the target variable bad as a blue circle for cases where bad = 0 and a red triangle where bad = 1. Program 7.2 provides the code to develop this graph.

Program 7.2: Scatter Plot of Predictor Variables

```
ods graphics / attrpriority=none;
proc sgplot data=TRAIN (obs=1000);
styleattrs datasymbols=(circlefilled trianglefilled) ;
      scatter x=loan_amnt y=int_rate / group=bad;
      title 'Scatter Plot of Loan Data';
run;
```

The first thing that we notice when we examine Output 7.2 is that the target variable appears to be randomly scattered throughout the decision space. There does not appear to be a strong separation between the "goods" and the "bads" in relation to these two variables.

Output 7.2: Scatter Plot of Loan Data

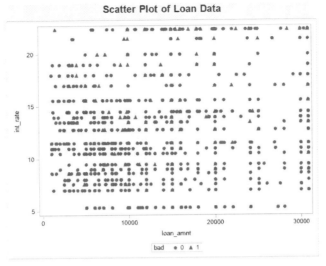

Maybe this issue is just the result of these particular variables. In order to get a broader understanding of the issue, we can develop a scatter plot matrix that contains several variables and plot them against each other. This approach can provide us with different views of the target variable, and we can gain additional information on what our expectations should be for any model that we develop.

Program 7.3 provides the code to develop the scatter plot matrix with each variable grouped by the target variable.

Program 7.3: Scatter Plot Matrix of Predictor Variables

```
proc sgscatter data=TRAIN (obs=250);
  title "Scatterplot Matrix for Loan Data";
  matrix loan_amnt total_bc_limit dti int_rate / group=bad;
run;
```

Output 7.3 shows the scatter plot matrix for four of the predictor variables where each has been grouped by the target variable. In this plot, the blue circles indicate where bad = 0 and the red plus signs represent where bad = 1.

A scatter plot matrix can easily get visually overwhelming. A lot is going on in one chart. Notice that I've included only 250 observations in the chart. Keep in mind that with a sample this small, we can expect some bias in the results. However, this does show us that the same issue of a non-distinct decision boundary between the goods and bads is prevalent across all these predictor variables.

Output 7.3: Scatter Plot Matrix of Predictor Variables

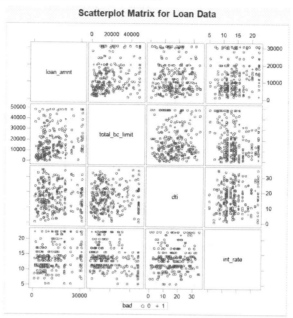

Most books about data science rely on examples where there are clear decision boundaries between the "goods" and the "bads" and that each predictor variable is a strongly significant predictor. However, in the real world, data is messy. In fact, most of the time, it will be a challenge to find a significant predictive relationship between your target and a list of predictor variables.

This challenge is especially true when there are restrictions (such as regulatory restrictions) put in place about what types of variables you are allowed to use (such as age, race, sex, location, and so on). There are also modeling issues of *data bleed*, which is where direct information about your target variable is contained in a predictor variable. There are other technical issues of data availability and data refresh schedules and the ability to move certain variables into a production environment that will limit your ability to build the best model possible. All of these restrictions need to be taken into account when developing your model.

Now that we have taken all of our restrictions into account and we have an *a priori* idea about how effective a model will be in separating our goods from our bads, we can expect that a binary classifier model will have a moderate level of effectiveness. We should not be surprised if we get a Gini score of around 40 and an overall accuracy of around 80%. Don't worry, the concepts of Gini and accuracy will be explained in the next couple of sections.

Logistic Regression Model

We have stressed the importance of variable selection prior to any modeling efforts. This selection process ensures that the variables that we will include in our model are appropriate (no data bleed) and permitted (allowed by regulation standards) and available (allowed by an IT department that controls the data infrastructure). Once these restrictions have been met, we can develop our predictive model.

Remember that the business goal of our model is to predict whether a loan will result in a bad status at some point in the future. We would like to implement this model at the point of the loan application, so all variables that we will feed into our model must be available at the point of application. When someone applies for a loan, we would not know if they have missed any payments yet or if they are delinquent or if they have a collection recovery fee. We wouldn't know any of this information because, at the point of application, these variables do not exist, so we must not include them in the model.

If we did include those variables, this would be an issue of *data bleed*, which is also known as *information leakage*. This is when you have variables that are **directly** related to the target variable in the model. If you were to include these variables, your model would be highly accurate, but it is a false accuracy because you could not implement that model due to those variables not being available at the point of application.

I have taken the liberty of examining the list of all variables in the Lending Club data set and selecting only those that are available at the point of application. Table 7.1 shows the list of 45 variables that meet our criteria.

Table 7.1: Variables Available at the Point of Application

acc_open_past_24mths	grade_F	purpose_other
annual_inc	grade_G	revol_bal
app_individual	home_mort	term_36
app_joint	home_own	term_60
bc_util	home_rent	tot_hi_cred_lim
dti	inq_last_6mths	total_bc_limit
emp_10	int_rate	ver_not
emp_0to4	loan_amnt	ver_source
emp_5to9	mo_sin_old_il_acct	ver_verified
emp_NA	mo_sin_rcnt_tl	num_actv_bc_tl
grade_A	mort_acc	num_bc_tl
grade_B	mths_since_recent_bc	num_il_tl
grade_C	mths_since_recent_inq	open_acc
grade_D	purpose_dc	pct_tl_nvr_dlq
grade_E	purpose_hi	purpose_cc

These variables represent a mixture of loan attributes that include information about the borrower (annual income, length of employment, homeownership), loan information (loan grade, purpose, term length), prior borrower behavior (number of accounts open in that previous 24 months, loan inquiries in the last 6 months, percent of trades never delinquent), along with several other descriptive variables.

I can easily place these variables into a global variable by utilizing the LET statement. Program 7.4 puts the variables into a global variable labeled num_vars.

Program 7.4: Create Macro Variable That Contains Model Variable Names

```
%LET num_vars = acc_open_past_24mths annual_inc app_individual app_joint
bc_util dti emp_10 emp_0to4 emp_5to9 emp_NA grade_A grade_B grade_C
grade_D grade_E grade_F grade_G home_mort home_own home_rent
inq_last_6mths int_rate loan_amnt mo_sin_old_il_acct mo_sin_rcnt_tl
mort_acc mths_since_recent_bc mths_since_recent_inq num_actv_bc_tl
num_bc_tl num_il_tl open_acc pct_tl_nvr_dlq purpose_cc purpose_dc
purpose_hi purpose_other revol_bal term_36 term_60 tot_hi_cred_lim
total_bc_limit ver_not ver_source ver_verified ;
```

PROC LOGISTIC Code

Now that we have our training data set constructed and we have placed the predictors into a global variable, we are ready to develop the logistic regression algorithm. Program 7.5 develops a standard logistic regression model with the target variable bad and the predictors contained in the global num_var macro.

Program 7.5: Logistic Regression Model

```
ODS GRAPHICS ON;
PROC LOGISTIC DATA=TRAIN DESCENDING PLOTS=ALL;
        MODEL BAD = &num_vars. / SELECTION=STEPWISE
SLE=0.01 SLS=0.01 CORRB OUTROC=performance;
        OUTPUT OUT=MYDATA.LOG_REG_PROB PROB=score;
RUN;
```

Notes on Program 7.5:

- The ODS GRAPHICS statement is set to ON. This will provide us with all the output graphics that we specify in the logistic regression options.

- PROC LOGISTIC is used to develop the model. This is a highly flexible procedure that can be used to predict binary, ordinal, or nominal responses. There are several options available that allow the researcher to customize the specifications of their model:

    - The DESCENDING option reverses the sorting order for the levels of the response variable. This ensures that the model is predicting the event where BAD = 1. If this option is not selected, then the model will predict where BAD = 0.

    - The PLOTS option is set to ALL. You can specify which plots you want to appear in the output. The ALL option states that we want all available plots to appear in the output.

- The MODEL statement specifies the target and predictor values. This is the core part of the model where we specify that the target variable is BAD, and the predictors are the variables contained in the global variable num_vars. Remember that it is not necessary to have a global variable. You can easily place the individual predictor variables directly in the PROC LOGISTIC code. (Make sure that they are separated by a space and do not include commas to separate them.)

- The SELECTION method is set to STEPWISE. This selection is similar to the FORWARD selection method, but variables are not guaranteed to remain in the model. They can be replaced with new variables that are introduced further in the selection cycle.

- The SLE option specifies the Chi-Square significance level to enter the model with the FORWARD or STEPWISE selection methods.

- The SLS option specifies the Chi-Square significance level to remain in the model in the BACKWARDS elimination step.

- The CORRB statement displays the correlation matrix for the parameter estimates.

- The OUTROC statement creates an output data set that contains the information that we will need to develop the Receiver Operating Characteristic (ROC) curve.

- The OUTPUT OUT= statement specifies that we want to create a new data set that contains the target variable and all of the predictors as well as the newly developed model output predictive score.

- The SCORE option specifies that we want to name the newly created predictive score variable "score."

Program 7.5 may seem like a lot of code to develop for a simple logistic regression. Most of the code has been created to specify the options available in the LOGISTIC procedure. However, the code does not need to be complicated at all. Program 7.6 develops a logistic regression in a single line of code.

Program 7.6: Simple Logistic Regression Program

```
PROC LOGISTIC DATA=TRAIN DESCENDING; MODEL BAD = &num_vars.; RUN;
```

That's all you really need to develop a logistic regression in SAS. However, all of the available options allow you to customize your model according to your needs.

PROC LOGISTIC Model Output

PROC LOGISTIC creates a variety of output, including summary information about the modeling data set, summary information for each step in our stepwise selection, maximum likelihood estimates, odds ratio estimates, model fit statistics, and any graphs that we specified in the PLOTS statement.

Model Summary Information

The first set of outputs provides you verification of your model inputs. Output 7.4 shows that the model is developed on the WORK.TRAIN data set and that target variable is BAD. It also specifies that this is a binary response model that was optimized with the Fisher's scoring technique.

The model used all 65,252 observations. This means that there were no missing values in the data set. The Response Profile shows that the model is specified where the target variable BAD = 1.

Output 7.4: Logistic Regression Output

Model Information	
Data Set	WORK.TRAIN
Response Variable	bad
Number of Response Levels	2
Model	binary logit
Optimization Technique	Fisher's scoring

Number of Observations Read	65252
Number of Observations Used	65252

Response Profile		
Ordered Value	bad	Total Frequency
1	1	11754
2	0	53498

Stepwise Selection Summary

The next section of the model output shows each step of the stepwise selection technique. The predictor variables are added to the model one at a time and evaluated for their predictive power as defined by the Chi-Square metric. Output 7.5 shows the summary of the stepwise selection.

Output 7.5: Logistic Regression Stepwise Selection Table

Summary of Stepwise Selection						
	Effect				Score	
Step	Entered	Removed	DF	Number In	Chi-Square	Pr > ChiSq
1	int_rate		1	1	4387.7371	<.0001
2	acc_open_past_24mths		1	2	378.4419	<.0001
3	tot_hi_cred_lim		1	3	310.9002	<.0001
4	dti		1	4	131.341	<.0001
5	emp_NA		1	5	77.7841	<.0001
6	loan_amnt		1	6	54.8411	<.0001
7	grade_A		1	7	48.8296	<.0001
8	home_mort		1	8	39.9212	<.0001
9	total_bc_limit		1	9	20.5846	<.0001
10	num_actv_bc_tl		1	10	47.8554	<.0001
11	term_36		1	11	20.8089	<.0001
12	inq_last_6mths		1	12	23.3802	<.0001
13	mort_acc		1	13	20.3845	<.0001
14	grade_C		1	14	12.6847	0.0004
15	ver_not		1	15	9.4022	0.0022
16	home_own		1	16	8.7725	0.0031
17	grade_D		1	17	6.9997	0.0082

This table of information shows that there were 17 variables that made it into the final model. These variables are ordered by their respective predictive power as defined by their Chi-Square value. Although we specified that the selection method was stepwise, in this particular model, none of the variables that were initially added to the model were replaced by new variables being added to the model. The Removed column would show where a new variable replaced a previous variable and at which step in the model that activity occurred.

Maximum Likelihood Estimates

The Maximum Likelihood Estimates table provides the information that we would typically use to state our model. The standard output for this table is that the intercept value is stated first, and then the model predictors are listed in alphabetical order. However, I have reordered the list of predictors by sorting them by their Chi-Square values. This adjustment allows us to see which variables carry the most predictive power in the model. Output 7.6 shows the re-sorted Analysis of Maximum Likelihood Estimates table.

Output 7.6: Logistic Regression Maximum Likelihood Estimates

Analysis of Maximum Likelihood Estimates					
Parameter	DF	Estimate	Standard Error	Wald Chi-Square	Pr > ChiSq
Intercept	1	-3.5418	0.0758	2182.8133	<.0001
int_rate	1	0.1144	0.00379	913.5426	<.0001
acc_open_past_24mths	1	0.0744	0.00421	311.9744	<.0001
dti	1	0.013	0.00128	102.5576	<.0001
emp_NA	1	0.4312	0.0426	102.5457	<.0001
total_bc_limit	1	-8.48E-06	1.12E-06	57.261	<.0001
tot_hi_cred_lim	1	-9.90E-07	1.32E-07	56.2152	<.0001
loan_amnt	1	0.000012	1.72E-06	46.2241	<.0001
num_actv_bc_tl	1	0.044	0.00676	42.4342	<.0001
home_mort	1	-0.1802	0.0293	37.7032	<.0001
term_36	1	-0.1451	0.0268	29.2797	<.0001
inq_last_6mths	1	0.0903	0.0187	23.2999	<.0001
grade_A	1	-0.2291	0.0518	19.575	<.0001
grade_C	1	0.109	0.0259	17.74	<.0001
mort_acc	1	-0.04	0.0095	17.6877	<.0001
ver_not	1	-0.0832	0.0275	9.1287	0.0025
home_own	1	-0.1067	0.0363	8.6406	0.0033
grade_D	1	0.0776	0.0293	6.9983	0.0082

We can further refine this information to make it more user-friendly with some data manipulation. Output 7.7 shows a new column labeled "Percent Contribution." This newly calculated field is simply each of the predictor's Chi-Square value divided by the sum of the Wald Chi-Square values (excluding the intercept value).

Notice that the variable int_rate contains 50.7% of the model's predictive value. This makes intuitive sense since the interest rate is based on either a separate predictive model or a set of heuristic rules that reflect the riskiness of the borrower. It would be a reasonable approach to remove this variable from the list of predictors that are fed into the model and rerun the algorithm. We would expect that a few new variables could replace the overbearing int_rate variable, and we should expect that the model's predictive power will decrease slightly due to the removal of this powerful variable.

I have also rescaled three of the predictors to make their interpretation clearer. The variables total_bc_limit, total_hi_cred_limit, and loan_amnt have model estimates that are very small. This is because a single dollar increase in a borrower's loan amount would impact the dependent variable by only 0.000012 points. We can easily divide these values by 10,000 so that the current variable loan_amnt is transformed into a new variable "loan amount per $10,000," and the new model estimate is 0.12 points. This adjustment can be interpreted as the dependent variable BAD will increase 0.12 points for every $10,000 borrowed with everything else being held constant.

Output 7.7: Transformed Maximum Likelihood Estimates

Analysis of Maximum Likelihood Estimates					
Parameter	DF	Estimate	Standard Error	Wald Chi-Square	Percent Contribution
Intercept	1	-3.541800	0.08	2,182.81	
int_rate	1	0.114400	0.00	913.54	50.7%
acc_open_past_24mths	1	0.074400	0.00	311.97	17.3%
dti	1	0.013000	0.00	102.56	5.7%
emp_NA	1	0.431200	0.04	102.55	5.7%
total_bc_limit / 10000	1	-0.084800	0.00	57.26	3.2%
tot_hi_cred_lim / 10000	1	-0.009900	0.00	56.22	3.1%
loan_amnt / 10000	1	0.120000	0.00	46.22	2.6%
num_actv_bc_tl	1	0.044000	0.01	42.43	2.4%
home_mort	1	-0.180200	0.03	37.70	2.1%
term_36	1	-0.145100	0.03	29.28	1.6%
inq_last_6mths	1	0.090300	0.02	23.30	1.3%
grade_A	1	-0.229100	0.05	19.58	1.1%
grade_C	1	0.109000	0.03	17.74	1.0%
mort_acc	1	-0.040000	0.01	17.69	1.0%
ver_not	1	-0.083200	0.03	9.13	0.5%
home_own	1	-0.106700	0.04	8.64	0.5%
grade_D	1	0.077600	0.03	7.00	0.4%

Output 7.7 also shows us that if we wanted to develop a parsimonious model and select only the variables that significantly contribute to the overall predictive power of the model, we could comfortably retain the top 5 or 6 variables and still have nearly the same overall strength of the model.

Odds Ratio Estimates

The next section of the model output shows the table of Odds Ratio Estimates. The PLOTS=ALL option also provides a visual description of the table. These pieces of output are shown in Output 7.8.

Output 7.8: Logistic Regression Odds Ratios

Odds Ratio Estimates		
Effect	Point Estimate	95% Wald Confidence Limits
acc_open_past_24mths	1.077	1.068 1.086
dti	1.013	1.011 1.016
emp_NA	1.539	1.416 1.673
grade_A	0.795	0.719 0.880
grade_C	1.115	1.060 1.173
grade_D	1.081	1.020 1.145
home_mort	0.835	0.788 0.885
home_own	0.899	0.837 0.965
inq_last_6mths	1.094	1.055 1.135
int_rate	1.121	1.113 1.130
loan_amnt	1.000	1.000 1.000
mort_acc	0.961	0.943 0.979
num_actv_bc_tl	1.045	1.031 1.059
term_36	0.865	0.821 0.912
tot_hi_cred_lim	1.000	1.000 1.000
total_bc_limit	1.000	1.000 1.000
ver_not	0.920	0.872 0.971

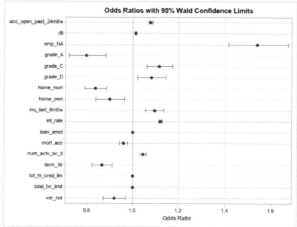

Odds ratios are easy to interpret. If a variable has an odds ratio of 1, this means that the variable has no influence on the target variable. An odds ratio greater than 1 means that there are higher odds of the outcome event happening when there is exposure to this variable. An odds ratio of less than 1 means that there are lower odds of the outcome happening when there is exposure to this variable.

Let's look at our example. The variables total_bc_limit, total_hi_cred_limit, and loan_amnt have odds ratios of one. This makes sense in their raw form because the model estimate for loan_amnt is 0.000012, which is nearly zero. If the odds ratios were extended to seven decimal places, then we would see a slight impact on the odds of the outcome event happening in relation to that variable. If the Odds Estimate table was constructed with the newly scaled version of these variables (example: loan amount per $10,000 = 0.12), then we would see distinct positive or negative odds ratios for those scaled variables.

The variable Grade_A has an odds ratio of 0.795. This can be interpreted as when the dummy variable Grade_A is 1, there is a reduced chance of the target variable BAD being positive. This makes sense because the variable Grade_A represents a loan category that has the least risky borrowers. If a loan is categorized as Grade_A, then there is less of a chance (lower odds) of it going bad.

In contrast, the variables Grade_C and Grade_D represent more risky loans. When either of these variables is positive, there is an increased chance that the response variable BAD will be positive.

Model Evaluation Metrics

Up to this point, we have seen SAS output related to several stages of the model development. These stages include what was fed into the model, how the model was constructed, and each step of the model selection process, point estimates, and odds ratios. These are all incredibly valuable pieces of information, but they do not answer one of the most important questions: Is my model any good?

For binary classification models, there are several methods of model evaluation. We will cover several of these methods in the chapter devoted to evaluating model output. For now, we will focus on the two main evaluation methods, which are standard outputs for PROC LOGISTIC:

- Gini metric and Somers' D score
- ROC and AUC curves

Gini Metric and Somers' D scores

One of the standard model output tables that the PROC LOGISTIC statement creates is titled "Association of Predicted Probabilities and Observed Responses." This table contains an important model evaluation metric and the information about how this metric was constructed. Output 7.9 shows this table and its associated components.

Output 7.9: Logistic Regression Evaluation Metrics

Association of Predicted Probabilities and Observed Responses			
Percent Concordant	71.1	Somers' D	0.422
Percent Discordant	28.9	Gamma	0.422
Percent Tied	0.0	Tau-a	0.125
Pairs	628815492	c	0.711

The main metric that this table of information displays is the Somers' D. This metric is also commonly called the Gini metric or the Accuracy Ratio. Although there are different ways of calculating these metrics, they all mean the same thing. The default methodology of calculating the Somers' D statistic in PROC LOGISTIC is through the concordance and tied percent. All of this information is contained in the above table, but let's review how this information is created and used.

> **Step 1:** The logistic regression output creates an output table that contains the actual event data and the predicted probability field. This data is separated into two data sets. The first data set contains all of the observations where the target event (BAD) = 1

along with the associated predicted probabilities for those observations. The second data set contains all of the observations where the target event (BAD) = 0 along with the associated predicted probabilities for those observations.

Step 2: SAS creates a matrix data set where each observation in the first data set is compared to each observation in the second data set. This is a Cartesian product (cross-join) of events and non-events. The volume of this matrix data set is displayed in Output 7.9 in the field titled Pairs. We can see that the matrix contains 628K observations.

Step 3: Concordance is evaluated. A pair of observations is considered **concordant** if the event =1 and the predicted probability is higher than the observation where event = 0. A pair of observations is considered **discordant** if the opposite is true. This is where the observation where event = 0 has a higher predicted probability than the observation where event = 1. A pair is tied if the predicted probability is tied for an observation where event = 1 and an observation where event = 0.

Step 4: Final percent values are calculated:

Percent Concordant = 100*[(Number of concordant pairs) / Total number of pairs]

Percent Discordant = 100*[(Number of discordant pairs) / Total number of pairs]

Percent Tied = 100*[(Number of tied pairs) / Total number of pairs]

Step 5: Evaluation metrics calculated:

Somers' D = 2 * AUC − 1 (also calculated as (Percent Concordant − Percent Discordant))

- This metric is used to determine the strength and direction of the relationship between pairs of variables. Its values range from -1.0 (all pairs disagree) to 1.0 (all pairs agree).
- This is very similar to the Gini metric produced by other binary classifiers.

Gamma − Utilizes nearly the same methodology as the Somers' D metric, but the Gamma metric does not penalize for ties. Because it does not penalize for ties, its value will be generally higher than the Somers' D value.

Tau-a = (2(number of concordant − number of discordant) / (N(N-1)))

- The denominator of this equation represents all possible pairs.
- This value is generally much lower than the Somers' D value since there are generally many paired observations with the same response.

Area Under the Curve (AUC) = (Percent Concordant + 0.5 * Percent Tied) / 100

- ○ This is also labeled as "c" in Output 7.10. This value is also often represented as a Receiver Operating Characteristic (ROC) curve.

- ○ This value ranges from 0.5 to 1.0 where 0.5 represents a model randomly selecting a response and 1.0 represents a model perfectly predicting a response.

- ○ Output 7.10 displays the ROC curve produced by PROC LOGISTIC.

Output 7.10: ROC Curve

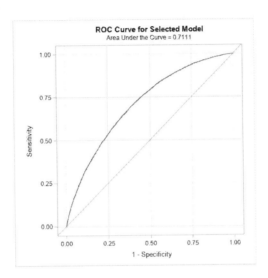

Detailed information about the ROC curve as well as several model evaluation metrics will be provided in the chapter dedicated to model evaluation.

Scoring the TEST Data Set

At this point, we have selected and transformed our TRAIN data set, developed our logistic regression model, and evaluated the results on the TRAIN data set. However, in order to truly evaluate the predictive accuracy of our model, we will need to apply it to a hold-out TEST population.

There are two main methods of applying our model to a data set that was not used for the development of the model.

1. The SCORE option in PROC LOGISTIC
2. Hard-coding the equation into a DATA step

Both of these methods will produce the same score for a given data set.

Transform the Hold-out TEST Data Set

The first step to scoring a hold-out TEST data set is to make sure that the data set has been exposed to the same treatments and filters that were applied to the TRAIN data set. For our example, many of the original data transformations (missing value imputation, feature engineering, outlier adjustments) were already applied to the TEST data set. This process was detailed in Chapter 5: Create a Modeling Data Set.

However, in this chapter, prior to developing the logistic regression model we made a few additional filters to the data. Due to a ramp-up period and a lag in the response variable, we made the decision to restrict the data to loan issue dates between Jan 1, 2015, and Dec 31, 2015.

If we do not restrict the data in the same way, then we will get very poor model results on the TEST data set. This is because the model was designed to calculate the probability of the dependent variable being positive given a set of independent variables during a time frame where the dependent variable has an event rate of 18.01% (Table 7.1). If the model is applied to earlier or later time periods where the event rate is much lower, the model will underperform.

Program 7.7 filters the MYDATA.MODEL_TEST data set to the same time period as the TRAIN data set. Again, the only reason that we are selecting these dates is because the event rate varies across the entire time period of the Lending Club data set.

Program 7.7: Limit the TEST Data Set by Time Frame

```
DATA TEST;
  SET MYDATA.MODEL_TEST;
  WHERE '01JAN2015'd le issue_date le '01DEC2015'd;
RUN;

PROC FREQ DATA=TEST; TABLES BAD; RUN;
```

Output 7.11 shows that the event rate for the TEST data set for this time period is 17.66%. This is within a half-percent range of the event rate of the TRAIN data set.

Output 7.11: TEST Data Set Target Value Frequency Distribution

bad	Frequency	Percent	Cumulative Frequency	Cumulative Percent
0	22866	82.34	22866	82.34
1	4905	17.66	27771	100.00

Now that we have selected the appropriate time frame for the TEST data set, we can apply the model to the TEST data set.

SCORE Option

PROC LOGISTIC includes an option called SCORE that allows you to specify a data set that you want to score with the model that was developed on the TRAIN data set. Program 7.8 shows this option in context with the original PROC LOGISTIC. Notice that the evaluation options (PLOTS, CORRB, OUTROC) have all been removed from the program. You can retain these options if you want, but they will just reproduce the same evaluation output that we already examined in the initial model development section.

Program 7.8: Score the TEST Data Set in the PROC LOGISTIC Program

```
PROC LOGISTIC DATA=TRAIN DESCENDING PLOTS=NONE;
      MODEL BAD = &num_vars. / SELECTION=STEPWISE SLE=0.01 SLS=0.01;
      SCORE DATA=TEST OUT=TEST_SCORE;
RUN;
```

The SCORE option allows you to specify the data set that you want to score. The DATA=TEST statement tells SAS that you want to score the hold-out TEST data set, and the OUT=TEST_SCORE tells SAS that you want to create an output data set that contains the probability scores and all of the original data from the TEST data set.

The default output of the SCORE option contains all of the original data from the TEST data set and two additional fields:

- P_1 – The probability that the observation has a dependent variable = 1

- P_0 – The probability that the observation has a dependent variable = 0

We can examine the scored TEST data with the use of PROC MEANS. Program 7.9 develops this program.

Program 7.9: Analyze Model Predicted Values

```
PROC MEANS DATA=TEST_SCORE N NMISS MIN MAX MEAN;
      VAR BAD P_0 P_1;
RUN;
```

Program 7.9 creates an analysis table that shows the values for the original target variable BAD along with the two predicted probability variables. Output 7.12 shows the analytical output.

Output 7.12: PROC MEANS Output

Variable	Label	N	N Miss	Minimum	Maximum	Mean
bad		27771	0	0	1.0000000	0.1766231
P_0	Predicted Probability: bad=0	27771	0	0.2895911	0.9858069	0.8204597
P_1	Predicted Probability: bad=1	27771	0	0.0141931	0.7104089	0.1795403

This table shows that the average rate of the actual target variable BAD is 17.66%. The variable P_1 shows the predicted probability of the event and the average predicted probability of the event is 17.95%. This analysis gives us an initial high-level analysis of the predictive accuracy of the model. The actual event rate and the predicted event rate are not too far from one another.

Evaluation Macros

We have seen that the standard LOGISTIC procedure provides evaluation metrics (Somers' D and ROC chart) for the data set that the model was developed on. However, the standard model output does not contain evaluation metrics for the scored data set. In order to evaluate the scored data set, you have to calculate the evaluation metrics yourself.

Luckily, there are many evaluation macros already developed and free to use on the internet. I will explore some of these in detail in the chapter on model evaluation metrics. But for now, I will quickly apply one of the model evaluation macros that I gathered from the internet and use it to assess the accuracy of the model on the TEST data set.

The model evaluation macro that I will use was developed by Wensui Liu and is labeled "separation." This easy-to-use macro creates several evaluation metrics and charts. I have placed this macro on my C drive, and I call it with a %INCLUDE statement. Program 7.10 shows the application of this macro.

Program 7.10: Application of Macro
```
%INCLUDE 'C:/Users/James Gearheart/Desktop/SAS Book
Stuff/Projects/separation.sas';
%separation(data = TEST_SCORE, score = P_1, y = bad);
```

The first line simply states where I placed the macro and the name of the macro. The actual macro is called with the *%separation* statement followed by specifications of your data set that you want to evaluate.

- The DATA statement allows you to specify the name of the data set that you want to evaluate.

- The SCORE statement allows you to specify the name of the predicted probability variable.

- The Y statement allows you to specify the name of the target variable.

With these three simple statements, the macro will develop a detailed analysis of the separation power and accuracy of your scored data set. Output 7.13 shows one of the output tables generated by this macro. This output table is called a *lift table* and will be reviewed in detail in the model evaluation metrics chapter.

The main takeaways from this output for our purposes are the AUC and Gini scores. In the header information in Output 7.13, we can see that the TEST data set has been evaluated with an AUC = 0.7097 and a Gini = 0.4193.

Output 7.13: TEST Data Set Lift Table

	MIN SCORE	MAX SCORE	GOOD #	BAD #	TOTAL #	ODDS	BAD RATE	CUMULATIVE BAD RATE	BAD PERCENT	CUMU. BAD PERCENT
	GOOD BAD SEPARATION REPORT FOR P_1 IN DATA TEST_SCORE									
	(AUC STATISTICS = 0.7097, GINI COEFFICIENT = 0.4193, DIVERGENCE = 0.5339)									
BAD	0.342	0.7104	1,689	1,088	2,777	1.55	39.18%	39.18%	22.18%	22.18%
		0.2708	0.342	1,947	830	2,777	2.35	29.89%	34.53%	16.92%	39.10%
	0.2239	0.2708	2,112	665	2,777	3.18	23.95%	31.00%	13.56%	52.66%
	0.1874	0.2239	2,196	581	2,777	3.78	20.92%	28.48%	11.85%	64.51%
	0.1562	0.1874	2,288	490	2,778	4.67	17.64%	26.31%	9.99%	74.50%

I	0.1284	0.1562	2,384	393	2,777	6.07	14.15%		24.29%	8.01%	82.51%
I	0.1021	0.1284	2,438	339	2,777	7.19	12.21%		22.56%	6.91%	89.42%
I	0.0766	0.1021	2,548	229	2,777	11.13	8.25%		20.77%	4.67%	94.09%
V	0.0533	0.0766	2,581	196	2,777	13.17	7.06%		19.25%	4.00%	98.08%
GOOD	0.0142	0.0533	2,683	94	2,777	28.54	3.38%		17.66%	1.92%	100.00%
	0.0142	0.7104	22,866	4,905	27,771						

The AUC for the development TRAIN data set was 0.7111, and the Somers' D score was 0.422. When we compare these scores to the scores that were generated on the hold-out TEST data set, we can see that the TEST metrics are slightly lower for both the AUC and the Gini metrics. This shows that the model is not overfitting the data and can be adequately applied to other data sets.

Hard-coding Scoring Method

This scoring method allows you to input all of the components of the logistic regression model directly into a DATA step. All of the information that we need to define the logistic regression equation is contained in the model output that was generated from the LOGISTIC procedure developed on the TRAIN data set (Output 7.6).

Program 7.11 shows the development of the logistic regression equation within the same data set that we used to filter the TEST data set.

Program 7.11: Hard-coding Scoring Method

```
DATA TEST_SCORE;
        SET MYDATA.MODEL_TEST;
        WHERE '01JAN2015'd le issue_date le '01DEC2015'd;

        /*Model variables and coefficients from TRAIN model output*/
        xb = (-3.5418) +
        int_rate * 0.1144 +
        acc_open_past_24mths * 0.0744 +
        dti * 0.013 +
        emp_NA * 0.4312 +
        (total_bc_limit / 10000) * -0.0848 +
        (tot_hi_cred_lim / 10000) * -0.0099 +
        (loan_amnt / 10000) * 0.12 +
        num_actv_bc_tl * 0.044 +
        home_mort * -0.1802 +
        term_36 * -0.1451 +
        inq_last_6mths * 0.0903 +
        grade_A* -0.2291 +
        grade_C* 0.109 +
        mort_acc * -0.04 +
        ver_not * -0.0832 +
        home_own * -0.1067 +
        grade_D * 0.0776;
```

```
score = exp(xb)/(1+exp(xb));
RUN;
```

Notes on Program 7.11:

- A DATA step is used to develop and process the logistic regression equation. This DATA step inputs data from the MYDATA.MODEL_TEST data set.

- The data is filtered to the defined date range in order to be aligned with the developmental data's event rate. At this point, the data set is exactly the same as the TEST data set that we fed into the previous PROC LOGISTIC with the SCORE option.

- The logistic regression equation is created by inputting the model intercept and each model variable along with their associated weighted values.

- Notice that the three variables with extremely small weights (total_bc_limit, tot_hi_cred_lim, loan_amnt) have been transformed by dividing each value by 10,000. Their associated weighted values have been adjusted accordingly.

- The final predicted score value is labeled "score". This value is based on the equation that was introduced in Equation 7.2:

$$p(X) = \frac{e^{\beta_0 + \beta_1 X}}{1 + e^{\beta_0 + \beta_1 X}}$$

The hard-coded scoring technique is very useful because you do not have to redevelop PROC LOGISTIC every time that you want to apply the model to a new data set. It is also very practical when you move your model into production and have to hand over the model to your IT team to implement the model in a live environment. It is impractical to run PROC LOGISTIC every time you want to score a new loan applicant.

Linear Discriminant Analysis

We just reviewed how the logistic regression model directly models the conditional distribution of the response variable Y given the predictors X (Equation 7.2). The Linear Discriminant Analysis (LDA) model also has the goal of estimating these conditional probabilities, but with a slightly different approach. The LDA algorithm models the distribution of the predictors (X) separately for each response class (Y). The algorithm then incorporates Bayes' theorem to transform these distributions into a form very similar to the logistic regression form.

The LDA algorithm develops a discriminant function that is also known as the classification criterion. The target variable defines a set of groups, and the discriminant function classifies each observation into one of the defined groups. A measure of generalized squared distance determines this discriminant function. These groups are projected onto a lower-dimensional plane that maximizes the separation between the groups. The discriminant function determines the minimum number of dimensions needed to describe the differences between the groups.

Because the LDA algorithm is essentially projecting the data set onto a lower-dimensional space, it is often used as a dimensionality reduction technique. It is very similar to Principle Component Analysis (PCA); however, PCA attempts to find the component axes that maximize the variance of the data, the LDA algorithm attempts to find the component axes that maximize the separation between groups.

Because of the projection mapping methodology, LDA can be used in two different ways:

1. **Descriptive Discriminant Analysis** – Data pre-processing dimensionality reduction methodology that reduces several independent variables onto a projected lower-dimensional plane. These newly created variables that maximize the separation between groups can be fed into other predictive models.
2. **Predictive Discriminant Analysis** – This is a machine learning classification technique that predicts the probability of two or more classes.

In this chapter, we will focus on the predictive discriminant analysis approach.

When to Use LDA for Prediction

Although logistic regression is the standard modeling approach for parametric classification models, there are specific instances when you might use the LDA model instead of a logistic regression model:

1. When there are more than two response classes.
2. When classes are well-separated. (In this case, the parameter estimates for the logistic regression model can be unstable, so the LDA is preferable.)
3. There is a small number of observations.
4. The distribution of the predictors is approximately normal.

If your data set contains one or more of the above characteristics, then the LDA model could provide significant predictive power with stable model coefficients.

PROC DISCRIM

The linear discriminant analysis predictive model can be created in SAS with PROC DISCRIM. This flexible procedure allows researchers to customize their model by specifying a variety of options, including whether the model will be parametric or non-parametric and whether the covariance matrices will be pooled. Researchers can also specify the threshold for classification, they can specify non-parametric methods, and they can select cross-validation methods.

For our purposes, we will develop a basic LDA predictive model on the same Lending Club data set that we used for the logistic regression model and the same target variable BAD. This will allow us to compare the logistic regression and LDA output.

Program 7.12 creates a global variable called "log_vars" that contains all of the predictors that were significant in the logistic regression model. This list of variables is fed into PROC DISCRIM.

Program 7.12: Create a Macro Variable That Contains All the Predictor Variables

```
%LET log_vars = int_rate acc_open_past_24mths dti emp_NA total_bc_limit
tot_hi_cred_lim loan_amnt num_actv_bc_tl home_mort term_36 inq_last_6mths
grade_A grade_C mort_acc ver_not home_own grade_D ;


PROC DISCRIM DATA=TRAIN OUTSTAT=DIS out=discrim_out
        TESTDATA=TEST TESTOUT=TEST_OUT;
        CLASS BAD;
        VAR &log_vars.;
RUN;
```

Notes on Program 7.12:

- PROC DISCRIM is used to create the LDA model on the TRAIN data set.

- The OUTSTAT statement tells SAS to create an output data set containing all of the various statistics such as means, standard deviations, and correlations.

- The OUT statement tells SAS to create an output data set that contains all of the TRAIN data set variables along with the model score (also called "posterior probabilities").

- The TESTDATA statement specifies that we want to score the hold-out TEST data set with the LDA model that was constructed on the TRAIN data set.

- The TESTOUT statement tells SAS to create an output data set that contains all of the TEST data set variables along with the model score.

- The CLASS statement specifies the groups for analysis.

- The VAR statement specifies the predictive variables for the model. In this example, I have limited the list of variables to the variables that were indicated as significant in the logistic regression model.

PROC DISCRIM Model Output

PROC DISCRIM creates a variety of output including summary information about the modeling data set, generalized squared distance, and the linear discriminant function for the target variable.

Model Summary Information

The first set of outputs provides you verification of your model inputs. Output 7.14 shows that the model is developed on the TRAIN data set that contains 17 predictors and a target variable that has two classes. It also specifies that the model used all 65,252 observations in the development of the model, and no observations were excluded.

The Class Level Information table shows the frequency and proportion of the target variable and the prior probability of that target variable.

Output 7.14: PROC DISCRIM Output

Total Sample Size	65252	DF Total	65251
Variables	17	DF Within Classes	65250
Classes	2	DF Between Classes	1

Number of Observations Read	65252
Number of Observations Used	65252

		Class Level Information			
bad	Variable Name	Frequency	Weight	Proportion	Prior Probability
0	0	53498	53498	0.819868	0.500000
1	1	11754	11754	0.180132	0.500000

Method Details

PROC DISCRIM allows you to specify whether you want to use the pooled or within-group covariance matrix to calculate the generalized squared distances. The default option is POOL=YES. This option specifies that the model will compute the linear discriminant function. If the option was changed to POOL=NO, then the procedure would use the within-group covariance matrix and the model would compute the quadratic discriminant function.

Output 7.15 shows the natural log of the determinant of the pooled covariance matrix.

Output 7.15: Pooled Covariance Matrix

Pooled Covariance Matrix Information	
Covariance Matrix Rank	Natural Log of the Determinant of the Covariance Matrix
17	51.55151

The procedure also allows you to specify whether you want to create a parametric or non-parametric model. This option is indicated with the METHOD statement. The default value is METHOD=NORMAL. This will create a parametric LDA model. If the option is changed to METHOD = NPAR, this will use a non-parametric approach to develop the model.

Linear Discriminant Function

The linear discriminant function is similar to the logistic regression model estimates. It shows how the data is used to classify an observation into one of the given groups (target levels). This example shows a binary classification of 0 and 1. However, if there were more than two classification groups, there would be a separate linear discriminant function for each level of classification. Output 7.16 shows the linear discriminant function for the binary target BAD.

Output 7.16: Linear Discriminant Function

Linear Discriminant Function for bad		
Variable	0	1
Constant	-23.94788	-26.37258
int_rate	1.99040	2.13349
acc_open_past_24mths	0.15253	0.23225
dti	0.16651	0.17927
emp_NA	1.25612	1.73797
total_bc_limit	0.0000796	0.0000721
tot_hi_cred_lim	-2.4447E-7	-1.0995E-6
loan_amnt	0.0003007	0.0003119
num_actv_bc_tl	0.46350	0.50453
home_mort	1.80890	1.61113
term_36	11.02448	10.86436
inq_last_6mths	-0.64790	-0.55137
grade_A	9.65924	9.86430
grade_C	2.01023	1.96407
mort_acc	0.35704	0.31732
ver_not	4.42172	4.35577
home_own	1.59143	1.46392
grade_D	-3.52515	-3.55918

Classification Matrix and Error Rate

PROC DISCRIM outputs a classification matrix (also called a confusion matrix). This table of information shows the **actual** number of observations for a given group (target level) and the **predicted** number of observations that were classified for a given group. The table also supplies the row percentage. These values allow the researcher to determine the number of predictions that the model got right and the number of predictions that the model got wrong.

If the actual value for an observation is 1 and the predicted value for an observation is categorized as 1, then it is an accurate prediction. Output 7.17 shows that when the actual value is 1, the model correctly predicts the value in 62.58% of the observations. However, when the actual value is 0, the model incorrectly predicts that it is 1 in 37.42% of the observations.

Classifications are determined by the 0.5 threshold value. If a predicted probability is less than 0.5, then the observation is classified as group 0. If a predicted probability is greater than or equal to 0.5, then the observation is classified as group 1. Output 7.17 displays the classification matrix.

Output 7.17: Confusion Matrix

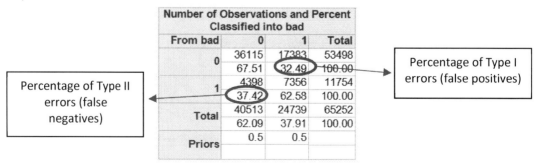

Number of Observations and Percent Classified into bad				
From bad	0	1	Total	
0	36115	17383	53498	
	67.51	32.49	100.00	
1	4398	7356	11754	
	37.42	62.58	100.00	
Total	40513	24739	65252	
	62.09	37.91	100.00	
Priors	0.5	0.5		

Percentage of Type II errors (false negatives)

Percentage of Type I errors (false positives)

Error Count Estimates for bad			
	0	1	Total
Rate	0.3249	0.3742	0.3495
Priors	0.5000	0.5000	

The Error Count Estimates table shows the percentage of errors compared to the prior probability values. This table shows that given a random assignment of a classification group, we would expect 50% of the observations to be incorrect. However, for observations where the actual value is 1, the model provides a predicted value that is incorrect in 37% of the observations. These are Type II errors that represent false negatives. Even though a relatively high percentage of the observations is incorrectly categorized, a comparison to the prior probabilities shows that the model provides a significant lift over a random assignment.

Output 7.18 shows the classification matrix for the scored hold-out TEST data set. The first part of the table verifies that all of the TEST data observations were able to be scored.

Output 7.18: TEST Data Set Confusion Matrix

Observation Profile for Test Data	
Number of Observations Read	27771
Number of Observations Used	27771

Number of Observations and Percent Classified into bad			
From bad	0	1	Total
0	15406	7460	22866
	67.38	32.62	100.00
1	1850	3055	4905
	37.72	62.28	100.00
Total	17256	10515	27771
	62.14	37.86	100.00
Priors	0.5	0.5	

Error Count Estimates for bad			
	0	1	Total
Rate	0.3262	0.3772	0.3517
Priors	0.5000	0.5000	

The remaining information in the classification matrix and the error count estimate are very similar to the data generated from the TRAIN data set. This shows that the model is not overfitting. If the error counts for the TRAIN data set were much lower than the error counts for the TEST data set, then we would have to be concerned that the model was overfitting the TRAIN data and not generalizing well to the hold-out TEST data.

Evaluation Macro

As a final look at the LDA predictive model, we can use the same evaluation macro that we applied to the logistic regression. These types of macros are flexible evaluation tools that can be applied to any data set that has a binary target variable and a continuous predicted probability score.

Program 7.13 shows the code that applies the macro created by Wensui Liu to the scored TEST data set.

Program 7.13: Application of Macro

```
%INCLUDE 'C:/Users/James Gearheart/Desktop/SAS Book
Stuff/Projects/separation.sas';
%separation(data = TEST_OUT, score = '1'N, y = BAD);
```

This is obviously very similar to the scoring code that we developed for the logistic regression model. However, notice that the score field is labeled '1'N. This odd naming convention is a result of the default predicted probability field created by the DISCRIM procedure. In this case, the field is labeled 1. In order to specify that field, SAS requires us to refer to the field as '1'N.

Output 7.19 shows the lift table generated by the evaluation macro. If you compare this lift table to the one applied to the logistic regression model output (Output 7.13), you will see that they are very similar. This shows that for this particular data set, the two modeling procedures (log reg and LDA) produce very similar results.

Output 7.19: Lift Table Generated by the Evaluation Macro

	MIN SCORE	MAX SCORE	GOOD #	BAD #	TOTAL #	ODDS	BAD RATE	CUMULATIVE BAD RATE	BAD PERCENT	CUMU. BAD PERCENT
\multicolumn{11}{c}{GOOD BAD SEPARATION REPORT FOR '1'N IN DATA TEST_OUT}										
\multicolumn{11}{c}{(AUC STATISTICS = 0.7097, GINI COEFFICIENT = 0.4193, DIVERGENCE = 0.5734)}										
BAD	0.7196	0.9393	1,685	1,092	2,777	1.54	39.32%	39.32%	22.26%	22.26%
I	0.6235	0.7195	1,967	810	2,777	2.43	29.17%	34.25%	16.51%	38.78%
I	0.5505	0.6235	2,093	684	2,777	3.06	24.63%	31.04%	13.94%	52.72%
I	0.4869	0.5505	2,200	577	2,777	3.81	20.78%	28.47%	11.76%	64.49%
I	0.4322	0.4868	2,291	487	2,778	4.7	17.53%	26.29%	9.93%	74.41%
I	0.3815	0.4321	2,400	377	2,777	6.37	13.58%	24.17%	7.69%	82.10%
I	0.332	0.3815	2,437	340	2,777	7.17	12.24%	22.46%	6.93%	89.03%
I	0.2819	0.332	2,531	246	2,777	10.29	8.86%	20.76%	5.02%	94.05%
V	0.2286	0.2819	2,584	193	2,777	13.39	6.95%	19.23%	3.93%	97.98%
GOOD	0.0812	0.2286	2,678	99	2,777	27.05	3.56%	17.66%	2.02%	100.00%
	0.0812	0.9393	22,866	4,905	27,771					

Chapter Review

The goal of this chapter was to introduce you to the concept of parametric classification models and demonstrate a few methods of producing those models in SAS. The logistic regression model is the go-to model for most binary target variable problems. This model design will deliver a high-performance model on large data sets with many predictors. Due to the parametric nature of the model design, the model can be generated quickly and efficiently.

However, the logistic regression and LDA model designs are not applicable for all binary target variable data sets. There are often cases where the target values are not well separated and cannot be segmented by a straight or curved line. This will be the subject of the next chapter on non-parametric classification models.

Chapter 8: Non-Parametric Models

Overview

Up to this point, we have reviewed parametric models. These models assume a pre-existing functional form, such as the linear regression equation (Equation 6.1) or the logistic regression equation (Equation 7.1). To apply these models to a data set, the data is assumed to be normally distributed, and for the linear regression model, the data is assumed to have a linear relationship with the target variable, and the variance is homogeneous. Because we have placed these assumptions on the data set, the problem of estimating the functional form of the data is greatly reduced. We do not need to explore every possible relationship between the target and the predictor variables; we only need to calculate the coefficients of the existing function.

The linear and logistic regression models are classified as parametric because the problem of estimating the functional form of the data is reduced to estimating the parameters of a given model. Due to these restrictions, parametric models are comparatively fast and easy to train and require minimal computational resources compared to non-parametric models. However, the relationship between the target and predictor variables is rarely linear. In fact, the linear regression model is appropriate only in a small fraction of modeling cases. It is often the case that the relationship between the target and predictor variables is anything but linear.

Non-parametric models do not have the restrictions associated with parametric models. They do not make assumptions about the functional form of the data; therefore, they are free to explore and develop all possible relationships between the target and the predictor variables. This freedom provides a great deal of flexibility for non-parametric models, but at the cost of complexity and computational resources.

Whereas the parametric model is at risk of the assumed functional form not representing the true functional form of the data, the non-parametric model does not run this risk. But that reduced risk of appropriate model fit comes at a cost. The non-parametric model requires a large number of observations to estimate the underlying functional form of the data accurately. Due to the increased number of observations and the need to search through the entire p-dimensional space of functional forms, the non-parametric modeling approach is very resource-intensive.

This chapter will review several different types of non-parametric models.

Modeling Data Set

Since the theme of this book is a hands-on approach to data science and machine learning, I will explain each of the non-parametric models in a practical sense and use the same modeling data set for each algorithm. This way, we can see the similarities and the differences between each of the algorithms while holding the underlying data constant.

The data that we will use for this chapter is found in the fantastic UCI Machine Learning Repository. The data set is titled "Bank Marketing Data Set," and it can be found here: http://archive.ics.uci.edu/ml/datasets/Bank+Marketing.

This data set represents a direct marketing campaign (phone calls) conducted by a Portuguese banking institution. The goal of the direct marketing campaign was to have customers subscribe to a term deposit product. The data set consists of 15 independent variables that represent customer attributes (age, job, marital status, education, and so on) and marketing campaign attributes (month, day of week, number of marketing campaigns, and so on).

The target variable in the data set is represented as "y." This variable is a binary indicator of whether the phone solicitation resulted in a sale of a term deposit product ("yes") or did not result in a sale ("no"). For our purposes, I will recode this variable and label it as "TARGET," and the binary outcomes will be 1 for "yes" and 0 for "no."

The code for importing the data and transforming the target variable can be found in the GitHub repository: https://github.com/Gearhj/End-to-End-Data-Science.

After the data has been imported, we can take a quick look at the numeric variables with a MEANS procedure. The output of the PROC MEANS is shown in Output 8.1.

Output 8.1: PROC MEANS Output

Variable	Label	N	N Miss	Minimum	Maximum	Mean	Median	Std Dev
age	age	41188	0	17.0000000	98.0000000	40.0240604	38.0000000	10.4212500
duration	duration	41188	0	0	4918.00	258.2850102	180.0000000	259.2792488
campaign	campaign	41188	0	1.0000000	56.0000000	2.5675925	2.0000000	2.7700135
pdays	pdays	41188	0	0	999.0000000	962.4754540	999.0000000	186.9109073
previous	previous	41188	0	0	7.0000000	0.1729630	0	0.4949011
TARGET		41188	0	0	1.0000000	0.1126542	0	0.3161734

This output shows us two critical variables that we need to be mindful of. The pdays variable represents the number of days after a client was contacted from a previous campaign. We can quickly see that the maximum value is 999. This is a good indicator that this variable contains a "special value." A special value is a numerical representation of an observation that is unlike the rest of the data. In this case, a value of 999 represents an observation where the client has not been previously exposed to a campaign. It would be a mistake to interpret the value as there have been 999 days since the last campaign contacted this client.

The second variable that we are even more concerned about is the duration variable. This variable is straightforward in its interpretation. It represents the number of minutes that a contact phone call lasted in relation to the campaign. This is obviously a very powerful predictive variable. However, we would not know this information beforehand. It would be a mistake to include this variable in any predictive model because it is an obvious case of severe data bleed. The only thing that we can do with this variable is to remove it from our modeling data set.

The data set contains ten character variables. Each of these variables has its own descriptive category. For example, the loan variable has three possible values, "no," "yes," and "unknown." Table 8.1 shows the number of levels for each of the character variables.

Table 8.1: Character Variable Levels

Variable	Levels
job	12
marital	4
education	8
default	3
housing	3
loan	3
contact	2
month	10
day_of_week	5
poutcome	3

Any of the tree-based algorithms will easily take character variables as model inputs without the need to transform them into numeric representations (dummy variables). However, since we are going to use this data set to demonstrate several different non-parametric algorithms, we will need to transform the character variables into dummy variables. For more detail on dummy variables and how they are constructed, see Chapter 5: Create a Modeling Data Set.

The code to develop the dummy variables can be found in the GitHub repository.

Now that we have transformed the data, we split the data into TRAIN and TEST data sets with a 70/30 ratio. Program 8.1 shows the PROC SURVEYSELECT method of splitting the data and building the TRAIN and TEST data sets.

Program 8.1: TRAIN/TEST Data Split

```
PROC SURVEYSELECT DATA=MYDATA.BANKFULL RATE=0.3 OUTALL OUT=class SEED=42;
RUN;
PROC FREQ DATA=class; TABLES selected; RUN;

DATA MYDATA.BANK_TRAIN MYDATA.BANK_TEST;
   SET class;
   IF selected = 0 THEN OUTPUT MYDATA.BANK_TRAIN; ELSE OUTPUT
MYDATA.BANK_TEST;
   DROP selected;
RUN;

PROC FREQ DATA=MYDATA.BANK_TRAIN; TABLES TARGET; RUN;
PROC FREQ DATA=MYDATA.BANK_TEST; TABLES TARGET; RUN;
```

A final look at the frequency distributions for the TRAIN and TEST data sets shows that the data has been randomly selected, and the event rate is comparable for both data sets.

Output 8.2: Frequency Distribution of Target Variable in TRAIN and TEST Data Sets

TARGET	Frequency	Percent	Cumulative Frequency	Cumulative Percent
0	25544	88.60	25544	88.60
1	3287	11.40	28831	100.00

TARGET	Frequency	Percent	Cumulative Frequency	Cumulative Percent
0	11004	89.05	11004	89.05
1	1353	10.95	12357	100.00

K-Nearest Neighbor Model

Birds of a feather flock together. – William Turner

You're the average of the five people you spend the most time with. – Jim Rohn

The K-Nearest Neighbor (KNN) model is perhaps the simplest modeling structure, yet it is very effective. It is highly versatile in that it can be used for classification or regression modeling and used across a wide range of nonlinear applications, from marketing to genomics. This modeling algorithm is classified as non-parametric because it does not make any assumptions about the functional form of the data. It is also called a **lazy learning algorithm** because it does not generalize based on training data. For this algorithm, there is a very minimal training phase.

As with all machine learning algorithms, there are pros and cons to the usage of KNN models. Table 8.2 lists some of the most relevant pros and cons of KNN models.

Table 8.2: KNN Model Pros and Cons

Pros	Cons
Simple to implement	Computationally intensive
Analytically tractable	Requires a lot of storage
Highly adaptive to local information to form nonlinear decision boundaries	Highly susceptible to the curse of dimensionality

The concept of the KNN model is simple. We will take a modeling data set and represent it on a grid. The grid will demonstrate each observation's location on an X-Y plane and show the target variable's value for each observation.

Figure 8.1 shows the basic concept of the data grid. The initial data to populate the grid is the training data. The figure on the left shows the distribution of the training data. Notice in this example that the data is clustered into specific groups and that these groups are color-coded to represent three levels of a classification target variable. We can see that categories of the target variable have similar distributions of the underlying data because they are clustered together.

Figure 8.1: Data Grid

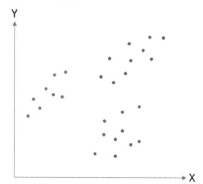 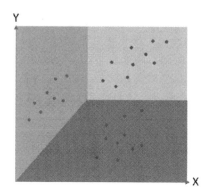

The initial training data distribution shows only the relationship between the X and Y variables and how they are grouped according to a target variable. For any new observation, we would simply need to place the new observation onto the grid according to its own X and Y coordinates and calculate the distance between the closest data points and the new observation.

The "k" in KNN represents the number of "neighbors" that we will use to determine the predicted target value for a new observation. If k = 1, we would simply determine which training data point is closest to the new observation and assign the target value of the nearest training data point to the new observation.

However, it is rarely useful to use k=1. This can lead to highly unstable predictions. If we increase the value of k, we will find the number of nearest neighbors represented by k and calculate the average for regression models (or the mode for classification models) to assign to the target value of the new observation. For example, if we selected k=5, then we would find the five closest training data points in relation to the new observation. If three out of five of those training data points had a target value of 1, then we would assign a target value of 1 to the new observation. This is how data is scored in a KNN algorithm.

The right-hand side of Figure 8.1 shows an example of *decision boundaries*. These color-coded spaces have been created based on a k=5 nearest neighbor algorithm. If the coordinates of a new data point would place it anywhere in the red area, then the new data point would be assigned a target value associated with the red group.

KNN Classification

In the previous chapter on parametric classification models, we reviewed PROC DISCRIM. This procedure was highly useful for classification problems where there are few observations or there are more than two levels of classification. This flexible procedure can also be used to develop KNN models for classification.

PROC DISCRIM has two key option statements that will allow us to develop KNN models. The METHOD option allows us to select NPAR, which will specify that we want to develop a non-parametric model. The K option allows us to specify the number of nearest neighbors that we will use for voting. Program 8.2 first places all of the numeric variables into a global variable and then it develops a KNN model using PROC DISCRIM.

Program 8.2: Create KNN Using PROC DISCRIM

```
/*Create global variables for variables to be included in KNN model*/
PROC CONTENTS NOPRINT DATA=MYDATA.BANK_TRAIN (KEEP=_NUMERIC_ drop=ROW_NUM
TARGET)
        OUT=VAR4 (KEEP=name);
RUN;

PROC SQL NOPRINT;
        SELECT name INTO: num_vars separated by " " FROM VAR4;
QUIT;

%PUT &num_vars;
/*KNN using PROC DISCRIM*/
PROC DISCRIM DATA=MYDATA.BANK_TRAIN METHOD=NPAR K=5
        TESTDATA=MYDATA.BANK_TEST TESTOUT=SCORED;
        CLASS TARGET;
        VAR &num_vars.;
RUN;
```

Notes on Program 8.2:

- PROC CONTENTS is used to select all numeric variables to be included in the list of predictors. Notice that the TARGET and ROW_NUM variables are excluded from the variable list.

- PROC SQL places the selected numeric variables into a global variable that we have named "num_vars".

- PROC DISCRIM is used to develop the KNN model. This procedure uses the MYDATA.BANK_TRAIN data set as the input training data.

- The METHOD statement is set to NPAR. This tells the model to use the non-parametric method for deriving the classification criterion.

- The K option determines the number of neighbors. Although we have initially set the option to 5, in the next section, I will show how to identify the optimal value for K.

- The TEST data set is specified in the TESTDATA statement, and the scored TEST output data set is specified with the TESTOUT statement.

- The CLASS statement specifies the target variable.

- The VAR statement specifies the predictors to use in the model.

Warning

One note of caution to remember when implementing a KNN model is that the model is very resource-heavy. This means that SAS must retain all the relationships (distances) between each of the observations in the training data set. If you have a relatively large training data set (over 100K), this can result in extended processing times and even result in insufficient storage capacity.

KNN Model Output

The default output for the PROC DISCRIM-derived KNN model contains summary information about the input data set and a confusion matrix for the TRAIN and TEST data sets. A *confusion matrix* is a table of information developed for classification models that summarizes the number of correct classifications and the number of incorrect classifications. This information can be used to develop specific metrics that will be reviewed in the next section.

Output 8.3 shows the first part of the model output. Most SAS modeling procedures produce this type of summary information. The table of information provides the total number of observations, the number of predictor variables, and the number of levels for the classification variable. This section of information also provides the event rate shown as the proportion of observations for each level of classification.

Output 8.3: KNN Model Output

Total Sample Size	28831	DF Total	28830
Variables	57	DF Within Classes	28829
Classes	2	DF Between Classes	1

Number of Observations Read	28831
Number of Observations Used	28831

		Class Level Information			
TARGET	Variable Name	Frequency	Weight	Proportion	Prior Probability
0	0	25544	25544	0.885991	0.500000
1	1	3287	3287	0.114009	0.500000

The next section of the model output is shown in Output 8.3. This section shows the confusion matrix for the training data set. The actual response values are listed vertically on the left-hand side as rows while the predicted response values are listed horizontally as columns on the top section of the table.

The intersection where the actual response equals 1 and the predicted response equals 1 shows that the model was accurate for the actual positive values. The intersection where the actual response value is 0 and the predicted response value is 0 shows that the model was accurate for the actual negative values.

False positives (Type 1 errors) are indicated where the actual value is 0 but the model predicted that the value is 1. *False negatives* (Type 2 errors) are indicated where the actual value is 1 but the model predicted that the value is 0. This information is highlighted in Output 8.4.

Output 8.4: Confusion Matrix

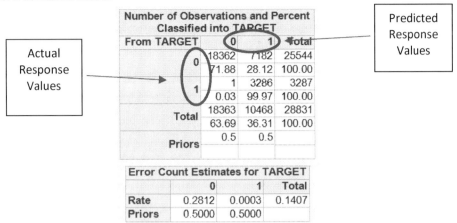

The above confusion matrix for the training data set shows that the model is highly overfit for positive response values. The Error Count Estimates table shows that the model misclassifies actual positive values in only three-tenths of a percent of cases. However, the model misclassifies negative responses in 28% of cases. Although this is still better than a random selection that would misclassify both positive and negative response values in 50% of cases (represented by the prior probability), we need to be aware that this model does not fit the data well.

Remember that we do not evaluate the accuracy of a model based on the training data set. We need to evaluate the confusion matrix developed on the hold-out testing data set. Output 8.5 shows the confusion matrix for the data set that was created by the TESTOUT = SCORED statement that we included in PROC DISCRIM.

Output 8.5: TEST Data Set Confusion Matrix

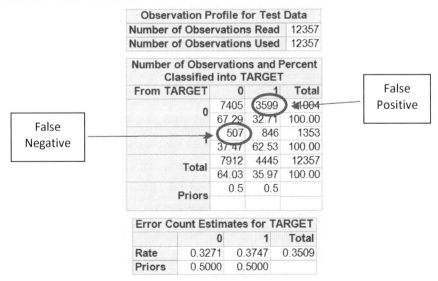

Notice that the Error Count Estimate table is drastically different for the hold-out TEST data set compared to the one developed on the TRAIN data set. The error rate for positive response values is 37% for the hold-out TEST data set. When we compare this value to the 0.03% error rate generated on the TRAIN data set, we can verify that the data is highly overfit to the training data.

Hyperparameter Tuning

One of the main reasons that the model is overfitting to the training data set is because we have not performed hyperparameter tuning. Hyperparameters are values that the data scientist selects prior to running the model. Each machine learning algorithm has its own list of available hyperparameters that the data scientist must decide before running the algorithm.

For example, in the regression chapter, we included the statement SLE=0.1. The SLE option specifies the significance level for a variable to enter the model. This value was selected BEFORE the model was run.

The difference between a model's parameters and hyperparameters is that the model generates parameters as output created by the algorithm. Hyperparameters are selected BEFORE the model is run and they define the limitations of the model.

The KNN example that was developed in Program 8.2 specified the number of nearest neighbors represented by K=5. There is no way to know a priori the correct value for K. We need to explore a range of values in order to optimize the model.

Program 8.3 creates a loop that cycles through K values 1 to 15 and creates summary metrics for each value of K.

Program 8.3: KNN Hyperparameter Tuning

```
/*Create a dataset to store the evaluation metrics*/
DATA MYDATA.MASTER;
   TP = 1; FP = 1; TN = 1; FN = 1; P = 1; N = 1;
RUN;

/*Create a DO LOOP that will cycle through K values 1 to 15*/
%MACRO KNN;
        %do k=1 %to 15;

/*A KNN model will be built for each value of K*/
                PROC DISCRIM DATA=MYDATA.BANK_TRAIN METHOD=NPAR K=&k.
                    TESTDATA=MYDATA.BANK_TEST TESTOUT=SCORED_&k.;
                    CLASS TARGET;
                    VAR &num_vars.;
                RUN;

/*Create indicators for metric creation*/
                DATA SUM;
                    SET SCORED_&k.;
                    if TARGET = 1 and _INTO_ = 1 then TP = 1;
                    if TARGET = 1 and _INTO_ = 0 then FN = 1;
                    if TARGET = 0 and _INTO_ = 0 then TN = 1;
                    if TARGET = 0 and _INTO_ = 1 then FP = 1;
```

```
                    if TARGET = 1 then P = 1;
                    if TARGET = 0 then N = 1;
                RUN;

/*Summarize indicators*/
                PROC SUMMARY DATA=SUM;
                    VAR TP FN TN FP P N;
                OUTPUT OUT=SUM2 SUM=;

/*Append summarized indicators to evaluation dataset*/
                PROC APPEND DATA=SUM2 BASE=MYDATA.MASTER force nowarn; RUN;
%END;
%MEND;

%KNN;
```

Notes on Program 8.3:

- The first DATA step creates a data set with placeholders for the summary metrics that we will create.

- A DO LOOP is created inside of a MACRO. This DO LOOP will cycle through each value of K from 1 to 15 and create a KNN model for each value. This algorithm will create 15 separate KNN models and output the scored TEST data set for each model.

- An additional data set is created that develops indicators for each of the model results. The SUM data set contains indicators for False Positives, False Negatives, True Positives, True Negatives, Total Positives, and Total Negatives.

- PROC SUMMARY summarizes all of the evaluation metrics for each model.

- PROC APPEND places the results of each model into a final data set.

The final output data set created in MYDATA.MASTER is shown in Output 8.6. This data set contains the various summary performance indicators for each iteration of the DO LOOP. For example, where K=5, there were 846 True Positives and 4040 False Positives.

These summary indicators will provide us with the information that we need to develop our performance metrics.

Output 8.6: KNN Performance Metrics

K	TP	FP	TN	FN	P	N
1	395	1063	9941	958	1353	11004
2	613	1892	9112	740	1353	11004
3	727	2532	8472	626	1353	11004
4	794	3072	7932	559	1353	11004
5	846	3599	7405	507	1353	11004
6	895	4040	6964	458	1353	11004
7	928	4431	6573	425	1353	11004
8	945	4655	6349	408	1353	11004
9	722	1981	9023	631	1353	11004

K	TP	FP	TN	FN	P	N
10	751	2229	8775	602	1353	11004
11	773	2470	8534	580	1353	11004
12	792	2734	8270	561	1353	11004
13	813	2978	8026	540	1353	11004
14	839	3203	7801	514	1353	11004
15	859	3443	7561	494	1353	11004

Program 8.4 calculates several standard performance metrics that are commonly used to evaluate the performance of a classification model.

Program 8.4: Create Performance Metrics
```
DATA METRICS;
  SET MYDATA.MASTER;
  ERROR_RATE = (FP+FN)/(P+N);
  ACCURACY = (TP+TN)/(P+N);
  SENSITIVITY = TP/P;
  SPECIFICITY = TN/N;
  PRECISION = TP/(TP+FP);
  FALSE_POSITIVE_RATE = 1-SPECIFICITY;
RUN;
```

We will review each of these performance metrics in detail in the chapter dedicated to model evaluation, but for now, let's focus on the metrics "sensitivity" and "specificity."

Sensitivity (also called "Recall") is the true positive rate. This metric demonstrates the percentage of actual positive values that the model got right.

Specificity is the true negative rate. This metric demonstrates the percentage of actual negative values that the model got right.

Decision Time

Choosing the "correct" values of the various hyperparameters and the associated performance metrics that an algorithm has to offer is not a black and white decision. There is no absolute correct model. This is because models are created to solve a business problem. For example, if your model was created to predict fraud, you might want your model to be more conservative, and you would select the model hyperparameters that would maximize the true positive rate (sensitivity). If, however, the model was designed for marketing purposes, you might want to focus on the model specificity.

Data scientists and their business partners generally have to make trade-offs and balance their decisions based on business needs. Often, model values that balance specificity and sensitivity are selected. Output 8.7 shows the performance metrics created in Program 8.4.

Output 8.7: Performance Metrics

K	ERROR RATE	ACCURACY	SENSITIVITY	SPECIFICITY	PRECISION	FALSE POSITIVE RATE
1	16.4%	83.6%	29.2%	90.3%	27.1%	9.7%
2	21.3%	78.7%	45.3%	82.8%	24.5%	17.2%
3	25.6%	74.4%	53.7%	77.0%	22.3%	23.0%
4	29.4%	70.6%	58.7%	72.1%	20.5%	27.9%
5	33.2%	66.8%	62.5%	67.3%	19.0%	32.7%
6	36.4%	63.6%	66.1%	63.3%	18.1%	36.7%
7	39.3%	60.7%	68.6%	59.7%	17.3%	40.3%
8	41.0%	59.0%	69.8%	57.7%	16.9%	42.3%
9	21.1%	78.9%	53.4%	82.0%	26.7%	18.0%
10	22.9%	77.1%	55.5%	79.7%	25.2%	20.3%
11	24.7%	75.3%	57.1%	77.6%	23.8%	22.4%
12	26.7%	73.3%	58.5%	75.2%	22.5%	24.8%
13	28.5%	71.5%	60.1%	72.9%	21.4%	27.1%
14	30.1%	69.9%	62.0%	70.9%	20.8%	29.1%
15	31.9%	68.1%	63.5%	68.7%	20.0%	31.3%

Notice that when K is equal to 1 or 2, there is a wide discrepancy between sensitivity and specificity. This difference is generally because the model is overfitting to the most prevalent classification of the target variable. In our example, the true negative rate (specificity) is very high for those models, but the true positive rate (sensitivity) is much lower.

If we focus on the models where K is greater than 2, we can see that the difference between sensitivity and specificity steadily decreases. I have highlighted the optimal values for each of the performance metrics, where K is greater than 2. We can see that there is a balance in the Force (Star Wars reference) where K is equal to 8 or 9 (depending on which metric you want to focus on).

In our example data set, the target variable is a binary indicator of whether the phone solicitation resulted in a sale of a term deposit product ("yes") or did not result in a sale ("no"). In order to optimize our marketing dollars, I would suggest that we use K=9 to minimize the false-positive rate.

KNN Scoring
PROC DISCRIM allows you to specify a data set to score directly within the PROC DISCRIM algorithm. Program 8.5 demonstrates the scoring code.

Program 8.5: KNN Score TEST Data Set
```
/*KNN using PROC DISCRIM*/
PROC DISCRIM DATA=MYDATA.BANK_TRAIN METHOD=NPAR K=9
        TESTDATA=MYDATA.BANK_TEST TESTOUT=SCORED ;
        CLASS TARGET;
        VAR &num_vars.;
RUN;
```

```
%INCLUDE 'C:/Users/James Gearheart/Desktop/SAS Book
Stuff/Projects/separation.sas';
%separation(data = scored, score = '1'N, y = target);
```

Notes on Program 8.5:

- PROC DISCRIM is applied to the training data set to develop the KNN model.

- The value of K is set to 9.

- The TESTDATA option is specified to score the hold-out TEST data set and the TESTOUT option outputs a scored data set labeled SCORED.

- A lift table macro that we used previously in the logistic regression chapter is applied to the scored test data. Output 8.8 shows the output lift table.

Output 8.8: Applying a Lift Table Macro

	MIN SCORE	MAX SCORE	GOOD #	BAD #	TOTAL #	ODDS	BAD RATE	CUMULATIVE BAD RATE	BAD PERCENT	CUMU. BAD PERCENT
BAD	0.8993	1	21	149	170	0.14	87.65%	87.65%	10.80%	10.80%
|	0.7988	0.8882	35	186	221	0.19	84.16%	85.68%	13.48%	24.28%
|	0.6984	0.7765	64	183	247	0.35	74.09%	81.19%	13.26%	37.54%
|	0.5982	0.665	91	138	229	0.66	60.26%	75.66%	10.00%	47.54%
|	0.4982	0.5537	192	139	331	1.38	41.99%	66.36%	10.07%	57.61%
|	0.3982	0.4426	259	179	438	1.45	40.87%	59.54%	12.97%	70.58%
|	0.2713	0.3317	286	187	473	1.53	39.53%	55.05%	13.55%	84.13%
V	0.1988	0.2209	263	133	396	1.98	33.59%	51.66%	9.64%	93.77%
GOOD	0	0.1104	193	86	279	2.24	30.82%	49.57%	6.23%	100.00%
	0	1	1404	1380	2784					

GOOD BAD SEPARATION REPORT FOR '1'N IN DATA SCORED. MAXIMUM KS = 32.6490 AT SCORE POINT 0.5982. (AUC STATISTICS = 0.6944, GINI COEFFICIENT = 0.3888, DIVERGENCE = 0.5751)

We can see that the Gini score for the KNN model is only 38.88. This indicates a relatively weak model that does not significantly separate the "goods" from the "bads" very well. However, this should not be an indicator that KNN models are themselves a weak modeling procedure. In fact, for certain data sets, the KNN algorithm produces the highest levels of accuracy. But for this data set, the KNN model does not fit the data very well.

Tree-Based Models

One of the first things that we should do before we perform any modeling is to visualize the data. The goal of this step is to get a general understanding of the distribution of the data. If the data is apparently linear, we would probably start the modeling process by investigating linear models. However, most data sets look somewhat chaotic when we first visualize them. For these data sets, there is no discernable visual pattern.

The left-hand side of Figure 8.2 shows a hypothetical distribution of a balanced data set where there is an equal number of events represented by gold stars compared to non-events represented by blue dots.

Figure 8.2

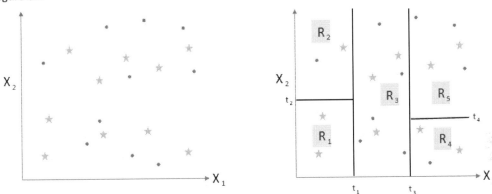

This example does not demonstrate visual cues that might indicate a linear relationship between the variables or a clustered relationship between those variables. The distribution pattern appears random.

Tree-based algorithms tackle this issue by segmenting the predictor space into several simple regions. These regions are then used to predict the values of new observations by taking the mean or the mode of a given region and inferring that value to a new observation that appears in that region. The mean is used for regression problems while the mode is used for classification problems.

The right-hand side of Figure 8.2 shows the predictor space divided into five distinct regions. These regions can be thought of as high-dimensional rectangular boxes. These regions are created by partitioning the feature space, where the Residual Sum of Squares (RSS) is minimized for each region.

Once the partitioning is complete, it is very easy and straightforward to predict the values of new unseen observations. This is performed by a series of IF-THEN questions. Figure 8.3 shows the logical steps for determining the value of a new observation.

Figure 8.3

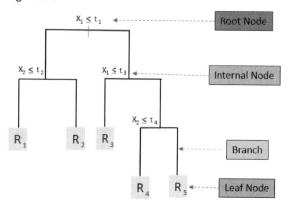

This tree-based model is constructed like an upside-down tree. The first part of the tree is called the root node. This provides the initial segmentation of the data. This is the first IF-THEN question that is asked of the data. For example, if the value of X_1 is less than or equal to a given value (t_1) then we will continue down the left-hand side of the tree. If, however, X_1 is greater than t_1 then we will proceed down the right-hand side of the tree.

The path that the decision algorithm follows is called the *branch*. This path shows the flow of the decision process from the root node to the next internal node to the final leaf node.

The next decision point is called the internal node. This is the next set of IF-THEN questions that will be asked of the data. For example, if the initial root node decision point followed the left-hand side of the tree, then the next IF-THEN question that is asked is whether X_2 is greater than or equal to t_2. If the answer is yes, then the data will be classified in region one, else the data will be classified in region two. These terminal sections of the tree are called the leaf nodes.

For classification problems, we would simply analyze each region and calculate the mode of the region. That mode will be the predicted value of any new observation that is in that region. For regression problems, we would calculate the mean of each region and impute that the value for any new observation in that region would be the mean value.

Pros and Cons

We can already see that decision trees provide an easy-to-understand decision path. It is a common language description of how data is classified, and new observations are scored. However, not all aspects of decision trees are beneficial. Table 8.3 shows a quick summary of the pros and cons of decision trees.

Table 8.3: Decision Tree Model Pros and Cons

Pros	Cons
Easy to understand	Greedy algorithm
Utilizes both numeric and categorical data	Tends to overfit
Requires little data pre-processing	Instability

Pros	Cons
Fast scoring	Biased to classes that have the majority

Pros

- **Easy to understand** – Decision trees are classified as "white boxes." This means that every decision point is easy to understand, and the researcher has complete knowledge of how decision points are constructed and how new observations are scored.

- **Utilizes both numeric and categorical data** – Decision trees can leverage a combination of both numeric and categorical data in the same model.

- **Requires little data pre-processing** – There is no need to normalize or standardize the input data. Nor do you have to create dummy variables, impute missing data, or adjust for outliers. Decision trees work well with raw data.

- **Fast scoring** – Once the decision tree has been constructed, new observations can be scored very quickly with little processing power.

Cons

- **Greedy algorithm** – It is computationally futile to consider every possible partition of the feature space. Therefore, the decision tree algorithm selects the best possible split of the data for each step of the tree. It does not, however, go back to reconsider previous divisions based on split points further down the tree. Decision trees use a top-down approach and do not reconsider previous splits.

- **Tends to overfit** – Unrestrained decision trees will develop very fine leaf nodes. These tend to be very deep decision trees that have many levels of decision points (internal nodes). These unrestrained trees will overfit the training data.

- **Instability** – Decision trees can be highly unstable. Small changes in the input data can result in drastically different decision trees.

- **Biased to classes that have the majority** – Unbalanced data can result in decision trees that favor the majority class.

Decision Tree Methodology

We have examined the general structure of the decision tree, but we need to understand how each of the nodes is determined.

There are two main methods that you can select to create decision trees: Entropy and Gini Impurity. Each of these metrics describes the amount of disorder or impurity in the data.

Equation 8.1: Entropy

$$I_H = -\sum_{j=i}^{C} p_j log_2(p_j)$$

Equation 8.2: Gini Impurity

$$I_G = 1 - \sum_{j=i}^{C} p_j^2$$

The first-order goal of these methods is to find the variable that has the most information about the target variable. This means that for numeric variables, the algorithm will search through the possible split points for each numeric variable and determine the optimal split point. The optimal split point is the one that creates segments that best separate the target variable. For character variables, the split points are already determined by the number of classes within the character variable.

Figure 8.4

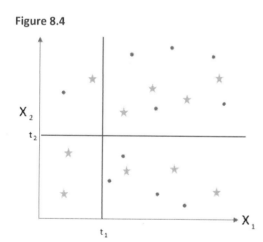

There is little practical difference between the two methods because they produce remarkably similar results. However, because the entropy method utilizes a logarithmic approach, this makes this method more resource-intensive.

Let's look at an example. Figure 8.4 shows the distribution of data that we presented earlier, but this time there are two possible split points that we will consider for the root node. The first split point is shown as t_1 and is represented as the blue line. Notice that this split point has three positive target variable observations (represented as gold stars) on the left-hand side and seven positive target variable observations on the right-hand side.

The second possible split point is shown as t_2 and is represented as the red line. This split point results in five positive observations on the left-hand side (top) and five positive observations on the right-hand side (bottom).

Since the goal of the splitting exercise is to create segments that best separate the target variable, we would select the first split point t_1 as the root node.

Decision Tree Construction

Decision trees are completely different from regression models. They take a non-parametric approach that attempts to split the feature space into distinct segments that best separate the target variable. These segments can take on nearly any contiguous form but they are generally represented by rectangular boxes. Since this is an entirely different approach from regression models, let's take the time to walk through an example from raw data to a finalized decision tree.

Table 8.4 shows a random sample of the data set that we will use for our demonstration. It is based on the same data set that we used for our KNN example; however, it has been modified for simplicity. I have created categorical variables with two levels for each of the four predictor variables, and I have balanced the data set so that there is an equal number of positive and negative outcome observations.

Table 8.4: Random Sample

Contact	Year	Campaign	Age Cat	Target
telephone	1st half	1 or 2	LE 45	no
telephone	1st half	1 or 2	45+	no
cellular	2nd half	1 or 2	45+	no
cellular	2nd half	1 or 2	LE 45	no
cellular	2nd half	1 or 2	45+	no
telephone	1st half	1 or 2	LE 45	no
cellular	2nd half	Greater than 2	45+	no
cellular	2nd half	1 or 2	LE 45	no
cellular	1st half	1 or 2	LE 45	no
cellular	1st half	Greater than 2	LE 45	no
cellular	1st half	1 or 2	LE 45	yes
cellular	1st half	Greater than 2	LE 45	yes
cellular	1st half	Greater than 2	45+	yes
cellular	1st half	1 or 2	LE 45	yes
cellular	1st half	1 or 2	LE 45	yes
cellular	2nd half	1 or 2	LE 45	yes
cellular	2nd half	1 or 2	LE 45	yes
telephone	1st half	1 or 2	45+	yes

Contact	Year	Campaign	Age Cat	Target
cellular	2nd half	1 or 2	LE 45	yes
cellular	2nd half	1 or 2	LE 45	yes

The process to construct a classification decision tree consists of four main steps:

1. Calculate the Gini impurity score for each variable.
2. Select the variable that best separates the data for the root node.
3. Recursively split the data to build a full decision tree.
4. Prune the decision tree to avoid overfitting.

In order to build a decision tree by hand, we would first create a cross-tabulation of each predictor variable and the target variable. Figure 8.5 shows the results of a PROC FREQ between each predictor and the target variable. We can see that each predictor has only two levels and that there is an equal number of positive and negative outcome observations.

Figure 8.5: PROC FREQ Results

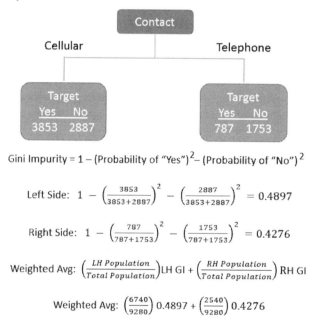

Gini Impurity = 1 – (Probability of "Yes")^2– (Probability of "No")^2

$$\text{Left Side: } 1 - \left(\frac{3853}{3853+2887}\right)^2 - \left(\frac{2887}{3853+2887}\right)^2 = 0.4897$$

$$\text{Right Side: } 1 - \left(\frac{787}{787+1753}\right)^2 - \left(\frac{1753}{787+1753}\right)^2 = 0.4276$$

$$\text{Weighted Avg: } \left(\frac{LH\ Population}{Total\ Population}\right)\text{LH GI} + \left(\frac{RH\ Population}{Total\ Population}\right)\text{RH GI}$$

$$\text{Weighted Avg: } \left(\frac{6740}{9280}\right) 0.4897 + \left(\frac{2540}{9280}\right) 0.4276$$

Contact Gini Impurity = 0.4727

Figure 8.6: Frequency Distribution and Splitting Calculation

Contact	no	yes	Total
cellular	2887	3853	6740
telephone	1753	787	2540
Total	4640	4640	9280

Year	no	yes	Total
1st half	2527	2260	4787
2nd half	2113	2380	4493
Total	4640	4640	9280

Campaigns	no	yes	Total
1 or 2	3215	3511	6726
Greater than 2	1425	1129	2554
Total	4640	4640	9280

Age Cat	no	yes	Total
LE 45	3302	3182	6484
45+	1338	1458	2796
Total	4640	4640	9280

To determine which of the predictor variables should be at the top of the decision tree (root node), we first need to calculate the Gini impurity score for each variable. Once this calculation is complete, we can compare the scores and choose the predictor that has the lowest Gini impurity score to be the root node.

The right-hand side of Figure 8.5 shows the steps to calculate the Gini impurity score for the first predictor variable "contact." It is a three-step process where we first calculate the Gini impurity for the left-hand side of the variable (cellular). The second step is to perform the same calculation on the right-hand side of the predictor variable (telephone). Finally, we calculate the weighted average of the left and right-hand side of the predictor variable. The final Gini impurity score for the contact variable is 0.4727.

I will not torture you by demonstrating the same process for each variable. Instead, Table 8.5 contains the Gini impurity scores for each of the predictor variables.

Table 8.5: Gini Impurity Scores

Variable	GI Score
Contact	0.4727
Year	0.4983
Campaigns	0.4439
Age Cat	0.4443

We can see that the highlighted variable "campaigns" has the lowest Gini impurity score of all the predictor variables. This variable would be selected as the root node because it does the best job of separating the data.

Once we have determined the root node, it is a rote exercise to recursively build the decision tree by performing the same process on the populations created by each split point. This would be a painful process to perform by hand. That's why we let the computer do it for us.

When does the splitting process stop? Up until now, we have just reviewed the steps of how to build a decision tree, but there has to be a point were the recursive splitting stops and creates leaf nodes. A leaf node is created when the Gini impurity score for the next node is greater than the previous node. Once this occurs, the node with the lower Gini impurity score becomes the leaf node.

Continuous Variables

Split points for continuous variables are not as straightforward as categorical variables. For continuous variables, we must first sort the data from lowest to highest. Figure 8.7 demonstrates the process.

Figure 8.7: Continuous Variable Splits

Age	Target	
18	0	
21	1	Avg age = 19.5
33	1	Avg age = 27
35	0	Avg age = 34
38	0	Avg age = 36.5
45	0	Avg age = 41.5
51	1	Avg age = 48
55	0	Avg age = 53
66	1	Avg age = 60.5
76	1	Avg age = 71

Once the data is sorted, the average value between two adjacent values is calculated. Next, the Gini impurity score for each average value is calculated. Finally, the average score with the lowest Gini impurity score is selected to be the split point of the continuous variable.

Once the split point for each continuous variable is determined, the decision tree can be built similarly to the categorical data example given above. This methodology also allows decision trees to contain both categorical and continuous variables within the same tree.

Pruning a Decision Tree

One of the biggest concerns with decision trees is their tendency to overfit the model to the training data. This occurs because the algorithm will continue to build the tree and construct very fine leaf nodes if the model is left unrestrained. These are labeled as "deep trees" because there are several layers of internal nodes leading to the leaf node. We need a method of finding the optimal tree within the vast space of all possible trees.

One way of limiting the algorithm and preventing deep trees is to place a constraint on the model. This constraint should reduce the size of the decision tree without reducing the predictive accuracy.

There are two widely used methods of pruning:

1. **Reduced Error Pruning** – For each leaf of the decision tree, the leaf is replaced with a node that represents the prevalent class. If the prediction accuracy does not decrease, then the node is retained.
2. **Cost Complexity Pruning** – This technique makes trade-offs between the size of the tree and the error rate to help prevent overfitting. A complexity parameter labeled alpha (α) is introduced and represents the cost of each new leaf. The tuning parameter α controls a trade-off between the subtree's complexity and its fit to the training data.

Equation 8.3: Cost Complexity

$$Cost\ Complexity = Error\ Rate(\#\ of\ leaves) + \propto (\#\ of\ leaves)$$

The cost complexity metric penalizes the development of additional leaves that do not provide a significant reduction in the error rate. The error rate is defined differently depending on the type of model. For regression models, the **residual sum of squares** is used as the error rate. For classification models, the **misclassification rate** is used as the error rate.

When $\alpha = 0$, this is the full tree and no pruning is performed. As α increases, the subtrees decrease in complexity. To find the optimal subtree, the optimal value of α must be determined. The process of determining the optimal value of α is through a hold-out method such as a validation sample or cross-validation. The subtree with the minimum cost metric on the hold-out data set (either validation sample or cross-validation) has been constructed with the optimal value of α.

Decision Tree Model

SAS provides an intuitive and easy-to-understand procedure to build decision trees. PROC HPSPLIT is a high-performance procedure that allows data scientists to custom-build a variety of decision tree types utilizing a single framework.

To demonstrate PROC HPSPLIT, we will utilize the same data set that we used in the KNN modeling example. The bank marketing data contains a variety of predictive variables that represent customer characteristics and a target variable that is a binary indicator of whether a phone solicitation resulted in a sale of a term deposit product. Many of the character variables have been transformed into numeric dummy variables.

Program 8.6 demonstrates the general structure of PROC HPSPLIT.

Program 8.6: PROC HPSPLIT

```
ODS GRAPHICS ON;
PROC HPSPLIT DATA=mydata.bank_train(DROP=row_num);
   CLASS TARGET _CHARACTER_;
   MODEL TARGET(EVENT='1') = _NUMERIC_ _CHARACTER_;
   PRUNE costcomplexity;
```

```
   PARTITION FRACTION(VALIDATE=0.3 SEED=42);
   CODE FILE='C:/Users/James Gearheart/Desktop/SAS Book
Stuff/Data/bank_tree.sas';
   OUTPUT OUT = SCORED;
run;
```

Notes on Program 8.6:

- The ODS GRAPHICS ON statement is included to provide all the visual elements of the decision tree.

- PROC HPSPLIT is used to develop the decision tree on the MYDATA.BANK_TRAIN data set. This data set had been previously balanced to ensure that there is an equal number of positive and negative target values. This will prevent the decision tree from overestimating the majority class.

- The CLASS statement specifies the target variable and any character variables that will be included in the model.

- The MODEL statement is required for PROC HPSPLIT. This statement spells out the variables that will be included in the model. The target variable is specified first, and the additional EVENT statement specifies the value of the target variable that we want to model. The predictor variables are included after the equals sign. For this model, I have included all numeric variables (since the character variables were previously transformed into numeric dummy variables). Any variables that could result in data bleed had been previously removed from the data set.

- The PRUNE statement specifies how we want to prune the decision tree to prevent overfitting.

- The PARTITION statement specifies how we want to apply the PRUNE statement. Instead of the PARTITION statement, we could have chosen to use a cross-validation approach by including the CVMODELFIT statement just after the DATA statement.

- The CODE FILE statement will output a SAS script that contains the logic of the decision tree. We will use this logic to score the hold-out TEST data set.

- The OUTPUT OUT statement will output the scored TRAIN data set.

PROC HPSPLIT provides a lot of options to custom design your decision tree including options to specify the maximum tree depth, maximum number of branches, how you want the tree to grow, if you want to bin the continuous variables, output display options, and a lot more.

For the tree structure that we selected, Output 8.9 shows the high-level information about the tree. Notice in the Model Information section that the PROC HPSPLIT procedure used the entropy method to select the split points. This is the default option, but we could have included the GROW statement and selected GINI or a variety of other options to grow the decision tree.

Also notice that in the Model Information section, the decision tree initially grew to 142 leaves before pruning. This large tree was reduced to just 17 leaves after the cost-complexity pruning occurred.

Output 8.9: PROC HPSPLIT Output

Performance Information	
Execution Mode	Single-Machine
Number of Threads	4

Data Access Information			
Data	**Engine**	**Role**	**Path**
MYDATA.BANK_TRAIN	BASE	Input	On Client
WORK.SCORED	V9	Output	On Client

Model Information	
Split Criterion Used	Entropy
Pruning Method	Cost-Complexity
Subtree Evaluation Criterion	Cost-Complexity
Number of Branches	2
Maximum Tree Depth Requested	10
Maximum Tree Depth Achieved	10
Tree Depth	10
Number of Leaves Before Pruning	142
Number of Leaves After Pruning	17
Model Event Level	1

Number of Observations Read	6496
Number of Observations Used	6496
Number of Training Observations Used	4541
Number of Validation Observations Used	1955

The next section of the PROC HPSPLIT output contains the visual representation of the decision tree. This is the visual that most people think about when they think of decision trees.

The left side of Output 8.10 shows a visual representation of the full decision tree. This representation also provides some visual cues of the volume of the population in each stage of the decision tree. The thickness of the line that connects the branch nodes represents the volume of the population and the bar chart represents the distribution of the target value within each branch node.

The right side of Output 8.10 shows more detail for the top section of the decision tree. This visualization provides the name of each branch node and the split point information. It also provides the actual volume of observations in each node and the distribution of the target variable within each node.

Output 8.10: PROC HPSPLIT Tree Visualization

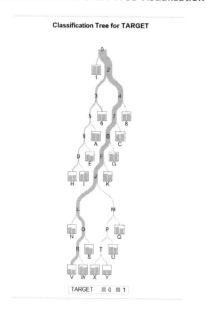

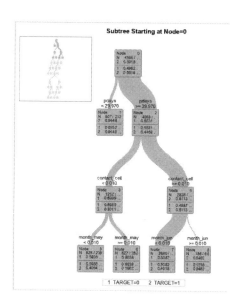

The next section of the output contains the confusion matrix for the training and validation data sets. This table shows the actual versus predicted target values and the corresponding error rate. Notice that the validation error rate is very similar to the training set error rate. This is a good sign that the model is not overfitting.

Output 8.11: PROC HPSPLIT Evaluation Metrics

		Confusion Matrices		
		Predicted		Error
	Actual	0	1	Rate
Training	0	2122	167	0.0730
	1	1153	1153	0.5000
Validation	0	875	72	0.0760
	1	511	443	0.5356

	N Leaves	ASE	Mis-class	Sensitivity	Specificity	Entropy	Gini	RSS	AUC
				Fit Statistics for Selected Tree					
Training	18	0.1868	0.2873	0.5000	0.9270	0.7954	0.3736	1716.8	0.7698
Validation	18	0.1960	0.3067	0.4644	0.9240	0.8171	0.3876	745.1	0.7483

The Fit Statistics for Selected Tree table shows the fit statistics for both the training and validation data sets. This information also provides a quality check to verify that the model is not overfitting to the TRAIN data set. The average squared error (ASE) and misclassification rate are both slightly lower for the TRAIN data set compared to the VALIDATION data set. The sensitivity, specificity, and area under the curve (AUC) are all slightly higher for the TRAIN data set compared to the VALIDATION data set.

Output 8.12 shows the ROC curve for both the training and validation data sets. This information is also contained in the Fit Statistics table above in the AUC column.

Output 8.12: ROC Curve

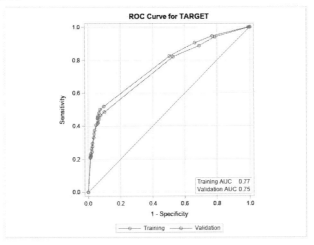

Output 8.13 shows us the Variable Importance table. This table provides us critical information on the power of each variable in the final model and their relative importance to predicting the target variable. It is important to remember that the most important variables might not be at the top of the tree. Variable importance is determined through four metrics:

- **Count** – The number of times a variable was used as a splitting rule.

- **Surrogate Count** – The number of times a variable was used in a surrogate splitting rule.

- **Reduction in RSS** – The change in the residual sum of squares when a spit is found at a node.

- **Relative Importance** – The individual variable RSS-based importance divided by the maximum RSS importance.

Output 8.13: Variable Importance Table

| | | Variable Importance | | | | | |
| | | Training | | Validation | | Relative | |
Variable	Variable Label	Relative	Importance	Relative	Importance	Ratio	Count
pdays	pdays	1.0000	14.9532	1.0000	9.5421	1.0000	1
contact_cell		0.5858	8.7594	0.6561	6.2607	1.1201	1
age	age	0.4263	6.3741	0.4370	4.1697	1.0251	2
month_mar		0.3918	5.8590	0.4176	3.9848	1.0658	2
month_jun		0.4069	6.0847	0.4118	3.9290	1.0119	1
month_oct		0.4626	6.9180	0.3291	3.1404	0.7114	2
month_apr		0.3787	5.6626	0.3135	2.9914	0.8278	2
month_sep		0.2342	3.5023	0.1765	1.6842	0.7536	1
edu_basic9		0.1919	2.8691	0.1440	1.3743	0.7506	1
month_dec		0.2119	3.1691	0.1342	1.2802	0.6330	1
default_no		0.2724	4.0729	0.1296	1.2365	0.4757	1
month_may		0.3518	5.2599	0.0997	0.9516	0.2835	1
day_thu		0.2470	3.6942	0.0000	0	0.0000	1

Output 8.14 shows the cost-complexity pruning for the target variable graphic. This graphic compares the number of leaves for the full decision tree (prior to pruning) and plots them against the misclassification rate (or classification models). This is performed for both training

and validation data sets. The optimal number of leaves is shown as the vertical blue line that specifies the point where the validation data set has the lowest misclassification rate. If this were a regression model, the y-axis would be the RSS value.

Output 8.14: Cost Complexity Chart

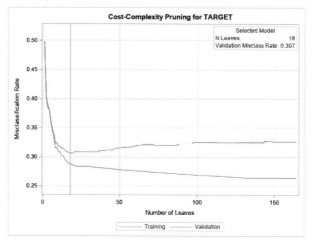

Scoring the TEST Data Set

PROC HPSPLIT does not have the internal ability to score a hold-out TEST data set within the procedure. However, it can output the scoring code that we can apply to the TEST data set in a DATA step.

Program 8.7 shows the code to score the hold-out TEST data set.

Program 8.7: Scoring the TEST Data Set

```
DATA test_scored;
  SET MYDATA.bank_test;
  %INCLUDE 'C:/Users/James Gearheart/Desktop/SAS Book
Stuff/Data/bank_tree.sas';
RUN;

%INCLUDE 'C:/Users/James Gearheart/Desktop/SAS Book
Stuff/Projects/separation.sas';
%separation(data = test_scored, score = P_TARGET1, y = target);
```

The score script that was generated from the CODE FILE statement in PROC HPSPLIT is applied to the hold-out TEST data set through the use of the %INCLUDE statement.

There are several ways to evaluate the performance of the model on the TEST data set. I've included the same macro that we used in the KNN example. The output of this evaluation macro (Output 8.15) shows that the decision tree algorithm produces a Gini score of 48.78 on the TEST data set. We can compare this score to the score that was produced by the KNN model to see which approach works better. When I applied the KNN model to the balanced data set (the previous KNN model was built on an unbalanced data set). The optimal value for k was 11. I then applied the %separation macro to the KNN scored TEST data set and the resulting Gini score was

38.88. This shows that the decision tree approach does a better job of separating the goods from the bads in the TEST data set.

Output 8.15: TEST Data Set Lift Table

GOOD BAD SEPARATION REPORT FOR P_TARGET1 IN DATA TEST_SCORED										
MAXIMUM KS = 38.6957 AT SCORE POINT 0.4639										
(AUC STATISTICS = 0.7439, GINI COEFFICIENT = 0.4878, DIVERGENCE = 1.0496)										
	MIN SCORE	MAX SCORE	GOOD #	BAD #	TOTAL #	ODDS	BAD RATE	CUMULATIVE BAD RATE	BAD PERCENT	CUMU. BAD PERCENT
BAD	0.8462	0.9448	69	471	540	0.15	87.22%	87.22%	34.13%	34.13%
I	0.75	0.8276	48	178	226	0.27	78.76%	84.73%	12.90%	47.03%
I	0.4639	0.4639	43	42	85	1.02	49.41%	81.20%	3.04%	50.07%
I	0.4281	0.4281	561	425	986	1.32	43.10%	60.75%	30.80%	80.87%
I	0.3413	0.3413	228	93	321	2.45	28.97%	56.02%	6.74%	87.61%
V	0.2762	0.2762	157	79	236	1.99	33.47%	53.80%	5.72%	93.33%
GOOD	0.1481	0.1962	298	92	390	3.24	23.59%	49.57%	6.67%	100.00%
	0.1481	0.9448	1404	1380	2784					

Random Forest

The main weakness of a single decision tree model is that it is a "greedy algorithm." This means that it selects the best variable and split point at each stage of the tree development, but it never looks forward or backward to determine whether alternative splits would have produced a better overall outcome. This process leads to a static tree that is not guaranteed to be the best possible tree-based approach.

The random forest algorithm is an attempt to mitigate this inherent weakness of decision trees. It is an ensemble approach that constructs several different decision trees and averages the results together. It is the algorithmic equivalent of "wisdom of the crowds."

The general construction of a random forest begins with building a bootstrapped data set. Figure 8.8 demonstrates the general construction of a bootstrapped data set. We will use the same data table from Table 8.4 to demonstrate the process of constructing a bootstrapped data set. This process has two parts:

1. **Randomly select predictors** – In the example, there are only four predictors in the data set. Normally, we would have many more predictors in a real data set. The general rule of thumb for randomly selecting the appropriate number of predictors is to take the square root of the number of predictors ($\sqrt{p}$). Later, when we discuss hyperparameter tuning, this value can be adjusted to find the optimal value.

2. **Randomly select observations** – Randomly sample the base data set to create a new bootstrapped data set with the same number of observations as the original base data

set. An important thing to remember is that this is sampling with replacement. So a single observation can be included more than once.

Figure 8.8: Bootstrapped Data Set Construction

Randomly select predictors

Contact	Year	Campaign	Age Cat	Target
telephone	1st half	1 or 2	LE 45	no
telephone	1st half	1 or 2	45+	no
cellular	2nd half	1 or 2	45+	no
cellular	2nd half	1 or 2	LE 45	no
cellular	2nd half	1 or 2	45+	yes
telephone	1st half	1 or 2	LE 45	no
cellular	2nd half	Greater than 2	45+	no
cellular	2nd half	1 or 2	LE 45	no
cellular	1st half	1 or 2	LE 45	no
cellular	1st half	Greater than 2	LE 45	yes

Bootstrapped Dataset

Year	Age Cat	Target
1st half	45+	no
2nd half	45+	yes
1st half	LE 45	no
1st half	LE 45	no
2nd half	LE 45	no
1st half	45+	no
1st half	LE 45	no
1st half	LE 45	no
2nd half	LE 45	no
2nd half	45+	yes

Randomly select observations

Figure 8.8 shows that the predictors Year and Age Cat have been randomly selected as the predictors for the bootstrapped data set. The observations for the base data set were then randomly sampled to create a bootstrapped data set with the same volume of observations as the base data set. Notice that the gray highlighted observations have each been selected twice and that the dark gray observation was selected four times.

Once the bootstrapped data set has been constructed, a decision tree is developed on this data set. The first step to constructing an individual decision tree in a random forest model is to randomly select a subset of available predictors to evaluate for the root node. After the root node has been determined, another set of random variables are selected to determine the branch node. This random selection process continues throughout the building of the tree. The random forest algorithm considers only a random subset of variables at each step of the tree construction.

The above process of developing an individual tree is repeated hundreds of times. Due to the random nature of the tree construction, this results in a wide variety of trees.

Scoring Unseen Observations

Once all of the decision trees have been constructed, a new unseen observation is subjected to all the decision trees and the results for each tree are tallied into a total across all trees. If, for example, there are 100 decision trees in a classification random forest model, then the results may look like Table 8.6.

Table 8.6: Random Forest Summary Example

Yes	No
85	15

In this example, 85 individual decision trees in the random forest resulted in the final categorical response of "Yes" and 15 individual decision trees that results in "No." The final predictive result of the random forest model is achieved through a voting method for classification models. Therefore, in this example, the final predicted value would be Yes.

For classification trees, a voting method determines the final result; for regression trees, the average determines the final result. The process of using a bootstrapped data set and using the aggregate to make a decision is called *bagging*.

Assessing Model Accuracy

Due to the random selection of observations during the construction of the bootstrapped data set, typically, about 1/3 of the original data set does not end up in the bootstrapped data set. This is called the "out-of-bag" data set. We can use this data set as the hold-out test data set and run it through the random forest to assess accuracy. Figure 8.9 shows how the data set is split between out-of-bag observations and observations used in the random forest.

Figure 8.9: Out of Bag Observations Example

We can measure the accuracy of the random forest by the proportion of out-of-bag (OOB) samples that were correctly classified by the random forest. The proportion of OOB samples that were incorrectly classified is the "out-of-bag error."

One of the key strengths of a random forest model is that you can use the entire data set as the training data set. There is no need to split the full data set into separate TRAIN and TEST data sets. This is because the algorithm inherently samples the data set and creates an out-of-bag data set that is essentially a hold-out TEST data set. Therefore, you get the benefit of a rigorous TRAIN/TEST split while using all of the observations.

Random forest models have a lot of options to custom design your algorithm to fit your needs. Each of these options can have a significant impact on the accuracy and performance of the model. Therefore, hyperparameter tuning is very important. You can adjust any of the hyperparameters including the number of variables to sample, the max tree depth, the value of alpha, the number of trees, the in-bag fraction, the number of interval bins, leaf size, the minimum number of observations to include in a category, and many more.

Random Forest Model

SAS provides a high-performance procedure to implement random forests. PROC HPFOREST is a flexible procedure that allows you to customize your model through the selection of hyperparameter values. Program 8.8 demonstrates the general structure of the procedure and several of the hyperparameter options.

For consistency, we will continue to use the bank marketing data set that we have used throughout this chapter.

Program 8.8: Random Forest Example

```
PROC HPFOREST DATA=mydata.bank_train
        VARS_TO_TRY=8 MAXTREES=300 TRAINFRACTION=0.6
        MAXDEPTH=15 LEAFSIZE=10
        ALPHA=0.1;
        TARGET target/LEVEL=binary;
        INPUT &num_vars. / LEVEL=interval;
/*      INPUT &char_vars. / LEVEL=nominal;*/
        SAVE FILE = 'C:/Users/James Gearheart/Desktop/SAS Book
Stuff/Data/bank_RF.bin';
        ODS OUTPUT FITSTATISTICS = FITSTATS(rename=(Ntrees=Trees));
run;
```

Notes on Program 8.8:

- PROC HPFOREST is utilized to develop the random forest. This procedure is applied to the MYDATA.BANK_TRAIN data set.

- Several hyperparameter values are specified in the PROC HPFOREST options:

  ○ VARS_TO_TRY – Specifies the number of variables to consider splitting on in a node.

  ○ MAXTREES – Specifies the number of trees in the forest.

  ○ TRAINFRACTION – Specifies the fraction of training observations to train a tree.

  ○ MAXDEPTH – Specifies the maximum depth of a node in any tree.

  ○ LEAFSIZE – Specifies the smallest number of training observations a new branch can have.

  ○ ALPHA – Specifies a threshold p-value for the significance level of a test of association of a candidate variable with the target.

- The TARGET variable is specified. The data type must be specified for all input variables including the target variable. In this case, the target variable is a numeric binary indicator of 1 or 0.

- The INPUT statement specifies the predictor variables to be included in the model. PROC HPSPLIT requires that the numeric and character variables be specified separately. Since I had previously created separate macro variables for the numeric and character variables, I used the numeric macro variable num_vars to specify the numeric variables. The LEVEL statement specifies that these variables are interval variables.

- Although I had transformed the character variables to numeric when I was preparing the data for modeling, I have included a statement of how to specify the character variables and set their values to nominal. This statement has been commented out.

- The SAVE FILE option has been included so that we can score other data sets with the random forest model. I am saving this score logic in a space on my C drive. Notice that this file is a .bin file and not a .sas file.

- The OUT statement creates an output file for the fit statistics created by PROC HPSPLIT. I have renamed the NTREES field to TREES.

Random Forest Model Output

PROC HPSPLIT provides several important output tables to evaluate the performance of the model. The Model Information table provides a summary of the hyperparameter values that the developer has selected and the default values that SAS provided. Output 8.16 shows the Model Information table for the model that we have developed. Directly after the Model Information table, SAS provides additional tables that include the Number of Observations table and the Baseline Fit Statistics tables. This last table provides the average squared error, misclassification rate, and the log loss for the training data. The Baseline Fit Statistics table describes the data prior to the model build.

Output 8.16: PROC HPFOREST Output

Model Information		
Parameter	Value	
Variables to Try	8	
Maximum Trees	300	
Actual Trees	300	
Inbag Fraction	0.6	
Prune Fraction	0	(Default)
Prune Threshold	0.1	(Default)
Leaf Fraction	0.00001	(Default)
Leaf Size Setting	10	
Leaf Size Used	10	
Category Bins	30	(Default)
Interval Bins	100	
Minimum Category Size	5	(Default)
Node Size	100000	(Default)
Maximum Depth	15	
Alpha	0.1	
Exhaustive	5000	(Default)
Rows of Sequence to Skip	5	(Default)
Split Criterion		Gini
Preselection Method		BinnedSearch
Missing Value Handling		Valid value

Number of Observations	
Type	**N**
Number of Observations Read	6496
Number of Observations Used	6496

Baseline Fit Statistics	
Statistic	**Value**
Average Square Error	0.250
Misclassification Rate	0.498
Log Loss	0.693

Output 8.17 shows the Fit Statistics table for each tree that was developed as part of the random forest. The table will contain information for all 300 trees that were developed; however, due to space limitations, I have shown only the first 20 trees.

Output 8.17: PROC HPFOREST Fit Statistics Table

		Fit Statistics					
Number of Trees	Number of Leaves	Average Square Error (Train)	Average Square Error (OOB)	Misclassification Rate (Train)	Misclassification Rate (OOB)	Log Loss (Train)	Log Loss (OOB)
1	149	0.199	0.214	0.326	0.361	0.627	0.746
2	333	0.186	0.209	0.279	0.332	0.550	0.659
3	460	0.185	0.207	0.280	0.329	0.545	0.641
4	606	0.183	0.206	0.278	0.322	0.543	0.656
5	777	0.182	0.205	0.274	0.319	0.542	0.633
6	936	0.181	0.203	0.271	0.315	0.540	0.617
7	1072	0.181	0.202	0.272	0.316	0.539	0.610
8	1228	0.181	0.201	0.269	0.314	0.537	0.615
9	1388	0.180	0.201	0.269	0.311	0.536	0.607
10	1554	0.180	0.199	0.269	0.309	0.535	0.597
11	1733	0.179	0.199	0.268	0.311	0.535	0.597
12	1903	0.179	0.199	0.269	0.308	0.535	0.584
13	2063	0.179	0.199	0.266	0.309	0.535	0.584
14	2231	0.179	0.198	0.266	0.308	0.534	0.582
15	2352	0.179	0.198	0.267	0.306	0.533	0.581
16	2509	0.179	0.198	0.264	0.307	0.534	0.580
17	2671	0.178	0.197	0.265	0.306	0.533	0.580
18	2800	0.179	0.197	0.264	0.305	0.533	0.579
19	2975	0.178	0.197	0.264	0.302	0.532	0.579
20	3154	0.178	0.197	0.265	0.305	0.532	0.579

The first column shows the number of trees added to the random forest. This is a cumulative process where each additional tree is combined with all of the previous trees. Therefore, we can see the cumulative benefit of each additional tree to the overall forest.

The second column shows the number of leaves of the random forest. Notice that this number continually increases as we add more trees to the forest.

The third and fourth columns show the average squared error (ASE) for both the training and the out-of-bag (OOB) data sets. We can see that the ASE continues to decrease as we add more trees to the forest.

The fifth and sixth columns show the misclassification rate for the training and the OOB data sets, while the seventh and eighth columns show the log loss for the training and OOB data sets. Notice that all of the error metrics continue to decrease as we add more trees.

It might occur to you that if we continue to add more trees, then the error rate might shrink to zero. Unfortunately, that is not the case. There is a point of diminishing returns where the addition of more trees does not affect the accuracy of the model.

Warning

It is a common misconception that random forests cannot overfit the data. Although it is true that the addition of more trees will not result in overfitting, the model can overfit in the same manner as simple decision trees. That is, if the tree depth is too deep or the minimum number of observations allowed in a given category is too small, then the model will overfit to the training data and not generalize well to unseen observations.

Variable Importance

One of the most important pieces of output from PROC HPSPLIT is the Loss Reduction Variable Importance table. This table shows the relative importance of each variable in the data set. Although we cannot assess the actual value for each variable in the same manner that we can in regression models, the variable importance table allows the researcher to look inside the massive amount of data generated from hundreds of trees and pull out the relative importance of each variable.

Output 8.18 shows the top 10 variables in the Loss Reduction Variable Importance table.

Output 8.18: PROC HPFOREST Variable Importance Table

	Loss Reduction Variable Importance				
Variable	Number of Rules	Gini	OOB Gini	Margin	OOB Margin
pdays	725	0.014401	0.01365	0.028802	0.02785
pout_succ	371	0.011043	0.01097	0.022087	0.02200
contact_tele	741	0.008268	0.00764	0.016536	0.01588
contact_cell	538	0.006911	0.00622	0.013823	0.01310
pout_non	373	0.006311	0.00603	0.012623	0.01239
previous	792	0.006871	0.00595	0.013742	0.01272
month_oct	501	0.004674	0.00423	0.009348	0.00878
month_may	1292	0.005275	0.00422	0.010550	0.00956
month_mar	410	0.004470	0.00400	0.008941	0.00831
month_jun	877	0.004608	0.00380	0.009216	0.00826

There are two measures that determine variable importance.

1. How much the accuracy decreases when the variable is excluded.
2. The decrease in Gini impurity when the variable is chosen to split a node.

Random forests are considered "black-box" models because we do not know exactly how the predictions are generated. We cannot say with certainty that the value for the variable pdays is exactly 0.375. This is because of the random nature of the bootstrapping process, the value of that specific variable changes for each tree in the random forest and in several of those trees, that variable is not included.

The variable importance table provides some level of insight into the relative importance of each variable in the model. The table is sorted by the OOB Gini column.

Scoring Algorithm

PROC HPSPLIT does not have the option to score a new data set directly within the procedure. Instead, the procedure allows you to output a SCORE FILE that you can apply to unseen data within a HP4SCORE procedure. Program 8.9 demonstrates PROC HP4SCORE.

Program 8.9: Score the TEST Data Set with the Random Forest Model

```
PROC HP4SCORE DATA=mydata.bank_test;
  ID ROW_NUM;
  SCORE FILE = 'C:/Users/James Gearheart/Desktop/SAS Book
Stuff/Data/bank_RF.bin'
  OUT = RF_SCORED;
RUN;
```

Notes on Program 8.9:

- PROC HP4SCORE is applied to the MYDATA.BANK_TEST data set. This data set is the hold-out TEST data set that was not used to build the random forest model.

- The ID option allows you to specify the unique identifier in your data set. This is often an account number or a customer number. In our case, we created a unique row identifier when we built the initial TEST data set.

- The SCORE FILE statement specifies the location, file name, and type to be applied to the data. This score file contains all of the logic to apply the random forest to unseen data that contains the same structure as the training data set.

- The OUT statement allows you to create an output data set of the scored file.

Once we have scored the hold-out TEST data set, we can assess the accuracy of the model with the same macro that we applied to the KNN and simple decision tree models. This will provide us a consistent metric to evaluate the accuracy of the model and compare it to the previous models built on the bank marketing data set. The random forest model applied to the hold-out TEST data set results in a Gini score of 51.60.

Output 8.19: TEST Data Set Lift Table

GOOD BAD SEPARATION REPORT FOR P_TARGET1 IN DATA RF_SCORED

MAXIMUM KS = 41.9881 AT SCORE POINT 0.5207

(AUC STATISTICS = 0.7580, GINI COEFFICIENT = 0.5160, DIVERGENCE = 1.0999)

	MIN SCORE	MAX SCORE	GOOD #	BAD #	TOTAL #	ODDS	BAD RATE	CUMULATIVE BAD RATE	BAD PERCENT	CUMU. BAD PERCENT
BAD	0.8605	0.9778	19	259	278	0.07	93.17%	93.17%	18.77%	18.77%
|	0.7199	0.8596	55	224	279	0.25	80.29%	86.71%	16.23%	35.00%
|	0.5801	0.7187	65	213	278	0.31	76.62%	83.35%	15.43%	50.43%
|	0.4914	0.58	144	135	279	1.07	48.39%	74.60%	9.78%	60.22%
|	0.4495	0.4913	167	111	278	1.5	39.93%	67.67%	8.04%	68.26%
|	0.4149	0.4494	162	117	279	1.38	41.94%	63.38%	8.48%	76.74%
|	0.3675	0.4148	175	103	278	1.7	37.05%	59.62%	7.46%	84.20%
|	0.3134	0.3674	202	77	279	2.62	27.60%	55.61%	5.58%	89.78%
V	0.2589	0.3133	204	74	278	2.76	26.62%	52.39%	5.36%	95.14%
GOOD	0.1184	0.2587	211	67	278	3.15	24.10%	49.57%	4.86%	100.00%
	0.1184	0.9778	1,404	1,380	2,784					

Hyperparameter Tuning Algorithm

With all of the possible options available in PROC HPSPLIT, how do you know which values to select that will produce the optimal tree? How many trees should be in your random forest? How many variables should the algorithm randomly sample? These types of questions are answered with the concept of hyperparameter tuning. The main approach to hyperparameter tuning is to try a range of values for each option and select the value that produces the best result. Let's take a look at two examples that I pulled directly from the excellent online SAS documentation website: https://documentation.sas.com/.

Evaluate the Optimal Number of Trees

In the original PROC HPSPLIT in Program 8.7, we created an output statement that placed the fit statistics into a data set that we called "fitstats." We can now leverage that output data set to examine the change in the misclassification rate as we add more trees. Program 8.10 demonstrates the development of this analysis.

Program 8.10: Tune the "Number of Trees" Hyperparameter

```
data fitstats;
   set fitstats;
   label Trees = 'Number of Trees';
   label MiscAll = 'Full Data';
   label Miscoob = 'OOB';
run;
```

```
proc sgplot data=fitstats;
    title "OOB vs Training";
    series x=Trees y=MiscAll;
    series x=Trees y=MiscOob/lineattrs=(pattern=shortdash thickness=2);
    yaxis label='Misclassification Rate';
run;
```

This program simply relabels a few attributes to make the interpretation easier to understand and then creates a line chart that visualizes the data. Output 8.20 shows the chart developed from PROC SGPLOT.

Output 8.20: Misclassification Rate for Full Data Set and OOB Data Set

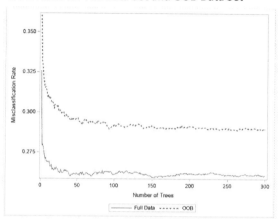

This chart shows the misclassification rate for both the full data and the OOB data set. We can see that the misclassification rate begins to drop rapidly when the first dozen trees are added to the model. After that point, the misclassification rate continues to decrease until about 150 trees are added to the model. At that point, the misclassification rate trend flattens out. We can determine from this analysis that 150 trees is the optimal number to include in the random forest.

Determine the Optimal Number of Variables

Other approaches to hyperparameter tuning can be slightly more involved. When trying to determine the optimal number of variables to sample, we will need to create a program that builds the random forest on a few values and determine which of those values produced the optimal result. Program 8.11 shows the development of this analysis.

Program 8.11: Tune the "Number of Variables" Hyperparameter

```
%macro hpforest(Vars=);
proc hpforest data=mydata.bank_train  maxtrees=300
    vars_to_try=&Vars.;
        TARGET target/LEVEL=binary;
        INPUT &num_vars. / LEVEL=interval;
    ods output
    FitStatistics = fitstats_vars&Vars.(rename=(Miscoob=VarsToTry&Vars.));
run;
```

```
%mend;

%hpforest(vars=all);
%hpforest(vars=40);
%hpforest(vars=26);
%hpforest(vars=7);
%hpforest(vars=2);

data fitstats;
   merge
   fitstats_varsall fitstats_vars40 fitstats_vars26 fitstats_vars7
fitstats_vars2;
   rename Ntrees=Trees;
   label VarsToTryAll = "Vars=All";
   label VarsToTry40 = "Vars=40";
   label VarsToTry26 = "Vars=26";
   label VarsToTry7 = "Vars=7";
   label VarsToTry2 = "Vars=2";
run;

proc sgplot data=fitstats;
   title "Misclassification Rate for Various VarsToTry Values";
   series x=Trees y = VarsToTryAll/lineattrs=(Color=black);
   series x=Trees y=VarsToTry40/lineattrs=(Pattern=ShortDash Thickness=2);
   series x=Trees y=VarsToTry26/lineattrs=(Pattern=ShortDash Thickness=2);
   series x=Trees y=VarsToTry7/lineattrs=(Pattern=MediumDashDotDot
Thickness=2);
   series x=Trees y=VarsToTry2/lineattrs=(Pattern=LongDash Thickness=2);
   yaxis label='OOB Misclassification Rate';
run;
```

Notes on Program 8.11:

- The first section of code develops a macro that loops through various values that we will apply to the vars_to_try hyperparameter. The range of values includes all variables at the high end and only two variabes at the low end.

- The next two sections are similar to the way that we analyzed the number of trees hyperparameter. The fit statistics have been placed into a data set labeled "fitstats_varX," where X is the number of variables that were sampled. These five data sets were then set together into a single data set labeled "fitstats".

- PROC SGPLOT creates a line plot of the OOB misclassification rate against the number of trees in the model. This approach developed separate lines for each of the variables that represent the number of variables that were sampled. Output 8.21 shows the output from PROC SGPLOT.

Output 8.21: Output from PROC SGPLOT

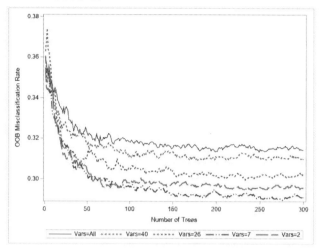

Output 8.21 shows that at 150 trees, the variable that represents the values when the model randomly sampled 7 variables results in the lowest OOB misclassification rate. So, for this data set, the optimal value for the number of trees to include in the model is 150 and the optimal value of the number of variables to try in the model is 7.

Gradient Boosting

Random forest is classified as a bagging technique because it randomly samples the observations and predictors to create a final prediction based on a voting method for classification models or the average for regression models. However, bagging is not the only approach that we can take to develop an ensemble of decision trees. The boosting technique produces a series of trees and creates weights based on the residuals of previous trees. Prediction is based on the sum of the final weights.

Although both random forest and gradient boosting are powerful machine learning techniques, both are considered black-box models. However, because the target value of the gradient boosting algorithm continually changes, and the strength of the observations are constantly updated by adjusting weights, the gradient boosting algorithm is deep into black-box territory.

The difference between random forests and gradient boosting is summarized in Table 8.7. This table shows that the two approaches are very different.

Table 8.7: Random Forest Versus Gradient Boosting

Random Forest	Gradient Boosting
Trees are independent	Trees are sequential
Trees are deep	Trees are shallow
Trees are strong learners	Trees are weak learners
Observations are sampled	All observations are used
Predictors are sampled	All predictors are used
All trees have equal say in final decision	Trees have weighted say in final decision
Predictions based on voting/average	Predictions based on sum of weights

The gradient boosting approach builds trees *sequentially*. This means that the trees are developed one at a time and the results of one tree are input to the next tree. Let's look at the development of a regression gradient boosting model.

Steps to build a regression gradient boosting model:

1. Assign initial weights to all of the observations. The initial weights are of equal value.
2. Take the average of the continuous target variable and assume that is the initial prediction.
3. Calculate the observed target value minus the average value to create the residual value.
4. Use the residual value as the updated target value and build a shallow decision tree against this target value. The shallow decision tree is specified in the hyperparameters where the number of leaves is limited to a value between 8 and 32.
5. Gradient boosting scales the trees but the algorithm scales all trees by the same amount. Then gradient boosting builds another tree based on the errors of the previous tree and then it scales that tree. This continues until the algorithm builds the number of trees that you asked for or additional trees do not improve the model fit.
6. The average value for the continuous target variable is taken as the initial weight. The residuals are created by taking the actual value and subtracting the average value. This creates a series of residuals. Now a decision tree is constructed to predict the residuals.
7. Gradient boosting adds a learning rate to scale the contribution of a new tree. This is to avoid overfitting. The addition of the learning rate forces the algorithm to take small

steps towards the final prediction (in a gradient descent fashion). This results in better predictions of the testing data set.

8. Then we add another tree based on the residuals from the previous tree and continue this process of adding trees based on the residuals of the previous tree.

9. For classification, the initial prediction is the log of the odds. We convert the log odds to a probability with the use of the logistic function.

$$probability = \frac{e^{\log(odds)}}{1 + e^{\log(odds)}}$$

10. We then calculate the residuals from the observed values and continue to build a decision tree on the residual values.

Gradient Boosting Model

SAS provides the TREEBOOST procedure for building gradient boosting decision trees. This procedure is structured similarly to the decision tree and random forest procedures, although PROC TREEBOOST has several more options available than a simple decision tree.

Program 8.12 demonstrates the structure and options of PROC TREEBOOST.

Program 8.12

```
ODS GRAPHICS ON;

PROC TREEBOOST DATA = mydata.bank_train
        CATEGORICALBINS = 10
        INTERVALBINS = 100
        EXHAUSTIVE = 5000
        INTERVALDECIMALS = MAX
        LEAFSIZE = 32
        MAXBRANCHES = 2
        ITERATIONS = 1000
        MINCATSIZE = 50
        MISSING = USEINSEARCH
        SEED = 42
        SHRINKAGE = 0.1
        SPLITSIZE = 100
        TRAINPROPORTION = 0.6;
        INPUT &num_vars. / LEVEL = INTERVAL;
/*      INPUT &charx. / LEVEL = NOMINAL;*/
        TARGET TARGET / LEVEL = BINARY;
        IMPORTANCE NVARS = 50 OUTFIT = BASE_VARS;
        SUBSERIES BEST;
        CODE FILE = 'C:/Users/James Gearheart/Desktop/SAS Book
Stuff/Data/bank_GB.bin';
        SAVE MODEL = GBS_TEST FIT = FIT_STATS
             IMPORTANCE = IMPORTANCE RULES = RULES;
RUN;
```

Notes on Program 8.12 (these definitions are taken directly from the *SAS Enterprise Miner and Text Miner Procedures Reference for SAS 9.3*) :

- PROC TREEBOOST is called to develop a gradient boosting algorithm on the MYDATA.TRAIN data set.

- The CATEGORICALBINS option is set to 10. This option specifies the number of preliminary bins that are used to collect categorical input values just before the search for a split.

- The INTERVALBINS option is set to 100. This option specifies the preliminary number of bins to create for the input interval values.

- The EXHAUSTIVE option is set to 5000. This option specifies the maximum number of splits that are allowed in a complete enumeration of all possible splits.

- The INTERVALDECIMALS option is set to MAX. This option specifies the precision, in decimals, of the split point for an interval input variable.

- The LEAFSIZE option is set to 32. This option specifies the minimum number of observations that are necessary to form a new branch.

- The MAXBRANCHES option is set to 2. This option specifies the maximum number of subsets that a splitting rule can produce.

- The ITERATIONS option is set to 1000. This option specifies the number of terms in the boosting series. For interval and binary targets, the number of iterations equals the number of trees.

- The MINCATSIZE option is set to 50. In order to create a splitting rule for a particular value of a nominal variable, there must be number of observations of that value.

- The MISSING option is set to USEINSEARCH. This argument specifies the policy that is used to handle missing values.

- The SEED option is set to 42. This option specifies the seed for the random number generator.

- The SHRINKAGE option is set to 0.1. This option specifies how much, as a percentage, to reduce the prediction of each tree. The value of the number must be between 0 and 1 and the default is 0.2.

- The SPLITSIZE option is set to 100. The TREEBOOST procedure will split a node only when it contains at least this number observations. The default value is twice the size of the value specified in the LEAFSIZE= argument.

- The TRAINPROPORTION is set to 0.6. This option specifies the proportion of observations that are used to train each tree. If you use less than all of the available data, this might improve the generalization error.

- The INPUT value specifies a global variable that contains all of the numeric variables. The LEVEL option is set to INTERVAL.

- The TARGET option specifies the name of the target variable. In this data set, we have named the target variable TARGET and set the LEVEL to be BINARY.

- The IMPORTANCE statement uses an observation-based approach to evaluate the importance of a variable or a pair of variables to the predictions of the model. For each observation, the IMPORTANCE statement outputs the prediction once with the actual variable value and once with an uninformative variable value.

- The OUTFIT statement produces a data set that contains the goodness-of-fit statistics. The number of observations in this data set is the number of variables plus the number of pairs of variables plus one. This data set contains the same variables as the output data set in the SCORE statement, plus one or two more variables. These variables contain the names of the uninformative variables.

- The SUBSERIES statement specifies how many iterations in the series to use in the model. For a binary or interval target, the number of iterations is the number of trees in the series. For a nominal target with k categories, k > 2, each iteration contains k trees.

- If you want to score a data set with a previously trained neural network, you can use the CODE statement. The CODE statement writes the SAS DATA step code to file or catalog entry. This code can be included in a DATA step that reads the scored data set with a SET statement.

- The final statements of the TREEBOOST procedure create output data sets for the fit statistics, the variable importance table, and the rules to create the decision trees.

One of the unfortunate characteristics of PROC TREEBOOST is that it does not output the traditional presentation-ready beautiful output tables and graphics like we see in most SAS procedures. Instead, we can look at the output tables that we specified in the code.

Output 8.22 shows the first ten rows of the fit statistics table. This table contains a row for each of the 1000 iterations that we specified in the code. We can see how the SSE, ASE, and RASE metrics all decrease with each iteration of the algorithm.

Output 8.22: PROC TREEBOOST Fit Statistics Table

	ITERATIO		_NOBS_		_SUMW_		_NW_		_MISC_		_MAX_		_SSE_		_ASE_		_RASE_		_DIV_		_DFT_
1	1		6496		12992		4		0.3879310345		0.5483234943		3164.7986789		0.2435959574		0.4935544118		12992		6496
2	2		6496		12992		8		0.3879310345		0.589616361		3098.078731		0.2384604935		0.4883241684		12992		6496
3	3		6496		12992		12		0.3879310345		0.6249351125		3045.9942924		0.2344515311		0.4842019528		12992		6496
4	4		6496		12992		16		0.3588362069		0.658024414		3002.5433448		0.2311070924		0.4807359904		12992		6496
5	5		6496		12992		20		0.3814655172		0.6879615301		2963.515629		0.2281031118		0.4776014152		12992		6496
6	6		6496		12992		24		0.3483682266		0.7163834439		2929.9793264		0.2255218078		0.4748913642		12992		6496
7	7		6496		12992		28		0.3485221675		0.7229699552		2901.067963		0.223295718		0.4725417632		12992		6496
8	8		6496		12992		32		0.3482142857		0.7455360406		2874.3126973		0.2212371227		0.4703535044		12992		6496
9	9		6496		12992		36		0.3482142857		0.7663356574		2849.7196608		0.2193441857		0.4683419538		12992		6496
10	10		6496		12992		40		0.3474445813		0.7867763813		2826.5087303		0.2175576301		0.4664307345		12992		6496

Output 8.23 shows the top 10 features in the importance table. We can see that this table is very similar to the importance table generated in the random forest algorithm.

Output 8.23: PROC TREEBOOST Variable Importance Table

	NAME	LABEL	NRULES	IMPORTANCE
1	pdays	pdays	42	1
2	age	age	612	0.9514090946
3	campaign	campaign	308	0.6187671732
4	contact_tele		39	0.540203351
5	month_may		62	0.4483990502
6	month_oct		30	0.4356217076
7	month_apr		75	0.433350337
8	month_jun		60	0.4186440384
9	default_unkn		27	0.4034422442
10	month_mar		22	0.4032608764

Output 8.24 shows the first tree of the gradient boosting algorithm. Remember that these are a series of shallow trees that are designed to be "weak learners." This first tree has only three nodes and two variables.

Output 8.24: PROC TREEBOOST Tree Logic Example

	TREE	NODE	ROLE	RANK	STAT	NUMERIC_VALUE	CHARACTER_VALUE
1	1	1	PRIMARY	1	VARIABLE		pdays
2	1	1	PRIMARY	1	LABEL		pdays
3	1	1	PRIMARY	1	NEWNODE	2	
4	1	1	PRIMARY	1	MISSING	2	
5	1	1	PRIMARY	1	WORTH	0.1021506563	
6	1	1	PRIMARY	1	BRANCHES	2	
7	1	1	PRIMARY	1	INTERVAL	508.5	
8	1	2	PRIMARY	1	VARIABLE	.	pdays
9	1	2	PRIMARY	1	LABEL		pdays
10	1	2	PRIMARY	1	NEWNODE	4	
11	1	2	PRIMARY	1	MISSING	1	
12	1	2	PRIMARY	1	WORTH	0.0056522029	
13	1	2	PRIMARY	1	BRANCHES	2	
14	1	2	PRIMARY	1	INTERVAL	8.5	
15	1	3	PRIMARY	1	VARIABLE	.	contact_tele
16	1	3	PRIMARY	1	NEWNODE	6	
17	1	3	PRIMARY	1	MISSING	1	
18	1	3	PRIMARY	1	WORTH	0.0407466878	
19	1	3	PRIMARY	1	BRANCHES	2	
20	1	3	PRIMARY	1	INTERVAL	0.5	

Gradient Boosting Scoring

PROC TREEBOOST does not inherently score new data sets. There is not a SCORE option available for this algorithm. Instead, the scoring is performed separately in the same manner as the decision tree scoring procedure is performed.

PROC TREEBOOST allows you to create an output SCORE FILE that you can apply to any data set that has the same structure as the input data set to PROC TREEBOOST. This score file can be called with a %INCLUDE statement. Program 8.13 demonstrates how to apply the scoring algorithm to a separate data set.

Program 8.13: Score TEST Data Set with PROC TREEBOOST Model

```
DATA GB_TEST;
  SET mydata.bank_test;
```

```
    %INCLUDE 'C:/Users/James Gearheart/Desktop/SAS Book
Stuff/Data/bank_GB.bin';
RUN;

%INCLUDE 'C:/Users/James Gearheart/Desktop/SAS Book
Stuff/Projects/separation.sas';
%separation(data = GB_SCORED, score = P_TARGET1, y = target);
```

This program applies the stored score code to the hold-out TEST data set, and then I apply the lift table macro to evaluate the performance of the model on the TEST data set.

Output 8.25 shows the lift table generated from the lift macro. This table shows that the gradient boosting algorithm does a good job of separating the goods from the bads with a Gini score of 49.11.

Output 8.25: TEST Data Set Lift Table

<table>
<tr><td colspan="11">GOOD BAD SEPARATION REPORT FOR P_TARGET1 IN DATA GB_TEST</td></tr>
<tr><td colspan="11">MAXIMUM KS = 39.5621 AT SCORE POINT 0.5837</td></tr>
<tr><td colspan="11">(AUC STATISTICS = 0.7456, GINI COEFFICIENT = 0.4911, DIVERGENCE = 1.0044)</td></tr>
<tr><td></td><td>MIN SCORE</td><td>MAX SCORE</td><td>GOOD #</td><td>BAD #</td><td>TOTAL #</td><td>ODDS</td><td>BAD RATE</td><td>CUMULATIVE BAD RATE</td><td>BAD PERCENT</td><td>CUMU. BAD PERCENT</td></tr>
<tr><td>BAD</td><td>0.9303</td><td>0.994</td><td>19</td><td>259</td><td>278</td><td>0.07</td><td>93.17%</td><td>93.17%</td><td>18.77%</td><td>18.77%</td></tr>
<tr><td>|</td><td>0.8182</td><td>0.9301</td><td>47</td><td>232</td><td>279</td><td>0.2</td><td>83.15%</td><td>88.15%</td><td>16.81%</td><td>35.58%</td></tr>
<tr><td>|</td><td>0.6168</td><td>0.8179</td><td>82</td><td>196</td><td>278</td><td>0.42</td><td>70.50%</td><td>82.28%</td><td>14.20%</td><td>49.78%</td></tr>
<tr><td>|</td><td>0.505</td><td>0.6165</td><td>153</td><td>126</td><td>279</td><td>1.21</td><td>45.16%</td><td>72.98%</td><td>9.13%</td><td>58.91%</td></tr>
<tr><td>|</td><td>0.4374</td><td>0.5049</td><td>149</td><td>129</td><td>278</td><td>1.16</td><td>46.40%</td><td>67.67%</td><td>9.35%</td><td>68.26%</td></tr>
<tr><td>|</td><td>0.3828</td><td>0.4369</td><td>180</td><td>99</td><td>279</td><td>1.82</td><td>35.48%</td><td>62.30%</td><td>7.17%</td><td>75.43%</td></tr>
<tr><td>|</td><td>0.3219</td><td>0.3828</td><td>177</td><td>101</td><td>278</td><td>1.75</td><td>36.33%</td><td>58.59%</td><td>7.32%</td><td>82.75%</td></tr>
<tr><td>|</td><td>0.262</td><td>0.3217</td><td>187</td><td>92</td><td>279</td><td>2.03</td><td>32.97%</td><td>55.39%</td><td>6.67%</td><td>89.42%</td></tr>
<tr><td>V</td><td>0.1913</td><td>0.2618</td><td>208</td><td>70</td><td>278</td><td>2.97</td><td>25.18%</td><td>52.04%</td><td>5.07%</td><td>94.49%</td></tr>
<tr><td>GOOD</td><td>0.0248</td><td>0.1909</td><td>202</td><td>76</td><td>278</td><td>2.66</td><td>27.34%</td><td>49.57%</td><td>5.51%</td><td>100.00%</td></tr>
<tr><td></td><td>0.0248</td><td>0.994</td><td>1,404</td><td>1,380</td><td>2,784</td><td></td><td></td><td></td><td></td><td></td></tr>
</table>

One of the main points to remember when working with gradient boosting decision trees is that hyperparameter tuning is very important. Although the initial setting that we applied to the gradient boosting algorithm produced a Gini score that is slightly lower than the random forest score (49.11 vs 51.60), we could tune the hyperparameters of the gradient boosting model to perform better and possibly outperform the random forest model.

Support Vector Machine (SVM)

Up to this point, the non-parametric models that we have studied have relied on concepts that we had previously discussed. The KNN models can be thought of as the same family as clustering, and the tree-based models all have a common approach of recursive partitioning of the data. Support Vector Machines (SVMs) take a fresh look at the problem of classifying data. The goal of SVMs is to find a dividing point, whether that be a single point, a line, or a hyperplane, that distinctly separates the classes of the observations. The idea of separating classes is taken further through the use of "kernels," where the separation becomes non-linear.

Figure 8.10 shows a hypothetical data distribution of observations with two classes. The left side of the figure shows the raw data distribution. There are many ways that we can separate the two classes. Our goal is to find the point of separation that provides the maximum distance between a pair of data points of both classes. This is called the maximum margin.

The right side of the figure shows the same data distribution with the optimal boundary that provides the maximum separation between the two closest points of each class.

Figure 8.10: Data Distribution Boundaries

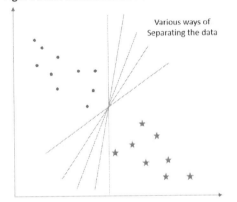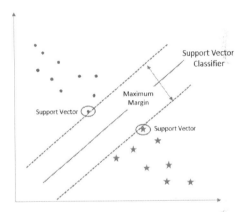

The line that provides the maximum space between the two classes provides us some comfort that new observations will be classified with more confidence. If a new observation is on one or the other side of the support vector classifier, then we can comfortably classify that observation.

The observations that are the closest to the support vector classifier are called support vectors. These observations define the position of the support vector classifier. They influence the position and orientation of the line or hyperplane. Due to the key role that these specific observations play in creating the decision boundaries of the Support Vector Classifier (SVC), the remaining observations are nearly unimportant. The entire model can be derived from just a few data points. This makes the Support Vector Machine one of the "lightest" models available because it only requires a few observations to make predictions.

When the classes are clearly separated, the support vector classifier is very easy to determine. However, most data sets are not neatly separated. Figure 8.11 shows an example where a few outlier observations destroy the perfect separation of the classes.

Figure 8.11: Outliers within the Boundary Specifications

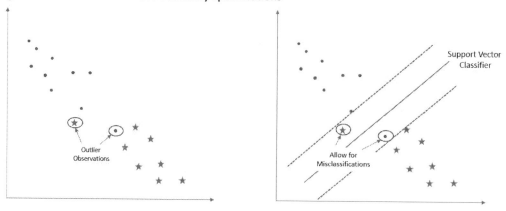

Choosing the threshold that allows for misclassification is an example of the bias-variance tradeoff. If the model is too sensitive to the training data, it will result in a high bias towards the training data and a low variance to new observations. By allowing misclassifications, we reduce the bias towards the training data but increase the variance towards new observations. When we allow misclassifications, the distance between the threshold (SVC) and the observations is called the soft margin. This soft margin is determined through cross-validation. The cross-validation technique will determine which of all possible soft margins has the lowest misclassification rate.

So, SVCs are flexible because they can handle outliers and misclassifications. They have an inherent tolerance built into the algorithm.

We use the hyperparameter C to specify how much misclassification that the model will allow. This is a regularization parameter that controls the specificity of the model. A low value of C will allow only a small number of misclassifications while a higher value of C will allow more misclassifications.

Kernel Trick

The unfortunate truth is that a linear decision boundary cannot separate most data distributions. Figure 8.12 demonstrates an example of a non-linear classification problem. The left-hand side of the figure shows the data distributed on the x- and y-axis. There is clearly no linear solution that will separate the classes.

Figure 8.12: Transform the Data by Moving It to a Higher Dimension

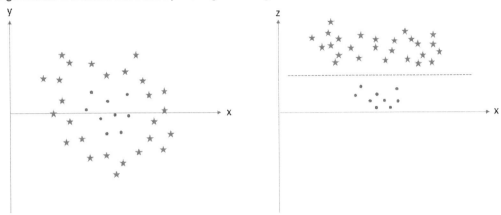

If the data is distributed where there are bad observations on each side of the good observations, then Support Vector Classifiers do not work very well. Instead, we need to use Support Vector Machines (SVMs). We can transform the data by moving it to a higher dimension (for example, by squaring it) and create a Support Vector Classifier in that view of the data. By adding non-linear features to the representation of the data, we can make linear models much more powerful. The data is now projected onto a three-dimensional axis (Z), which shows a clear separation of the classes.

How do we decide how to transform the data? In order to make the mathematics possible, SVMs use something called kernel functions to systematically find SVC in higher dimensions. This is referred to as the "kernel trick." The reason that it is a trick is that it would be very computationally expensive to calculate all possible interactions in a 100+ dimensional feature space. Instead, the algorithm can learn a classifier in a higher-dimensional space without actually performing the calculations of each representation. It works by calculating the distance of the data points for the range of feature representations without actually computing those features.

There are two different methods of mapping the data into a higher-dimensional space, the polynomial kernel and the radial basis function (RBF). The polynomial kernel computes all possible polynomials up to a certain degree while the RBF computes all possible polynomials of all degrees, but the importance of the features decreases for higher degrees. It behaves like a weighted nearest neighbors model.

SVM Model

Before we jump into the coding aspect of SVMs, it is important to visualize the data so that we have an *a priori* idea of how well a model will be able to separate the goods from the bads. If there is a clear visual separation of the data, then we could expect that the model will provide strong results. However, if the data is not well separated, then a model like SVMs will have a much poorer classification performance than tree-based models. Program 8.14 develops a scatter plot of the only two continuous features of the model: pdays and age.

Program 8.14: Scatter Plot of Predictor Variables

```
ods graphics / attrpriority=none;
proc sgplot data=mydata.bank_train (where=(pdays ne 999));
styleattrs datasymbols=(circlefilled trianglefilled) ;
      scatter x=pdays y=age / group=target;
      title 'Scatter Plot of Bank Marketing Data';
run;
```

The results of the program are shown in Output 8.26. We can see that there is not a clear distinction between the goods and bads in the data distribution. For the two variables that we have chosen to visualize, the target variable does not show any signs of separation or groupings. We should expect that this would make an SVM model underperform compared to tree-based models or KNNs.

Output 8.26: Scatter Plot of Predictor Variables

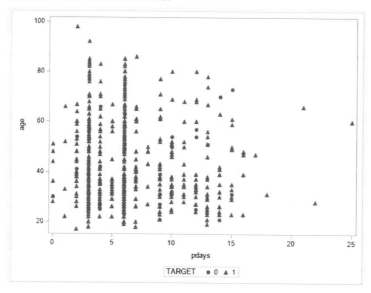

Polynomial Model Design

Program 8.15 develops the polynomial SVM model on the bank marketing data set.

Program 8.15: Support Vector Machine Example

```
PROC HPSVM DATA=mydata.bank_train;
      KERNEL POLYNOM;
    INPUT pdays age pout_succ previous contact_tele / LEVEL=interval;
    TARGET target / LEVEL=binary;
    PENALTY C=0.1 to 0.5 by 0.05;
    SELECT FOLD=3 CV=SPLIT;
    OUTPUT OUTCLASS=outclass OUTFIT=outfit OUTTEST=outest;
RUN;
```

Notes on Program 8.15:

- PROC HPSVM is applied to the MYDATA.BANK_TRAIN data set. This procedure is a high-performance algorithm that provides maximum processing efficiency.

- The KERNEL statement is set to POLYNOM. This tells the algorithm to develop the polynomial SVM model. The other options include LINEAR, RBF, and SIGMOID.

- The INPUT statement specifies the numeric variables and assigns the LEVEL to interval. If the data set contained character variables, they would have a separate INPUT statement and the LEVEL would be set to "nominal".

- The TARGET statement specifies the target variable and the LEVEL is set to binary.

- The PENALTY statement specifies a range of values for C (the regularization parameter). I have chosen a range of values from 0.1 to 0.5 with 0.05 intervals. This will help us determine the optimal value for C.

- The SELECT FOLD statement combined with the CV=SPLIT statement specifies that we want to use three-fold cross-validation to find the optimal value of C.

- The OUTPUT statements specify the output data sets that will be created.

PROC HPSVM provides a lot of information that allows you to know exactly what the model is doing and provides you with evaluation metrics.

Output 8.27 shows the Model Information table. This table shows you that the data was automatically scaled from 0 to 1 and that the kernel function was polynomial. The value of C was optimized at 0.1 and the algorithm cycled through 25 iterations.

Output 8.27: PROC HPSVM Output

Model Information	
Task Type	C_CLAS
Optimization Technique	Interior Point
Scale	YES
Kernel Function	Polynomial
Kernel Degree	2
Penalty Method	C
Penalty Parameter	0.1
Maximum Iterations	25
Tolerance	1e-06

Output 8.28 shows the Penalty Selection table. This table displays the hyperparameter tuning methodology. Cross-validation was used to select the value of C that provided the maximum accuracy. Remember, in the code that we input a range of values for C, from 0.1 to 0.5 in increments of 0.05. The Penalty Selection table provides the model evaluation metrics for each incremental C value.

Output 8.28: PROC HPSVM Penalty Selection Table

					Penalty Selection	
					Cross-Validation, Fold=3, Best C=0.1	
Penalty	True Positive	True Negative	False Negative	False Positive	Misclassification	Accuracy
0.100000	2748	1228	512	2008	2520	0.6121
0.150000	2748	1228	512	2008	2520	0.6121
0.200000	2748	1228	512	2008	2520	0.6121
0.250000	2748	1228	512	2008	2520	0.6121
0.300000	2748	1228	512	2008	2520	0.6121
0.350000	2748	1228	512	2008	2520	0.6121
0.400000	2748	1228	512	2008	2520	0.6121
0.450000	2748	1228	512	2008	2520	0.6121
0.500000	2748	1228	512	2008	2520	0.6121

Output 8.29 provides the final Classification Matrix and Fit Statistics tables. The classification matrix is structured in the standard manner as all of the other classification matrix tables that we have seen with the observed values on the left-hand side and the predicted values on top.

Output 8.29: PROC HPSVM Evaluation Metrics

Classification Matrix			
	Training Prediction		
Observed	1	0	Total
1	2748	512	3260
0	2008	1228	3236
Total	4756	1740	6496

Fit Statistics	
Statistic	Training
Accuracy	0.6121
Error	0.3879
Sensitivity	0.8429
Specificity	0.3795

The Fit Statistics table shows the standard evaluation metrics for classification models.

RBF Model Design

Program 8.16 develops the RBF model design.

Program 8.16: Support Vector Machine RBF Design

```
PROC HPSVM DATA=mydata.bank_train METHOD=activeset;
    KERNAL RBF / K_PAR = 1.5;
    INPUT pdays age pout_succ previous contact_tele  /LEVEL=interval;
    TARGET target / LEVEL=binary;
    OUTPUT OUTCLASS=outclass OUTFIT=outfit OUTEST=outest;
RUN;
```

Notes on Program 8.16:

- PROC HPSVM is applied to the MYDATA.BANK_TRAIN data set. The METHOD statement specifies which method to use during training.

- The KERNEL option is set to RBF. The K_PAR option specifies the kernel parameter.

- The INPUT statement specifies the numeric variables and assigns the LEVEL to interval. If the data set contained character variables, they would have a separate INPUT statement and the LEVEL would be set to "nominal."

- The TARGET statement specifies the target variable and the LEVEL is set to binary.

- The OUTPUT statements specify the output data sets that will be created.

Output 8.30 shows the Model Information table for the RBF model. We can see that the optimization technique was changed to "Active Set" and the kernel function is now RBF. The optimal penalty parameter for this model is 1.0.

Output 8.30: PROC HPSVM RBG Design Model Output

Model Information	
Task Type	C_CLAS
Optimization Technique	Active Set
Scale	YES
Kernel Function	RBF
Penalty Method	C
Penalty Parameter	1
Maximum Iterations	25
Tolerance	1e-06

Output 8.31 shows the Classification Matrix and the Fit Statistics table for the RBF model.

Output 8.31: PROC HPSVM RBG Design Evaluation Metrics

Classification Matrix			
	Training Prediction		
Observed	1	0	Total
1	2748	512	3260
0	2008	1228	3236
Total	4756	1740	6496

Fit Statistics	
Statistic	Training
Accuracy	0.6121
Error	0.3879
Sensitivity	0.8429
Specificity	0.3795

The fit statistics for the RBF model is exactly the same as the polynomial model. This shows that changing the modeling technique did not improve the SVM model fit.

Neural Networks

Neural networks have certainly captured the headlines in the machine learning news stories. Whether it is image recognition, speech to text, teaching a bot to chat, creating a machine to beat world champions in any number of games, or making breakthroughs in the field of artificial intelligence, neural networks are the go-to algorithms for these deep learning challenges.

What is deep learning? Deep learning refers to training deep neural networks on large amounts of data. It is the application of a multi-node neural network on a very large data set with the goal of correctly classifying or predicting an outcome.

Figure 8.13 shows the performance gains of adding more data and additional hidden nodes to the neural networks. Other types of machine learning programs plateau at a certain amount of data. But neural networks have the unique ability to continue to learn more information and make more complex predictions when exposed to additional data and added complexity within the neural network by the addition of layers of hidden nodes.

Figure 8.13: Performance Gains of Additional Data

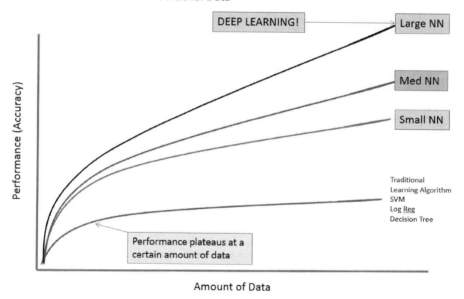

Neural Network Structure

Neural networks do not have to be very complicated. They can be as simple as a standard simple linear regression. Figure 8.14 shows a simple linear regression example that predicts the price of a car using a single predictor, horsepower.

Figure 8.14: Simple Linear Regression Example

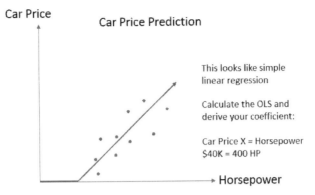

The figure shows a simple linear regression line that does a decent job of predicting car prices. This relationship between the predictors and the target value can be represented in a traditional linear regression equation. However, we can also represent the relationship in an alternative manner.

Figure 8.15 represents the same equation in the form of a neural network.

Figure 8.15: Neural Network Form of a Regression Model

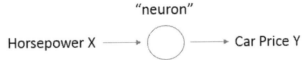

For this model, the neuron represents a simple linear equation that expresses the relationship between the predictor and the target variable. This may seem like a mere simplification of the linear regression model, but a neural network model is not limited to a single linear regression equation. We can stack several of these neurons together to create complex relationships between many predictors and a single target variable.

Figure 8.16 demonstrates a simple neural network with four input features and one hidden layer of nodes.

Figure 8.16: Hidden Nodes Example

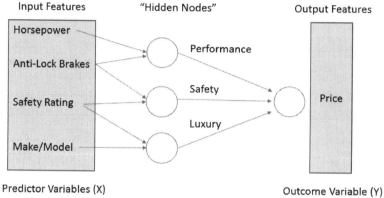

We can still think of the initial structure like a simple linear regression model. We have four input features (x) that are trying to predict the output feature (y). The main deviation occurs in the middle part of Figure 8.16. This space is where the hidden nodes appear. We do not explicitly tell the program what these hidden nodes are. The neural network figures this out for itself. The only information that we explicitly tell the program is the input and output features.

The neural network can assess all of the available features and create hidden nodes that represent rolled-up categories of these features. This process is a form of feature generation that the neural network automatically performs. In this example, the first two features are horsepower and anti-lock brakes. The neural network might find similarities within these features and create a hidden node that represents performance. This new node makes intuitive sense since more powerful vehicles would require anti-lock brakes.

The same approach can be found in the last two features of safety rating and make/model. The combination of these features could be rolled-up to create a hidden node of luxury. These hidden nodes are then used to predict the outcome variable.

In this example, the flow of information is forward. This type of neural network design is called a multilayer perceptron. The neural network can be thought of as multiple stages of processing where each stage consists of generalizations of linear models that predict an outcome.

If this were a simple linear regression, the equation would look like Equation 8.4.

Equation 8.4

$$Y \approx \beta_0 + \beta_1 X_1 + \beta_2 X_2 + \beta_3 X_3 + \beta_4 X_4$$

The coefficient weights are depicted as β_p in Equation 8.4. These weights are the input features of the hidden nodes. Figure 8.17 shows how these nodes output new weighted features that predict the outcome variable. The initial feature weights are shown as the connectors to the hidden nodes. The hidden nodes generate new features with their own weights that are fed into the final prediction.

Deep neural networks are algorithms with additional layers of hidden nodes. The more hidden layers of nodes, the more complex the algorithm becomes, and the more computationally intensive the algorithm becomes.

Figure 8.17: Coefficient Weights Example

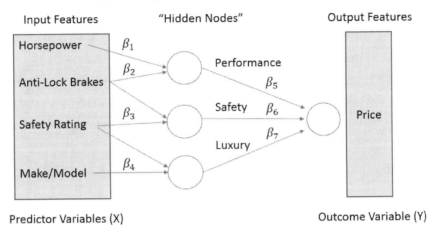

There is one final trick that the neural network performs before predicting the outcome variable. After computing the weighted sum for each hidden unit, a nonlinear function is applied to the result. This nonlinear function is usually the **rectifying nonlinearity** (ReLU) or the **tangens hyperbolicus** (tanh). The ReLU function forces the predicted result to be greater than zero while the tanh function acts like a logistic regression logit function and forces the predicted result to be between -1.0 and 1.0. These **activation functions** allow the neural network to learn much more complicated functions than a simple linear regression model could.

Types of Neural Networks

Although the details of all the different types of neural networks are beyond the scope of this book, we can quickly touch on the four basic types of neural networks:

- **Standard** (feed-forward) – This is the multilayer perceptron model described above.
- **Convolutional** – Convolutional neural networks (CNN) are designed to recognize images. The model has convolutions inside, which see the edges of an object recognized on the image.
- **Recurrent** – Recurrent neural networks (RNN) are designed to recognize sequences, for example, a speech signal or a text.
- **Hybrid** – This is a combined neural network that contains both convolutional and recurrent aspects. This is often found in self-driving cars.

The differences between the CNN and RNN model types are summarized in Table 8.8.

Table 8.8: CNN Versus RNN

CNN	RNN
Fixed sized inputs and outputs	Arbitrary input and output lengths
Feed-forward	Use internal memory to process arbitrary sequences of inputs
Uses connectivity pattern between its neurons	Uses time-series information
Ideal for images and video processing	Ideal for text and speech analysis

Neural Network Model

PROC HPNEURAL allows you to build feed-forward multilayer perceptron models in an easy-to-use framework. Program 8.17 demonstrates the development of a neural network utilizing PROC HPNEURAL.

Program 8.17: Neural Network Example

```
PROC HPNEURAL DATA=MYDATA.BANK_TRAIN;
   ARCHITECTURE MLP;
   INPUT &num_vars.;
   TARGET target / LEVEL=nom;
   HIDDEN 10;
   HIDDEN 5;
   TRAIN;
   SCORE OUT=scored_NN;
   CODE FILE= 'C:/Users/James Gearheart/Desktop/SAS Book
Stuff/Data/NN_Model.sas';
run;
```

Notes on Program 8.17:

- PROC HPNEURAL is applied to the MYDATA.TRAIN data set.

- The ARCHITECTURE is set to MLP. This statement specifies that the neural network design will be the multilayer perceptron.

- The INPUT specifies the numeric variables. If the data set contained character variables, then an additional INPUT statement would be included to specify the character variables.

- The TARGET statement specifies the target variable and the LEVEL is set to NOM. This specifies that the target variable is nominal, which, in this case, is a binary variable.

- There are two HIDDEN statements in this program. The first HIDDEN statement specifies the number of hidden neurons in the first hidden layer and the second HIDDEN statement specifies the number of hidden neurons in the second hidden layer. So this program has two hidden layers with 10 neurons in the first hidden layer and 5 neurons in the second hidden layer.

- The TRAIN statement causes PROC HPNEURAL to use the training data to train a neural network model that is defined in the ARCHITECTURE, INPUT, TARGET, and HIDDEN statements.

- The SCORE statement combined with the OUT statement creates a scored data set of the initial training data.

- The CODE FILE statement creates a SAS program that contains all of the scoring logic. This SAS program can be applied to new data sets with the same structure as the training data to score new observations.

Neural Network Model Output

PROC HPNEURAL provides several important output tables to evaluate the performance of the model. The Model Information table provides a summary of the hyperparameter values that the developer has selected.

Output 8.32 shows the Model Information table for the model that we have developed. This table specifies that the model was built on the MYDATA.BANK_TRAIN data set and that the neural network architecture is the multilayer perceptron. We developed two hidden layers with a total of 15 hidden neurons between them.

Directly after the Model Information table, there is a summary of the data usage where it shows the total number of observations read and used in the model. It also provides the breakout of the number of observations used for training and validation.

Output 8.32: PROC HPNEURAL Output

Model Information	
Data Source	MYDATA.BANK_TRAIN
Architecture	MLP
Number of Input Variables	57
Number of Hidden Layers	2
Number of Hidden Neurons	15
Number of Target Variables	1
Number of Weights	641
Optimization Technique	Limited Memory BFGS

Number of Observations Read	6496
Number of Observations Used	6496
Number Used for Training	4872
Number Used for Validation	1624

Output 8.33 shows the Fit Statistics table for PROC HPNEURAL. This table provides the absolute error and misclassification metrics for both the training and validation data sets.

Output 8.33: PROC HPNEURAL Evaluation Metrics

NAME	Train: Number of Observations	Valid: Number of Observations	L1 Norm of Weights	Train: Average Error Function	Valid: Average Error Function	Train: Average Absolute Error	Valid: Average Absolute Error
TARGET	4872	1624	68.897684	0.560088	0.561487	0.380936	0.381607

Train: Maximum Absolute Error	Valid: Maximum Absolute Error	Train: Number of Wrong Classifications	Valid: Number of Wrong Classifications	Train: Misclassification Rate	Valid: Misclassification Rate
0.966426	0.961053	1428	477	0.2931	0.2937

Scoring Algorithm

The SAS code that was created in the CODE FILE statement can be included in a DATA step to score new observations. Program 8.18 shows the implementation of the code file on the hold-out TEST data set.

Program 8.18: Score TEST Data Set with PROC HPNEURAL Model

```
DATA test_scored;
  SET MYDATA.bank_test;
   %INCLUDE 'C:/Users/James Gearheart/Desktop/SAS Book
Stuff/Data/NN_Model.sas';
RUN;

%INCLUDE 'C:/Users/James Gearheart/Desktop/SAS Book
Stuff/Projects/separation.sas';
%separation(data = test_scored, score = P_TARGET1, y = target);
```

The DATA step calls the stored code file with a %INCLUDE statement. This statement applies the logic contained in the code file to the TEST data set. The evaluation macro that we have used throughout this chapter is applied to the scored TEST data set to evaluate the accuracy of the model on the hold-out TEST data set. Output 8.34 shows the output of the evaluation macro.

Output 8.34: TEST Data Set Lift Table

	MIN SCORE	MAX SCORE	GOOD #	BAD #	TOTAL #	ODDS	BAD RATE	CUMULATIVE BAD RATE	BAD PERCENT	CUMU. BAD PERCENT
	GOOD BAD SEPARATION REPORT FOR P_TARGET1 IN DATA TEST_SCORED									
	MAXIMUM KS = 38.6938 AT SCORE POINT 0.5480									
	(AUC STATISTICS = 0.7409, GINI COEFFICIENT = 0.4819, DIVERGENCE = 0.9860)									
BAD	0.9329	0.9674	19	259	278	0.07	93.17%	93.17%	18.77%	18.77%
I	0.7767	0.9324	47	232	279	0.2	83.15%	88.15%	16.81%	35.58%
I	0.5851	0.7752	94	184	278	0.51	66.19%	80.84%	13.33%	48.91%
I	0.4761	0.5847	145	134	279	1.08	48.03%	72.62%	9.71%	58.62%
I	0.4257	0.4758	166	112	278	1.48	40.29%	66.16%	8.12%	66.74%
I	0.3836	0.4255	156	123	279	1.27	44.09%	62.48%	8.91%	75.65%
I	0.3363	0.3836	174	104	278	1.67	37.41%	58.90%	7.54%	83.19%
I	0.2788	0.3363	200	79	279	2.53	28.32%	55.07%	5.72%	88.91%
V	0.2292	0.2787	197	81	278	2.43	29.14%	52.19%	5.87%	94.78%
GOOD	0.1816	0.2289	206	72	278	2.86	25.90%	49.57%	5.22%	100.00%
	0.1816	0.9674	1,404	1,380	2,784					

We can see that the Gini score for the neural network model applied to the hold-out TEST data set is 48.19. This model is competitive with the tree-based models and is eclipsed only by the random forest Gini score of 51.60. Both of these models are considered black-box models due to the inability to explicitly explain how the predictions are made.

Chapter Review

This chapter covered a lot of material. Throughout this chapter we have seen the transition of highly interpretable models such as simple decision trees to increasingly opaque black-box models such as gradient boosting and neural network models. We have also seen the resulting increase in model evaluation metrics. This chapter demonstrates the trade-off between model interpretability and model accuracy. It is often the case that accuracy is more important than interpretability. In cases where the underlying data is non-linear and model interpretability is not paramount, the models covered in this chapter will provide the most accurate predictions possible.

Chapter 9: Model Evaluation Metrics

Overview

Model evaluation is essential for determining the accuracy and effectiveness of your model. Evaluation metrics can help a data scientist develop a robust model on the training and validation data sets while also providing a framework to evaluate the accuracy of the final model by applying these metrics to the hold-out test and out-of-time data sets. A data scientist must select the appropriate evaluation metric before developing their model and must understand the pros and cons of each evaluation metric.

This chapter will focus on many of the most common model evaluation metrics that are required in both the academic and corporate data science settings.

General Information

Before you create any model, you should first have a strong understanding of all the data assets that you will be using to develop your analysis and subsequent model. Not only is this very important for your own use, but once you build your model, you will need to demonstrate its quality and effectiveness to a team of people who were not involved in the model development process. They will require a start-to-finish explanation of the data sources, modeling techniques, and evaluation metrics before they can approve your model for production.

Data Source Statement

The first item that is generally required is a *data source statement*. This statement is a summary of information about all the data sets that you have pooled together to create your modeling data set. Table 9.1 shows a general structure of the data source statement.

Table 9.1: Data Source Statement Structure

Source Type	Structured / Unstructured	Database Type / File Type	Data Source Name	Table Name / File Name	Number of Columns	Number of Rows
Database	Structured	Teradata	EDW	wxmp.cust_att_1802	348	15,538,126
Database	Structured	Oracle	Delphi	wtrp.trans_acc_1802	792	222,739,511
Database	Unstructured	Teradata	EDW	pbrs.twitter_1802	43	18,576,329

The data source statement is usually in the form of a spreadsheet or a Word document. It contains all the information that a reviewer would need to understand what type of data you will be using, where it can be found, and some indication of the volume of data.

Data Dictionary

The next critical piece of information that a reviewer would need is the *data dictionary*. The data dictionary is a summary of all the variables that are used in the model. Some model governance organizations require that you submit a data dictionary for all variables that were even considered by the model, while other model governance bodies require only a data dictionary for those variables that were retained in the final model.

Table 9.2 shows the general structure of the data dictionary.

Table 9.2: Data Dictionary Structure

Variable Name	Business Name	Description
acceptD	Accepted	The date on which the borrower accepted the offer.
accNowDelinq	Delinquent Accounts	The number of accounts on which the borrower is now delinquent
accOpenPast24Mths	Trades Opened in the Past 24 Months	Number of trades opened in past 24 months
addrState	State	The state provided by the borrower in the loan application
all_util	Balance	Balance to credit limit on all trades
annual_inc_joint	Co-borrower Annual Income	The combined self-reported annual income provided by the co-borrowers during registration
annualInc	Annual Income	The self-reported annual income provided by the borrower during registration
application_type	Application Type	Indicates whether the loan is an individual application or a joint application with two co-borrowers
avg_cur_bal	Average Current Balance	Average current balance of all accounts

The table shows the variable name as represented in the data set, the actual business name (which is the common language name of the data asset), and a definition of the variable.

Variable Summaries

The last pieces of general information that we will touch on are the variable summaries, statistics, and graphs. These pieces of information provide the reviewer with detailed information about each variable in your data set.

We will use the Airbnb data set that we developed in Chapter 2 to demonstrate the variable summaries. This data set contains both continuous numeric variables and categorical character variables. For the numeric variables, we can run a simple PROC MEANS to get a general overview of these variables. Program 9.1 develops the numeric variable summaries.

Program 9.1: Numeric Variable Summaries
```
PROC MEANS DATA=TRAIN N NMISS MIN MAX MEAN STDDEV;
        VAR price bedrooms bathrooms accommodates square_feet;
RUN;
```

This program pulls only a few selected numeric variables for demonstration purposes. The data that is used is the raw data that has not been treated for missing values, outliers, or limits set on specific values. Output 9.1 shows the data output.

Output 9.1: Variable Summary for a Few Selected Variables

Variable	N	N Miss	Minimum	Maximum	Mean	Std Dev
price	39241	3	0	10000.00	151.1356999	210.0367293
bedrooms	39200	44	0	11.0000000	1.1789541	0.7490844
bathrooms	39183	61	0	17.0000000	1.1713498	0.4792557
accommodates	39241	3	1.0000000	16.0000000	2.8866492	1.8862519
square_feet	374	38870	0	5000.00	730.7967914	599.4075372

The raw data shows missing values and wide standard deviations of the data. The model reviewers will need to know what the data looked like prior to any treatments of the data.

Once the data has been treated, you can provide another variable summary of the final modeling data set. This summary provides the model reviewers with a before and after look at the modeling data set. Output 9.2 shows the same PROC MEANS applied to the final modeling data set.

Output 9.2: Variable Summary for the Final Modeling Data Set

Variable	N	N Miss	Minimum	Maximum	Mean	Std Dev
price	38527	0	30.0000000	750.0000000	139.2587017	102.1064689
bedrooms	38527	0	0	5.0000000	1.1660913	0.7159927
bathrooms	38527	0	0	4.0000000	1.1583305	0.4305045
accommodates	38527	0	1.0000000	16.0000000	2.8580736	1.8067483

By evaluating the before and after look at the data, the model reviewers can easily see that there no more missing values, there are thresholds placed on the target variable price, the standard deviations have been significantly reduced, and the variable square_feet has been removed due to a large number of missing values.

For critical variables such as the target variable, additional analysis may be required. This analysis would include a statistical review of the variable. The most common approach is to create a PROC UNIVARIATE of the target variable. This analysis will show all of the relevant information pertaining to that variable. Program 9.2 develops a statistical analysis of the price variable.

Program 9.2: Univariate Analysis of the Target Variable

```
PROC UNIVARIATE DATA=train_final;
    VAR price;
    HISTOGRAM;
RUN;
```

The output of PROC UNIVARIATE has been reviewed in both Chapter 2 and Chapter 3, so please refer to those chapters for more detail on the interpretation of the output. The model reviewers will generally inspect the Moments and Basic Statistical Measures tables shown in Output 9.3.

Output 9.3: PROC UNIVARIATE Output

Moments			
N	38527	Sum Weights	38527
Mean	139.258702	Sum Observations	5365220
Std Deviation	102.106469	Variance	10425.731
Skewness	2.1610293	Kurtosis	6.43560029
Uncorrected SS	1148815284	Corrected SS	401661713
Coeff Variation	73.3214282	Std Error Mean	0.52020038

Basic Statistical Measures			
Location		Variability	
Mean	139.2587	Std Deviation	102.10647
Median	110.0000	Variance	10426
Mode	150.0000	Range	720.00000
		Interquartile Range	105.00000

For character variables, PROC FREQ will provide the necessary information on the number of classes and the volume in each category for each character variable. Program 9.3 shows a sample PROC FREQ statement.

Program 9.3: Character Variable Analysis

```
PROC FREQ DATA=train_final;
  TABLES _CHARACTER_;
RUN;
```

The final piece of information that a model reviewer may require is a graphical depiction of the distribution of a set of variables. This chart is not generally required for all variables, but it is common to produce a graphical distribution for the target variable and a few of the critical predictive variables.

Output 9.4: Graphical Distribution for a Few Key Variables

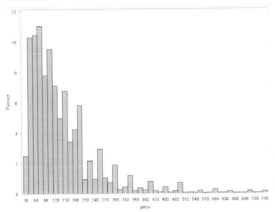

PROC UNIVARIATE in Program 9.2 included a HISTOGRAM statement that produces a graphical distribution of the data shown in Output 9.4.

This view of the target variable allows the model reviewer to see that the variable is skewed right with most of the values occurring between a price of $50 and $150 per night.

Model Output

Academic review and organizational model governance will require a detailed description of how the model was developed. There are standard templates that you can use for academic purposes, and most organizations have detailed forms that you need to complete. These forms walk you through the process of detailing your development process. Some parts of these forms will require you to provide model overview information and model assessment metrics. This section will focus on walking you through the explanation of each of the most common model metrics and what is expected in the model overview section.

Model Overview

Once a model has been developed, we can provide detailed information on certain features of the model. If the model that was developed is a linear regression, logistic regression or a simple decision tree, then we can provide a model overview table similar to Table 9.3.

Table 9.3: Model Overview Table

	Estimate	% Contribution	Description	Direction of Relationship	Business Description
Intercept	-3.542				
int_rate	0.114	57%	**Interest Rate** - Interest Rate on the loan.	Positive	As the interest rate increases, the bad rate increases.
acc_open_past_24mths	0.074	20%	**Accounts Opened in the Past 24 Months** - Number of trades opened in past 24 months.	Positive	As the number of accounts opened in the past 24 months increases, the bad rate increases.
dti	0.013	6%	**Debt to Income Ratio** - A ratio calculated using the borrower's total monthly debt payments on the total debt obligations.	Positive	As the debt-to-income ratio increases, the bad rate increases.
emp_NA	0.431	6%	**Employment Not Applicable** - Dummy variable created to indicate that no employment status was indicated.	Negative	When the employment-not-applicable dummy variable is set to one, the bad rate decreases.
total_bc_limit	0	4%	**Total Bankcard Limit** - Total bankcard high credit/credit limit.	Positive	As the total bankcard limit increases, the bad rate increases.
tot_hi_cred_lim	0	4%	**Total High Credit Limit** - Total high credit/credit limit.	Positive	As the total high credit limit increases, the bad rate increases.
loan_amnt	0	3%	**Loan Amount** - The listed amount of the loan applied for by the borrower.	Negative	As the requested loan amount increases, the bad rate decreases.

This table is very useful for "white-box" models. These models allow us to know precisely what is going on inside the model at the variable level. Therefore, we can list the relevant variables and provide information on each variable such as the coefficient value, percent contribution based on the Wald Chi-Square value, the variable description, the direction of the relationship between the variable and the target variable and the business description that defines how this variable works in relation to the target variable.

"Black-box" models will require some alternative methods of explanation that we will explore throughout this chapter.

Accuracy Statistics

Model accuracy metrics can be divided into two classes, regression and classification. Regression models contain a target variable that is a continuous numeric value, while classification models contain a categorical target variable. Because of this difference, the way that the model accuracy is assessed is different depending on which of these model designs are being used.

Regression Models

There are different stages of model accuracy that we need to inspect during the construction and review of regression models. During the construction phase, we need to assess the training error rate that compares the actual observation values with the predicted value (for example, MAE and RMSE). Once the given error metric is minimized, we will need to determine which of a range of models will perform best on the testing data set (for example, AIC and BIC). Finally, once a model is selected, we need to determine the overall accuracy of the model (for example, R^2 and Adjusted R^2).

RSS, MAE, MSE, RMSE, and MAPE

In Chapter 6, we reviewed linear regression models and we introduced the subject of accuracy metrics such as the Residual Sum of Squares (RSS). The RSS is simply the sum of the squared values of the actual minus the predicted value. Equation 9.1 shows the formula for the RSS. This metric is used to construct the coefficient weights of the regression model. These weights are selected where the RSS is minimized.

Equation 9.1: Residual Sum of Squares Equation

$$RSS = \sum_{i=1}^{n} (y_i - \hat{y}_i)^2$$

Although this is an important error metric that we need to calculate to understand the predictive accuracy of the model, it is by no means the only error metric that we can calculate by using the difference between the actual and the predicted values.

Figure 9.1 shows us an example of the actual versus the predicted values for a sample data set.

Figure 9.1: Actual vs. Predicted Values

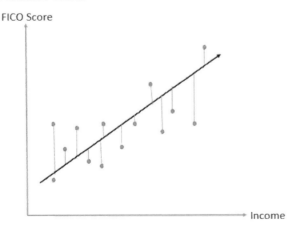

The *Mean Absolute Error* (MAE) is calculated by taking the absolute value of the difference between the actual and predicted values.

Equation 9.2: Mean Absolute Error Equation

$$MAE = \frac{1}{n} \sum_{i=1}^{n} |y_i - \hat{y}_i|$$

This metric mitigates the impact that outliers can have on your model performance metric because each residual contributes proportionally to the total amount of error. This means that outliers contribute linearly to the overall error.

The *Mean Squared Error* (MSE) can be thought of as a combination of the RSS and MAE approaches. This equation takes the RSS formula and divides it by the total number of observations.

Equation 9.3: Mean Squared Error Equation

$$MSE = \frac{1}{n} \sum_{i=1}^{n} (y_i - \hat{y}_i)^2$$

Because we are squaring the difference of the terms, the MSE will almost always be greater than the MAE. Because the MAE and MSE are computationally different, we cannot justly compare the two results. For the MSE metric, the square term magnifies the impact of outliers. This means that the error term will grow quadratically in relation to outliers.

The *Root Mean Squared Error* (RMSE) is the square root of the MSE metric. This metric normalizes the units to be on the same scale as the target variable. If the MSE can be thought of as the variance of the model, then the RMSE can be thought of as the standard deviation of the model.

Equation 9.4: Root Mean Squared Error Equation

$$RMSE = \frac{1}{n} \sum_{i=1}^{n} \sqrt{(y_i - \hat{y}_i)^2}$$

The *Mean Absolute Percent Error* (MAPE) is calculated by converting the MAE into a percentage. The main benefit of the MAPE is that people understand percentages, so the interpretation of this metric is much easier to understand. We still get the linear relation of outliers to the overall error, just like the MAE. Where the MAE is the average magnitude of error produced by the model, the MAPE is how far the model's predictions are off from their corresponding outputs on average.

Equation 9.5: Mean Absolute Percent Error Equation

$$MAPE = \frac{1}{n} \sum_{i=1}^{n} \frac{|y_i - \hat{y}_i|}{y_i}$$

Mallow's C_p, AIC, and BIC

When we built our regression model, we selected a method that specifies how the variables will be added to the model. The possible methods included full, forward, backward, and stepwise. Each of these approaches results in a set of models that contain subsets of a different number of predictors. We can evaluate the model errors on the training data set using the model error metrics discussed in the previous section (MAE, MSE, RMSE, MAPE).

Those metrics are beneficial in determining the best model for the training data. However, we select the overall best model based on the TEST data. To evaluate the error metrics on the TEST data set, we can either create separate hold-out test data sets and investigate the accuracy statistics on those data sets, or we can adjust the training error for the model size, which will simulate a test data set performance metric. This approach can help us select the best model among a set of models with a different number of variables.

Mallows's C_p adds a penalty factor to the training RSS to adjust for the training error underestimating the test error. Equation 9.6 shows that Mallows's C_p adds a penalty factor of $2d\hat{\sigma}^2$.

Equation 9.6: Mallows's C_p Equation

$$C_p = \frac{1}{n}(RSS + 2d\hat{\sigma}^2)$$

This penalty factor has two main effects:

1. As more variables are added to the model (represented by d), the penalty increases.
2. The $\hat{\sigma}^2$ term is an estimate of the variance of the error associated with each response measurement.

The C_p statistic can be interpreted as "lower is better." This interpretation is because the value of C_p tends to be small for models with a low test error.

The *Akaike Information Criterion* (AIC) functions similarly to the Mallows's C_p statistic. Equation 9.7 shows that the difference between the AIC and the C_p statistic is that the AIC includes the variance in the denominator.

Equation 9.7: Akaike Information Criterion Equation

$$AIC = \frac{1}{n\hat{\sigma}^2}(RSS + 2d\hat{\sigma}^2)$$

An alternative formulation of AIC is shown in Equation 9.8.

Equation 9.8: Alternative Formulation of AIC

$$AIC = -2\ln(L) + 2k$$

This approach highlights that the AIC uses a model's maximum likelihood estimation (log-likelihood) as a measure of fit (where L is the likelihood and k is the number of parameters).

AIC can be interpreted in the same manner as the Mallows's C_p statistic. Lower is better.

The Bayesian Information Criterion (BIC) derives very similar results as the Mallows's C_p and the AIC. The BIC replaces the $2d\hat{\sigma}^2$ used by Mallows's C_p with a $\log{(n)}d\hat{\sigma}^2$. This replacement forces the BIC to place heavier penalties on models with more predictors and can result in more conservative models compared to the Mallows's C_p and AIC approaches.

Equation 9.9: Bayesian Information Criterion Equation

$$BIC = \frac{1}{n}(RSS + \log{(n)}d\hat{\sigma}^2)$$

R^2 and Adjusted R^2

The above metrics allow us to evaluate and choose the best model across a range of model designs. But how do we evaluate our overall model fit? For regression models, the model fit is generally measured by a variety of metrics including R^2 and Adjusted R^2.

The R^2 metric represents the percentage of variation of the observations explained by the model. Equation 9.10 shows that R^2 is calculated by the ratio of the Residual Sum of Squares (RSS) to the Total Sum of Squares (TSS).

Equation 9.10: R^2 Equation

$$R^2 = \frac{RSS}{TSS}$$

It is tempting to use this metric to evaluate your model. It is straightforward and easy to understand. However, the R^2 metric has some inherent problems with it:

- The R^2 metric will always increase when you add more predictors to the model. This is the case even when these predictors are random variables with no relation to the target variable.

- The R^2 metric can misrepresent the strength of the model. It does not measure goodness-of-fit and can be artificially low when the model is entirely correct. If the standard deviation of the data is large, this will drive R^2 towards zero, even when the model is correctly specified.

- The R^2 metric can be artificially high even when the model is wrong. This often occurs when the data is clearly non-linear, as demonstrated by a scatter plot of the data. A straight line through the data might capture many observations and produce a high R^2 value, but the most appropriate model would be a non-linear approach.

- If you change the range of your predictor variables, it can have a dramatic effect on the R^2 value.

A key component of the regression model building process is that the model is trying to reduce the RSS value of the training data set. It does this by adjusting the coefficients of the model and selects the coefficients that result in the lowest training RSS. However, this does not mean that this is the lowest RSS of the testing data set. Therefore, the training RSS and the training R^2 cannot be used to select from among a set of models with different numbers of variables.

Instead of using the R^2, you can instead use the **Adjusted** R^2. This error metric penalizes the R^2 for each additional term added to the model. Therefore, you cannot artificially improve model performance by merely adding more features to your model. The Adjusted R^2 requires that each additional feature must add a significant amount of predictive power to the model to overcome an inherent adjustment based on degrees of freedom.

Equation 9.11: Adjusted R^2 Equation

$$Adjusted\ R^2 = 1 - \frac{\dfrac{RSS}{(n-d-1)}}{\dfrac{TSS}{(n-1)}}$$

The d term in the equation represents the number of variables in the model. The Adjusted R^2 is maximized when the numerator of Equation 9.11 is minimized. This equation demonstrates that the Adjusted R^2 metric is penalized for the inclusion of unwarranted variables in the model.

For most regression designs, SAS provides detailed output on each of the statistics reviewed above. These statistics include graphical representations such as the one shown in Figure 9.2.

Figure 9.2: Fit Criteria Graphics

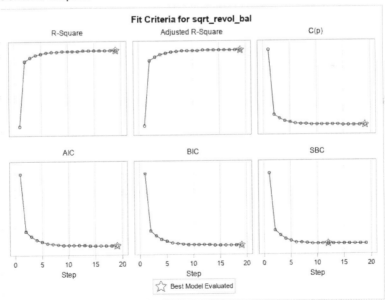

The graphical representation provides an easy-to-understand overview of each of the model fit statistics. These graphics show us that for the R^2 and Adjusted R^2 higher values are better, and for the remaining fit metrics, lower values are better. SAS also includes an indicator (a star on the graph) that shows where the number of predictors generates the lowest RSS value.

Variance Inflation Factor

This test measures the increase in an independent variable's variance due to other independent variables in the model. The variance inflation factor test is produced with the VIF option in the REG procedure. Although the issue of where to set the threshold for the VIF varies by project, a good rule of thumb is that the VIF for each of the variables in the model should be less than 5.

Program 9.4 shows the VIF statement included in the PROC REG model.

Program 9.4: Variance Inflation Factor Metric in a PROC REG Model

```
PROC REG DATA=train_final;
    MODEL price_log = r_entire log_accom n_manhattan
            p_group1 log_bath poly_accom / SELECTION=STEPWISE
        SLE=0.1 SLS=0.1 INCLUDE=0 COLLIN VIF;
RUN;
```

The standard output of the PROC REG model includes the Parameter Estimates table. Since we included the VIF statement in the program, the last column contains the VIF values.

Output 9.5: PROC REG Parameter Estimate Output

Parameter Estimates						
Variable	DF	Parameter Estimate	Standard Error	t Value	Pr > |t|	Variance Inflation
Intercept	1	3.45060	0.01385	249.18	<.0001	0
r_entire	1	0.55658	0.00527	105.67	<.0001	1.57864
log_accom	1	0.43619	0.00973	44.81	<.0001	3.33127
n_manhattan	1	0.35693	0.00429	83.25	<.0001	1.04368
p_group1	1	0.35417	0.01438	24.62	<.0001	1.00771
log_bath	1	0.31260	0.01362	22.96	<.0001	1.13162
poly_accom	1	0.00158	0.00017643	8.98	<.0001	2.64647

Classification Models

Warning

Data scientists who are new to the field often make a common mistake when evaluating the performance of a classification model. That is, they examine only the classification accuracy or misclassification rate of the training and test data sets. Although this metric is important, it can provide you with a false sense of accomplishment with misleading scores. For example, if you have an unbalanced data set where the event rate is only 1.3% of your total observations, it is very easy to get a low misclassification rate by simply predicting that all the observations are a non-event. In this case, your accuracy rate would be 98.7%. In many cases, models built on unbalanced data sets result in a bias towards the majority class.

A better approach is to create a *balanced data set* where there is an equal number of events and non-events for your training data set. If your data set is large enough, you can simply pull all the events and take a random sample of the non-events at a sample size equivalent to the event population. If your population is not large enough, you can create a bootstrapped data set by sampling with replacement to increase the size of your population.

Remember that the train/test split must occur **before** the creation of a balanced data set. This is because you will build your model on the balanced training data set, but its final accuracy assessment must be determined by the hold-out testing data set that contains the true event rate.

Classification Accuracy and Misclassification Rate

Classification accuracy is simply the ratio of the number of correct predictions to the total number of observations. Equation 9.12 shows this calculation.

Equation 9.12: Classification Accuracy

$$Classification\ Accuracy = \frac{Number\ of\ correct\ predictions}{Total\ number\ of\ observations}$$

The misclassification rate represents the ratio of incorrect predictions to the total number of observations. Equation 9.13 shows this calculation.

Equation 9.13: Misclassification Rate

$$Misclassification\ Rate = \frac{Number\ of\ incorrect\ predictions}{Total\ number\ of\ observations}$$

On a balanced data set, these metrics can provide a good overview of your model performance.

Classification Matrix and Error Rate

A classification matrix (also called a confusion matrix) is a table of information that shows a 2X2 matrix of the **actual** number of observations for a given group and the **predicted** number of observations that were classified for a given group. These values allow the researcher to determine the number of predictions that the model got right and the number of predictions that the model got wrong.

If the actual value for an observation is 1 and the predicted value for an observation is categorized as 1, then it is an accurate prediction. However, when the actual value is 0, and the model predicts that it is 1, then it is an incorrect prediction. This holds true in the opposite direction also.

Figure 9.3 displays the classification matrix.

Figure 9.3: Classification Matrix

	Predicted Positive	Predicted Negative	
True Positive	TP	FN	Condition Positive
True Negative	FP	TN	Condition Negative
	Predicted Condition Positive	Predicted Condition Negative	**Total Population**

Classification Accuracy	=(TP+TN)/Total Pop
Misclassification Rate	=(FP+FN)/Total Pop
Recall (Sensitivity)	=TP / Condition Positive
Precision (Specificity)	=TP / Predicted Condition Positive
F1 Score	=2 / ((1/Recall) + (1/Precision))

Figure 9.3 shows that the classification matrix can be used to develop critical model evaluation metrics for classification models. These metrics tell us more than the overall error rate.

- The **False Positive** (FP) cell is also known as the Type I Error.

- The **False Negative** (FN) cell is also known as the Type II Error.

- The **True Positive Rate** is also referred to as **Recall** or **Sensitivity**. This value answers the question, "when the value is actually positive, how often does the model predict that it is positive?"

- The **False Positive Rate** is calculated as (**1- Specificity**). This value answers the question, "when the value is actually negative, how often does the model predict that it is positive?"

- The **Positive Predicted Value** is also referred to as **Precision** or **Specificity**. This value answers the question, "when the value is predicted to be positive, how often is the value actually positive?"

- The **F1 Score** is the weighted average of the True Positive Rate and the True Negative Rate.

Receiver Operating Characteristic (ROC) and Area Under the Curve (AUC)

It is a common approach in classification models to create a probability threshold of 0.5 and judge any observation with a value greater than or equal to the threshold as positive, and any observation with a value less than the threshold as negative. It is a reasonable place to start; however, there is no hard and fast rule that your threshold must be 0.5. We can choose to set the threshold at any value between 0 and 1. With all the possible choices, how do we determine which point is the optimal place to set our threshold?

Figure 9.4: ROC Curve

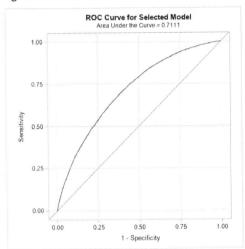

The ROC curve is a visual representation of all the possible choices between 0 and 1. This graphic displays the True Positive Rate (sensitivity) on the y-axis and the False Positive Rate (1-specificity) on the x-axis. Figure 9.4 shows a sample ROC graphic.

Both the x- and y-axis range from 0 to 1. The diagonal line that bisects the graph represents points where the True Positive Rate equals the False Positive Rate. That is, at each position across the diagonal line, the probability is 50% (a coin flip). Any point on this line means that the proportion of correctly classified samples is equal to the proportion of incorrectly classified samples.

The curved line represents the model's probability scores at various thresholds. Therefore, the ROC is a probability curve. The optimal threshold point can be determined where the curve is at its highest point towards the upper left and point of the graph. This location is the balance point where the True Positive Rate is maximized while the False Positive Rate is minimized.

The AUC is the area under the ROC's probability curve. This metric tells us the degree or measure of separability. The higher the AUC, the better the model is at separating the positives from the negatives.

Gini Score

The *Gini score* (also called the Somers' D score) is calculated by 2 * AUC -1. This formula provides us a single metric that represents how well a binary classifier model can separate the classes.

Depending on the subject matter that you are studying, the Gini score can be interpreted in different ways. A score of 40 may be weak for a marketing model, but it may be strong for a clinical model. For my own purposes of building marketing and risk models, I developed Table 9.4 that provides a very broad rule of thumb to interpret your Gini score results.

Table 9.4: Model Strength Table

Gini Score	Model Strength
0 to 20	Not a model
20 to 30	Very weak model
31 to 40	Mildly predictive
41 to 60	Intermediately predictive
61 to 70	Strongly predictive
71 to 80	Very strong model
Greater than 80	Suspiciously strong - check for data bleed

Lift Table

Lift tables provide additional information that has been summarized in the ROC chart. Remember that every point along the ROC chart is a probability threshold. The lift table provides detailed information for every point along the ROC curve.

The model evaluation macro that I have referenced throughout Chapters 7 and 8 was developed by Wensui Liu. This easy-to-use macro is labeled "separation" and can be applied to any binary classification model output to evaluate the model results.

I have placed this macro on my C drive, and I call it with a %INCLUDE statement. Program 9.5 shows the application of this macro.

Program 9.5: Lift Table Evaluation Macro

```
%INCLUDE 'C:/Users/James Gearheart/Desktop/SAS Book
Stuff/Projects/separation.sas';
%separation(data = TEST_SCORE, score = P_1, y = bad);
```

The first line simply states where I placed the macro and the name of the macro. The actual macro is called with the *%separation* statement followed by specifications of your data set that you want to evaluate.

- The DATA statement allows you to specify the name of the data set that you want to evaluate.

- The SCORE statement allows you to specify the name of the predicted probability variable.

- The Y statement allows you to specify the name of the target variable.

With these three simple statements, the macro will develop a detailed analysis of the separation power and accuracy of your scored data set. Output 9.6 shows the lift table generated by this macro.

Output 9.6: Lift Table Macro Output

	MIN SCORE	MAX SCORE	GOOD #	BAD #	TOTAL #	ODDS	BAD RATE	CUMULATIVE BAD RATE	BAD PERCENT	CUMU. BAD PERCENT

	MIN SCORE	MAX SCORE	GOOD #	BAD #	TOTAL #	ODDS	BAD RATE	CUMULATIVE BAD RATE	BAD PERCENT	CUMU. BAD PERCENT
BAD	0.342	0.7104	1,689	1,088	2,777	1.55	39.18%	39.18%	22.18%	22.18%
I	0.2708	0.342	1,947	830	2,777	2.35	29.89%	34.53%	16.92%	39.10%
I	0.2239	0.2708	2,112	665	2,777	3.18	23.95%	31.00%	13.56%	52.66%
I	0.1874	0.2239	2,196	581	2,777	3.78	20.92%	28.48%	11.85%	64.51%
I	0.1562	0.1874	2,288	490	2,778	4.67	17.64%	26.31%	9.99%	74.50%
I	0.1284	0.1562	2,384	393	2,777	6.07	14.15%	24.29%	8.01%	82.51%
I	0.1021	0.1284	2,438	339	2,777	7.19	12.21%	22.56%	6.91%	89.42%
I	0.0766	0.1021	2,548	229	2,777	11.13	8.25%	20.77%	4.67%	94.09%
V	0.0533	0.0766	2,581	196	2,777	13.17	7.06%	19.25%	4.00%	98.08%
GOOD	0.0142	0.0533	2,683	94	2,777	28.54	3.38%	17.66%	1.92%	100.00%
	0.0142	0.7104	22,866	4,905	27,771					

GOOD BAD SEPARATION REPORT FOR P_1 IN DATA TEST_SCORE

(AUC STATISTICS = 0.7097, GINI COEFFICIENT = 0.4193, DIVERGENCE = 0.5339)

This lift chart was constructed to create ten bins of data that are sorted by the max score. It is also common to specify for the program to develop twenty bins for even more detailed analysis. Although it is a common practice to set your threshold at the midpoint of the range of scores, the lift table allows you to make more strategic decisions by selecting a max score value based on your business strategy.

For example, if this was a credit risk model and I wanted to minimize my risk while not excluding good customers, I might select the maximum score that would choose the top two bins (max score = 0.342). Since there are ten bins, I am choosing the top 20% of the population sorted by the probability of their account going delinquent. The column labeled "Cumu. Bad Percent" shows that we would capture 39.10% of delinquent accounts.

If we examine the Gini score in the header information, we can see that the model has a Gini score of only 41.93. This is not a very strong risk model, so the "goods" and "bads" are not separated very well. Some risk models are very strong and have good separation of the good and bad accounts. The lift table for these models can help you determine thresholds where you can capture over 70% of predicted delinquent accounts in the top two deciles.

Population Stability Index (PSI)

The *Population Stability Index* measures a variable's distribution and compares it to the same variable's distribution of a different time period. The reason that this metric is valuable is because it is important to know if the distribution of the variable is changing over time. If it is changing over time, then the model that you developed will not be very effective in a different time period. This evaluation metric tries to determine whether the underlying data is stable across time periods or varies significantly.

After you have developed separate data sets for modeling and Out-Of-Time (OOT) based on distinct time periods, the PSI is calculated according to these steps:

1. Use PROC RANK to divide the numeric variables into an equal number of bins for both the modeling and OOT data sets. This is generally set to ten bins to create decile categories.
2. Calculate the percentage of records for each bin in the modeling sample.
3. Obtain the cutoff points for the intervals in the modeling sample.
4. Apply the cutoff points to the OOT sample.
5. Create the distributions for the OOT sample.
6. Calculate PSI from the statistics gathered from the modeling and OOT data sets.

Table 9.5 shows an example PSI table.

Table 9.5: Population Stability Index Table

	acc_open_past_24mths					
order_rank	acc_open_past_24mths	count_mod	count_oot	freq_mod	freq_oot	PSI
1	1	3791	5082	0.1365	0.1356	.000005024
2	2	3583	4981	0.1290	0.1329	.000120040
3	3	4051	5410	0.1458	0.1444	.000014126
4	4	3928	5038	0.1414	0.1345	.000348510
5	5	3376	4408	0.1215	0.1176	.000125695
6	6	2691	3542	0.0969	0.0945	.000056847
7	7	1969	2815	0.0709	0.0751	.000247914
8	8	2429	3312	0.0874	0.0884	.000010484
9	10	1964	2882	0.0707	0.0769	.000524787
Total	-	27782	37470	1.0000	1.0000	.001453000

This table was created for the variable acc_open_past_24mths. I had created two separate data sets that were specified by time period. The modeling data set contains records from Jan to Jun 2015 and the OOT data set contains records from Jul to Dec 2015.

The PSI is calculated by Equation 9.14.

Equation 9.14: Population Stability Index Equation

$$PSI = \sum ((\%Actual - \%Expected) \text{ X } ln \frac{\%Actual}{\%Expected})$$

For example, the top row PSI can be calculated as:

$$PSI = (0.1356 - 0.1365) \text{ X } ln \frac{0.1356}{0.1365}$$

The individual bins of the calculated PSI are summarized to create a single PSI metric for the variable. This metric can be interpreted with the following rule of thumb:

    <0.1: Very slight change

    0.1-0.2: Some minor change

    >0.2: Significant change

Figure 9.5 shows a graphical demonstration of the PSI output for the example above. The overall PSI for the variable acc_open_past_24mths is 0.001453. This is far below the range that would indicate significant change, so we can determine that this variable is stable across the modeling and OOT time frames.

Figure 9.5: PSI Macro Output

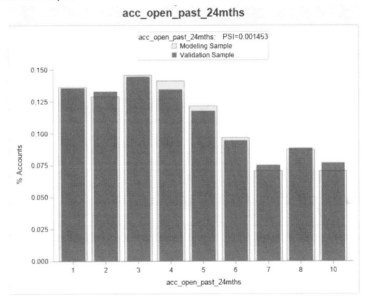

The table of information and the output graphic have been generated from an excellent macro created by Alec Zhixiao Lin. I have included this macro in the GitHub repository, and I have labeled it "PSI Macro." For further information on the population stability index and the development of this macro, check out Alec's excellent paper titled, "Examining Distributional Shifts by Using Population Stability Index (PSI) for Model Validation and Diagnosis."

Black-Box Evaluation Tools

Black-box models are models where we cannot say precisely how a value was generated. This lack of insight could be because of a randomization within the model (such as a random forest) or it could because of a shifting target value and constant rebalancing of coefficients (such as gradient boosting), or it could be because of complex hidden layers of non-linear models with changing weights (such as neural networks) or it could be because of several other factors.

Both academic and organizational model review boards must pay particular attention to black-box models because of these mysterious processes that occur within the model development period. In order to understand the contributing factors and the importance of these factors, we must be able to develop evaluation approaches that allow us to understand how the final output value is determined.

Variable Importance

Although we may not be able to determine the exact effect that a variable has on the development of an output variable (such as coefficient weights in a regression model), we can still create an importance metric that tells us the relative importance of each variable in a black-box model.

Variable Importance tables are commonly created as output from tree-based models. This output is a great help when evaluating the variables in random forests and gradient boosting algorithms.

Table 9.6 shows us the Variable Importance table. This table provides us critical information on the power of each variable in the model and its relative importance to predicting the target variable. It is important to remember that the most critical variables might not be at the top of the tree. Variable importance is determined through four metrics:

- **Count** – The number of times a variable was used as a splitting rule.

- **Surrogate Count** – The number of times a variable was used in a surrogate splitting rule.

- **Reduction in RSS** – The change in the residual sum of squares when a split is found at a node.

- **Relative Importance** – The individual variable RSS-based importance divided by the maximum RSS importance.

Table 9.6: Variable Importance Table

| | | Variable Importance | | | | | |
| | | Training | | Validation | | Relative | |
Variable	Variable Label	Relative	Importance	Relative	Importance	Ratio	Count
pdays	pdays	1.0000	14.9532	1.0000	9.5421	1.0000	1
contact_cell		0.5858	8.7594	0.6561	6.2607	1.1201	1
age	age	0.4263	6.3741	0.4370	4.1697	1.0251	2
month_mar		0.3918	5.8590	0.4176	3.9848	1.0658	2
month_jun		0.4069	6.0847	0.4118	3.9290	1.0119	1
month_oct		0.4626	6.9180	0.3291	3.1404	0.7114	2
month_apr		0.3787	5.6626	0.3135	2.9914	0.8278	2
month_sep		0.2342	3.5023	0.1765	1.6842	0.7536	1
edu_basic9		0.1919	2.8691	0.1440	1.3743	0.7506	1
month_dec		0.2119	3.1691	0.1342	1.2802	0.6330	1
default_no		0.2724	4.0729	0.1296	1.2365	0.4757	1
month_may		0.3518	5.2599	0.0997	0.9516	0.2835	1
day_thu		0.2470	3.6942	0.0000	0	0.0000	1

The variable importance can be interpreted as each predictor's ranking based on the contribution predictors make to the model. A relative importance of 0.000 can be interpreted to mean that since this variable was never used to split a column, it does not contribute to the predictive value of the model.

Variable importance can be used as a variable reduction technique. Since the table provides a ranked order of variables based on their usefulness, a data scientist can make selections on which variables to retain for a more parsimonious model based on their relative value.

Partial Dependence (PD) Plots

One of the most critical questions that we will need to answer to any model reviewer is, "what is the relationship between the model inputs and the prediction?" This question is easily answered with transparent models such as regression models and simple decision trees, but it becomes much more difficult to answer for black-box models. We know what the inputs are and because of the variable importance chart, we know which variables are the strongest drivers of the model prediction, but we still need to be able to express the actual relationship between the model inputs and the predicted value.

Partial Dependence Plots are graphs that depict the functional relationship between a model's inputs and its output. This plot can show whether the relationship between a single variable and the prediction is a linear relationship or a step function or some other kind of relationship.

The PD plot attempts to explain how the model's predictions vary depending on the value of the inputs. These plots are called "model agnostic" because they can be used across a wide variety of model designs. The PD plot is an ad hoc method of model interpretation because it shows how the model behaves when the inputs are changed, but it does not evaluate how the model creates the predictions.

The PD plot simply plots the average predicted value for each value of an input variable. This plot is a simple chart that visually demonstrates the relationship between an input variable and the prediction.

An excellent explanation and accompanying SAS code has been provided by Ray Wright, a Principle Machine Learning Developer at SAS, in his paper "Interpreting Black-Box Machine Learning Models Using Partial Dependence and Individual Conditional Expectation Plots." This paper and the accompanying macros can be found in my GitHub repository.

Let's develop an example using Ray's PD plot macro titled "%PDFunction." The example will be developed on the MYDATA.BANK_TRAIN data set that we used in Chapter 8.

The PD plot allows us to not only examine the relationship between a predictor and the output, but it can also allow us to compare the difference between model designs. For example, Program 9.6 develops a simple decision tree on the MYDATA.BANK_TRAIN data set with a small number of predictors for demonstration purposes.

Once you have downloaded the macro from either Ray's paper or through my GitHub site and you have run the macro, you can apply the %PDFunction macro with the appropriate specifications.

Program 9.6: Partial Dependence Macro Example

```
proc hpsplit data=MYDATA.BANK_TRAIN leafsize = 10;
      target target / level = interval;
      input age pdays pout_succ contact_tele
pout_non contact_cell previous / level = int;
      code file='C:/Users/James Gearheart/Desktop/SAS Book
Stuff/Data/treecode.sas';
run;
%PDFunction( dataset=MYDATA.BANK_TRAIN, target=target, PDVars=age,
otherIntervalInputs=pdays pout_succ contact_tele pout_non contact_cell
previous, otherClassInputs=,
scorecodeFile='C:/Users/James Gearheart/Desktop/SAS Book
Stuff/Data/treecode.sas', outPD=partialDependence );


proc sgplot data=partialDependence;
      series x = age y = AvgYHat;
run;
```

The %PDFunction uses the stored modeling code and creates a PD output data set of the variables that you defined in the macro. The final step is to apply a line plot to visualize the relationship developed in the PD output.

Output 9.7 shows the relationship between the variable "age" and the target variable. We can see that the relationship is a step function.

Output 9.7: Partial Dependence Plot

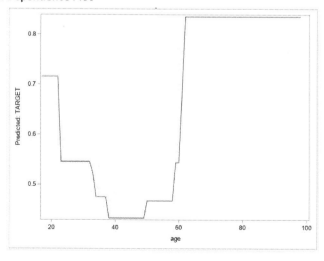

In order to compare model designs, we can create a new model and apply the PD plot macro to it so we can examine the relationship between the same two variables, but defined through a new model.

Program 9.7 develops a neural network model on the MYDATA.BANK_TRAIN data set with the same input variables that we used in the decision tree example. The model output code is input to the %PDFunction macro, and a line chart is developed to show the relationship between the same input variable and the target variable.

Program 9.7: Partial Dependence Macro Example

```
PROC HPNEURAL DATA=MYDATA.BANK_TRAIN;
   ARCHITECTURE MLP;
   INPUT age pdays pout_succ contact_tele
   pout_non contact_cell previous;
   TARGET target / LEVEL=nom;
   HIDDEN 10;
   HIDDEN 5;
   TRAIN;
   SCORE OUT=scored_NN;
   CODE FILE= 'C:/Users/James Gearheart/Desktop/SAS Book
Stuff/Data/NN_Model.sas';
run;

%PDFunction( dataset=mydata.bank_train, target=target, PDVars=age,
otherIntervalInputs= pdays pout_succ contact_tele pout_non contact_cell
previous, otherClassInputs=,
scorecodeFile='C:/Users/James Gearheart/Desktop/SAS Book
Stuff/Data/NN_Model.sas', outPD=partialDependence );

proc sgplot data=partialDependence;
      series x = age y = AvgYHat;
run;
```

Output 9.8 shows that the neural network model develops a smooth relationship between the two variables. The overall direction of the relationship is similar for both models. The average target value is at a midpoint for lower age ranges, then it decreases significantly for the middle age ranges, and then it increases significantly for older age ranges. Both models and their associated PD plots tell the same story, but we can easily see that the *functional* relationship is different between the models.

Output 9.8: Partial Dependence Plot

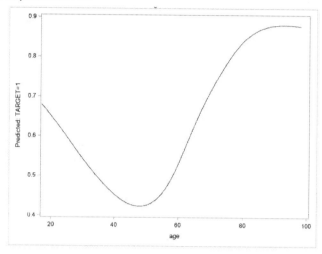

Individual Conditional Expectation (ICE) Plots

A concept that is closely associated with the partial dependency plots is *Individual Conditional Expectation* plots. The ICE plots allow a data scientist to dig deeper into the relationship between variables and discover subgroups and interactions between model inputs.

The PD plots examined the average value of the target variable and compared it to a given variable's values. The ICE plot drills down to the individual observation level. Individual observation plots can be overwhelming to look at. For a data set of even a hundred observations, examining a graph with one hundred different line plots would be challenging to comprehend. That is why the ICE plots either samples or clusters individual observations.

In the paper by Ray Wright referenced in the Partial Dependence section above, Ray also provides a macro for the development of ICE plots (thanks, Ray!). This macro can also be found in the GitHub repository for this book.

Program 9.8 shows that the %ICEPlot macro is a continuation of the %PDFunction macro. Once you have run the %PDFunction macro, the %ICEPlot macro will take the same data set, input features, and model prediction as inputs to the development of the ICE plot.

Program 9.8: Individual Conditional Expectation Macro Call

```
%ICEPlot( ICEVar=age, samples=10, YHatVar=p_target1 );
```

The %ICEPlot macro can be called with only a few statements. You need to specify only the plot variable, the number of observations to sample, and the prediction variable.

Output 9.9 shows the output of the ICE plot created from the neural network model.

Output 9.9: Individual Conditional Expectation Plot

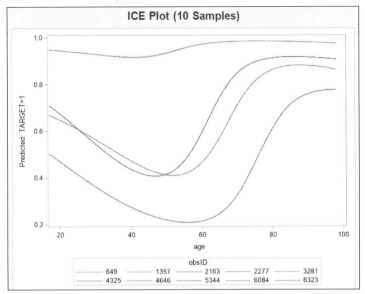

We can see that although we specified ten individual observations, there are only four represented in the chart. This difference is because some observations overlap with one another. This chart shows us that the predictive value is influenced by age in some cases, but the top line indicates that there are observations where age does not affect the predicted value.

If we were to increase the number of samples to fifty, we would get a chart like the one in Output 9.10.

Output 9.10: Individual Conditional Expectation Plot

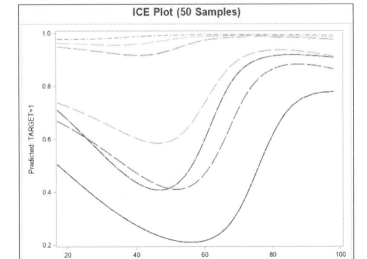

This chart clearly shows that there is a distinction between observations where the predicted value is a function of age and observations where the predicted value is not influenced by age.

Chapter Review

This chapter might be the most important in this book. This is because evaluation metrics are a way of holding ourselves accountable for the data science products that we produce. Properly developed evaluation metrics shine a light on all of our false assumptions, data mistakes, and biases. If the appropriate evaluations are made at each stage of the model development process, then there should be no surprises at the end of the project.

We can often tell how well a model will fit the data simply by visualizing the distribution of the data. We can also create histograms of the continuous target variables and frequency distributions of the binary target variables to gain some insight into how well a model will perform. We can look at scatter plots and bar charts of predictor variables and see how strongly they are associated with the target variable. These evaluations are performed before any modeling has occurred.

At this point, you should have a good idea of the strength of the relationship between the predictors and the target variable. Strong associations suggest that a predictive model will produce accurate predictions while weak associations suggest that a predictive model will produce poor predictions.

The next phase of the model development is the initial construction of the model. Through evaluation metrics such as AIC or the BIC, we can determine the influence of the predictors in the model outcome for regression models, and for classification models, we can gain the same insight through the Variable Importance metrics. Both of these techniques, among others, can provide us insight into how the target variable relates to the predictors within the confines of the modeling algorithm. The strength of the relationship between the target and the predictors can again be evaluated at this stage of model development.

Finally, the model that was developed on the TRAIN data set is applied to the hold-out TEST data set. The evaluation metrics that are applied to the hold-out TEST data set will determine your overall model fit. These metrics are often the RMSE for regression models and the Gini for classification models. At this point, you should have developed a good intuition of how well the model evaluation metrics will look. There is little chance that you would have seen weak relationships between the target and the predictors at each stage of the model development and somehow end up with a very strong model.

This chapter covered a variety of model evaluation techniques. It is important to align the proper technique with the associated model structure. You wouldn't want to evaluate a continuous regression model with a Gini metric, and you wouldn't want to evaluate a binary classifier with the RMSE metric. By understanding how each of the evaluation metrics is constructed, you can have a deeper understanding of how and when to apply each of these metrics.

Index

Ready to take your SAS® and JMP® skills up a notch?

Be among the first to know about new books,
special events, and exclusive discounts.
support.sas.com/newbooks

Share your expertise. Write a book with SAS.
support.sas.com/publish

sas.com/books
for additional books and resources.

THE POWER TO KNOW.

Made in the USA
Middletown, DE
15 October 2023